D0230472

UNIVERSITY *of* LIMERICK

TELEPHONE: 061 202158 / 202172 / 202163

Foundations of
General Linguistics

Also from Unwin Hyman:

English Word Stress
Erik Charles Fudge

Language and Literature
An Introductory Reader in Stylistics
Edited by Ronald Carter

On the Surface of Discourse
Michael Hoey

Psychology in Foreign Language Teaching
Second Edition
Steven H. McDonough

Rhetoric of Everyday English Texts
Michael P. Jordan

Towards a Contextual Grammar of English:
The Clause and Its Place in the Definition of Sentence
Eugene Winter

Vocabulary
Applied Linguistic Perspectives
Ronald Carter

Foundations of General Linguistics

Second Edition

Martin Atkinson
David Kilby
Iggy Roca

*Department of Language and Linguistics,
University of Essex*

London
UNWIN HYMAN
Boston   Sydney   Wellington

Published by the Academic Division of
Unwin Hyman Ltd
15/17 Broadwick Street, London W1V 1FP

Unwin Hyman Inc.,
955 Massachusetts Avenue, Cambridge, MA 02139, USA

Allen & Unwin (Australia) Ltd,
8 Napier Street, North Sydney, NSW 2060, Australia

Allen & Unwin (New Zealand) Ltd in association with the
Port Nicholson Press Ltd,
Compusales Building, 75 Ghuznee Street, Wellington 1, New Zealand

First published in 1982
Third edition 1989
Second impression 1991

British Library Cataloguing in Publication Data
Atkinson, Martin
Foundations of general linguistics.
1. Linguistics
I. Title   II. Kilby, David   III. Roca, Iggy
410   P121
ISBN 0–04–410005–1

Library of Congress Cataloging in Publication Data
Atkinson, Martin.
Foundations of general linguistics
1. Linguistics.   I. Kilby, David A.   II. Roca, Iggy.
III. Title.
P121.A85 1988 410 87–27043
ISBN 0–04–410005–1 9 pbk. : alk. paper.

Printed and bound in Great Britain by
Biddles Ltd, Guildford and King's Lynn

Contents

Preface to the Second Edition

As we send this second edition of *Foundations of General Linguistics* to the publisher we deplore the untimely death of our co-author David Kilby. As well as being a collaborator on the first edition, David was our friend and colleague, and his comradeship and expertise have been sorely missed as we prepared this manuscript. We dedicate this second edition to his memory.

In the five years which have elapsed since the book first saw the light of day, progress in linguistics has been swift, adding to the complexity and the excitement of the field. Nonetheless, we believe that both the original purpose and much of the previous material are still valid. In particular, there remains a vast range of unresolved problems which the reader can begin to tackle by making use of the techniques and terminology he or she will find in this book.

As before, we believe that the level of discussion in the text is such that it can be approached by students of both linguistics and allied disciplines, as well as by the interested layman. The exercises provide a testing ground for the ideas and formalisms in each chapter, and the annotated bibliographies direct the reader to more advanced and comprehensive texts and to relevant original sources. All in all, we remain confident that the book is appropriate both as a serious introduction for the beginner and as a reference work for the more advanced student.

We have completely rewritten chapters 6 and 8. Chapter 8 attempts to incorporate modern work and style of argument in the fields of syntax and phonology. We are conscious that this chapter is more difficult than the rest, but are optimistic that a determined student, aided by a conscientious teacher, will derive great benefit from reading it. The rewriting of Chapter 6 was necessary in order to provide an appropriate foundation for the more advanced syntactic material in Chapter 8. Additionally, Chapter 1, Section 5, has been extended to take account of recent work on primate language learning, and material has been added to Chapter 5 to make our discussion of morphology more comprehensive. New exercises are included to make contact with the new material where appropriate, and all the bibliographies have been updated. Finally, it has been our intention to correct all typographical errors from the first edition, but we have preserved our practice of ignoring vowel length and other such phonetic detail except when it is relevant to the point being made or when we are citing someone else's data.

Wivenhoe   MARTIN ATKINSON
July 1987   IGGY ROCA

Acknowledgements

The following are the sources of some of the passages in the exercises which accompany the chapters:

Abercrombie, D., *English Phonetic Texts* (London: Faber, 1964), pp. 54, 63 (in these texts the phonetic symbol a̱ has been changed to æ); Bailey, B. L., 'Jamaican Creole: can dialect boundaries be defined?', in D. Hymes (ed.), *Pidginization and Creolization of Languages* (Cambridge: Cambridge University Press, 1971), pp. 343, 346; Chomsky, N., 'Linguistics and politics', *New Left Review* 57 (1969), p. 31; Hawkins, P. R., *Social Class, the Nominal Group and Verbal Strategies* (London: Routledge & Kegan Paul, 1977), p. 81; Hughes, A., and Trudgill, P., *English Accents and Dialects* (London: Edward Arnold, 1979), pp. 63–4; Labov, W., 'The logic of non-standard English', in P. P. Giglioli, *Language and Social Context* (Harmondsworth: Penguin, 1972), pp. 194, 197; Lawton, D., *Social Class, Language and Education* (London: Routledge & Kegan Paul, 1968), pp. 124, 134–5. These passages, like the International Phonetic Alphabet and Figures 1.1, 3.7, 4.3 and Tables 3.2, 3.4, 3.5 and 3.7, are all reproduced by permission of their publishers.

THE INTERNATIONAL PHONETIC ALPHABET

		Bilabial	Labiodental	Dental, Alveolar, or Post-alveolar	Retroflex	Pala alveo
CONSONANTS (pulmonic air-stream mechanism)	*Nasal*	m	ɱ	n	ɳ	
	Plosive	p b		t d	ʈ ɖ	
	(Median) Fricative	ɸ β	f v	θ ð s z	ʂ ʐ	ʃ
	(Median) Approximant		ʋ	ɹ	ɻ	
	Lateral Fricative			ɬ ɮ		
	Lateral (Approximant)			l	ɭ	
	Trill			r		
	Tap or Flap			ɾ	ɽ	
CONSONANTS (non-pulmonic air-stream)	*Ejective*	pʼ		tʼ		
	Implosive	ɓ		ɗ		
	(Median) Click	ʘ		ʇ ʗ		
	Lateral Click			ʖ		

DIACRITICS

- ◌̥ Voiceless n̥ d̥
- ◌̬ Voiced s̬ t̬
- ʰ Aspirated tʰ
- Breathy-voiced b̤ a̤
- ◌̪ Dental t̪
- ◌̺ Labialized t̫
- ◌̡ Palatalized t̡
- ◌̴ Velarized or Pharyngealized t, ɫ
- ◌̩ Syllabic n̩ l̩
- ‿ or ◌̬ Simultaneous s͡f (but see also under the heading Affricates)

- ˑ or ◌̝ Raised e˔, ẹ, ẹ w
- ˏ or ◌̞ Lowered e˕, ẹ, e̞ ɤ
- ◌̟ Advanced u̟+, u̟
- ˍ or ◌̠ Retracted i̠, i-, t̠
- ◌̈ Centralized ë
- ◌̃ Nasalized ã
- ˞, ◌˞, ᴿ r-coloured a˞
- ː Long aː
- ˑ Half-long aˑ
- ◌̆ Non-syllabic ŭ
- ◌̹ More rounded ɔ̹
- ◌̜ Less rounded y̜

OTHER SYMBOLS

- ɕ, ʑ Alveolo-palatal fricativ
- ʃ̡, ʒ̡ Palatalized ʃ, ʒ
- ɼ Alveolar fricative trill
- ɺ Alveolar lateral flap
- ɧ Simultaneous ʃ and x
- ʃˢ Variety of ʃ resemblin etc.
- ɪ = ɩ
- ʊ = ɷ
- ɜ = Variety of ə
- ɚ = r-coloured ə

(Revised to 1979)

Palatal		Velar		Uvular		Labial-Palatal	Labial-Velar		Pharyngeal		Glottal	
ɲ		ŋ		ɴ								
c	ɟ	k	ɡ	q	ɢ		k͡p	ɡ͡b				ʔ
ç	ʝ	x	ɣ	χ	ʁ			ʍ	ħ	ʕ	h	ɦ
	j		ɰ			ɥ		w				
ʎ												
				ʀ								
				ʀ								
		ʞ										
		ɠ										

VOWELS

Front		Back		Front		Back
i		ɯ	Close	y	ʉ	u
ɪ				ʏ		ʊ
e		ɤ	Half-close	ø		o
	ə				ɵ	
ɛ		ʌ	Half-open	œ		ɔ
æ	ɐ					
	a	ɑ	Open	Œ		ɒ
Unrounded				Rounded		

STRESS, TONE (PITCH)

ˈ stress, placed at beginning of stressed syllable :
ˌ secondary stress : ˉ high level pitch, high tone :
˰ low level : ˊ high rising :
ˏ low rising : ˋ high falling :
ˎ low falling : ˆ rise-fall :
ˇ fall-rise.

AFFRICATES can be written as digraphs, as ligatures, or with slur marks ; thus ts, tʃ, dʒ : ƫs t͡ʃ d͡ʒ : t͡s t͡ʃ d͡ʒ.
c, ɟ may occasionally be used for tʃ, dʒ.

Part ONE

The Nature of Language

Chapter 1

Are Humans Unique?

1.1 On origins

When God created all birds and wild animals, says the Book of Genesis (2: 19), 'He brought them to the man to see what he would call them, and whatever the man called each living creature, that was its name.' Adam's language was lost in the midst of the confusion at Babel and, later, in a different vein, Herodotus tells of a curious experiment supposedly carried out by the Egyptian prince Psammitichus, in which two newly born children were brought up silently by a solitary shepherd, in the hope that the original language of Adam would spontaneously flow out of the babies' mouths. To Psammitichus' disappointment, the first utterance was the Phoenician word *bekos* ('bread'), thus disconfirming his hypothesis that the Egyptians were the oldest nation on earth. Similar experiments, including one by the Scottish king James IV, are reported to have been staged throughout the centuries, with Hebrew taking on the privileged position originally occupied by Phoenician.

Whatever the historical accuracy of these accounts, they highlight two beliefs which still persist in the layman's view of the nature of language. First, language is identified with naming, to the total exclusion of the myriad of other facets that constitute it and make up the subject-matter of this book. Secondly, the origin of language is regarded as a sudden event (as maintained by the *discontinuity theory*), rather than as the result of continuous evolution happening over thousands or millions of years (as held by the supporters of the *continuity theory*).

The biblical doctrines of divine creation received a serious blow with the advent of Darwin's theory of evolution in the mid-nineteenth century, according to which evolution consists of a series of random mutations, of which only the fittest for survival are preserved (note that, attractive as it is, Darwinism dangerously approaches tautology, since if only the fittest survives, then whatever survives must by definition be the fittest). The hypothetical reconstruction within biology of earlier states in the development of man has stimulated important recent research on the possible language abilities of primitive man.

The phonetician Philip Lieberman has constructed an argument for the non-existence of language as we know it in Neanderthal man, a relatively recent relation of modern man in the evolutionary scale. He notes that in both chimpanzees and newborn humans certain anatomically possible sounds do not occur, and he suggests that this may be due to their lack of an appropriate neural mechanism for decoding speech sounds as speech sounds. This lack can also be correlated with important differences in pharyngeal structure between chimpanzees and newborn humans, on the one hand, and adult humans, on the other (which makes production of the three most basic sounds in human speech – [a], roughly as in *bar*, [i], as in *bee*, and [u], as in *boo* – anatomically impossible for the former), since evolution proceeds in a unitary manner, embracing both the structure of organisms (bodily and cerebral) and their behaviour, and the only function of the pharyngeal cavities specific to humans appears to relate to speech production, while chimpanzees preserve structures which are better adapted to the prevention of choking by inhalation of food. Using complex reconstruction techniques aided by computer technology, Lieberman hypothesises that, because of parallels between the pharyngeal structures of Neanderthal man and chimpanzees and newborn humans, the first also did not possess the appropriate neural mechanisms and thus lacked the linguistic abilities of his modern counterpart. The question now is whether all this constitutes evidence for the discontinuity theory first embodied in the biblical account, one implication of which is that language is unique to man. Before we attempt to answer this, however, we must look at the nature of language itself.

1.2 Rules and creativity

Philosophers often select language as the cornerstone of the divide between man and other living creatures. Thus for Descartes ([1637] 1970, p. 42) 'it is a very remarkable thing that there are no men so dull and stupid, not even lunatics, that they cannot arrange various words and form a sentence to make their thoughts understood; but no other animal, however perfect or well bred, can do the like', a fact that 'is evidence that brutes not only have a smaller degree of reason than man, but are wholly lacking in it'. The presence of language in a non-human species would indeed be inconceivable for a Cartesian. Note, however, that so far we have not provided a definition of language, and therefore, strictly speaking, the question of its species-specificity has been begged, a problem which characterises much metaphysical speculation on language within philosophy. It is precisely one of the purposes of this book to construct a rigorous and explicit characterisation of what language is, and in what follows we shall proceed to the enumeration of a series of properties that can be attributed to human language and all together can be said to define it.

Language, like the information which is expressed by it, must be unpredictable (i.e. it cannot be obviously related to environmental factors or to internal states) and appropriate to the situation (note, moreover, that there is a conceivably infinite number of these, and this makes language unbounded), and if it were possible to program a computer in such a way that it produced a continuous stream of well-formed utterances in a language, we would not want to say that the computer was communicating or, indeed, using language in any straightforward sense. The American linguists Charles Hockett and Noam Chomsky, among others, regard such a property, or *creativity*, as one of the most crucial properties of human language, and Chomsky (1976, p. 40) states along Cartesian lines that 'the capacity for free, appropriate, and creative use of language as an expression of thought, with the means provided by the language faculty, is . . . a distinctive feature of the human species, having no significant analogue elsewhere'.

Note that the word 'creativity' has a special use here. Chomsky draws a distinction between 'rule-governed' and 'rule-changing' creativity. The latter corresponds to the everyday idea of creativity, as when we talk about an artist or a scientist being creative, while the former operates within the constraints of a set of rules, making a potentially infinite use of these finite means, as happens, for instance, with the game of chess. It is important to realise that rules of the type we are dealing with here (*constitutive rules*) must be kept separate from the more common *regulative rules*. These relate to the regulation of an activity which exists independently of the rules themselves (e.g. the rules of etiquette regulate social behaviour), while constitutive rules actually *constitute* (as well as regulate) the activity – chess would be meaningless without its rules. The distinction between constitutive and regulative rules is crucial to our understanding of what language is. Typical forms learnt at school may include prescriptions such as 'don't split your infinitives' or 'don't end a sentence with a preposition'. Perceptive critics have not been slow to point out that prescriptive grammarians often violate their own precepts, and a number of such regulative rules are now manifestly out of line with predominant usage (for instance, the rule governing the forms *who* and *whom*). As a discipline, linguistics is quite unconcerned with prescribing to the users what to do or not to do. Rather, it purports to describe the reality of language as it is – linguistics is a *descriptive* science, not a *prescriptive* activity.

1.3 Animal communication and the 'design features' of language

The findings of the ethologist Karl von Frisch, among others, in the field of communication systems of the honey-bee may be interpreted as casting some degree of doubt on the supposed human-specificity of language creativity. Honey-bees live in highly structured societies, and efficiency of communication is essential for the survival of the colony. Most important in their daily life is the recruitment by the scouting forager of other fellow workers for purposes of food collection. Important elements in the communication of information about a discovered food source are the environmental scents carried by the foraging bees on their return to the hive, the taste of the nectar regurgitated on arrival and the release of an attraction *pheromone* (i.e. a behaviour-triggering chemical) coupled with vigorous motion of the wings. An additional and most remarkable communication system specific to bees is dancing. In the simpler variety of the dance (*round dance*) the bee describes a narrow circle on the comb, now in one direction, now in the other – odour and taste of the source are directly transmitted to other bees, in close contact with the dancer by their outstretched feelers, while information on the quality of the source is conveyed through the amount of energy spent in the dance. Round dances are useful when the food source is located within a short distance of the hive (some 15 metres), but bees can travel several kilometres to a source and directional information becomes imperative as distance increases. This, the bee transmits by means of a *figure-of-eight dance*, where a straight run is followed by a semi-circle in one direction and back to the origin of the straight run, another straight run, and a

Table 1.1   *Summary of the Relationship between the Orientation of the Bee's Dance and the Location of the Food Source*

Location of Food Source	Direction of Straight Run
between the hive and the sun`	upwards along the vertical
behind the hive, in a straight line with the sun	downwards along the vertical
in front of the hive, to the left of the sun	upwards diagonally to the left of the vertical
in front of the hive, to the right of the sun	upwards diagonally to the right of the vertical
behind the hive, to the left of the sun	downwards diagonally to the left of the vertical
behind the hive, to the right of the sun	downwards diagonally to the right of the vertical

semi-circle in the opposite direction. If the weather is warm the dance is performed on a horizontal surface at the entrance of the hive and the straight run points in the direction of the food source. Otherwise, the dance takes place on the dark vertical surface of the comb, and the solar angle is translated into the gravitational angle, i.e. the angle between the vertical and the straight run on the comb equals the angle between the straight line from the hive to the sun and the straight line from the hive to the food source, as illustrated in Figure 1.1. Table 1.1 summarises the six possibilities for the location of the source in relation to the site of the hive and the position of the sun. This extremely ingenious system allows the honey-bee to locate easily the direction of the food source. In addition, the duration of the straight run and its accompanying buzzing give a direct indication of the distance, apparently computed by the bee on the basis of the amount of energy it uses up in the flight. Finally, the intensity of the waggling that takes place

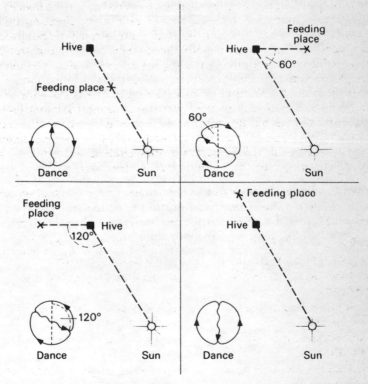

Figure 1.1 *Relationship between the angle between sun and food source, and the bee's figure-of-eight dance on a wall.*

Source: K. von Frisch [1927], *The Dancing Bees* (London: Methuen, 1966), p. 135.

during the straight run (from which derive the alternative names 'waggle' or 'tail-wagging' dance) directly correlates with the assessed quality of the source.

The claim that bee dancing possesses creativity does not appear unduly exaggerated, since, at least in theory, an infinite amount of unpredictable and appropriate information can be transmitted, mainly related to the parameters of direction and distance. True, the bee's creativity operates within extremely strong constraints (the idea of verticality, for instance, as conveyed by the English word 'up' is inexpressible, not to mention the complex thoughts and feelings present in human philosophy, literature and science), but the crucial question is whether the differences between this sort of creativity and human creativity are just a matter of degree or whether we are dealing with two qualitatively different properties, since quantitative differences of an otherwise identical ability would be consistent with the continuity theory of the origin of human language. On the other hand, despite his claim for the exclusiveness of language creativity to humans, Chomsky explicitly conceives of the possibility that certain things (ideas, concepts, feelings) may well be inexpressible in human language, a situation that would be reminiscent of the fact that there are many things which cannot be expressed in the 'language' of the bee.

Alongside creativity, another important and widely accepted property of human language is *arbitrariness*, i.e. the lack of a natural relation between the object and its name. To accept this characteristic is to oppose the belief of the *naturalists*, a belief originating in ancient Greek philosophy and amusingly discussed by Plato in *Cratylus*, that views names as stemming naturally from the properties of their bearers. In the early part of this century the Swiss linguist Ferdinand de Saussure, commonly regarded as the founder of modern linguistics, laid emphasis on the arbitrary nature of the connection between the two components of each linguistic unit (basically each word) or *linguistic sign*. Each linguistic sign is made up of a concept (*signified*) and sound-image (*signifier*), as illustrated in Figure 1.2. Apart from very minor exceptions relating to onomatopoeia and sound symbolism,

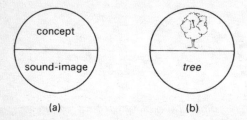

Figure 1.2 (*a*) *Diagram representing the internal structure of the linguistic sign.* (*b*) *Linguistic sign corresponding to the English word* tree.

according to Saussure ([1916] 1974, p. 67), 'the bond between the signifier and the signified is arbitrary'. Note that bee 'language' is also arbitrary in the choice of dancing as information-conveyer and in some of the particular aspects of the dance itself (e.g. the choice of the vertical to represent the line from the hive to the sun), but in other aspects it is *iconic* (i.e. the symbols bear a resemblance to the object), for instance, in so far as variations in the angle with the vertical relate to variations in the angle with the sun line, or in that duration of the straight run correlates with distance. On the other hand, the evolution of the dance from other non-communicative events associated with the bee's life through *ritualisation* (a term used in ethology and animal psychology to describe a process whereby an initially non-communicative behaviour sequence takes on communicative significance) appears reasonable, a fact that suggests that arbitrariness must not be equated with total randomness.

Also in the field of animal communication, it will be useful to consider briefly the facial and vocal signals of the chimpanzee, our closest non-human relation. These are presented in Tables 1.2 and 1.3 respectively, where each signal is associated with a specific set of circumstances.

Table 1.2   *The Significance of the Facial Signals of the Chimpanzee*

Signal	*Circumstances*
tooth-covered open mouth	threatening, fright-free behaviour
closed mouth with tightly pressed lips	precedes copulation and the chase of a subordinate
pout	anxiety or frustration (e.g. when an infant searches for the nipple or when a strange sound is heard or a strange object detected)
grin with lip retraction	submissive behaviour; also used as a reassuring signal or to indicate attachment
relaxed open mouth	playful behaviour involving physical contact
lip-smacking	grooming

A brief note on evolution will be fitting here. According to the ethologist J. A. R. A. M. van Hooff, the chimpanzee's grin and relaxed open mouth are the direct antecedents of human smile and laughter respectively, since, apart from the obvious morphological correlates, research into judgemental correlates shows smile associated with an

Table 1.3   *The Significance of the Vocal Signals of the Chimpanzee*

Signal	Circumstances
high-pitched, far-carrying *scream*	as in submissive grin (cf. Table 1.2)
pant-shriek and roar in a sequence	general communication within the group (e.g. when a chimpanzee becomes stranded or when a general arousal of the group is intended)
low-pitched *pant-grunt*	subordination
laughter	play
short *squeak*	stress
loud and sharp *short bark*	annoyance
long bark	apprehension and aggression
rough grunt	presence of (favourite) food
rapid panting	copulation
short, *soft grunts*	mild general excitement
whimper	as in pout (cf. Table 1.2)
cough	mild threat to subordinates
wraaa (variant of long bark)	threat and alarm (e.g. when predators are detected, dead chimpanzees are found, etc.)

affinitive mood (reassurance, attachment), and laughter with a playful mood. Moreover, smiles and laughter are usually social activities, and thus part of a code of social communication, rather than a mere means of discharging surplus tension, and this too points in the direction of evolutionary development. Continuity can therefore be claimed for at least some aspects of human non-verbal communication.

Unlike the pheromones used by bees and other insects, both communication systems of chimpanzees possess the property of *rapid fading*, i.e. the signal vanishes fast, thus freeing the channel for the next unit of transmission, a trait with an obvious functional value. On the other hand, a very important difference between the system of facial gestures (as with the dancing of the honey-bee or the visual signalling of humans) and that of vocal signals (as with human language) is that only the latter uses the *vocal-auditory channel* with its properties of *broadcast transmission and directional reception*. Broadcast transmission refers to the fact that the transmission of sound, but not its reception, is omnidirectional, thus increasing the efficiency of the signal, albeit at the expense of privacy, a potentially disadvantageous fact. Directional reception, on the other hand, permits the location of the sender by the receiver. Chimpanzee cries also possess *discreteness*, each particular cry standing for a specific set of circumstances rather than having signal variations correlate with different degrees of any one emotion.

Rapid fading, use of the vocal-auditory channel, broadcast transmission and directional reception, and discreteness are, alongside creativity and arbitrariness, among the sixteen *design features* proposed by Hockett to define human language. The usefulness of the features resides in the fact that they permit a fair characterisation of human language as well as a reasonably straightforward means of comparison with other communication systems, but it must be noted that their choice is ultimately motivated by the arbitrary decision of the individual researcher at a particular time, the list having undergone various changes over the years, and there is no indication that it has reached its final format. As will be seen in Section 5 below, recent developments in chimpanzee communication have been taken by some to suggest that human language may not be qualitatively different from some types of artificially-induced animal communication systems.

1.4 Genetic transmission of language

One of the aspects of human language most strongly emphasised by Chomsky is its supposed innateness, an issue that will be pursued in some detail in the next chapter. Chomsky's view has received some biological support through the work of Eric Lenneberg, and according to it the human mind is equipped from birth with a blueprint for language, i.e. it is endowed with certain genetically transmitted neurological structures which underlie the acquisition and subsequent use of human-like languages. Hockett also agrees that human genes are a necessary condition for language acquisition, but his main emphasis is on the environment, as indicated by the label of his design feature *cultural transmission*. For Chomsky, the role of the environment is one of providing the basic language material for the genetically pre-programmed human being to process it into a grammar (for more discussion see Chapter 10, Section 8). A quote from Lenneberg (1967, p. 375) will make this clear:

> the situation is somewhat analogous to the relationship between nourishment and growth. The food that the individual takes in as architectural raw material must be chemically broken down and reconstituted before it enters the synthesis that produces tissues and organs. The information on how the organs are to be structured does not come in the food but is latent in the individual's own cellular components. The raw material for the individual's language synthesis is the language spoken by the adults surrounding the child. The

presence of the raw material seems to function like a releaser for the developmental language synthesizing process.

Whether the social environment or the genetic endowment is taken as the primary cause of the individual's language acquisition, it is commonly held that both factors must be present during the process (but see Chapter 10, Section 8 for some interesting recent evidence about language emerging without linguistic input). It follows from both Hockett's and Chomsky's views that neither a non-human animal nor a human child reared in isolation can acquire language. Interesting evidence in this connection is provided by the so-called 'feral men' or 'wolf children'.

One of the best-known cases of wolf children is that of the late eighteenth-century *enfant sauvage* of Aveyron, Victor. He was approximately 12 years of age at the time of his capture and must have spent at least seven years in complete isolation from humans. He was only able to produce a single guttural, uniform sound, and despite the efforts of his mentor, Dr Itard, a convinced empiricist, he reportedly only succeeded in pronouncing the word *lait*, which he associated with various objects related to his act of milk-drinking, his desire to do it and his ensuing joy, the exclamation *oh Dieu*, which contains the first speech sound (the vowel *o*) that elicited a reaction from the boy, and a few other monosyllables and isolated sounds. This performance does not appear to constitute flattering evidence for the innateness hypothesis, but it must be noted that, as just mentioned, in Chomsky's conception the biologically determined prerequisites must be complemented by an adequate social environment to act as a trigger, so that as the combined result of both factors speech usually emerges before the age of 5, during the so-called critical period for language acquisition. Moreover, Victor's failure is even more mysterious from an empiricist viewpoint bound to the idea of an exclusively cultural transmission, since he was a mentally alert child who greatly benefited from Itard's tuition in other areas.

Despite its drastic poverty, Victor's language behaviour shows an incipient degree of semanticity in his usage of the word *lait*. *Semanticity* is a design feature that refers to the existence of associative ties between elements in the linguistic system and things or situations in the environment. On the other hand, other features as yet unmentioned are absent, such as *displacement* (the ability to refer to things or events remote in time or space), *reflexiveness* (the capacity to use language to talk about language itself) and *prevarication* (the ability to deliberately tell lies or talk nonsense). Note that the scarcity of information on Victor's day-to-day language behaviour (or lack of it) in Itard's otherwise irreproachable report makes it unwise to lend disproportionate weight to the event.

More successful than Victor was the Indian girl Kamala, discovered together with her sister Amala in the company of wolves at the beginning of the century. She must have been about 8 when she was discovered and after some time she began to use a booing noise to demand water, before attempting several phonetic approximations to the Bengali forms she was exposed to. At the time of her death, nine years later, she had reportedly gained mastery of some fifty words, which she could string together to form sentences, used appropriately and creatively in a way that gave evidence of her intellectual growth. This compares favourably with Victor but is still a long way from the language development of normal children. A more successful story is that of Kaspar Hauser, a nineteenth-century German teenager who spent his childhood years in domestic imprisonment and seems to have eventually acquired almost normal speech. Interestingly, in contrast to Victor and Kamala, he could already utter a few words at the time of his discovery, a fact that seems to indicate that he had not been kept in total isolation, but rather as a prisoner not deprived of occasional contact with his warders. This is consistent with the existence of a critical period for spontaneous and normal language acquisition and with the innateness of the language faculty. If language were entirely contingent on tradition the difference between Kaspar and the other two cases would certainly be difficult to explain.

A more recent case of language deprivation is that of the American girl Genie, discovered at the age of 13, in 1970, after having been kept a prisoner by her father more or less since her birth. She had been confined in a small room where her movement was severely impeded, and production of any sound, linguistic or not, would result in physical punishment. After receiving the appropriate care, she was sent to live with a foster family where her as yet uncompleted development is being observed by psychologists and linguists. At the time of her discovery, Genie showed total lack of comprehension of language, with the possible exception of a few isolated words. Also, she had almost no control over the organs associated with speech, even for such purely vegetative functions as chewing or swallowing. A detailed account of the various stages in the linguistic development of Genie is beyond the scope of this book, but a few general remarks on her differences from and similarities to normal children in the early stages of language development will be in order. Genie exhibits a definite advantage with regard to rate of acquisition of vocabulary and in the accuracy of her word usage. This might be related to her quite considerable cognitive development, which keeps well ahead of what is normal for children at a similar language stage, as evidenced, for instance, by her acquisition of the ability to comprehend questions containing the words *how*, *why*, or *when* at the same time as those with *who*, *what*, or *where*, the former set usually being acquired later in the case of normal children. On the other hand, Genie lags behind in her ability to string words together (i.e. in syntax, see Chapter 6). Interesting in this connection is Lenneberg's claim that the critical period for language acquisition is linked to the specialisation of functions between the two brain hemispheres, the completion of lateralisation at puberty marking the end of the critical period. Tests applied to Genie indicate that the right, rather than the more usual left, hemisphere is active in her acquisition of language, and this may explain some of her linguistic anomalies. Subject to future developments, the case of Genie seemingly supports Chomsky's hypothesis that both nature (i.e. innate basic language structures) and nurture (i.e. a linguistic environment to trigger off the innate linguistic abilities) are necessary for adequate language development.

1.5   Human-like language in higher primates?

Considerations such as those just mentioned are supportive of the long-held belief that non-human animals simply do not possess the innate mental structures which are essential for the acquisition of language. If so, it would appear to follow that no amount of training can lead to the use of a human language by animals. Undeterred by such inauspicious prospects, two American couples, the Kelloggs and the Hayseses, attempted to train two young chimpanzees (Gua and Viki) in their own family environments, in the 1930s and 1950s, respectively. The choice of the chimpanzee as a subject was of course not random, since, besides their well-attested intelligence, these animals are closest to humans anatomically, genetically and even emotionally. The results were none the less disappointing; Gua did not learn any word, and Viki barely managed to pronounce *mama, papa, cup* and *up*.

In the mid-1960s another American couple, the psychologists Allen and Beatrice Gardner, speculated that possibly the responsibility for these failures ought to be apportioned not so much to the animals themselves as to the medium, speech simply being inappropriate for the chimpanzee (cf. e.g. the research by Lieberman mentioned in Section 1).

The Gardners embarked on a project designed to exploit the renowned manual dexterity of the chimpanzee, adopting as a medium American Sign Language (ASL), the communication system used by the deaf in most of North America. Crucially, although articulated with the hands and thus lacking the feature 'vocal-auditory channel', ASL shows very strong parallels with ordinary vocal language: largely arbitrary relationships between signifier and signified, meaningful word order differences, regional divergences, incomprehensibility to other deaf communities, translation difficulties, and so on.

The subject of the experiment was a female chimpanzee named Washoe, captured wild in Africa and about 1 year old when the training began in 1966. All efforts were made to provide an environment conducive to spontaneous and creative behaviour, and Washoe enjoyed a freedom of movement similar to that of human children. The use of ASL was strictly adhered to in Washoe's presence, to the extent of repressing all human sound not vocalisable by chimpanzees. The instruction procedures were deliberately eclectic, and included imitation (immediate or delayed), instrumental conditioning (the 'shaping' into ASL of apparently random signals; cf. Chapter 2, Section 5, for a general discussion of this technique, pioneered by the psychologist B. F. Skinner) and moulding (the direct physical guiding of the animal's hands into the target sign).

Before enumerating and evaluating the results, we shall briefly refer to a few of the growing number of studies prompted by Washoe's apparent success.

In the Gardners' tradition is the experiment by Herbert Terrace with Nim Chimpsky (the name is hardly coincidental!), a 2-month-old male chimpanzee born in captivity. Here, too, eclectic teaching was adopted, with the emphasis on moulding and imitation, and the ape was provided with an informal environment where socialisation and emotional bonding with his trainers (about sixty in all) could take place. Possibly the most significant difference was the subjection of Nim to a daily sign-tuition routine on a school-like schedule in a special cell-type 'classroom', bare but for a few objects related to the learning task, to prevent distraction, and where the basic pedagogic principle was to focus on only one activity at a time.

Similarly, Francine (Penny) Patterson's Koko, a 1-year-old captive-born female gorilla, lived mostly in a house-trailer in conditions comparable to those of her chimpanzee counterparts, including a substantial amount of daily sign instruction (ten hours on average), which Patterson purposely describes as 'non-regimented'. The specific interest of this experiment is of course the extension of the investigation to a different (if very closely related) biological species, one which has traditionally been regarded (perhaps unfairly) as inferior to the chimpanzee in both intelligence and social adaptation. The series was then completed with the addition of the orang-utan, the third of the great apes. Departing slightly from his predecessors, Lyn Miles's Chantek, a 9-month-old captive-born male, was deliberately treated as a wild, if sociable, creature (i.e. not as a human child), and a 'jungle-gym' was accordingly provided adjacent to the house-trailer where he was lodged.

The last two experiments to be reported on here represent a

dramatic departure environmentally, linguistically and pedagogically. In one, conducted by the psychologist David Premack, a 6-year-old wild-born chimpanzee (Sarah) was taught to communicate by placing metal-backed plastic chips representing words on a magnetised board. In the other, the 2-year-old Lana (also a female chimpanzee) was trained by Duane Rumbaugh to utilise a keyboard linked to a computer to produce on a screen geometrical configurations ordered in accordance with the rules of a language especially devised for the purposes of the experiment. Both animals were placed in a confined space where strict conditioning techniques could be easily implemented.

Sarah's training consisted in the matching of a social situation with a language presentation. A transaction was first established through the offer of a fruit by a friendly trainer. When the transaction was well established, additional fruits were placed out of the reach of the animal, while a plastic chip was left in her vicinity. If Sarah placed the chip on the board, she was immediately rewarded with the fruit. Sarah's target sentences ultimately consisted of four elements (donor + action + object + recipient, as in 'Mary give apple Sarah'), and the training typically proceeded step by step, substituting only one element at a time in the sentence (and, correspondingly, in the situation), in such a way that all but one of the elements would be known to the ape. Notice that Premack's design minimises the number of variables; vocabulary size is directly controllable, memory as an extraneous factor is dispensed with (the plastic chips do not possess 'rapid fading'), and it is relatively easy to ascertain what type of difficulty may be involved in any particular problem.

Lana's 'room' contained several objects and goods-dispensers, a screen for the projection of slides and motion pictures, stereo equipment, a sliding door and an outside window, which was normally closed. Her interaction with this environment took place exclusively through the manipulation of her linguistic facilities. In addition, conversations could be held between ape and trainer, who had access to a similar computer-linked keyboard. Like Sarah's, Lana's training was based on conditioning, although guiding, both verbal and direct, was also used.

Taken at face value, the results of these and other similar experiments are impressive. In all cases precautions were taken to ensure the objectivity and robustness of the field observations. Thus the Gardners stipulated that, in order for a sign to be 'officially' declared acquired, it had to have been reported by three independent observers as occurring unprompted daily over a fifteen-day period under conditions of contextual appropriateness. Such a strict control was somewhat relaxed in other studies, in ways which were deemed not to jeopardise the significance of the results (Terrace, for instance, required a period of only five days). A particular misinterpretation risk is presented by the so-called 'Clever Hans' phenomenon, so named after a German horse that tapped numbers with his hoof in tune with visual cues unconsciously given out by his trainer. Accordingly, the Gardners chose a 'double-blind' testing procedure, where the stimulus is out of the visual field of the judge, and Premack used testers ignorant of the chip language. Finally, the apes were generally submitted to routine psychological testing with the aim of ascertaining the general cognitive or perceptual strategies which may underlie their linguistic performance.

The number of signs mastered by the apes over the average four-year training period falls typically between 100 and 150. Moreover, after the initial learning period, the signs are reported to have been transferred to other objects of the same class and used creatively and appropriately, in a manner which resembles the communicative activities of young children. Much quoted, for instance, is Washoe's utterance *water-bird* at the sight of a duck. Errors are relatively infrequent (Sarah's and Lana's test performances are reported often to have been over 80 per cent accurate) and, when they occur, they are open to alternative interpretations, such as breaking up boring situations (Terrace on Nim) or indulging in verbal abuse (Patterson on Koko). Terrace also reports on Nim's capacity for duplicity, and Patterson on Koko's for humour.

Word order, a significant trait of human language (cf. Chapter 6 on syntax), including ASL, was strictly required of Sarah and Lana, and, interestingly, the sign sequences produced by the 'natural' apes show a spontaneous preference for certain permutations. Because of the controlled nature of Sarah's experiment, the list of her overall achievements is particularly detailed and will be given here as exemplification: naming, sentence formation (including compound sentences: 'Sarah insert banana pail apple dish'), comparison ('same' v. 'different'), questioning, negation, pluralisation, quantification (use of 'all', 'none', 'several'), conjunction ('and'), logical connection ('*if* Sarah take apple, *then* Mary give Sarah chocolate') and expression of spatial relations (as in 'red *on* green' on presentation of the appropriate visual stimulus).

Sarah has also shown a capacity to *name* classes such as colour, shape, or size. Also, more interestingly for the linguist, she exhibited some metalinguistic ability (cf. the design feature 'reflexiveness') by performing an activity involving linking a symbol with an object by means of the operator 'name of' (also represented by a symbol). Another design feature worthy of mention in the context of the present experiments is *learnability*, a property of all human languages, including ASL, which, rather obviously, can be said to be *learnable* by human organisms (some other system, such as a computer program, might not be). The interest of the ape research is of course that it directly addresses the question of the biological prerequisites of such learning. More specifically, the argument could be made that, if ASL is learnable by both humans and apes, then apes must share the appropriate biological structures with humans. And if the list of design features defines the scope of human language, it would appear that at least the 'natural' apes have successfully acquired one such language. The only feature open to question appears to be 'displacement', but even here Patterson explicitly mentions reference to past and future events by the animal.

The argument above assumes that the apes have indeed acquired ASL, and we shall now review some of the criticisms which question both aspects of this assumption: that the system they learnt is ASL, and that, whatever the learnt system is, it was indeed acquired as a human-like language.

It is important to realise that the structure of ASL exhibits a considerable degree of complexity, and, in addition to hand configuration and movement in a structured space, signs are defined by means of eye gaze, facial expression and head and body shifts. Crucially, ASL sentences do not have a direct correspondence with English. Now, with very few exceptions, the personnel involved in the ape projects were not fluent signers, their output being thus closer to 'signed English' than to true ASL. Moreover, signs were frequently simplified, or the ape's natural gestures simply taken over, all in an effort to adapt to the animal's abilities, which manifestly are not suited for any of the complex aspects of standard ASL. Given these facts, it is perhaps more accurate to describe the system used by the apes as 'pidgin' sign language. While 'pidgins' (cf. Chapter 12, Section 8) are also used by humans and share at least some of the characteristics of natural human languages, the level of achievement of the primates is thus somewhat reduced.

The next question relates to the true nature of the animals' feats. In particular, is there evidence that they used the system in a manner approximating language? It is questionable whether the apes involved in the 'artificial' experiments did, their performance being probably explainable as a chain of conditioned responses (cf. Chapter 2); pigeons also have been shown to be able to peck a sequence of coloured keys (reminiscent of Lana's 'sentences', e.g. 'please machine make window open'), but it is not clear that it is legitimate to interpret this behaviour as 'language'.

The 'natural' apes, on the other hand, invariably produced unrequested sign sequences. For instance, some 20,000 such utterances by Nim with anything up to sixteen signs in each were recorded over a two-year period. However, the critics of the experiments (and, interestingly, these include Nim's trainers Herbert

Terrace and Laura Petitto) have forcefully pointed out a collection of flaws which seriously vitiate the interpretation of this output as language.

First, it is not always easy to establish what the accomplishments of the animals really are, since the data are typically under-reported and 'cleaned up'. In particular, errors are hardly mentioned, and repetitions are deleted as a matter of general policy. For instance, an utterance like Nim's 'give orange me give eat orange me eat orange give me eat orange give me you' could well have been transcribed as 'give orange me eat, you!'. This of course gives the false impression of a carefully thought-out sentence, similar to that of a human child. In actual fact, however, not only are children's utterances free of such redundancies, but typically they are drastically reduced (cf. Chapter 10, Section 3). It has been suggested that the strategy underlying the apes' overproduction might be one of maximising signing correspondingly to maximise the reward. Obviously, this has little to do with the expression of meaning, the primary aim of language as normally used by humans, children included.

The apes' tendency to repetition extends to the domain of discourse, where it has been observed that a substantial proportion of their utterances simply echo the trainer's output. The consequences of this are fairly serious, critically undermining the claims made in the literature about the contextual appropriateness of their use of signs. It also highlights another shortcoming of the animals' performance, namely, their general lack of motivation and spontaneity, since they usually require considerable prodding by the trainers before an adequate response is elicited. Finally, they have difficulties as regards conversational structure, typically interrupting the trainer in mid-discourse. These trends stand in sharp contrast with the behaviour of human children (including deaf children learning ASL), who are known to initiate conversations and to take turns in diadic exchanges.

As hinted at above, one of the most characteristic traits of human language relates to the use of word order to express different meanings. Importantly, each such order is relatable to the semantic classes present in the sentence, and is thus not contingent on the specific identity of the lexical items. The best documented case of syntactic tendencies in the 'natural' experiments is provided by Nim. It is telling, however, that for each putative 'semantic role' in his sentences, only one lexical item was normally used, thus weakening the likelihood that a general semantic base underlay his performance. Also, and perhaps not unrelatedly, the average length of his utterances failed to show any significant increase throughout his training. Finally, because of the redundancies mentioned above, greater sentence length did not necessarily result in greater information content. Once more, these traits contrast sharply with those found in the speech of human children, whose sentences, even when reduced, also exhibit hierarchical structure, as is typical of human syntax (cf. Chapter 6, Section 2).

In the face of such unfavourable assessment of the apes' performance, it would appear that only their ability to name remains as a solid achievement. But here again the differences with children are significant. In effect, while the latter go through a 'naming stage' of relentless questioning, the animals have to be submitted to intensive teaching, sometimes involving thousands of hours for any one sign. Moreover, particularly in the habitual absence of 'displacement', it is not obvious that their comprehension of the meaning of individual words greatly exceeds that of lower organisms conditioned to particular behaviours in the presence of certain stimuli (cf. Chapter 2). Thus, while the apes have undoubtedly grasped the utility of the signs (e.g. 'banana' can bring about the obtainment of the fruit), it appears unlikely that they have understood that the signs *refer* to particular objects (on 'reference' cf. Chapter 7, p. 201). Accordingly, it seems more parsimonious and perhaps more realistic to adopt a pragmatic (cf. Chapter 7, Section 6) rather than a linguistic interpretation of their sign behaviour, reminiscent of children's *earliest* steps in language.

Faced with this barrage of criticism, the advocates of the linguistic ape have striven for a higher level of refinement in experimental design, which allegedly has overcome some of the shortcomings of previous attempts, and have examined critically some of their opponents' charges. A typical strategy has been to remove the burden of failure from the biology of the animal to the experimental procedures. In the context of the social and communicational aspects of language, the stilted learning conditions prevailing in the 'artificial' experiments and to some extent also in Nim's have been the target of special attack. Also, possession of language has been claimed to be a gradient, rather than an all-or-nothing, affair, and this would subtract legitimacy from the use of a rigid defining set of necessary conditions such as the design features. Finally, and importantly, there are reports of the spontaneous teaching of signs by Washoe (now 'retired' at the Institute for Primate Studies, in Norman, Oklahoma) to her adopted infant, who has apparently begun to use them. All this leads us to conclude that the ape language controversy is still very much alive, and that it will probably take years of patient but dispassionate research and interpretation before the final word on the matter is said.

1.6 The functional significance of Hockett's design features

Four of Hockett's features have not yet been mentioned. *Interchangeability* means that all healthy adults can be both transmitters and receivers of the signal (cf. the situation existing in species where there is, for example, sex specialisation for song, visual display, chemical trail, etc.). *Complete feedback* implies that the speaker himself can perceive the totality of his own signal, through the sense of hearing (cf., for instance, facial gesturing, where unaided visual feedback is not possible for the sender). *Specialisation* refers to that property of communication systems whereby the production of elements in the system has effects ('triggering effects') which are distinct from their immediate physical consequences. Thus, for instance, if a drunk leaves a bar propelled by a bouncer, the bouncer's action is not seen as communication; but if he leaves after receiving a threatening gesture or an utterance 'you'd better leave', the drunk's action is not a direct physical consequence of the bouncer's activity, but rather it is *triggered* by it. Finally, *duality of structure* refers to the independence of the internal sound-structure of the basic structural units of language, such as words (but cf. Chapter 5), from the laws governing the way words are strung together. Thus the rule that prevents the sequence *table the big is* in English (but not necessarily in some other language) is unrelated to the principle that rules out a word like *bnick*, despite its being objectively very similar to *brick* (an actual English word) and to *blick* (a possible English word).

It is our contention that it is possible to regard all of Hockett's features as different manifestations of two fundamental traits – efficiency and distance. We shall examine them in turn.

Regarding *efficiency*, the use of the vocal-auditory channel implies that darkness is no obstacle for the transmission and reception of the signal. Broadcast transmission facilitates the diffusion of the signal, while directional reception improves the accuracy of perception and makes the source more easily locatable. Rapid fading implies that the channel will immediately be free for further transmission, thus increasing rapidity and, consequently, quantity of signals. Interchangeability permits any member of the species to act as sender or receiver at any point in time, hence a greater flexibility and adaptability in the system. Complete feedback provides a very efficient and particularly fast checking procedure, while duality of structure (which implies the existence of structure itself, i.e. the fact that human languages are rule-governed systems) has the effect of drastically increasing the economy of the system. Creativity introduces (questionably total) flexibility regarding the number of transmitted messages, and both discreteness and semanticity reduce potential ambiguity, thus making the system more accurate and efficient. Flexibility in signifier-signified pairings

(arbitrariness) and independence of the signifier from biological determination (specialisation) also have the effect of increasing efficiency. Hockett (1960, p. 426) ascribes to cultural transmission an efficiency value as regards survival, since 'it allows a species to learn through experience and to adapt to new living conditions, at a rate much greater than is possible purely with the genetic mechanism'. From a Chomskyan angle, on the other hand, the genetic blueprint would enable the organism to acquire the knowledge it requires in a remarkably short timespan, thus making possible the mastery of the environment in a way that satisfies the intrinsic needs of the organism itself.

Both arbitrariness and specialisation imply that the user can take psychological distance from his own life experience and consequently manipulate the code independently of events in the outside world (cf., for instance, the facial expression of horror at the sight of a disaster, which is connected to muscular feelings of withdrawal and flight induced by the event itself). This independence between code and experience characterises the second group of features, all sharing a property that can be given the label *distance*. Thus prevarication implies that the user can utilise the code in ways that are at variance with its primary function. Displacement enables manipulation of both spatial and temporal distance between outside events and their linguistic expression. Thanks to reflexiveness the code can schizophrenically analyse itself, while learnability provides the user with sufficient independence to separate himself from the code, which can therefore be switched. Arbitrariness frees the signifier from the signified, and specialisation distances the expression from the physical limitations of the users.

Possession of all of Hockett's design features places human language in a privileged position regarding both efficiency and distance, but it does not necessarily imply that language as a qualitatively unique communication system is exclusive to the human species, since the feats by chimpanzees previously examined perilously approach the area formerly monopolised by humans, if not in quantity of output at least with regard to the qualitative traits manifested in their performance. The quantitative differences may, of course, turn out to be crucial in ways as yet unforeseen, but in the meantime the safest bet for the human uniqueness of language seems to lie in the Chomskyan feature 'genetic transmission' (what Chomsky calls 'innateness', an expression that has philosophical overtones and may be potentially misleading), since in no other species in the animal kingdom does language emerge with such precision and regularity. In the case of the 'talking' chimpanzees the role of cultural (as against genetic) transmission is obvious – in all cases a training schedule was followed and rewards were introduced to ensure the establishment of language connections. Chomsky contends that the situation with humans is otherwise, culture and the environment only acting as triggers which activate the biologically conditioned language development of the child (see Chapter 10, Section 8, for some discussion of the necessity and role of a linguistic environment in first language acquisition). If this is so, one would expect that the emergence and development of language would follow its own genetic blueprint independently of the communicative needs of the child. It is to the interaction (if any) between language and communication that we turn next.

1.7 Structure and function in language

Chomsky's views on language appear peculiar and eccentric to the American philosopher John Searle, who, because of the interrelation between structure and function, views the study of language independently from communication as a 'perversity' similar to studying the structure of the heart with disregard of its blood-pumping activity. The British linguist M. A. K. Halliday holds a similar opinion and advocates the study of both structure and function in order to achieve a good understanding of what language is. This synthetic approach is undoubtedly commendable, but in practice it is difficult not to give priority to one of these two aspects of language, and Halliday's sympathies seem to be with function rather than structure: 'we try to explain the nature of language, its internal organisation and patterning, in terms of the functions that it has evolved to serve' (1974, p. 13). According to this view, language is best understood in the context of communication, communication being a natural and genetically determined function of the human being. For Halliday, an act of communication typically consists of the encoding of meaning, and meaning will therefore be at the basis of language. He finds six distinct communicative functions characterising the child's early communicative development, all of them relating to aspects of social life, such as the satisfaction of his material needs, the regulation of other people's behaviour, the expression of the self, the exploration of the outside world, and so on (see Chapter 10 for a more detailed discussion). From these six functional categories (later supplemented by a seventh) evolve the three *macrofunctions* of the adult linguistic system.

The first macrofunction, which Halliday calls *ideational*, relates to the expression of propositional content. The second, the *interpersonal* function, establishes links with the social participants in the communication act. The third, the *textual* function, provides the language with an internal structure and relates it to the context of situation. An example will clarify all this. In the sentence *kick that ball*, the meaning of the words *kick* ('hit with the foot') and *ball* ('round object') is part of the ideational function. At the interpersonal level, such an utterance expresses a relationship between speaker and hearer, that is, the former requests (or commands, depending on extralinguistic social factors) the latter to do something. Finally, the particle *that* has the textual function of relating the sentence to the particular situation in which it is uttered in the presence of an actual ball (otherwise the sentence would be inappropriate). Associated with each of these three functions are one or more networks of structural relations (*that*, for instance, patterns with *this* in that they both express degrees of physical distance in relation to the speaker), and the choice of options within these networks enables the participants to encode meaning and thus to engage successfully in an act of communication. Thus, according to Halliday (1974, p. 42), the grammar of any particular language is only 'the linguistic device for hooking up the selections in meaning which are derived from the various functions of language', in such a way that they are realised 'in a unified structural form'.

The main problem in Halliday's approach is to account for the developmental discontinuity between the child's proto-language and the adult's grammar, a fact which is consistent with the Chomskyan hypothesis that there are genetically determined mental structures programmed for the acquisition of a system with precisely the characteristics of human language. Also, it is far from clear how a functional approach could deal with such phenomena as the overlap between the forms used to express statements, requests and questions in English. The declarative form is usually said to express statements ('he passed the vinegar'), the imperative form expresses orders and requests ('pass the vinegar') and the interrogative form expresses questions ('did he pass the vinegar?'), but the declarative form in English may express requests ('I wish you'd pass the vinegar', 'I wonder if you'd mind passing the vinegar') and the interrogative form may also express requests ('would you pass the vinegar?') or even statements ('but would he pass the vinegar?'). At least in the intuitively clear sense of 'structure' (i.e. declarative, imperative and interrogative) and 'function' (i.e. statement, request, question) there seems to be precious little correlation between the two in such examples.

Caution is called for when considering the possible causal relationship between language and communication in humans. Newborn babies, severely handicapped people, persons out of voice-range, speakers of two mutually incomprehensible languages, all manage to communicate through non-linguistic means, many of which are also generously used in everyday social intercourse. And the converse is also true, since language can be and often is used for non-communicative purposes. We all sometimes think in words, and some go as far as articulating sound to themselves, an activity that Searle views as communication with oneself, but Chomsky rightly retorts that nothing much is gained by robbing the word 'communication' of its common everyday sense, which implies the presence of at least two people. This function of language seems rather related to thinking and, whether or not language is an essential prerequisite for thinking (disparate opinions abound on this matter; see Chapters 9 and 10 for some discussion), it is undoubtedly a powerful encoding device of great potential as a thinking aid, much in the way algebra helps us perform complex numerical operations. Another non-communicative function of language is play: from childhood to adulthood, humans take obvious enjoyment in sounds and words, rhythms and rhymes, puns and poetry, and the pleasure appears to be connected to language itself, quite independently of whether it is communicated to someone else or not. Finally, and most importantly, it appears reasonable that we use language to impose a structure on the world – in Halliday's own words, 'a child's construction of language is at once a part of, and a means of, his construction of reality' (1978, p. 89).

1.8 Saussure's structuralist linguistics

The idea that language is structure is at the basis of the linguistic theories of Ferdinand de Saussure. In a famous analogy, he likens language to the game of chess ([1916] 1974, pp. 22–3):

> language is a system that has its own arrangement . . . In chess what is external can be separated relatively easily from what is internal . . . If I use ivory chessmen instead of wooden ones, the change has no effect on the system; but if I decrease or increase the number of chessmen, this change has a profound effect on the 'grammar' of the game . . . In each instance one can determine the nature of the phenomenon by applying this rule: everything that changes the system in any way is internal.

Similarly, within the structure of language the meaning of words depends on their relationship to other words, not on their form. Thus if *fruit* in English were to be entirely replaced by a word *glep*, there would be no change in the system of word-meanings, but if *fruit* were extended in such a way that it could now be used to refer to nuts as well, or if it were contracted to exclude such things as strawberries, gooseberries, etc., then a whole range of words would be in a different relationship to one another. Note that these examples are not chosen at random: Chinese has a word *gwo* whose reference covers fruit and nuts, while the Russian word *frukty* does not include berries. The applicability of a word is therefore determined by the relationship it has to other words (in English 'apple' and 'gooseberry' are two sorts of the same thing, while in Russian they are not).

Thus language is nothing but differences between the elements that constitute the system. But this system is not lying somewhere, like diamonds in a mine, ready for the linguist to go and dig it out. Rather, our first task is to characterise such a system, and this Saussure does by setting up a dichotomy between what he calls *langue* and *parole*, two well-nigh untranslatable terms reflecting a distinction drawn by the French sociologist Émile Durkheim between what is social and what is individual. Thus while *parole* is similar to individual speech, *langue* 'exists in the form of a sum of impressions deposited in the brain of each member of the community, almost like a dictionary of which identical copies have been distributed to each individual' (Saussure, [1916] 1974, p. 19). Saussure's dichotomy is similar, though not identical, to Chomsky's distinction between *competence* and *performance* (see Chapter 2, p. 40) (Saussure's *langue* has an explicit social orientation), and both Chomskyan and Saussurean linguistics focus on the more idealised side of language (competence, *langue*) often at the expense of its concrete manifestation (performance, *parole*), a fact that has been seen by some as a shortcoming.

Saussure's is the first of the linguistic revolutions of the twentieth century, and the subsequent work of Chomsky is inconceivable without the methodological avenues he opened up. Nineteenth-century linguistics was chiefly oriented towards language history, and Saussure emphatically advocates a shift from the study of *diachrony* (i.e. the historical evolution of a language) to the study of *synchrony* (i.e. the system of oppositions that constitute the *langue* at any one time). Once more he uses chess as the basis for an analogy to contend that any state of a game can be perfectly understood without any knowledge of the previous moves. To take a real example from language, the meaning of *nice* is given in the system of contemporary English by its relationships with other elements (e.g. it is the opposite of *nasty*, and so on), and the fact that etymologically it means 'ignorant' (it derives from the Latin *nescius*, a compound from *ne-*, 'not', and *scire*, 'to know') can be completely disregarded. Like other Saussurean dichotomies, the distinction between synchrony and diachrony has subsequently been found to be less strict than in the original formulation (see Chapters 11 and 12 for some discussion).

We can now identify the object of study of linguistics in Saussure's formulation as being a synchronic state of *langue*, defined as a system of oppositions between linguistic signs, each of them made up of the arbitrary pairing of a concept and a sound-image. As yet undecided is the issue of how the linguist can get at the structure of the system (*langue* or competence) from the individual acts of *parole*, since only the latter are directly accessible to the senses. A solution to this problem presupposes an answer to the question of which of the multifarious aspects of *parole* must be selected for study, i.e. the question of what are the data of linguistics. Each of the possible approaches to these issues leaves a rich trail of psychological and philosophical implications, and it is with these problems that the next chapter is concerned.

Exercises: Chapter 1

1   It has been suggested that speech perception may take place by mentally relating the actual sound heard to the movement of the organs involved in its production. In this light:

(*a*) explain how the chimpanzee's systematic failure to produce speech sounds for which he is anatomically equipped (e.g. *p*, *t*, *s*) can be taken as evidence that he lacks the appropriate language-related neural structures;
(*b*) advance some explanation for Viki's acquisition of words such as *up*, and for Victor's striking poverty of language.

2   State which of the following sentences are best interpreted as expressing a constitutive rule and which as expressing a regulative rule. Explain why.

(*a*) thou shalt not kill; (*b*) have a light breakfast, such as muesli and fruit juice; (*c*) 15 × 15 = 225; (*d*) it is forbidden to park in front of the gate; (*e*) a penalty is given for handling the ball in the penalty area; (*f*) plurals are usually formed by adding an *s* to the singular; (*g*) headlights must be dipped when a vehicle is coming from the opposite direction; (*h*) the final stanza in a sonnet must be a tercet; (*i*) flags are flown at half mast following the death of the head of state; (*j*) keep off the grass; (*k*) for a stew, simmer for four hours with the lid on; (*l*) four-letter words are not used; (*m*) silence must be respected in the House of the Lord; (*n*) all applications must be typed; (*o*) officials wear red caps.

3   Collect a few materials illustrative of language prescriptivism, such as letters to the media, quotes from school grammars, personal anecdotes (advice given by parents to their children, etc.). Point out any inconsistencies between such regulations and actual behaviour. Advance some hypotheses to account for the existence of linguistic prescriptivism.

4   A threefold classification of signs is usually made according to the type of relationship existing between signifier and signified, as follows: *symbols* (the relationship is arbitrary and conventional), *icons* (the signifier resembles the signified) and *indices* (the signifier is caused by the signified). Where possible, assign the following signifiers to sign-categories.

(*a*) the V-gesture made with the index and middle fingers; (*b*) an immaculately trimmed gentleman; (*c*) an ordnance survey map; (*d*) the usual traffic sign for 'school'; (*e*) the usual traffic sign for 'no entry'; (*f*) blushing; (*g*) a pointer with the word *toilets* on it; (*h*) the index finger held vertically to the lips to indicate silence; (*i*) a smile; (*j*) a skin rash; (*k*) a cigarette advertisement showing a man on horseback in the middle of a lush valley; (*l*) clearing one's throat; (*m*) the smell of incense; (*n*) the traffic policeman's stop signal; (*o*) a wheelchair drawn on a toilet door; (*p*) a statue of Queen Victoria; (*q*) a painting of Jesus; (*r*) nodding.

5   On the basis of the words below comment on the alleged arbitrariness of the linguistic sign, bringing in further examples and/or counter-examples to strengthen your arguments. Remember that 'signifier' refers to sound, and thus the orthography may be distracting, particularly in the case of foreign words.

slosh, liquid, crack, flow, ouâ-ouâ (French), slide, glacial, fluctuate, bau-bau (Italian), crackle, fluvial, glimpse, glue, glass, grate, chichirichì (Italian), slight, glance, scratch, glow, flush, cuckoo, glist, fluent, smack, cock-a-doodle-doo, slape, glare, cocorico (French), slush, glide, ¡ay! (Spanish), liquor, shriek, gleen, sleek, kukuriku (Russian), smash, screech, mew, crow, crunch, guau-guau (Spanish), slime, slippery, slap, crush, glucose, cricket, quiquiriquí (Spanish), fluid, glister, crisp, flux, slick, crash, gloat, grit, kikeriki (German), glare, groan, slash, glitter, glycerin, creak, glaze, wau-wau (German), sludgy, sleet, slop, glossy, scream, caw, slough, aïe! (French), glutinous, screak, cry, crump, grind, glimmer, glisten, growl, gleam, sluice, croak, slob, ouch!, glint, crust, bow-wow, crinkle.

6   Each of the following can be thought of as a 'language' used in, for example, British society: the traffic light system, money, a card game such as poker or whist, an art form such as music or painting. Establish the basic sign unit(s) for one or more of these systems, and analyse them within the framework of Hockett's design features. How would the system have to be modified so that it would possess the design features it currently lacks?

7   The following sentences illustrate the fact that language can be put to a variety of uses. You are asked to elucidate what the functional value(s) of each of them would be in an ordinary, everyday context.

(*a*) I find it hard to believe; (*b*) I pronounce you man and wife; (*c*) you are dismissed; (*d*) it must be rather late; (*e*) your marriage is hereby annulled; (*f*) am I on the right bus, I wonder?; (*g*) you shall be taken to one of Her Majesty's prisons and detained there for the next twenty years; (*h*) I christen this child Sarah Jo; (*i*) haven't I seen you before?; (*j*) I challenge you to supply some proof; (*k*) how very awful!; (*l*) apples and pears; (*m*) take care; (*n*) hello!; (*o*) come off it!; (*p*) push the door to; (*q*) Grosvenor Square!; (*r*) beautiful day, isn't it?; (*s*) I do apologise; (*t*) don't you think it's time we stopped quarrelling?; (*u*) tiger! tiger! burning bright in the forests of the night; (*v*) let's see, four and four is eight, three and six is nine, and one and four is five, so it's five pounds ninety eight, sir; (*w*) your salad looks most appetising; (*x*) doobidoobidoo; (*y*) can't you feel the draught?; (*z*) you're the cream in my coffee.

8   The paraphrases below correspond to language behaviour associated with Sarah (S), Lana (L), or Nigel (N), the child investigated by Halliday. Here you are asked to analyse the linguistic functions they fulfil, paying particular attention to possible ambiguities resulting from the indeterminacy of the context of the situation. In the light of your findings draw some conclusions regarding the nature of each of the studies.

do that again (N), red colour-of apple (S), please Lana groom Tim (L), please machine give name-of this (L), no don't let's do that (N), Tim give bowl to Lana? (L), you move behind room? (L), let me play with the cat (N), a bus! (N), several apple is PLURAL green (S), yes I want that (N), Tim move into room? (L), that's nice (N), Tim tickle Lana out of room? (L), tra-la-la (N), Daddy! (N), no Sarah take honey cracker (S), round is shape (S), look: a picture (N), Tim put milk in machine (L), let's pretend to go to sleep (N), 'apple' is name-of apple (S), please Tim groom Lana (L), Anna! (N), Lana drink this out-of room? (L), don't be cross with me (N), blue on green (S), yes Lana want drink milk (L), Lana want ball which-is orange (L), please machine give water (L), nice to see you (N), Lana want drink milk eat bread (L), round is not colour (S), Mary give Sarah yellow (S), round, square is PLURAL shape (S), look: that's interesting (N), Mary give apple Gussie (S), please machine make window open (L), Mary give peach Sarah (S), yes, it's me (N), 'banana' is not name-of apple (S), no name-of this bowl (L), 'milk' name-of this (L).

9   Using Saussurean constructs such as signifier and signified, diachrony and synchrony, *langue* and *parole*, etc., comment on the linguistic implications of the differences between 'Newspeak' as described by George Orwell in *Nineteen Eighty-Four* and ordinary English, from which it supposedly evolved. The following is a summary of the main traits of Newspeak:

GENERAL FEATURES:
   drastic reduction of vocabulary;
   suppression of 'heterodox' words;
   only 'orthodox' meanings allowed (e.g. *free* is legitimate in *the dog is free of lice* but not in *politically free*).

DESCRIPTION OF STYLES:
   Style A (for everyday words):
   small number of words;
   no ambiguities or shades of meaning (each word is spoken with one staccato sound that expresses one clear concept);
   regular morphology: *-ful* = adjective; *-wise* = adverb; un- = negative; *plus-*, *doubleplus-* = strengthening; *ante-*, *post-*, *up-*, *down-* are also prefixes and have the obvious meanings; *-ed* = preterite or past participle; *-(e)s* = plural; *-er*, *-est* = comparison;
   almost complete interchangeability between parts of speech (differentiated by the above affixes).
   Style B (for political words):
   all compound words (NB there are no rules of compounding, any existing word, integral or mutilated, being a candidate for compounding, in any order);
   a full understanding of the principles ruling the new society is a prerequisite for appropriate use of these words (e.g. *sexcrime* can refer to fornication, adultery, homosexuality and intercourse for its own sake, while *goodsex* only refers to matrimonial intercourse with no female gratification);
   semantic ambivalence, with good or bad connotations contingent on political affiliation of referent; abundance of euphemisms (e.g. *joycamp* = forced-labour camp) and telescoped words (e.g. *Minipax* = Ministry of Peace, i.e. War).
   Style C (for supplementary technical terms):
   all rigorously defined;
   very few words common to all three styles – most C-style words have no currency in the other two styles.

Bibliography: Chapter 1

Chomsky, N., *Cartesian Linguistics* (New York: Harper & Row, 1966). A collection of studies relating Chomsky's theories on language to ideas current in the Cartesian tradition. Of particular relevance here are the chapters entitled 'Creative aspect of language use' and 'Acquisition and use of language'. Chomsky's claim for a Cartesian pedigree has been vigorously opposed by some.

Chomsky, N., *Language and Mind* (New York: Harcourt Brace Jovanovich, 1972, enlarged edn). Chs 1, 2 and 3 are directly relevant to the issue of innateness, but rather technical in parts, especially ch. 2, best read after Chapters 4, 6 and 8 in this book. See also Chapter 2.

Chomsky, N., *Reflections on Language* (London: Temple Smith, 1976). See also Chapter 2.

Chomsky, N., *Rules and Representations* (Oxford: Blackwell, 1980). Contains a clear, up-to-date statement of Chomsky's position on many of the issues discussed in this chapter and in Chapter 2, in particular the nature of the competent speaker's knowledge of language and its relation to the biology of the human organism.

Culler, J., *Saussure* (London: Fontana/Collins, 1976). A reasonable summary and exposition of Saussure's ideas and of their relationship to other intellectual currents of the time; it includes references to the current impact of Saussure's doctrine.

Den Ouden, B. D., *Language and Creativity* (Lisse: Peter de Ridder Press, 1975). A useful summary of Chomsky's ideas on creativity and their relationship to philosophy and psychology; probably more profitably read after completing Chapter 2 in this book.

Descartes, R., 'Discourse on method' [1637], in E. Anscombe and P. T. Geach (eds), *Descartes. Philosophical Writings* (London: Nelson, 1970).

Halliday, M. A. K., *Explorations in the Functions of Language* (London: Edward Arnold, 1973). A reasonable presentation of the author's functionalist ideas of language; it touches on a variety of topics included in this book, especially in Chapters 10 and 12, but the exposition is kept at a fairly simple level and the book can probably be tackled at this stage.

Halliday, M. A. K., *Language and Social Man* (London: Longman, 1974). A concise presentation of the functionalist view relating language to social structure, worth examining critically in the light of biological and structural evidence suggestive of an independent language faculty.

Halliday, M. A. K., 'Meaning and the construction of reality in early childhood', in H. L. Pick and E. Saltzman (eds), *Modes of Perceiving and Processing Information* (Hillsdale, NJ: Lawrence Erlbaum, 1978), pp. 67–96.

Hinde, R. A. (ed.), *Non-verbal Communication* (Cambridge: Cambridge University Press, 1972). A very accessible collection of papers on Hockett's design features, various forms of animal communication and non-verbal communication in man.

Hockett, C. F., 'Logical considerations in the study of animal communication', in W. E. Lanyon and W. N. Tavolga (eds), *Animal Sounds and Communication* (Washington, DC: American Institute of Biological Sciences, 1960), pp. 392–430.

Lenneberg, E. H., *Biological Foundations of Language* (New York: Wiley, 1967). This is an impressive study of the biological correlates of aspects of language such as production, growth and pathology, and of the inferences that can be drawn concerning the emergence of language in ontogeny and in phylogeny, and is thus directly relevant to the innateness issue; the science-based nature of the subject may make reading difficult for the arts-oriented reader, and facilitation is to be expected from a close study of this book, especially most of Part Two and Chapters 9 and 10. See also Chapter 2.

Lieberman, P., *On the Origins of Language* (New York: Macmillan, 1975). A good exposition of the reconstruction techniques mentioned in this chapter, but it anticipates some of the material to be presented later in this book, especially in Chapter 3, and reading it at this stage may be too difficult.

Saussure, F., *Course in General Linguistics* [1916] (London: Fontana/Collins, 1974). English translation and original preface of the compilation of Saussure's lectures published in French by his pupils in 1916; it marks the beginning of 'modern' linguistics and is currently regaining topicality, particularly in the areas of semiotics and sociolinguistics; the style, and some of the chapters, are definitely old-fashioned and point at the desirability of a guided reading.

Schrier, A. M., and Stollnitz, F. (eds), *Behaviour of Nonhuman Apes*, Vol. 4 (New York: Academic Press, 1971). It includes important papers by Hayes and Nissen on Viki, by the Gardners on Washoe and by Premack on Sarah.

Searle, J. R. (ed.), *The Philosophy of Language* (London: Oxford University Press, 1971). A collection of papers by various authors, including Chomsky, related to innateness and other topics mentioned in this book, e.g. semantic and pragmatic meaning (Chapter 7) and transformational grammar (Chapter 8); in ch. III Searle discusses briefly the issue of rules in connection with speech acts.

Sebeok, T. A. (ed.), *How Animals Communicate* (Bloomington, Ind.: Indiana University Press, 1977). A most impressive collection of thirty-eight papers by specialists on different aspects of the topic, including studies by Lieberman on the phylogeny of language, Marler on the evolution of communication, Hölldobler on communication in bees and other social insects, Marler and Tenaza on the signalling behaviour of apes and Fouts and Rigby on communication between man and chimpanzee.

Sebeok, T. A., and Umiker-Sebeok, J. U. (eds), *Speaking of Apes* (New York: Plenum Press, 1980). A very useful collection of papers on various experiments on teaching human language to chimpanzees, on the differences and similarities between human child and chimpanzee performance and on language and communication, by specialists like the Sebeoks, Lenneberg, Rumbaugh, the Gardners, Chomsky, and many others.

Seidenberg, M. S. and Petitto, L. A., 'Signing behaviour in apes: a critical review', *Cognition*, 7 (1979), pp. 177–215. Presents the other side of the coin in relation to signing achievements in apes. Specifically, the authors are highly critical of the research with Washoe and with the gorilla Koko regarding both accessibility and interpretation of data, strongly suggesting that the behaviour exhibited by the animals is *not* linguistic. A welcome complement to the sanguine reports of the experimenters.

Chapter 2

The Data of Linguistics and the Nature of Learning

2.1 Structuralist linguistics and behaviourist psychology

According to one popular position the data of the linguist have been considered to be a sample of utterances collected from a native speaker or native speakers of the language under investigation. This was the view advanced by the school of American structuralists following Leonard Bloomfield, which flourished in the USA between the 1930s and 1950s, and to adopt it has immediate implications for how we view the nature of language and the goals of linguistics. As far as the former is concerned, it seems natural to view this collection of utterances (*corpus*) as a 'bit' of language and thus to see the language being studied simply as a large corpus consisting of all the utterances which have ever been made and, presumably, ever will be made within a particular speech-community. This is the type of definition of a language which Bloomfield himself envisaged and which, despite a crucial vagueness in the notion 'speech-community' (see Chapter 12), tended to ossify in the introductory paragraphs of structuralist texts. The linguist of this persuasion must, of course, hope that the corpus he collects is *representative* of the language as a whole and he must believe that he has some way of knowing when this is the case. Regarding the goals of linguistics, these are seen as involving the description of *regularities* in the corpus according to well-defined procedures (see Chapters 4 and 6) and, while it is intended, via the representativeness of the corpus, that these regularities should extend to the language as a whole, predictions of language-patterns not appearing in the corpus are not a feature of this sort of work. Thus, it seems not unreasonable to see the goal of structuralist linguistics as the *rearrangement* of primary data, the corpus, in as economical a way as possible. Indeed, one notable structuralist, Zellig Harris, in his *Methods in Structural Linguistics* explicitly limits his ambition in this fashion.

The relationship between this approach to language and psychological behaviourism is not difficult to see, but first we need to say something about the latter. Initiated by J. B. Watson in the early years of this century and having its roots in a number of diverse traditions (most important in this connection is the Russian school of physiology with its best-known figure, Ivan Pavlov), behaviourism is best viewed as a reaction to introspectionism, the previously dominant methodology in psychology. The data of the introspectionist psychologist were typically verbal reports by subjects of events taking place in their consciousness or 'mental life', and this consciousness was viewed as the subject-matter of the investigation. For example, a standard experiment involves a subject in judging which of two weights is heavier. In addition to the judgement, however, the subject is asked to report verbally everything that goes on in his consciousness from the point at which he is presented with the weights to the point at which he makes the judgement. Resort to data of this kind has two immediate limitations. On the one hand, there was a lack of consistency and objectivity leading to endless disputes concerning the 'elements' of consciousness and the status of these elements. For example, Wilhelm Wundt, the best-known figure of the period, concerned himself with whether a feeling was a sensation or an attribute of a sensation; even without an initiation into Wundtian terminology, we can see the opaqueness surrounding this sort of question. On the other hand, non-verbal organisms, i.e. all non-human and some human organisms, could not be investigated by such methods. Watson swept these strictures aside by insisting that the data of the psychologist should be *behaviour*, which had the advantage of being publicly observable, and in terms of which non-verbal organisms can be investigated. It was an initial step which caught the imagination of the vast majority of psychologists in North America and led to behaviourism being the dominant psychological paradigm for most of the rest of this century.

From this initial revolutionary move there is a number of further steps which can be entertained and which can be seen as leading to different versions of behaviourism. So, as well as insisting that the *data* of psychology are observable 'chunks' of behaviour, it is possible to maintain that behaviour constitutes the *subject-matter* of psychology. Someone accepting this will see his task as the description of regularities in behaviour and of connections between stimuli in the environment and organisms' responses to these stimuli (i.e. S-R connections). He will deny that behaviour can tell us anything about mental states or mind. Construing the corpus collected by the linguist as a segment of behaviour, albeit complicated, aligns the structuralist linguist firmly with this tradition, although it is important to note that it is not necessary for such a linguist to take this or any other stance on the psychological significance of his work.

A less radical step in the move away from introspectionism is to see the subject-matter of psychology as mental states and to assume that only overt (and hence observable) behaviour can provide evidence on the nature of these mental states. This amounts to subscribing to a materialistic view of such states and to the assumption that they are causally related to behavioural events. Much modern cognitive psychology can be seen as accepting this framework, and what distinguishes it (represented, say, by George Miller) from the neo-behaviourism of Charles Osgood seems to revolve around the complexity of mental states allowed into psychological theories. Thus, the latter assumes that such states are limited to covert (and hence unobservable) stimulus-response connections while the former puts no *a priori* restriction on complexity. A further relaxation of the original behaviourist constraints extends the class of data beyond that which is publicly observable by allowing for the consultation of an organism's intuitions concerning stimuli from a certain domain. Of course, this again restricts psychological inquiry to verbal organisms. Yet it is not to be seen as a full-scale reversion to introspectionism, as consultation of intuitions is only *one* source of data which the psychologist might use. We can summarise the above discussion as in Table 2.1.

Table 2.1 *The Data and Subject-Matter of Different Schools of Psychology*

School of Psychology	Data of Psychology	Subject-matter of Psychology
Introspectionism (Wundt)	verbal reports	consciousness
Radical behaviourism (Watson)	behaviour	behavioural regularities
Neo-behaviourism (Osgood)	behaviour	mental states (highly restricted)
Cognitive psychology (Miller)	behaviour	mental states
Neo-rationalism (Chomsky)	behaviour and intuitions	mental states

The objections that have been raised to a corpus-based approach have not been on the grounds that it fails to lead to hypotheses concerning the behaviour (or even mental states) of the language-user. Interpreted within a non-radical behaviourism it can lead to such hypotheses. What we now consider are objections which originate with the linguist in his capacity of someone trying to understand the structure of a language. Only after we have given these matters the attention they deserve shall we return to the question of psychological interpretation.

2.2 Objections to a corpus-based approach

A corpus provides at once too much and too little for us to see it as presenting the way into the structure of a language. It contains too much because native speakers do not always perform as 'correctly' as they should. So we have such phenomena as false starts, hesitations, incomplete utterances and interruptions, all of which may leave their mark on a corpus of utterances collected in the field. Chomsky has made much of this and has been criticised for making too much, the counter-suggestion being that everyday talk does not contain anything like the proportion of speech errors that Chomsky would have us believe. This may be so and will be of some importance in Section 6 below, but for the point at issue we only need to be able to identify a single utterance in a corpus as containing a speech error for the argument to stand. For the linguist starting from an undifferentiated corpus this utterance must be analysed along with the majority of error-free utterances and it must impinge on the analysis. But the speaker's failure to complete a sentence because his attention is diverted is of no interest to the linguist probing language-structure. It has recently been convincingly argued, for example, by the American linguist Victoria Fromkin, that such phenomena as hesitations and slips of the tongue are related to language-structure in a revealing way (see Chapter 4), but it is vital to realise that such an argument only makes sense in a framework which recognises these occurrences as aberrant in some way and does not treat them as having the same status as perfectly well-formed utterances. The corpus, in order to be of any use to the linguist, must be 'cleaned up', i.e. there must be a certain amount of *idealisation* with respect to the data. The alternative is to have an analysis cluttered with phenomena which have no rightful place in it.

The second aspect of the objection that a corpus contains too little can best be illustrated with examples. We assert that sentences (1) and (2) will never occur in a corpus of collected English utterances (unless the corpus is collected on the basis of examination of linguistics articles and books!):

(1) Whenever a tortoise dies or disappears it behoves its owner or the parent or guardian of its owner to submit a written report to the Ministry of Tortoises and Turtles stating the sex and date of birth of the tortoise together with any disease it may have contracted during the fifty-three days preceding its death or disappearance and which appears on the list of reportable tortoise diseases obtainable at Post Offices and good tortoise shops.
(2) The tortoise the child the teacher the school employs hates owns is lost.

Obviously this assertion would be difficult to prove, but its denial would be hard to justify. The reason why such sentences would not occur deserves discussion. In the case of (1) its content is quite bizarre and also it is fairly long. Nevertheless, it is a well-formed English sentence which can be interpreted by any adult native speaker of English. For (2) the problems are not quite so easy to articulate and, indeed, the first response of the reader is probably to deny that it is a sentence of English. Faith in this judgement may be shaken a little by indicating the subject-verb relationships as shown in

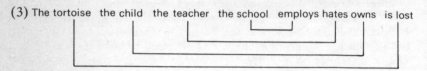

(3) The tortoise   the child   the teacher   the school   employs hates owns   is lost

where the lines indicate that the school employs the teacher, the teacher hates the child, the child owns the tortoise and the tortoise is lost. Similarly, we could 'paraphrase' (2) as in

(4) The tortoise which is owned by the child who is hated by the teacher which the school employs is lost.

but, even so, the reader may still insist that all that has been demonstrated is that (2) can be *made sense of* with help of a particular sort, and not that it is a well-formed sentence of English. In response to this, consider

(5) Tortoise the the hates the school lost employs the teacher child owns

and compare its status with that of (2). It is clearly a random string of words and although each of them happens to occur in (2) it none the less makes a quite different impression on us. The reader may persist by noting that (5) is unintelligible and that it remains that all we have demonstrated is that (2) is intelligible, given certain aids, whereas (5) is not; and this still says nothing about well-formedness. But now consider

(6) The tortoise the child the teacher the school employs hates owns are lost.

We submit that (6) is as intelligible as (2) and the help we enlisted in understanding (2) could be brought to bear on (6); but, unlike (2), (6) is not constructed according to the principles of English sentence-structure; there is a violation of the principle that a verb must agree in number with its subject, i.e. *the tortoise* cannot be the subject of *are*. On the basis of this argument we can draw a distinction between *acceptability* and *well-formedness* saying that (2) is well-formed but unacceptable whereas (5) and (6) are each both ill-formed and unacceptable. The unacceptability of (2) and (6) can be reduced using the techniques we mention. What makes (2) unacceptable is still largely a matter of conjecture, but one aspect of its structure which is usually assumed to be involved is that whereby grammatical subjects are separated from their verbs by a considerable amount of similarly structured linguistic material. In comprehending the sentence we have to keep a subject in our memory while performing operations on the rest of the sentence and having to do this for a number of subjects as in (2) means that we tend to lose track of which subject goes with which verb.

The above arguments are only a particularisation of a more general point of objection against the corpus-based approach. This is that the well-formed sentences of any human language are infinite in number (see Chapter 1); the point can be illustrated for English using any number of examples, but the sets of sentences in (7), (8) and (9) will serve our purposes.

(7) One is a number
 Two is a number
 . . . .
 . . . .
 One thousand, five hundred and sixty-two is a number
 . . . .
 etc.

(8) John likes coffee
 John and Mary like coffee
 John, Mary and George like coffee
 . . . .
 . . . .
 etc.

(9) This is the house that Jack built
 This is the malt that lay in the house that Jack built
 This is the rat that ate the malt that lay in the house that Jack built
 . . . .
 . . . .
 etc.

Again, an objection might be that, in each of these sequences, and any other of a similar nature, we reach a point where the string of words we are considering can no longer plausibly be regarded as a sentence of English. But exactly where is this point? Is there anyone who would seriously suggest that there is a number, n, such that *n is a number* is a sentence of English and *n +1 is a number* is not a sentence of English; or that *John, Mary, George, Henry, Sally, David and Aloysius like coffee* is a sentence of English but *John, Mary, George, Henry, Sally, David, Aloysius and Kate like coffee* is not? What could Kate have done wrong? On this basis we take it as conclusively demonstrated that the number of English sentences is infinite and, therefore, that English cannot be equated with any corpus no matter how large. From this simple argument we can get an alternative perspective to that adopted by the American structuralists on both the nature of language and the goals of linguistics.

2.3   Rules and intuitions – mentalist linguistics

If a language consists of an infinite number of sentences we can no longer identify it with a corpus. We can, however, identify it with a finite set of principles or *rules* which determine membership of strings of words in the language (see Chapter 1, p. 5). For example, consider the artificial language which has only two 'words', *a* and *b*, and sentences, *ab*, *abab*, *ababab*, *abababab*, . . . the dots indicating that the set of sentences can be indefinitely extended. The sentences of this language can be characterised by two rules.

(i) *ab* is a sentence in the language
(ii) if S is a sentence in the language, S*ab* is also a sentence in the language.

The linguist studying such a language has done at least part of his job when he has formulated these rules. Similarly, for a natural language the goal of the linguist is to produce a finite theory consisting of a set of rules which will characterise the well-formed sentences of the language. As we have seen, reference to a corpus is going to be of minimal value in this enterprise but, assuming that the linguist is a native speaker of the language he is investigating, there is now another course open to him. This is to refer to his own abilities to distinguish between well-formed and ill-formed strings of words, abilities we have already referred to in discussing the process of idealisation which is a necessary part of any linguistic methodology. In short, as a native speaker of the language, he is entitled to *invent* sentences and non-sentences in helping him to formulate and test his hypotheses. These abilities are usually referred to as *linguistic intuitions* and are important in that they form an essential part of the data-base of a Chomskyan approach to linguistics which will contain not only utterances but judgements about such utterances. Not surprisingly, in an age where we are still labouring under the stringencies of a positivistic view of science with its emphasis on observationality and objectivity, the use of such data has caused a certain amount of concern, and there are those who believe that it undermines the scientific status of Chomskyan linguistics (see our earlier discussion of the data of psychology in this chapter and also Chapter 12).

There are two immediate consequences of the above discussion. The first is that once we have allowed the use of linguistic intuitions into our methodology there is no need to stop at intuitions of well- and ill-formedness. There are many other facts about linguistic expressions with which native speakers seem to be acquainted. Thus, confronted with

(10) The tortoise chased the turtle

a native speaker will agree that *the tortoise* and *the turtle* are expressions of the same type; he may well not know them as noun phrases but that is beside the point. He will also agree that *the tortoise*, *the turtle* and *chased the turtle* have a status which is distinct from that of *tortoise chased the*; the former set appears to comprise significant syntactic units (see Chapter 6) while this is not true of the last example. He will probably say that (11) and (12) are synonymous (identical in meaning)

(11) John read the book quietly
(12) John quietly read the book

but that (13) and (14) differ in meaning

(13) John read the book carelessly
(14) John carelessly read the book.

And he will say that (15) and (16) are ambiguous (having at least two meanings)

(15) John met Mary near the bank
(16) Loving tortoises can be exciting

agreeing that, whereas in (15) the source of the ambiguity can be traced to the ambiguity of a particular word, *bank*, thus showing that we have a case of lexical ambiguity (i.e. based on two or more different meanings of a single word) this is not so in (16) where the ambiguity appears to reside in there being two distinct ways in which the words in the sentence can be related to each other. This can be made explicit by the paraphrases *To love tortoises can be exciting* and *Tortoises which love can be exciting*.

Referring back now to the goal of linguistics under the conception of the discipline we are currently exploring, we can see a way in which this might be enriched. We demand not only that the linguist articulates a set of rules which will characterise the sentences of the language in question, but also that the rules should do this in such a way as to accord with the linguistic intuitions of the native speaker. Without access to some of the formal ideas developed in Chapters 4, 6 and 8 it is difficult to see exactly what is involved here but, by way of preliminary illustration, we might consider the sets of simple sentences in (17) and (18).

(17) John loves Mary
      John eats sweets at school
      Mary hits John regularly
      etc.
(18) Mary is loved by John
      Sweets are eaten by John at school
      John is hit by Mary regularly
      etc.

A native speaker of English, confronted with a sentence from the list in (17), will have no difficulty in producing the corresponding sentence from the list in (18) if such a sentence exists, and vice versa. This can be seen as a reflection of the native speaker's linguistic intuitions concerning the relationship between active (as in 17) and passive (as in 18) sentences, and an adequate system of rules will not only characterise all the sentences in (17) and (18) as sentences of English but will also contain some statement of the relationship between the two sets of sentences.

The second consequence of admitting intuitions as data is that the way is now clear to define a goal for linguistics in explicitly mentalistic (as against purely behaviouristic) terms. Not only do the rules describe and characterise an infinite set of sentences together with regularities appearing within and between them, but they do this by reference to what the native speaker *knows* about his language. The goal of linguistics, then, is not simply that of producing a theory of an infinite set of sentences but rather that of producing a theory of the native speaker's knowledge of his language. Chomsky's famous distinction between competence and performance is best stated in his own words: 'We thus make a fundamental distinction between *competence* (the speaker-hearer's knowledge of his language) and *performance* (the actual use of language in concrete situations)' (Chomsky, 1965, p. 4).

It is clear that there are *two* aspects of the transition from performance (which is instanced by the utterances in a corpus) to competence. On the one hand, we have idealisation away from slips of the tongue, false starts, etc., and, on the other hand, we have the introduction of *knowledge*, knowledge which is claimed to *underlie* the native speaker's ability to produce and comprehend (perform with) sentences of his language. It is this latter aspect of the transition which has rendered this approach to linguistics of such interest to psychologists and upon which Chomsky's claim that linguistics should be seen as belonging to cognitive psychology rests.

Before moving on to examine some of the arguments which have been raised against the competence-performance distinction, there are two remarks to make. The first is that linguistics could be practised in the way in which Chomsky envisages without making mentalistic claims and there have been linguists who have urged that this should be the case. It is extremely doubtful whether meaningful progress could be made in understanding language-structure without a measure of idealisation and, therefore, some aspects of the distinction would appear to be vital, but the mentalistic claim that the linguist is describing a mental structure which would in some sense underlie language behaviour is quite independent of this. Chomsky takes the view that this characterisation of a mental faculty is one of the most important aspects of linguistics and without such an emphasis the interest of linguistics for the psychologist and social scientist would undoubtedly be diluted. Nevertheless, the question of whether linguistics can be significantly pursued along Chomskyan lines within a non-mentalistic framework remains an interesting one.

The second remark is that distinctions similar in spirit to that between competence and performance have proved necessary in the history of experimental psychology and, interestingly, they have been drawn most explicitly by psychologists who are regarded as pillars of the behaviourist establishment. Thus Clark Hull, the leading behaviourist psychologist in the 1930s and 1940s, distinguished between what an organism did and what it had learned, recognising that the former need not always be an accurate reflection of the latter. In a somewhat different vein E. E. Tolman, working within a tradition which regarded stimulus-response connections as the basic building-blocks of all learning, invoked stimulus-stimulus connections, what we might regard as a 'mental map', in order to explain such phenomena as organisms being able to swim through mazes having previously only learned to run through them. Clearly such stimulus-stimulus connections are not directly tied to behaviour and can be construed as a form of knowledge which the organism possesses about its environment and which it puts to use in moving around in that environment. Again, this knowledge need not be directly reflected in the organism's behaviour because of, for example, shifts of attention which might lead it not to find its way through a maze despite controlling the relevant stimulus-stimulus connections. Thus, we can see that notions akin to Chomsky's idea of competence have a considerable pedigree.

2.4   Objections to mentalist linguistics

Objections have been raised at one time or another to virtually every aspect of the competence-performance distinction with its mentalistic implications. The idealisation involved in the distinction has been the target of sociolinguists while philosophers have been disturbed by the reference to 'knowledge' as a characteristic of competence. The sense in which competence underlies performance and leads to predictions about behaviour is the aspect of the distinction which has been explored by psychologists and which, after some initial successes, has given them cause for concern. We briefly consider these sets of objections in turn.

From sociolinguists, e.g. William Labov, has come the claim that the idealisation to a homogeneous speech community – an aspect of the idealisation not discussed above but which appears to make sense if we are interested in understanding language rather than one individual's use of it – is too savage. They have observed that there is a wide range of systematic variation in the linguistic performance of even an individual depending on the social environment in which he finds himself (see Chapter 12 for more details).

An objection of a slightly different kind has been most frequently voiced by Dell Hymes, arguing that the idealisation to linguistic competence or, as is often the case in Chomsky's work, grammatical competence, misses out on the competence we really ought to be interested in. Hymes refers to this as 'communicative competence'. Whether any sense can be attached to Hymes's own notion of communicative competence is not something we shall discuss here, but two things seem to be clear. In the same way that it makes sense to talk about a sentence being well-formed, ambiguous, etc., it also makes sense to talk about a sentence being *appropriate* to encode a particular message under certain circumstances; and, in the same way that it makes sense to talk about a native speaker's knowledge in connection with well-formedness, ambiguity, etc., it is also intelligible to talk about appropriateness in similar terms. Thus, it appears to be correct that if it is the whole gamut of conversational and communicative behaviour in which we are interested, there is more to it than mere linguistic competence. But what follows from this? A realisation that the engine is not the only part vital to the functioning of the car does not lead us to reject it as a part, not does it lead us to insist that those people who focus their attention exclusively on engines should switch their interests to cars-as-a-whole. It might, of course, be the case that our understanding of engines will be enriched by studying cars-as-a-whole just as it may be the case that our understanding of language-structure will be enriched by studying communication-as-a-whole (see Chapter 1) but this is not self-evidently true and both strategies must be extensively explored in order for the protagonists to have any leverage.

Turning now to 'knowledge', this has been vociferously attacked in the context of the competence-performance distinction by a number of philosophers. The principal worry seems to be that the knowledge which is supposedly captured by the rules the linguist proposes cannot be assimilated to paradigmatic cases of knowledge such as knowing that $2 + 2 = 4$ or that dinner is ready. Thus, it has been argued that, in such paradigmatic cases, the knower can readily formulate a version of his knowledge, will assent to an appropriate formulation of it by others, etc., and that this is obviously not the case with the rules which linguists propose. This is perfectly true but there is an important modifier of 'knowledge' which is claimed to answer this objection. This modifier is 'tacit' and so it is claimed that linguistic competence is tacit knowlege of rules, which explicitly removes it from paradigmatic cases of knowledge. But still the objection may be pursued: why credit the native speaker even with tacit knowledge of the rules? What is gained by such a procedure? In answer to this we must remember what needs to be explained. Among other things, this includes the native speaker's *explicit* knowledge concerning linguistic expressions, e.g. that *the tortoise chased the turtle* is a well-formed sentence of English, that *tortoise the the chased turtle* is not a well-formed sentence of English, etc. Crediting him with tacit knowledge of the rules formulated by the linguist may enable us to account for this explicit knowledge by seeing it as following from the tacit knowledge. Whether one calls the latter knowledge, tacit or otherwise, seems to be a purely verbal issue and Chomsky, in his recent writings, coins a verb, 'cognise', to replace the offending phrase, 'tacitly know'.

To get some perspective on this issue we can consider the case of visual perception. Our visual perception of the external world is undoubtedly governed by complex and poorly understood principles which are somehow represented in our visual systems – consider, for example, the phenomena of size and colour constancy where the size and colour of an object are perceptually constant despite marked changes in viewing and lighting conditions. The visual system of the brain must somehow abstract away from certain objective changes and it seems to do justice to Chomsky's position to say that a human *cognises* these principles of abstraction or, to resort to the old idiom, tacitly knows them, and that the task of the theorist of visual perception is to discover them. The point of discovering them is to explain a human's perception of his visual world and there is surely nothing objectionable here except, perhaps, labels.

The third set of objections can be raised naturally from the above. It was pointed out there that one of the reasons for crediting the native speaker with tacit knowledge of rules is that it enables us to explain his explicit knowledge of certain properties of linguistic expressions and relationships between linguistic expressions. In addition, however, the native speaker's competence is claimed to underlie his performance, i.e. his everyday linguistic behaviour, and to be an essential part of such performance, making the comprehension and production of sentences possible. A straightforward interpretation of a claim such as this (and note that we would expect a theory of visual competence as discussed above to be useful in explaining everyday aspects of seeing) is that the rules which comprise the theory of competence are somehow involved in linguistic production and comprehension, and it was to an investigation of this 'somehow' that psychologists turned their attention in the 1960s. In retrospect it is easy to see that there were some rather naïve attempts to interpret linguistic theorising in the psychological laboratory; some of these were remarkably successful but later and more sophisticated experimentation has forced on us the conclusion that fifteen years of intensive investigation have failed to find a niche in a performance theory where a theory of native speaker competence can comfortably sit, interacting with whatever other psychological mechanisms are involved in the task situation in a particular experiment, e.g. attention, short-term memory (see Chapter 9 for further discussion). This is an important conclusion and calls into question either the competence-performance distinction under this interpretation or the details of the particular theories of native speaker competence which have been scrutinised experimentally. Unfortunately, such theories have always been effectively insulated against the negative conclusions of experimental testing by the ignorance which surrounds the other psychological mechanisms interacting with the linguistic competence of the experimental subjects and the way has always been open to the conclusion that negative results are the product of some little-understood aspect of, for example, the retrieval of information from long-term memory rather than amounting to a refutation of the mentalistic interpretation of the linguistic theory. What emerges from all this is that there is no clear need to reject a competence-performance distinction on the basis of experimental evidence. At the same time, without some more precise specification of how whatever knowledge is represented in the competence theory gets implemented in a performance theory, the holder of the distinction is going to be accused of mere hand-waving.

2.5 Native language learning; empiricism *versus* rationalism

In this section we assume that we have linguistic theories of certain kinds and consider the implications of these theories for the acquisition of his native language by a small child. Recalling Section 1 above, let us begin by adopting the structuralist methodology and assume that, having studied a corpus of utterances, we end up with a set of regularities concerning the distribution of linguistic elements in the corpus. Just as the Chomskyan framework led us to formulate a psychological hypothesis as to what the native speaker knows, a mentalistic hypothesis, so from the point of view of the structuralist we could give a psychological interpretation to the statements of regularities. In this case, we might expect a behavioural interpretation in terms of such constructs as 'habits' or 'dispositions to respond'. For example, the fact that linguistic elements from a particular class typically follow elements from another class (e.g. nouns follow adjectives in English) is correlated with the behavioural interpretation that speakers of the language under investigation have a disposition to produce elements from the former class following, or in response to, elements from the latter class.

We can now ask how the native speaker would have acquired such dispositions given his exposure to data as a first language learner and the typical response of a behaviourist would mention principles of discrimination and generalisation leading to behaviour which is suitably rewarded or reinforced by members of the speech-community in which the child is being brought up. Such constructs as 'habit' and 'disposition to respond' are the product of behaviourist thinking and it would be surprising if they could not be derived from behaviourist learning principles. Thus, if the structuralist view of language is correct and if we interpret such a theory in terms of habits and dispositions, it follows that the acquisition of language can be accounted for on the basis of some fairly limited learning principles.

The programme just outlined was, without reference to any particular linguistic theory, that envisaged by Skinner – an attempt to explain the whole of language development by reference to principles of reinforcement of responses initially made at random and subsequently moulded by the linguistic community so that the child used them appropriately. The credibility of the approach was destroyed in a famous review by Chomsky of Skinner's book *Verbal Behaviour*, in which Chomsky pointed not only to the lack of linguistic sophistication in Skinner's treatment but also to the pseudo-objectivity to which he is driven in his attempt to extrapolate a highly restricted laboratory methodology to the normal first language learning situation. Of course, to demonstrate the poverty of Skinner's approach does not disqualify all behaviourist theorising on these issues but it is a fact that, at the time of writing, no viable behaviourist theory of first language acquisition has been advanced. Equally, a demonstration of the misguided nature of behaviourist approaches in general would not amount to a justification of the Chomskyan alternative. Before turning to this alternative, however, it is necessary to make contact with another dichotomy which is relevant to the debate, that between empiricism and rationalism.

Obviously, we cannot hope to do justice here to an enormous and sophisticated body of philosophical discussion but we can draw some broad strokes. Empiricism and rationalism are philosophical positions concerning the question of the acquisition of knowledge, where the term 'knowledge' is construed quite generally – traditional examples which have been considered in connection with this question include speculation as to how we come to know that every effect has a cause or that the angles of a triangle add up to 180°. Rather than representing distinct positions they are best seen as labelling two ends of a continuum with positions being more or less empiricist and rationalist, and most debates assuming some arbitrary cut-off point for the application of the labels. They come apart most clearly on the issue of innate ideas – ideas or knowledge which the knower has independently of experience – with the empiricist position tending to minimise the role of such ideas and the rationalist trying to give some innate ideas a more central and vital position in this issue. It is important to realise that the empiricist does not do away with innate ideas altogether but restricts the apparatus the child brings to the acquisition of knowledge. He may, for example, assume that the child is capable of *comparing* sensory inputs and noting similarities and dissimilarities between them, perhaps with respect to particular sensory dimensions such as hue, orientation, frequency (of sound), etc. – at this point the closeness of this position to the behaviourist views on learning mentioned above should be obvious. The rationalist does not strip the child of these abilities. Rather, in addition to such general abilities as the empiricist countenances, the rationalist wishes to credit the child with certain specific ideas, such as that of 'triangularity' or that 'every event has a cause', because he is convinced that these ideas cannot arise from the interaction of experience and the minimal empiricist assumptions.

Why should an issue such as this be regarded as important? To see this, assume that the empiricist is correct and that the human infant is only equipped with a minimal set of learning procedures. There is ample evidence that species other than humans can discriminate complex stimuli and generalise along various dimensions, evidence which would indicate that non-human organisms have exactly the same *kind* of mental powers as man. Of course, no one is suggesting that they have these powers in the same abundance as man, but the immediate implication would be that all of mankind's knowledge, that of everyday events, of language, of relativity theory and of Keynesian economics, is of the same general kind as that possessed by a rat which has learned to turn left in a maze for reward. The importance of the question requires no further comment.

A structuralist approach to language is, as we have seen, amenable to interpretation as a behaviourist theory of linguistic behaviour and as a similar theory of language acquisition. It is also consistent with empiricist views on the acquisition of knowledge and, indeed, the operations which the structuralist will perform on his corpus in deriving his statements of regularities can, without too much imagination, be reinterpreted as those performed by a child equipped with a fairly rudimentary set of empiricist learning procedures on exposure to data. The alternative offered by Chomskyan linguistics goes well beyond the statement of superficial regularities. The adult native speaker is credited with a complex set of rules which are intended to characterise his linguistic competence and, again, assuming that such a view is correct, we can ask how a child could have acquired such a system given his exposure to data. Chomsky and his followers have presented a number of arguments in this connection, all of which are taken to indicate that a child endowed only with empiricist learning principles *could not* learn such a system in the time and manner in which all children do learn it. The conclusion is that the child must be initially acquainted with the general form of the system he is to acquire, that is, he must possess a special innate language faculty which makes language acquisition possible. It is vital to realise that it is the general form or 'blueprint' of the system which is assumed to be innate. Clearly a child is not predisposed to learn any particular language and, therefore, the 'blueprint' must be quite neutral between actual languages.

2.6 External evidence for language innateness

Most of the arguments for Chomsky's position proceed from the vague premise that a human language is extremely complicated and involves much more than the superficial regularities systematised in structuralist linguistics. Let us grant this premise and consider some of the arguments. One has it that a native language is learned remarkably quickly and certainly this might be the impression of someone reflecting on the issue for the first time. Figures which were commonly cited not long ago suggested that language learning starts at about 1½ years, and is complete in all essential respects by about 4 years – a period of two and a half years. If these figures were accurate what would be the force of the argument? It is difficult to answer this because we have no yardstick against which we can compare the rate of acquisition of a first language. The learning of a second language might be suggested as a roughly comparable achievement but the conditions of learning in the two cases are sufficiently different to render any such comparison opaque. Still, it is true that something very complicated is learned by an infant at an age when he is achieving nothing comparable in other domains of his activity. But can we be sure about this? As Chomsky has pointed out, psychologists have not found it necessary to postulate rule-systems of the sort he advocates in order to explain any other sphere of human activity, but against this we must note that such studies are in their infancy, that information-processing capacities of considerable complexity are being discovered, particularly in the domain of visual perception, and that there is no *a priori* reason to believe that the theory of visual space with which we eventually credit the adult human will be intrinsically simpler than the sort of system Chomsky envisages for linguistic competence. And this, presumably, is a theory which the child has already learned to a large extent when he approaches language acquisition. Finally, we should note that the figure of two and a half years has recently been questioned, with the beginnings of language acquisition being pushed back into the first year of life and the demonstration that aspects of the development which cannot be regarded as peripheral are not complete in 9-year-olds. Clearly, parts of this debate revolve around questions concerning the definition of language (see Chapter 1) and it is not our intention to take a stand on this issue here. We are merely concerned to point out the controversial nature of what looks like an initially plausible suggestion and to conclude that this first argument cannot be taken as providing any more than weak support for the idea of an innate language faculty. Also, of course, in itself this argument says nothing about the contents of such an innate faculty.

A second argument which is often cited concerns instruction and is most easily presented in comparison to second language learning in school. Memory tells us that the latter is an arduous and demanding procedure yielding rather unspectacular results. Nor are the efforts simply on the part of the learner. Yet the child learns his first language with, apparently, little effort and no explicit instruction. The reference to 'little effort' can be disposed of in terms similar to those of the previous paragraph, i.e. we lack a yardstick for comparing 'efforts', and it is the lack of explicit instruction which we wish to emphasise here. Chomsky reinforces this argument with a general remark on the degenerate nature of the data to which the child is exposed, referring again to false starts, hesitations, etc. (see Section 1 above). However, recent research has demonstrated that Chomsky's emphasis is quite misleading here, particularly if we restrict ourselves to speech directed at the child. Studies by, for example, Catherine Snow have shown that this speech is remarkably free from grammatical errors, simple in grammatical structure and semantically relevant to the immediate spatio-temporal environment of the child. A new generation of child language workers is studying 'Motherese', and the results promise to be very interesting although, no doubt, their relevance to the argument under discussion will be difficult to assess in detail (see Chapter 10 for further discussion). Again, though, it seems that we are justified in urging caution.

An argument of a rather different sort points to the uniformity of language acquisition across children and across languages and its apparent independence of general intelligence level except in extreme cases. While this latter point can be interpreted as an argument in favour of language being independent of general cognitive capacities, it does not amount to an argument for aspects of it being innate. As for the former point, while such uniformity is consistent with an innate language faculty it is equally consistent with there being universal aspects of teaching (cf. the previous argument) and of environment.

Linguistic universals (see Chapter 11) have been used as a basis for an argument for innateness, the suggestion being that those features which are common to all languages are just those which are given to the child as part of his innate endowment. But again we can look to universals of social interaction and environment (see the discussion of functionalist theories in Chapter 1) for alternative explanations, and without further argument and research it is impossible to distinguish between these suggestions. In the other direction, of course, a demonstration that some property of language is innate would entail that that property is also universal since, before learning his native language, the child is equally capable of learning any language and, therefore, the contents of the language faculty will be reflected in any language, i.e. be universal. The difficulty here is that we have no independent way of showing that any such aspect of language is innate.

A different sort of argument advanced, for example, by Lenneberg comes from the observation that various linguistic milestones fit neatly into developmental sequences which include aspects of behaviour which are clearly maturational in the sense that they do not depend on any form of teaching or moulding by the environment, e.g. the ability to walk. Coupled to this is the phenomenon of lateralisation whereby one of man's cerebral hemispheres becomes specialised for language, a fact which may be related to the so-called 'critical period' in language acquisition (see the discussion of linguistically disadvantaged children in Chapter 1). Evidence such as this seems to point to a maturational, rather than environmental, aspect of language development but, as with all the arguments above except for that using universals, it tells us nothing about the content of the language faculty if it exists.

2.7 An internal argument for innateness

Taken together a battery of arguments such as those of the previous section might convince the uncommitted reader but they would be unlikely to impress the sceptic. We would like to close this chapter by constructing the outline of an argument which, if a concrete example of it could be found, would lend further credence to the innateness position. Let us suppose that the investigation proceeds in a number of steps:

1   We construct a theory of language structure. The terms in such a theory will be formally related in certain ways. We describe this by saying that the theory has a set of formal properties which we can designate as $P_1, P_2, \ldots, P_n$.

2   We credit the adult native speaker with the theory in terms of either tacit knowledge or dispositions to respond, i.e. we give the theory a psychological interpretation.

3   We make a minimal (empiricist) set of assumptions about the learning abilities of the human infant – recall that even an extreme form of empiricism will make some such assumptions. These might include such abilities as discrimination and generalisation along certain dimensions, segmentation of sequences, and so on.

4   We make assumptions about the data which are input to the child, say, we can represent them as D (e.g. we might assume that the small child is presented with a 'simple' corpus of language data where 'simple' means that the corpus is free from errors, false starts and hesitations, consists of short sentences and is transparently related to the situation of utterance).

5   We assume that a device with the abilities in 3 has D input to it and ask what sort of theory of the data such a device will construct. Diagrammatically, we can represent this stage of the inquiry as in Figure 2.1. What we are interested in is whether the theory which is the output of the device has the properties, $P_1, P_2, \ldots, P_n$ of our original linguistic theory.

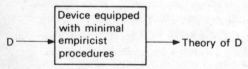

Figure 2.1   *A minimal theory of language learning.*

6   Assume that we can demonstrate that under these assumptions the theory of D does not have all the properties $P_1, P_2, \ldots, P_n$. There are a number of alternatives open to us:

6(*a*) Assume that the original linguistic theory is incorrect. Our reason for doing this would be that it could not be learned by a device equipped with minimal empiricist assumptions.

6(*b*) Assume that our views on D are incorrect.

6(*c*) Equip our learning device with the relevant properties, i.e. let those properties which cannot be learned by the minimal assumptions be part of the child's innate endowment. This is the alternative which the rationalist might readily adopt.

To consider a particular example, we can begin from the fact that most theories of sentence structure assume some notion of hierarchisation (see Chapter 6, p. 160ff.) and so we can let P have the value 'contains hierarchical structures'. It is possible to construct an argument that a device equipped with the abilities to discriminate and generalise with respect to linear position in a string of sounds would be capable of arriving at theories with this property (see the exercises at the end of this chapter). This could be seen as the first step in a demonstration that the property of containing hierarchical structures is not beyond empiricist learning principles. It is, perhaps, no accident that other systems of human and animal cognition are believed to manifest this property. This example, then, would not require modification of Figure 2.1. On the other hand, if we were driven to accept 6(c) above, then we would be subscribing to the picture in Figure 2.2.

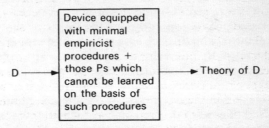

Figure 2.2   *An enriched theory of language learning.*

Let us take the discussion one step further and assume that we have indeed discovered a property, P, which has led us to accept 6(c). We can now pursue two fundamental questions. The first concerns whether P also proves to be necessary in characterising the child's acquisition of knowledge in some other, non-linguistic, domain, e.g. spatial perception. If it does not, then we may feel justified in concluding that P properly belongs to the language faculty alone and can be seen as part of the definition of human language. Human language would be shown to be unique in a quite non-trivial sense. If P does arise in other connections and if this proves to be the case for all the properties on our original list, then we have an argument for there not being a specialised language faculty and for language learning being just one part of the general phenomenon of *human* learning. Note that such a conclusion is quite independent of the question of innateness. It could be the case that there is no special language faculty, yet that certain properties of human language are innately specified. In these circumstances such properties would also play a role in other cognitive systems.

The second question is of even grander status. It requires that we consider, within the same mode of analysis, non-human organisms. The question is whether P is necessary in characterising any abilities in any domain of activity of any non-human organism (in an empirical investigation we would be justified, at least initially, in restricting our activities to organisms which are phylogenetically close to man, e.g. chimpanzees). A positive answer for each of the properties on our original list would show that human language, in its essential features, is not even characteristically human as all those features are shared by systems of 'knowledge' acquired by non-human organisms. A negative answer for any property would show that property as part of the general definition of man and here resides the most far-reaching significance of linguistics; it has brought us to a position where we can begin to conceptualise what answers to this sort of question would look like. Note further than an inquiry in these terms need not be restricted to human beings or to human languages. Just as we can examine the properties necessary to explain the fact of language acquisition in the human infant, so we can examine the properties necessary to explain the fact of space perception in the human infant or the fact of space perception in the pigeon. In each case we may find properties which are unique in the sense that they are not required in any other domain of psychological inquiry. In the former case we would have grounds for regarding these properties as being definitive of human space and human beings and in the latter case of pigeon space and pigeons. We simply do not know what the outcome of such an investigation would be nor, at the moment, do we possess the analytical tools to begin the investigation in an optimistic way. But the questions can be raised and understood and it is Chomsky who has led the way in this respect.

The above discussion has been rather abstract and it would be useful to conclude it with another concrete example. Unfortunately these are few and far between, but one reasonably accessible one which has been discussed by Chomsky is that of the (hierarchical) structure-dependence of rules. Consider (19) and (20) and how we might describe the difference between them.

(19) John is here
(20) Is John here?

A first guess might be that we can scan (19), find the first occurrence of *is* and move it to the front of the sentence to yield (20). This will work in some cases and is an example of a rule that involves only the linear (i.e. non-hierarchical) structure of the string of words in (19). It is a reasonable assumption to make about the way in which questions correspond to statements on the basis of a limited amount of data but, of course, in general it does not work because not all sentences which have corresponding questions of the type shown in (20) contain *is*, e.g. *John has a car* and, even for sentences which do contain *is*, it sometimes fails, as in (21) and (22):

(21) The man who is married to Clara is here
(22) *Is the man who married to Clara is here?

The point is that the correct version of the rule relating such sentence pairs requires reference to more than the *linear* structure of the string and needs to be able to recognise, for example, *the man who is married to Clara* in (21) as a grammatical unit constituting the subject of the sentence and, on this basis, to ignore any occurrence of *is* (or any other verb) in it. Chomsky argues that there is no logical reason why questions should be formed in this way rather than, say, by moving the third word, whatever it happens to be, to the front of the sentence; there is nothing inherently simple about the facts we find in English nor do they seem to be reducible to the needs of communication in any revealing way. He goes on to suggest that the fact that languages contain structure-dependent rules is not one which children could hit on so infallibly unless they were initially informed in this regard. So, for P in the above discussion we could substitute 'has structure-dependent rules' and it is clear now where the lines of conflict are to be drawn. For the empiricist, assuming he accepts the primary analysis, it is necessary to show that a system with structure-dependent rules can plausibly be induced from data by a device equipped with empiricist principles. If Chomsky wishes to insist that possessing structure-dependent rules is part of the essence of human language or even of man, then non-linguistic domains of human and non-human activity must be examined and the presence or absence of such rules ascertained. Nothing is known in this regard but the prospects are fascinating.

Exercises: Chapter 2

1   Collect samples of speech in a number of different situations, e.g. a lecture, a television interview, casual conversation. Describe the errors (e.g. false starts, hesitations, grammatical errors) which appear in your speech samples and discuss whether any differences in type or frequency of error exist depending on the situation.

2   Observe a mother interacting and talking with her child (age 1–2 years). Describe any features of the mother's speech which you find remarkable, e.g. quality of enunciation, sentence length, syntactic complexity, vocabulary.

3 As for Exercise 2 but using a 2–3-year-old child.

4 Using the results of Exercises 2 and 3 describe and discuss any differences in the speech of mothers to 1–2-year-olds and that of mothers to 2–3-year-olds.

5 Try to collect some data relevant to the distinction between grammaticality and acceptability (p. 35). Construct sentences of the form

The rat the cat the dog chased bit died

which have different numbers of sentences embedded in the middle and present them to native speakers of English together with a question, the exact form of which might be varied. You might like to consider such questions as 'Is this an English sentence?', 'Would you ever say this?', or 'Does this make sense?'. Summarise your results paying particular attention to whether there is any consistency in the degree of embedding tolerated by native speakers (see Chapter 9, Exercise 10, for further variables you might like to try to take account of).

6 As for Exercise 5 but using sentences of the form

The doctor took *the bandages which had become encrusted with blood* off

where the italicised portion may be made more or less complex. Be sure to consider further verb-particle constructions such as ring . . . up, hand . . . out.

7 Assume that a rat is to learn to run through a simple maze for food reward. The maze is T-shaped and the rat, initially placed at the bottom of the T, has to learn to turn left at the single choice point. Imagine that the following sequence of behaviour is observed, where L means 'the rat turns left' and R means 'the rat turns right', on a trial.

LRRLLLRLRLLRRRLLLLLLLLLLRLRLLLLLLLLLLLLLLLRLLLLLLLLLLLLLRLLLL
* *   *   *

Using whatever terminology you can find in introductory psychology texts or using your own terms, provide a description of what you think might be going on, paying particular attention to the responses marked *, and keeping in mind the distinction between 'knowledge' and behaviour.

8 Imagine that a device is equipped with the following 'abilities':

 (i) to segment a linguistic utterance into words;
 (ii) to recognise two instances of a word as *the same word*;
(iii) to recognise words (or sequences of words) as occurring in *the same position relative to other words* (or sequences of words).

Abilities (ii) and (iii) can be seen as types of generalisation. Now assume that the machine is presented with the following utterances in the order given and that it will store information about the utterances, producing a 'theory' of the structure of the language from which the utterances come on the basis of (i)–(iii).

(a) John walks
(b) Mary walks
(c) John runs
(d) Sally runs
(e) Sally eats

Specify the theory that the machine will construct.

9   Show how a device constructed as in Exercise 8 could manifest *creativity* (see Chapter 1) in the sense of 'knowing' that some particular utterances to which it has never been exposed are well-formed in accordance with the 'theory'.

10   Imagine that the following data are now presented to the machine of Exercise 8 after sentences (a)–(e).

(f) The man walks
(g) The woman walks
(h) A man runs
(i) John walks quickly
(j) The man walks slowly
(k) Sally runs elegantly

State how the machine's theory will change, paying particular attention to the notion of hierarchical structure.

Bibliography: Chapter 2

Bracken, H., 'Minds and learning: the Chomskyan revolution', *Metaphilosophy*, 4 (1973), pp. 229–45. A sympathetic review of Chomsky's political views tied to his position on innateness. Quite readable.

Chomsky, N., *Aspects of the Theory of Syntax* (Cambridge Mass.: MIT Press, 1965). Chapters 2–4 are also relevant for Chapter 8.

Chomsky, N., *Language and Mind* (New York: Harcourt Brace Jovanovich, 1972, enlarged edn). Contains a systematic treatment of Chomsky's views on the relationship between linguistics, psychology and philosophy of mind. Difficult in places. See also Chapter 1.

Chomsky, N., *Reflections on Language* (London: Temple Smith, 1976). First chapter presents Chomsky's views on innateness in terms more similar to those used in this book than in his earlier writings. In the remainder of the book Chomsky takes issue with some philosophers who have objected to his views on language and their implications for the study of mind. Some more technical sections are difficult. See also Chapter 1.

Chomsky, N., and Katz, J. J., 'What the linguist is talking about', *Journal of Philosophy*, 71 (1974), pp. 347–67. An attempt to take on a group of philosophical objections and justify the rationalist linguistics of Chomsky.

Derwing, B. L., *Transformational Grammar as a Theory of Language Acquisition* (Cambridge: Cambridge University Press, 1973). Sets out several points of difference between pre- and post-Chomskyan American linguists.

Also contains a good deal of polemical discussion of innateness and the competence-performing distinction.

Edgeley, R., 'Innate ideas', in G. Vesey (ed.), *Knowledge and Necessity*, Vol. 3 of Royal Institute of Philosophy Lectures (London: Macmillan, 1968–9), pp. 1–33. A difficult but scholarly and accurate investigation of the similarities and differences between classical and Chomskyan rationalism.

Harris, Z., *Methods in Structural Linguistics* (Chicago: University of Chicago Press, 1951). Introductory chapters give a clear statement of the structuralist view that the aim of linguistics is restricted to the rearrangement of primary data. The rest of the book requires a good deal of stamina. See also Chapter 5.

Leiber, J., *Noam Chomsky: A Philosophic Overview* (New York: St Martin's Press, 1975). A clear introductory discussion of structuralist linguistics and the changes in methodology promoted by Chomsky's influence. Also introduces some of Chomsky's more formal ideas.

Lenneberg, E. H., *Biological Foundations of Language* (New York: Wiley, 1967). The best introduction to biological considerations in language development. Discusses linguistic milestones in terms of other aspects of growth and maturation and presents a wealth of evidence from disadvantaged children. See also Chapter 1.

Lyons J., *Chomsky* (London: Fontana/Collins, 1977, 2nd edn). An introductory overview of North American structuralism and the effect of Chomsky's work on linguistics. A good place to start if you find Chomsky in the original formidable.

Pylyshyn, Z. W., 'The role of competence theories in cognitive psychology', *Journal of Psycholinguistic Research*, 2 (1973), pp. 21–50. An argument that notions akin to Chomskyan competence should be central to any sort of psychological inquiry. Difficult in places.

Sampson, G., *The Form of Language* (London: Weidenfeld & Nicolson, 1975). Idiosyncratic in many ways but contains a balanced discussion of arguments for an innate language faculty and objections to such arguments. See also Chapter 8.

Stitch, S., 'What every speaker knows', *Philosophical Review*, 80 (1971), pp. 476–96. A discussion of paradigmatic cases of knowing and the argument that talking about knowledge in the context of linguistic rules does not add anything of substance to the debate.

Watson, J. B., *Behaviourism* (New York: Norton, 1930). Watson's popularisation of his views on psychology contains a central chapter on thought and language. Earlier chapters can easily be read to get the flavour of behaviourism and many of the anecdotes are delightfully unscientific.

Part TWO

The Structure of Language

Chapter 3

Phonetics

3.1 Primacy of spoken language

In this chapter we shall be concerned with the medium in which language operates. In the previous chapter it was stated that the subject of study of linguistics in the Chomskyan paradigm is the (abstract) representation of language in the mind (i.e. linguistic competence), which makes linguistics a branch of psychology. Obviously, direct access to this mental reality is denied to both the linguist and the hearer and so if language is to have public status it must be encoded in a medium accessible to the senses.

The medium of encoding of this book is writing, which has the virtues of transportability and durability. Although the most frequently used form of language encoding for all of us is speech, there are at least four well-known encoding systems for language employing three distinct modalities: the visual modality (writing and also signs, as, for example, in the systems used by the deaf), the tactile modality (e.g. Braille, the 'reading' system of the blind) and the auditory modality (speech). Leaving aside those systems which are only used by disadvantaged sections of the population, the contest for the primary medium of language is only between speech and writing.

The study of writing systems and of the art of writing itself is, of course, a legitimate subject of study, but in the context of language it is worth pointing out that writing is parasitic on speech. Two weighty arguments support this view. First, a large proportion of the world's population is illiterate (the Unesco figures for 1970 give 783 million, i.e. 34·2 per cent of the world's population; the figure for the developing countries was 50·2 per cent). Further, the emergence of worldwide literacy is only a recent phenomenon and the past is still with us to some extent, as even in these later years of the second millennium A D the odd 'primitive' tribe is still found which is innocent of Western civilisation and of the written word. So it is not difficult to imagine the time when absolutely everyone was illiterate – writing, in effect, is not part of nature, but an invention, a conscious product of man's ingenuity, just like the wheel or the silicon chip. Speaking, on the other hand, appears to be biologically rooted.

The second argument for the primacy of speech relies on the fact that while speaking is acquired without apparent instruction by every normal human child between the ages of 1 and 5 (see Chapter 10), reading and writing have to be learned and are usually taught within the formal framework of the school. Thus both phylogeny (the history of the species) and ontogeny (the history of any particular individual) provide very strong evidence to the effect that speech, and not writing, is the primary medium for language encoding.

Although the regularity of speech acquisition breaks down in cases of deafness, lack of hearing does not interfere with the bodily movements that generate sound, and even the most severely deaf can, for example, clap their hands without difficulty. The reason for the special difficulty the deaf face in making the bodily movements appropriate to speech is to be found in the fact that, by and large, speech sound is generated by organs which are out of sight. Miraculous as it is that normal children learn to move these organs on the basis of what they hear, it is little wonder that the deaf will find the task beyond their reach.

The observations just made indicate that some non-visual sensory input absent in the deaf must be present in the hearing. In order to clarify this, it is necessary to differentiate three stages in the life of a sound – generation, which requires movement of a physical body, transmission, which requires a medium capable of carrying the sound (a sound generated in a vacuum is not heard) and reception, which requires a device sensitive enough to pick up the signal. In the case of normal hearing, the ear picks up the signal from the surrounding air and transmits it to the brain, where the sensation of hearing is felt. In the case of the deaf person, the receiving system (the ear or the auditory paths in the brain) is faulty and the signal in the air fails to reach the final target in the brain.

3.2 Sound waves

We must now go into the analysis of sound in some detail, given the crucial role that it performs in human language. As suggested in the previous section, sound is generated by the vibration of a physical body, e.g. a tuning fork or, at least in principle, any other physical body. Vibration is induced by the application of a force to the body. This force displaces the body from its state of rest. After reaching the maximum displacement point, the body falls back to the point of rest, but movement does not stop here, since the action of inertia carries it beyond the point of rest, in the direction opposite to that of the initial displacement until it is counteracted by the action of elasticity and returned to the point of rest. This to-and-fro motion repeats itself until it is cancelled out by the opposing forces of friction.

The type of motion just described, namely, vibration that, in the ideal case without friction, repeats itself exactly, is the simplest one and is known as *periodic motion*. A particularly important subtype of periodic vibration is *simple harmonic motion* and we now turn to the description of it.

We can approach simple harmonic motion by means of an analogy. Imagine an electric bulb placed at the end of one of the spokes of a cart wheel, right on the rim. Imagine that we position the wheel in front of a mirror and perpendicular to it. Now if we rotate the wheel at a *constant speed* in a dark room, we will see the reflection of the lit bulb drawing a straight line in the mirror. Moreover, the speed of the light will be greatest in the middle of the line and smallest at either end – in fact, it will be zero at the point where it changes direction. Also, each trip of the light along the line will take the same amount of time, since the wheel is being rotated at a constant speed. The essential aspects of this arrangement are represented in Figure 3.1.

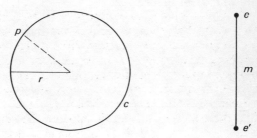

Figure 3.1   *Illustration of simple harmonic motion. As point p moves clockwise round circle c at a constant speed, its projection on line e–e' replicates the movement of a pendulum or of a tuning fork.*

This analogy provides us with the basic concepts for the analysis of vibration. Their importance for the understanding of sound waves and speech sounds will be more fully appreciated as we proceed.

amplitude   The length of each spoke in the wheel, or, equivalently, the distance between the end and the middle of the line in the mirror.

cycle   One complete turn of the wheel, or, equivalently, the trajectory of the light from the middle of the line to one end, back to the middle, out to the other end and back to the middle again.

frequency   The number of cycles per second (the label *hertz*, abbreviated *Hz*, is commonly used for the expression 'cycles per second').

period   The time taken to complete one cycle.

Note that the above concepts can be given a more rigorous interpretation if the wheel analogy is thought of as a geometrical construct (cf. Figure 3.1) – the spoke of the wheel will now be equivalent to the radius (*r*) and the line in the mirror will now be a geometrical line (*l*), the light being any one point (*p*) in the circle, the projection of which describes a trajectory along the line as the circle rotates.

The importance of these notions can begin to be seen if we consider that the perception of *loudness* is mainly related to amplitude and that of *pitch* to frequency.

From the discussion above it can readily be noted that the crucial relationship in sound is that between displacement of the vibrating body and time. Given a set of values for these two variables for any given body (including air in the case of speech sounds, as will be discussed below), one can straightforwardly plot displacement as a function of time along two axes, thus obtaining a graphic representation of the vibration known as a *waveform*. If the vibration plotted corresponds to simple harmonic motion, the resulting waveform is known as a *sinusoid*, as in Figure 3.2.

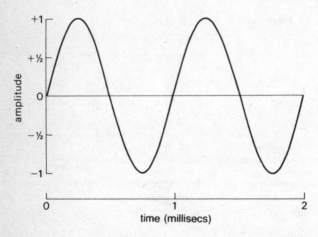

Figure 3.2   *A sinusoid, i.e. the waveform corresponding to simple harmonic motion. The amplitude is plotted along the vertical axis ('ordinate') and corresponds to maximum displacement (the distance* m–e *or the length of* r *in Figure 3.1). The time is here given in milliseconds along the horizontal axis ('abscissa').*

The type of vibration considered so far is a simple one (simple periodic motion), but several sinusoids can be added together to produce a *complex wave*. The frequency of a complex wave equals the largest common divisor of the frequencies of its component sinusoids, which is known as the *fundamental frequency* of the wave. Components of a complex wave are known as *harmonics* when their frequency is an integral multiple of that of the fundamental – each harmonic is usually identified by the ordinal number that expresses the numerical relationship between its frequency and the frequency of the fundamental. As for the amplitude of the complex wave, displacement at any given time t is determined by the sum of the displacements of all the component sine waves present (i.e. the various harmonics including the fundamental) at t. A complex wave and its components are represented in Figure 3.3. Note that it is easier to make up complex waves from sinusoids than to break down a complex wave into its basic components. Fortunately, in 1822 the French mathematician Fourier discovered a method which can do precisely this. The analysis of complex waves does not therefore present a major problem and the analysis of simple waves is, as has been seen, a relatively easy matter.

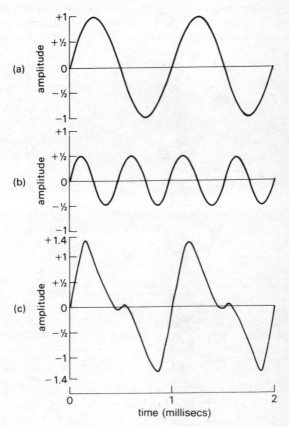

Figure 3.3 *Building up a complex wave from two sinusoids. Sinusoid (b) has twice the frequency of (a) and half its amplitude. The result of combining both sinusoids is complex wave (c), which has the same fundamental frequency as (a) and whose displacement is a function of the combined displacements of both (a) and (b).*

Figure 3.4 *Waveform corresponding to random noise. Note the total aperiodicity of the vibrations.*

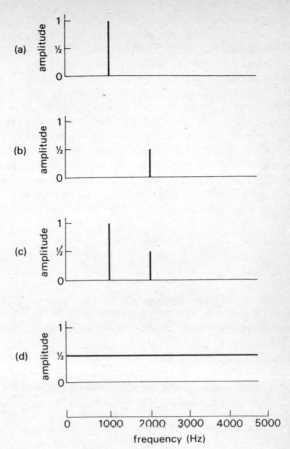

Figure 3.5 *Spectra of various types of wave.*

(a) *Sinusoid (a) in Figure 3.3 – note that the period is a thousandth of a second, and thus the frequency is 1,000 cycles per second.*

(b) *Sinusoid (b) in Figure 3.3 – its amplitude is only half that of (a) and its frequency twice as great.*

(c) *Complex wave (c) in Figure 3.3 – note that each of its two component waves is represented in the spectrum.*

In each of (a)–(c) the amplitude of the component frequencies is represented by the length of the line drawn at those frequences.

(d) *Spectrum of random noise as in Figure 3.4 – note the characteristic continuous spectrum indicating that all the frequencies are making an equal contribution to the aperiodic wave.*

If a wave is aperiodic it must be made up of an infinite number of components and, correspondingly, cannot be represented by a line spectrum as in (a)–(c).

Our discussion so far has been limited to repetitive waves. But nature's patterns are seldom straightforward and it will come as no surprise that the actual occurrence of periodic waves (simple or complex) is not as frequent as that of *aperiodic waves*, where the vibrations do not repeat themselves regularly. A common everyday instance of aperiodic vibration is *random noise* (also called *white noise* by analogy with white light, because in both cases all wavelengths are present), as with radio interference. The waveform of random noise is completely irregular (see Figure 3.4). It is therefore not very revealing of its components, and a more useful representation results from comparing the contribution of each frequency to the overall sound and plotting the frequency against the amplitude. This graph is known as a *sound spectrum*. In Figure 3.5 the sound spectra of the periodic waves considered in Figure 3.3 are compared with the sound spectrum of random noise.

3.3 Air vibration

As suggested above, transmission of the vibrations of the generating source is essential if sound is to be perceived by the ear. The transmission medium for speech sound (and for the overwhelming majority of the sounds perceived in the course of our everyday life) is air. Air is made up of molecules floating near each other in a void and when a vibrating body displaces the adjacent layer of particles, these in turn will exert a force on those in the neighbouring layer setting them in motion, and so on, in a manner analogous to the fall of a set of dominoes.

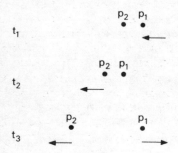

Figure 3.6   *The mechanism of air vibration*

It is important to look at this process in some detail. As the motion of the sound-generating body changes direction, the particles immediately adjacent to it, having transmitted their momentum to the second set of particles, will be free to move backwards to and beyond their original point of rest. This is illustrated in Figure 3.6 for two imaginary particles P_1 and P_2 at three successive instances t_1, t_2 and t_3. At t_1, P_1 has received a blow from the vibrating source and is moving towards the stationary P_2. At t_2, P_1 has struck P_2 transmitting its (linear) momentum to it; as a result, P_2 is now moving off away from the source and P_1 has stopped moving. At t_3, P_2 is continuing to move away, but, as the vibrating source has now reversed its direction of movement, P_1 has begun to move back towards it in the direction of reduced pressure – remember how air escapes from a punctured tyre. Figure 3.6 makes clear that, for any particular spatial point, there will be a series of alternations between a state of *condensation* (more molecules per unit volume) and a state of *rarefaction* (fewer molecules per unit volume). Thus changes of *pressure* (note that pressure is directly proportional to the number of molecules per unit volume) occur which correlate with the actual physical movement of the molecules. For purposes of graphical representation, either particle displacement or pressure variation can be plotted against time to give the appropriate soundwave.

In all the cases presented so far, the assumption has been that a force was applied to the vibrating element only once, and that the element was then left to vibrate without further interference. This type of vibration is known as *free vibration* and a common instance of it is the plucking of a string on a guitar. This mode of vibration contrasts with *forced vibration*, where the vibrations of a body B_1 are constantly driven by the action of another body B_2, as in the case of a sustained note played on the violin, where the movement of the bow directly causes the string to vibrate. Each physical body is particularly prone to vibrate at a specific frequency, depending on its physical characteristics, and it is at this *natural frequency* that free vibrations will occur. In a situation of forced vibration, however, the driven body can only vibrate at its natural frequency if allowed to do so by the driving element, i.e. if the driving element vibrates at precisely the natural frequency of the driven object. When this condition obtains we talk about *resonance*, that is, the situation where the frequency of the driving force is identical with the natural frequency of the driven body, which therefore vibrates at its maximum amplitude, with minimum initial *damping* (damping is due to the existence of frictional forces which have a dissipating effect on the energy expended on the vibrating body, whose movement will therefore tend to die away more or less rapidly depending on the characteristics of the body).

Bodies of air are susceptible to vibration just as solid bodies are and they can thus be found in a situation of forced vibration where resonance can occur. A case in point is that of the mass of air contained in the body of some musical instruments, say, the guitar and the lute. While the plucked string engages in free vibration, the trapped air must follow the driving force provided by the string. The natural frequency of the mass of air is contingent on the shape and size of the instrument's body, so that different instruments will have different natural frequencies and the auditory effects will vary accordingly. As will be seen below, a similar mechanism is directly responsible for the differences we perceive in speech sounds.

3.4 Voice production

So far we have been concerned with aspects of sound which relate to *acoustic phonetics*. Acoustics is a branch of physics which studies the properties of sound. The generation of actual speech sound involves the manipulation of certain anatomical structures, and this constitutes the subject-matter of *articulatory phonetics*.

The basic generator of speech sound is contained within the *larynx*. The larynx can be thought of as a box situated at the top of the *trachea* or windpipe, in the neck (part of it is often visible in men as the Adam's apple), and it is made up of soft tissues held by a system of cartilages linked to each other by joints that allow movement. The cartilages are: at the base, the *cricoid*, which is ring-shaped and also constitutes the top of the trachea; in front, the *thyroid*, made up of two flattish plates that join together at one end to form a V-angle, thus giving the thyroid a plough-like appearance, and which connects with the vertical plate of the back of the cricoid; at the back, the two *arytenoids*, two small independent cartilages in a shape reminiscent of a prehistoric handaxe, and also connected to the back of the cricoid. The arytenoids can engage in gliding motion and also rotate within an angle of about 30°, thus being able to move towards the midsaggital plane (*adduction*) or away from it (*abduction*). A pictorial representation of the larynx and its various parts is given in Figure 3.7.

The gaps between the laryngeal cartilages are filled by a membrane known as the *conus elasticus*, which continues above the cricoid and closes up the space enclosed within it. To allow respiration, there is a slit at the top of the conus elasticus and each of the two thick edges of this slit constitutes a *vocal fold* (also known, somewhat confusingly, as 'vocal ligament' and 'vocal cord'); one end of each vocal fold is attached to the thyroid and the other to the base of the arytenoid, at the opposite end to the one which links with the cricoid. The vocal folds have such basic functions as the prevention of choking, and the trapping of air in the chest to help with lifting weights and similar exertions, but they also play a crucial role in speech. During respiration they come apart to allow the air through. The vocal fold opening is known as the *glottis* and it is produced by abduction of the arytenoid cartilages.

As we have already said, the existence of sound requires the presence of a vibrating body at the source. The most important source of

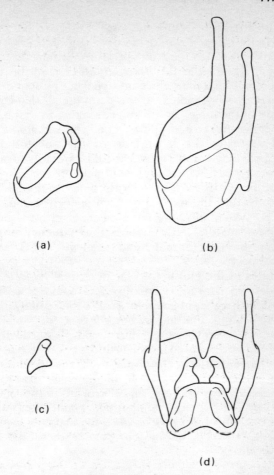

Figure 3.7   *The larynx and its component cartilages. (a) The cricoid. (b) The thyroid. (c) One arytenoid. (d) Articulated laryngeal cartilages.*

Source: Adapted from W. M. Shearer, *Illustrated Speech Anatomy* (Springfield, Ill.: C. C. Thomas, 1968), p. 41.

speech sound is vocal fold vibration. If the glottis is not too widely open or too tightly closed and if air comes out of the lungs at a sufficient speed, the vocal folds will be set in motion, thus creating an open and a closed glottis in succession. The outgoing airflow is therefore not a continuous one – rather, the air comes out in successive puffs which, as will be seen below, will cause forced vibration in the bodies of air contained in the vocal cavities.

The mechanism of vocal fold vibration is important enough to warrant closer attention. When the vocal folds are held loosely in relative proximity to each other, the outgoing air causes a drop in *intraglottal* air pressure (i.e. air pressure within the space of the glottis itself), known as the *Bernoulli effect*, and this causes the vocal folds to come together, since no opposing muscular forces are being exerted on the arytenoids. At this point the air that continues to be pumped out of the lungs can no longer escape, so that air pressure builds up below the closed glottis (i.e. the *subglottal* pressure increases). Eventually the magnitude of the subglottal pressure reaches a critical point and the vocal folds are forced apart. The process can now restart. As already mentioned, the successive opening and closing of the glottis causes the air to come out in rapid puffs and these puffs constitute the most important speech sound, known as *voice*. (This is, incidentally, the basic mechanism involved in humming.) Because of anatomical differences, the frequency range of vocal fold vibration is different for males and females – 120 Hz and 240 Hz on average, respectively.

The two states of the glottis thus far described (*voicelessness*, i.e. glottis too widely open for the Bernoulli effect to take place, and *voice*) do not exhaust the number of possibilities. We shall briefly mention the three next most important states. For *whisper* the vocal folds are brought near each other forming a narrow slit. Acoustically, whisper consists of glottal noise caused by the turbulence created at the glottis by the rapidly moving airflow. For *breathy voice* the arytenoids are kept apart, while the vocal folds form a slit still narrower than for whisper. The vocal folds can now vibrate, and the result is the simultaneous production of periodic sound and aperiodic sound (i.e. noise, in the technical sense). Finally, for *creaky voice* the arytenoids are pressed tightly together and only the anterior portion of the vocal folds is allowed to vibrate.

3.5 Respiration and speech airstream mechanism

The force that brings about the vibration of the vocal folds is provided by the outgoing air which is being pumped out of the lungs. *Respiration* is therefore temporally prior to *phonation* (i.e. vocal fold vibration). We now turn to the study of respiration.

The existence of an inverse relationship between volume and pressure has already been mentioned (p. 67) – for the same number of particles, the greater the volume is, the lower the pressure, and conversely. This is crucial for the understanding of respiration. Masses of air are set in circulation by the action of aerodynamic forces, because of the basic fact that air flows spontaneously from areas of high pressure to areas of low pressure, analogously to water contained within locks in a canal system (cf. the generation of winds due to variations in atmospheric pressure).

At the respiratory rest position, lung air pressure equals atmospheric pressure. In order for inspiration to occur, lung air pressure must be lowered to set the outside air in motion into the lungs. This is achieved by increasing lung volume through the action of the diaphragm and various chest muscles expanding the thoracic cage where the lungs are housed. Expiration mainly occurs by the recoil action of the lungs.

In the case of speech voice production, the subglottal pressure (roughly equivalent to lung pressure) must be made greater than the supraglottal pressure (roughly equivalent to atmospheric pressure), so that the Bernoulli effect can take place. This is achieved by reducing the thoracic volume and by blocking the glottal exit until the subglottal pressure reaches the critical point and forces the glottis open.

The type of airstream mechanism just described is called *pulmonic egressive*, and it is by far the most common one in the sound-systems of human languages. Three other types of airstream are also used in some languages and will be mentioned here.

An *egressive pharyngeal* (or *glottalic*) airstream is created by closing the glottis (which cuts the airflow from the lungs) and raising the larynx (which decreases pharyngeal volume and thus increases pharyngeal air pressure). When a closure made farther forward in the mouth is released, this pressurised air rushes out, producing a type of sounds usually known as *ejectives*, and common, for example, in the native languages of North America. The combination of an *ingressive pharyngeal* (or *glottalic*) airstream (produced by lowering the larynx, which causes a decrease of pharyngeal air pressure) with a slight pulmonic egressive airstream leaked through the glottis is the source of the sounds known as *implosives*, which are mainly found among African languages. Finally, an *oral* (or *velaric*) airstream results from the closure of the vocal cavity by the action of the back of the tongue at the back of the mouth (i.e. on the soft palate; see p. 79). The tongue then moves backwards, thus increasing buccal volume and decreasing buccal air pressure. When another closure farther forward is released, atmospheric air flows into the rarefied mouth, producing a type of sound usually known as *clicks*, occurring in certain Southern African languages.

3.6 Analysis and classification of vowels

From several points of view, the simplest sounds used in language are the vowels and we shall begin our discussion of speech sounds with them. *Vowels* are *tones* (i.e. periodic sounds) which are produced by the combined effect of glottal voice and of resonance in the vocal cavities. The puffs of air escaping from the glottis cause forced vibrations in the bodies of air contained in the vocal tract. The glottal wave is extremely rich in harmonics (some forty of them), but the frequencies that do not approach the natural frequencies of the air masses in the mouth will be impeded (*impedance* is a technical term which refers to the characteristic possessed in different degrees by all media that hinders the free flow of the wave). The result is a complex modification of the original glottal wave, determined by the size and shape of the air volumes in the vocal tract.

Of particular importance for the understanding of the differences between vowel sounds is the physical model known as a *Helmholtz resonator*. It consists of a volume of gas enclosed in a spherical container. The gas only meets the external medium by means of a small circular tube. A two-dimensional representation of a Helmholtz resonator is given in Figure 3.8. The *natural* (or 'resonant') *frequency*

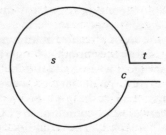

Figure 3.8   *A two-dimensional representation of a Helmholtz resonator. The natural frequency stands in direct proportion to the area of the circular opening c and in inverse proportion to the volume of the sphere s and the length of the tube t.*

of such a resonator bears a direct relationship to the area of the circular opening and an inverse relationship to both the volume of the sphere and the length of the tube. During the production of vowels, the vocal tract can be likened to a system made up of *two* Helmholtz resonators. First, there is a clear parallel between the Helmholtz resonator and the vocal tract during the period of vocal fold closure – only one opening, at the lips, and, for some sounds at least, a labial protrusion. Now, if the words *he*, *who* are pronounced several times in succession paying particular attention to the movement of the tongue, it will be realised that the tongue moves backwards between production of *he* and *who* and forwards again for the next production of *he*. Also, in the production of both vowels, the highest part of the tongue moves close to the roof of the mouth, narrowing the air passage. The result is that the vocal cavity is divided into two smaller subcavities, in a way analogous to a system made up of two coupled Helmholtz resonators. The place where the tongue is closest to the roof of the mouth will determine the respective volume of both resonators and will therefore play a major role in determining the resonant frequencies of both cavities.

The areas of concentration of the harmonic frequencies of the glottal spectrum that remain unimpeded due to the resonance properties of the air volumes in the vocal cavities are known as *formants*. Because the vocal cavities corresponding to each vowel have several natural frequencies, each vowel sound is made up of several formants, but the frequency of some of them hardly varies from one vowel to the next. Differences between vowels are mainly associated with differences in the frequency-range of the three formants with the lowest frequencies. Formant one (the formant with the lowest frequency) is related most directly to the size and shape of the pharyngeal cavity (which is defined by the volume between the highest point of the tongue and the larynx), formant two to those of the front cavity (the cavity in front of the highest point of the tongue) and formant three to more complex interactions between volumes in the vocal tract and other resonances.

If the words *heed*, *had* are pronounced in succession, it will be observed that the tongue moves vertically from a position of closed-ness (i.e. nearer the roof of the mouth) to one of openness. These changes in vowel *height* have an important effect on the volumes of both the pharyngeal and front cavities and on the coupling relationship between them and thus on their acoustic and perceptual correlates. Finally, a third basic articulatory parameter for vowels besides back-ness (or, equivalently, frontness) and height refers to the degree of lip-rounding (consider the difference between *he* and *who* once more), its increase resulting in a decrease in frequency for the first two formants (remember that the longer the tube in a Helmholtz resonator, the lower the resonant frequency of the resonator).

The mechanical analysis of formant frequencies was made possible by the invention shortly before 1950 of the *sound spectrograph*. The input to the device is the sound signal picked up by a microphone and the output is a visual representation of the component formant frequencies of the sound wave, displayed on a sheet of special paper mounted on a revolving drum and known as a *sound spectrogram*. A spectrogram shows formant frequencies as a function of time. In addition, it gives the relative intensity (which, as mentioned earlier, is a function of the amplitude) of each component frequency – the blacker the mark, the greater the intensity at the corresponding frequency. Spectrograms are therefore three-dimensional graphs. Also, in addition to formant frequency, intensity and time, spectrograms show the presence of glottal voice in the sound waves in the form of striations in the formant bars. The distance between striations provides a measure of the pitch – the closer the striations are to each other, the higher the pitch. As will become apparent as we proceed, spectrographic analysis is an invaluable tool in the study of speech sounds.

On the basis of the parameters mentioned above, vowels can be divided into front, back and central (in relation to the front–back axis), high, low and mid (in relation to height) and rounded and unrounded (in relation to labial rounding). These labels delimit a number of regions in the articulatory space, each with its own characteristic acoustic profile. Each of these areas could be systematically referred to by the full list of its defining labels, either articulatory or acoustic or both. For example, the vowel in *he* could be named 'the high/front/ unrounded vowel', or 'the vowel with the first three formants at frequencies of 280, 2,620 and 3,380 Hz', but this is obviously cumbersome and the most common systems for referring to speech sounds make use of one letter for each area instead. It is crucial to bear in mind, however, that the phonetic value of these letters is given by universal convention – they are defined within each system in terms of the articulatory and/or acoustic parameters referred to above and not by the parochial spelling conventions of any particular language (note that these conventions usually include a certain degree of arbitrariness, as is brought to light in the case of English by Bernard Shaw's well-known witticism that *fish* ought to be spelled *ghoti*: *gh* as in *enough*, *o* as in *women* and *ti* as in *nation*).

The most widely used of these systems (phonetic alphabets) is that of the International Phonetic Association (IPA). In common with other phonetic alphabets, the pivotal principle is that each sound (i.e. each area in the articulatory space) is consistently represented by only one symbol and, reciprocally, that each symbol stands for only one sound, so that there is a constant one-to-one relationship between sound and

Table 3.1   *Classification of English RP Vowels in Terms of the Relevant Articulatory Parameters*

	Front	Central	Back Round	Back Unrounded
High	i		u	
Lowered high	ɪ		ɑ	
Mid-high		3		
Mid-low	ɛ	ə	ɔ	
Low	æ	ʌ	ɒ	ɑ

Note: Identity of labelling does not, of course, guarantee absolute identity at the articulatory level, as can be seen more obviously in Figure 3.9. The following words illustrate the sounds in the table, from top to bottom and from left to right: *heat, hit, head, hat, hurt*, the first sound in *allow, hut, hoot, hood, horde, hot, hart*. Note that there are differences in length as well as quality between some of these vowels.

graphic representation. The IPA symbols for the vowels of English are given in Table 3.1. Note that for the sake of familiarity the present discussion has been restricted to the system of the prestigious British accent known as *Received Pronunciation* (RP). This is a slightly ideal-ised standard (see Chapter 12, p. 391) set up by the English phoneti-cian Daniel Jones on the basis of his own southern English speech, claimed to coincide roughly with the pronunciation used in English preparatory and public schools.

Table 3.2 *Average Frequencies in Hertz for the First Three Formants of RP English Vowels (excepting the 'neutral vowel' [ə], the formants of which are more variable but have a similar value to those of [ɜ])*

Vowel	F1	F2	F3
i	280	2,620	3,380
ɪ	360	2,220	2,960
ɛ	600	2,060	2,840
æ	800	1,760	2,500
ʌ	760	1,320	2,500
ɑ	740	1,180	2,640
ɒ	560	920	2,560
ɔ	480	760	2,620
ʊ	380	940	2,300
u	320	920	2,200
ɜ	560	1,480	2,520

Source: Gimson, 1970, pp. 98–9.

On the basis of this taxonomy, a geometrical analogue of the articulat-ory space for English vowels can be drawn, as in Figure 3.9. The formant specifications of vowels in RP English are given in Table 3.2.

Although English is comparatively rich in vowel sounds, the list of RP vowels is far from exhausting the total inventory of attested vowel sounds. Cardinal vowels 2 ([e]) and 7 ([o]) (see Figure 3.9) are quite common – they are the vowels of French *thé* ([te]) 'tea' and *tôt* ([to]) 'early', and they also represent the pronunciation of words like *day* ([de]) and *dough* ([do]) in many northern English and Scottish varieties of English. (Note that phonetic symbols are enclosed within square brackets to distinguish them from the phonological representations (see Chapter 4, p. 100) and from ordinary spelling.) Cardinal vowel 4 ([a]) corresponds to probably the most widespread vowel of all – it appears in the Spanish word *pan* ([pan]) 'bread' and also in the northern English pronunciation of *pan* ([pan]). In addition to the eight primary cardinal vowels, it is possible to create a number of secondary vowels

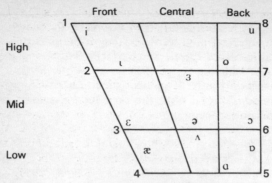

Figure 3.9 *Diagram showing the approximate positions occupied by the RP English vowels in the articulatory space, represented here by means of a quadrilateral. (NB indications of the length which usually accompany some of the vowels have been left out). The intersections numbered 1–8 are the points of the so-called 'cardinal vowels', which represent the official standard of measurement and point of reference laid down by the IPA. The symbols for the cardinal vowels are as follows: 1 [i], 2 [e], 3 [ɛ], 4 [a], 5 [ɑ], 6 [ɔ], 7 [o], 8 [u]. The cardinal vowels as recorded by Daniel Jones are available from the Linguaphone Institute. Note the idiosyncratic use of the symbol [ʌ] in the chart above, which would represent the unrounded counterpart of [ɔ] in the IPA system.*

by altering the rounding parameter, thus giving rise to pairs parallel to that of RP English [ɒ] [ɑ] (strictly speaking, however, there are also differences in place of articulation between these two vowels). The rounded counterpart of [i] is [y], as in German *süss* ([zys]) 'sweet' or French *su* ([sy]) 'known', that of [e] is [ø], as in German *Höhle* ([høːlə]) 'cave' or French (*jeu* [ʒø]) 'game' and that of [ɛ] is [œ] as in German *Hölle* ([hœlə]) 'hell' or French *jeune* ([ʒœn]), 'young'. A central sound [ʉ] intermediate between [y] and [u] occurs in certain Scottish dialects in words like *book* ([bʉk]), as it does in Norwegian *hus* ([hʉs]) 'house'. Unrounding of non-low back vowels is less common than front vowel rounding. The unrounded [u] ([ɯ]) occurs in Japanese and a central vowel [ɨ], intermediate between [ɯ] and [i], in Russian and in northern Welsh (*un* [ɨn] 'one'). The unrounded counterparts of [o] and [ɔ] ([ɤ] and [ʌ], respectively) are quite rare. A low central vowel [ɐ] can appear in final unstressed position in English, as in *manner* ([mænɐ]), and is common in languages like Portuguese and Catalan, as in *català* [kɐtɐˈla] 'Catalan' (the diacritic ˈ indicates stress on the following syllable; see Section 11 for a brief discussion on stress and on the syllable).

Very closely related to vowels both articulatorily and acoustically, are *glides*, also known as 'semivowels' and, sometimes, 'semiconsonants', and exemplified by the initial sound in the English words *yell* and *well*. The production of the front glide [j] of *yell* is practically identical to that of the vowel [i], and that of the back glide [w] (as in *well*) to that of [u]. Glides differ from vowels in that the vocal tract changes shape more rapidly. This increased speed is only possible when the transition takes place to or from a vowel and thus glides always occur next to a vowel sound.

Also, in addition to pure vowels, English possesses a number of complex vocalic sounds or *diphthongs*. For the production of a diphthong the articulators effect a rapid movement from an onset target to an offset target, as in the English word *eye*, [aɪ], which contains a transition from a position roughly equivalent to that for [a] to approximately that for [ɪ] (a word like *eye* would be transcribed [aj] by some writers, with a glide in the second position; strictly speaking, however, diphthongs are independent unitary sounds characterised by the presence of a transient state, thus contrasting with the steady state of pure vowels). Spectrograms of diphthongs show the corresponding movement from one formant region to another. The chief English diphthongs are listed in Table 3.3.

Table 3.3 *Principal English Diphthongs*

eɪ	əʊ
aɪ	aʊ
ɔɪ	

Note: The transcription given here corresponds to the sound of the diphthongs in RP English. Note that in the three diphthongs in the left column the closing element is front and unround (as in the words *bay*, *buy* and *boy*), while in the two in the right column it is back and round (cf. *bow*, as in *bow tie*, and *bow*, as in *bow of the boat*). The RP diphthong [əʊ] corresponds to [oʊ] in many standard accents.

3.7 Liquids and fricatives

The width of the narrowed vocal tract for vowels is such that free, unconstricted air passage is allowed. *Consonants*, on the other hand, are characterised by the presence of an obstacle in the way of the airflow. For instance, if *l* as in *lay* is pronounced in isolation, it will be observed that, while air flows out freely through the spaces left open by the sides of the tongue, the tongue tip resting on the upper tooth ridge (see Figure 3.10) stops the airflow in the midsagittal (i.e. central) region of the mouth. This explains the mixed character of *l*, which shares properties with both consonants and vowels – articulatorily, it is a consonant because the air does not flow out completely unconstrained; acoustically, it is associated with three formants, like vowels, although their frequencies are specific to *l* (F1: 360+ Hz; F2: 840–1,800 Hz; F3: 1,920 + Hz; (Gimson, 1970, p. 200)).

Consonants like *l* which occupy a middle ground between vowels and consonants are known as *liquids*. Another common liquid is *r*, as in *ray*. Although the spelling *r* can be found in most languages, the actual sound it represents varies quite considerably even within any one language. In both RP and American English, for instance, *r* is an *approximant*, since the tongue never constricts or interrupts the airflow, and it will be represented as [ɹ] in IPA script. In Scottish English, on the other hand, *r* can be a *tap*, produced by the rapid contact of the tongue tip with the upper tooth ridge ([ɾ]) or even a full *trill*, i.e. a series of vibrations of the tongue tip near the upper tooth ridge ([r]). These two varieties of *r* are common in many well-known languages (e.g. Spanish, Italian, Russian), but the variety [ɹ] present in most English dialects is less frequent. A different type of trill occurs when the vibratory organ is the uvula (see p. 79). This or a similar type of sound is also fairly common among the world's languages (e.g. French, Portuguese, German) and is given the IPA representation [R].

The only source of linguistic sound identified so far has been glottal vibration. An easy check on the presence of glottal voice consists in placing a finger on the Adam's apple and feeling the vibrations on the fingertip. If this check is carried out on the *s* in *say*, it will be found that this sound is voiceless. This being so, it must have a different sound source from vowels.

Let us consider briefly the articulatory and acoustic properties of this consonant. A constriction is created between the tongue tip or blade and the upper tooth ridge which produces a difference in air pressure on either side, in a manner parallel to the one described for vocal fold vibration. The orifice is very small and the air particles collide with each other as they go across it at high speed. These collisions slow them down into irregular patterns of turbulent air, thus originating aperiodic waves, i.e. acoustic noise. Sounds that make use of this friction mechanism are known as *fricatives* or *spirants* – the action of the two articulators is such that the airflow is never completely stopped, though it is severely constricted, with the concomitant creation of noise.

It can be easily observed that the pitch of the English fricative [s] as in *same* is considerably higher than that of [ʃ] as in *shame*. This can be accounted for if we remember that the resonant frequency of a Helmholtz resonator (which, as has already been said, is a useful analogue for the human vocal cavities) is inversely proportional to the volume of the resonator and to the length of the protrusion. Now, the constriction is farther to the front of the mouth for [s] than for [ʃ], and thus the air volume in the front cavity will be smaller and the frequency higher. English [ʃ], moreover, is often accompanied by a certain degree of lip protrusion, which has the effect of further lowering the frequency for this consonant. A list of English fricatives and their corresponding frequencies appears in Table 3.4.

Table 3.4   *Frequency Regions in Hertz for RP English Fricatives (as in the words* fee, thigh, sign, shy *and* high)

IPA Symbol	Frequency Range
f	1,500–7,000
θ	1,400–8,000
s	3,600–8,000
ʃ	2,000–7,000
h	500–6,500

Note: Fricatives are noises and thus lack the clear formant structure of vocalic sounds. The noise concentrates in a different frequency region depending on the resonance characteristics of the vocal tract.

Source: Gimson, 1970, p. 180.

3.8   Places of articulation

Before proceeding to the exposition of the articulatory properties of English fricatives, it will be best to look at the topology of the human mouth and to mention the labels customarily attached to the various areas relevant for purposes of speech production.

The *vocal tract* contains two main chambers or cavities – the oral cavity and the pharyngeal cavity. The *oral cavity* is formed by the hard and soft palates at the top (the latter ending in the *uvula*, a small appendage that hangs at the entrance to the throat), the teeth and tooth ridges at the sides, the lips and central incisors at the front and the tongue at the bottom. The *pharyngeal cavity* can be thought of as a tube that crosses the oral cavity vertically at the back, its bottom being the glottis and its top the base of the skull. A diagram of the parts of the mouth relevant to the articulation of linguistic sounds is given in Figure 3.10.

The production of speech normally requires the action of two articulators, one active and one passive. The *tongue* is made up of a highly complex series of muscles, hence its great mobility and adaptability, which make it the most frequently used of all active articulators. Because of this prominent role, the area of the tongue is usually divided into several articulatory regions, each defined by reference to the area of the mouth it faces when at rest.

The three main parts of the tongue are the *tip* – the area closest to the front teeth; the *root* – the posterior part of the tongue, attached to the muscles near the epiglottis (a leaf-shaped cartilage attached by the base to the inner surface of the thyroid V-angle); and the *body* – the remaining area. The body itself is divided into the *blade* – the part

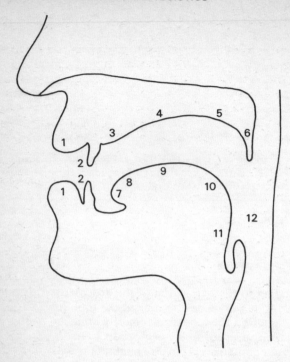

Figure 3.10   *The vocal tract and its articulatory regions: 1 lips, 2 teeth, 3 upper tooth ridge, 4 hard palate, 5 soft palate, 6 uvula, 7 tongue tip, 8 tongue blade, 9 tongue front, 10 tongue back, 11 tongue root, 12 pharynx.*

opposite the upper tooth ridge; the *front* – which rests against the hard palate; and the *back* – the area opposite the soft palate. In order to avoid terminological confusion, the reader must pay particular attention to the fact that the 'back' of the tongue is not the backmost area (the 'root' is), and that the 'front' of the tongue is not frontmost either (the 'tip' is the frontmost part of the tongue and the 'blade' is the frontmost part of the 'body').

The English fricatives listed in Table 3.4 can now be differentiated according to their *place of articulation*. Each sound is usually labelled by means of a compound made up of the Latinate names of the two articulators involved in its production. Mention of the tongue as an active articulator, however, is often omitted. The following English–Latin glossary will be of assistance.

English	*Latin*
lips	labia
teeth	dentes

English	Latin
tooth ridge	alveoli
hard palate	palatum
soft palate	velum
tongue	lingua
blade	lamina

In addition, the following prefixes are in common use:

English	Latin
both	bi-
between	inter-
before	pre-
after	post-

The articulatory specification of English fricatives can now be given:

[f]	labiodental	lower lip on the upper teeth edge
[θ]	(linguo-)interdental	tongue tip between the teeth
[s]	(linguo-)alveolar	tongue tip (or blade) near the upper tooth ridge
[ʃ]	(linguo-)palatoalveolar	tongue blade near the junction of the hard palate and the upper tooth ridge
[h]	glottal	vocal folds partially apart

3.9 Stops and affricates

The set of stop consonants will be considered next. In the production of *stops* the outflow of air is completely cut off by the action of the articulators, which come together and make a complete *occlusion* (hence the name 'occlusives', which is also given to stops) of the air passage. During the occlusion phase there is no vibrating source and consequently no acoustic wave, but during the *release* stage an explosion is caused that produces a sudden burst of air turbulence. The release is normally executed by the sudden separation of the articulators, which causes the explosion (hence the name 'explosives', which is also used for stops), but in some cases the articulators play no role in the release, which is instead implemented by lowering the soft palate. This type of stop lacks the air burst characteristic of explosives and the name *implosives* is used instead (note that this word is also ambiguously applied to sounds with an ingressive pharyngeal airstream, as discussed on p. 71; the derived term *plosives* is also given to occlusives in general).

The three stop sounds of English are kept apart by differences in the size and shape of the resonating chambers. The velar articulation of [k] entails a larger volume for the front cavity, and thus a lower frequency range for the burst, than that of the alveolar [t]. Paradoxically, the frequencies for [p] concentrate on the lower regions, as with [k], although the bilabial articulation of this consonant implies that no front cavity is involved in its production. A possible explanation for this parallel between [p] and [k] is that the burst caused by the sudden lip-opening in [p] induces a resonance effect along the entire length of the vocal tract.

The acoustic identification of stops is chiefly achieved by the *transition* (the frequency shift they induce in the formants of the neighbouring vowel) which is characteristic of each of them. A transition can be described as a movement from a particular point in the frequency-scale which is associated with each plosive (i.e. the *locus*) to the steady-state level of the vowel, or vice versa. A *minus* transition has the locus at a frequency lower than that of the steady state of the vowel and a *plus* transition has the locus higher. The frequency-range for the burst and the type of transition associated with each English stop is given in Table 3.5. Articulatorily, English stops have the following specifications:

[p]	bilabial	both lips together
[t]	(linguo-)alveolar	tongue tip on the upper tooth ridge
[k]	(linguo-)velar	tongue back on the soft palate

Fricatives and stops do not exhaust the inventory of English consonant sounds proper (i.e. the inventory of *obstruents*, as opposed to *sonorants*, which comprise vowels, glides and liquids, and also, nasals; see p. 84). A third category of obstruents is the *affricates*, which share with the stops the presence of an occlusion, but where the release is

Table 3.5 *Acoustic Specification of RP English Plosives*

IPA Symbol	Noise Burst Frequency-Range	F2 Transition
p	360–2,000	minus
t	3,000–4,000	minus for [i] etc. plus for [u] etc.
k	700–3,000	plus

Note: There exist some contextually bound variations in the direction of the transition. The magnitude of the transition is also subject to variation depending on the nature of the neighbouring vowel.

Source: Gimson, 1970, pp. 154–5.

delayed rather than sudden. Thus affricates can be regarded as consisting of a stop immediately followed by a homorganic fricative (i.e. a fricative produced at the same place of articulation as the stop). An English affricate is *ch* [ʧ], as in *church*: [ʧ] (linguo-)palatoalveolar composed of [t]+[ʃ].

3.10 Voicing and nasalisation

Two types of sound source have been identified so far – the glottal wave associated with vocal fold vibration and the noise characteristic of stops and fricatives. These two sources are not necessarily exclusive and can co-occur. The consonants described above are all voiceless, but voiced consonants also exist, where supraglottal noise is superimposed on the voice generated by the vocal folds. Apart from this difference in voicing, voiced consonants are practically identical to their voiceless counterparts from the point of view both of articulation and of acoustics, and their detailed description can therefore be safely omitted. Table 3.6 gives an inventory of English voiced obstruents, each presented alongside its voiceless analogue.

Table 3.6 *Chart of the Main English Obstruents in IPA Symbols*

Place of Articulation	Stop		Fricative		Affricate	
Bilabial	b	p				
Labiodental			v	f		
Dental			ð	θ		
Alveolar	d	t	z	s		
Palatoalveolar			ʒ	ʃ	ʤ	ʧ
Velar	g	k				
Glottal				h		

Note: The first sound in each pair is voiced. The one on its right is its voiceless correlate. The following words exemplify these sounds, from left t to right and from top to bottom: *bill*, *pill*, *vill*, *fill*, *this*, *thill*, *dill*, *till*, *zip*, *sill*, *pleasure, assure, gill* (as in measuring), *chill*, *gill* (as in a fish), *kill*, *hill*.

So voice provides a third parameter in the classification of consonants, alongside manner and place of articulation. A fourth parameter will be introduced now, but first a brief anatomical diversion is in order.

The hard palate is made of bone and is thus rigidly fixed, but the soft palate is a muscular flap of tissue which can move up and down, and in so doing close the passage between the oral and the nasal tracts (i.e. the 'velopharyngeal port'). During quiet breathing, the soft palate ordinarily remains lowered to permit the air inhaled through the nostrils to find free passage down to the larynx, the trachea and, ultimately, the lungs. During speech production, however, the soft palate performs a crucial linguistic function in differentiating *oral* sounds (produced with a raised soft palate and thus with no nasal resonance) from *nasal* sounds (produced with a lowered palate and thus with nasal resonance).

Acoustically, the opening of the passage to the nasal cavity represents the addition of an extra resonator, of greater volume than the oral resonator and, therefore, associated with lower frequencies. Nasalisation is also accompanied by an important reduction in amplitude because of the damping caused by the soft tissues lining the inside of the nasal cavities and by the presence of antiresonances (i.e. frequency-ranges of particularly low energy) that debilitate and sometimes cancel out altogether some of the formants. Note, furthermore, that, in marked contrast with non-nasal sounds, the size of the oral resonator during production of nasal sounds increases as the location of the closure moves away from the glottis, because the air has no exit at the lips. Consequently, an increase in the length of the oral tube will result in a lower frequency for the second formant.

English has at least three nasal consonants, but no nasal vowels as such, although a certain amount of vowel nasalisation can occur in the vicinity of nasal consonants as a result of coarticulation (see Chapter 4, p. 93). Moreover, in some dialects (e.g. many North American ones) nasalisation spreads throughout the utterance due to the incomplete closure of the velopharyngeal port during production of normally oral sounds. Table 3.7 gives the acoustic characteristics of the common

Table 3.7 *Synthetically Produced and Perceptually Tested Frequencies for English Nasal Consonants*

IPA Symbol	Frequencies		
	F1	*F2*	*F3*
m	200	1,100	2,500
n	200	1,700	2,500
ŋ	200	2,300	2,500

Source: Gimson, 1970, p. 193.

English nasal consonants. In Figure 3.11 a general inventory of English consonantal sounds is displayed in a tree form.

There are, of course, other consonants besides those found in English. Some languages have palatal stops (Basque [bicor], Victor, and

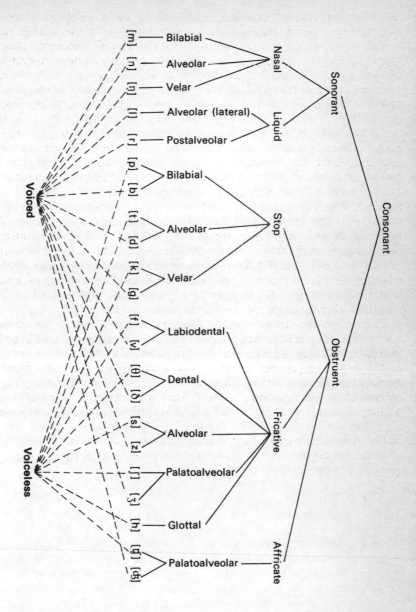

Figure 3.11 *General inventory of chief English consonants. The tree format brings out the hierarchical organisation of the different classificatory parameters. The complete labelling of any particular sound can be easily worked out by following the path from the phonetic symbol to the root of the tree.*

[maɹalen], Madelaine), and others like Arabic, uvular stops ([q], as in [qɑmus] 'dictionary', and [G], as in [Gɑmus] 'buffalo'). A glottal stop [ʔ] is common in many varieties of English, especially in British English, where it can replace [t] or even [p] or [k] in certain positions. All stops can have fricative counterparts and these are sometimes used as variants of the former in rapid speech in some pronunciations of English. In other languages they have an independent status, as happens with Arabic [χ] (homorganic with [q]) and [ʁ] (homorganic with [G] and which can be found in French corresponding to the spelling *r*), German [x] (homorganic with [k]), as in *doch* ([dɔx]) 'yes' (cf. the Scottish word *loch* [lɔx]), and [ç], as in *ich* ([ɪç]) 'I' (cf. the common English pronunciation of *Hugh* as [çju]). The bilabial fricative [Φ] (the counterpart of [p]) appears in Japanese, and its voiced analogue [β] in Greek and in Spanish, which also have the voiced velar [ɣ]. The pharyngeal fricative sounds [ħ] and [ʕ], formed by placing the tongue root in the proximity of the back wall of the pharynx, are common in Arabic.

Retraction of the tongue tip towards the palate can add an element of *retroflexion* to dental and alveolar consonants, a phenomenon which is particularly common in the languages of the Indian subcontinent and which accounts for one important aspect of the pronunciation of English by some native speakers of those languages (as in [ʈi] for *tea*). Retroflexion is also the rule for the English sound [ɜ] in some American and south-western British varieties of English (cf. the pronunciation of words like *bird* [bɜ˞d] in these accents, with *rhotacisation* or r-colouring of the vowel represented by the diacritic ˞. A final category of consonants unrepresented in English is the nasal and lateral palatals. The former occurs in French *signe* [siɲ], Spanish *señal* [seɲal] and Italian *segno* [seɲo] (all meaning 'signal'). The voiced lateral palatal is found in Italian *taglio* [taʎo] and Portuguese *talho* [taʎu] both meaning 'cut' and also in some varieties of Spanish (*tallo* [taʎo], 'stem'). A voiceless alveolar lateral fricative occurs in Welsh represented by the digraph *ll*, as in *llan* [ɬan], 'church' or 'village'.

3.11 Suprasegmentals

As was mentioned in the previous section, nasalisation is not necessarily limited to individual sounds – the failure of the soft palate to close the velopharyngeal port can affect several sounds in succession. Thus nasalisation can take on a suprasegmental character, i.e. it can span units larger than the *segment* (the individual sound). This final section will turn to the study of *suprasegmentals*.

The rate of vibration of the vocal folds is controllable within a certain range contingent on variables such as age and sex. This control is carried out by regulation of the tension of the vocal folds and of subglottal pressure. Perceptually, changes in fundamental frequency result in variations in pitch which constitute the underlying mechanism for intonation and tone.

Intonation is a device commonly used in language to differentiate, for instance, statements from questions, as well as to bring out idiosyncratic emotional states of the speaker. In the following two English utterances, for instance,

(*a*) go on holiday this summer

(*b*) go on holiday this summer

the difference in intonation impressionistically shown by the two underlining contours has the effect of altering the functional status of the sentence, such that (*a*) can best be viewed as a piece of advice by the speaker to the hearer to perform a particular action (go on holiday) at a particular time (this summer), whereas (*b*) questions whether such an action took place at such a time. Note that, in addition to this obvious change in illocutionary force (see Chapter 7, p. 215), the referent of the phrase 'this summer' also varies with intonation – in (*a*) the summer being talked about is still to come, while in (*b*) (which is of course a colloquial abbreviation for 'did you go on holiday this summer?') it must be the summer already elapsed prior to the conversation.

Deviations from the speaker's average frequency level are also responsible for *tone*, the counterpart of intonation at word level (this use of the word 'tone' must not be confused with its utilisation as a synonym of 'periodic sound', see p. 71, in which case it contrasts with 'noise'). English does not use tone, but most South-East Asian, African and native American languages do. The only European languages that possess tone are Serbo-Croat, Lithuanian, Norwegian and Swedish. In a manner parallel to intonation for whole utterances, tone serves to differentiate the meaning of individual words. In Mandarin Chinese, for instance, the sequence [ma] can have four different meanings, depending on the tone contour associated with it:

ma	'mother'
— level tone	
ma	'hemp'
/ rising tone	
ma	'horse'
∨ falling-rising tone	
ma	'scold'
\ falling tone	

A second suprasegmental worth mentioning here is *stress*, or relative emphasis of a vowel or syllable with respect to the neighbouring segments. Stress is a suprasegmental in that it can (and usually does) span a whole syllable comprising more than one segment. Note that the definition of the *syllable* is one of the most elusive in phonetics and no existing theory of the syllable is fully satisfactory. But whatever the rigorous theoretical interpretation of the construct might ultimately be, individual sounds in the speech chain do not stand in isolation but, rather, group themselves in units which are usually shorter than the word. Evidence for this abounds in all languages – particularly relevant are writing systems (e.g. the Japanese *kana*) where each graphic unit relates to a whole syllable rather than to one individual sound, as happens in European languages, thus arguably revealing the existence of an underlying intuition of the speakers for syllables. The suprasegmental nature of stress is also brought out by the fact that, perceptually, stress is defined as a prominence peak within a sequence of segments.

At the articulatory level, stress derives from a neurologically induced increase in muscular effort, which may result in higher levels of fundamental frequency and intensity, as well as in a longer duration of the sound. Note that *duration* is also commonly included under the heading of suprasegmentals. As is obvious from the name, it refers to the length (i.e. timespan) of segments in relation to each other. Duration is by no means uniform across segments, as careful observation of the vowel length in the (RP) English pronunciation of the words *hit* (short), *hid* (longer) and *heed* (longer still) will reveal.

The linguistic importance of stress can be illustrated by the two English sentences below, identical in all respects except in the location of accentual prominence (indicated by small capitals) in the underlined words.

(*a*) I <u>perMITted</u> the children to go abroad
(*b*) I <u>PERmitted</u> the children to go abroad

Sentence (*a*) expresses permission to do something and can be naturally associated with, for instance, a father allowing his children to travel, while (*b*) could have been uttered by a passport official reporting that a party of minors has been issued with permits to cross the frontier. Another, more common, instance of minimal differentiation based on stress is exemplified by the following two sentences.

(*a*) the LIGHThouse keeper fell
(*b*) the light HOUSEkeeper fell

The linguistic use of phonetic processes discussed in this section falls outside the scope of phonetics and leads naturally into *phonology*. This is the subject of the next chapter.

Exercises: Chapter 3

1   Construct sinusoids with the following values for amplitude and frequency respectively (values for amplitude are given with reference to the first sound-wave; values for frequency are given in Hz).

1   1, 4
2   ½,8
3   2, 2
4   1, 6
5   ⅓,12

2   If the sinusoids resulting from Exercise 1 are combined to form a complex waveform, which will be the fundamental and which the harmonics? What harmonics will be present?

3   The measurements for volume (in cm³), surface of tube opening (in cm²) and length of protrusion (in cm) are given for three Helmholtz resonators in each of the groups below. State with reasons which resonator within each group is likely to have the highest natural frequency.

1   (a) (27,000, 25, 6); (b) (1,000, 21, 3); (c) (64,000, 23, 5)
2   (a) (27,000, 12, 23); (b) (26,990, 13, 40); (c) (27,010, 12, 5)
3   (a) (12,005, 1, 13); (b); (11,090, 33, 12); (c) (12,000, 18, 11)

4   Indicate which of the words below have homophones (i.e. words with the same pronunciation which are spelled differently), which are homographs (i.e. correspond to more than one pronunciation without changes in the spelling) and which have a particularly deviant spelling with regard to the English norm:

colonel, have, lead, bow, urn, tomb, tyre, weigh, mown, aunt, read, sword, lone, fir, lieutenant, boar, sieve, thyme, yacht, bury, aisle, quay, witch, sow, court, due, pretty, ache, wring.

5   Render the following passage into ordinary spelling.

wi məst ˈlɜn tə bɪkʌm ˈmɔ ˈtɒlərənt əv ðə ˈwɜd əz ˈspoʊkən baɪ ə ˈmɛrɪkənz, kəneɪdiənz, ɒstreɪljənz ən saʊθ ˈæfrɪkənz; ənd ˈɪŋglɪʃ-spikɪŋ ˈlɪsnəz ɒn ðɪ ʌðə saɪd əv ðə ˈwɜldz ˈoʊʃnz məst rɪ ˈmɛmbə ðət ˈwɛn ɪt kʌmz tə ˈθroʊɪŋ ˈstoʊnz ət ðə ˈsoʊ-kɔld ˈbrɪtɪʃ ɪŋglɪʃ, ˈðeɪ, ˈtu, lɪv ɪn ˈglɑs ˈhaʊzɪz. ðɪ ˈɪŋglɪʃ ˈlæŋgwɪdʒ ɪz ə ˈvɛrɪ mʌtʃ mɔ ˈwaɪdsprɛd ˈlæŋgwɪdʒ ðən ðə ˈwɜld həz ˈjɛt ˈsin ɪn ɪts ˈhɪstrɪ, ən ðə ˈfɜst θɪŋ ðɪ ˈɪŋglɪʃ spikɪŋ ˈpiplz hæv tə ˈlɜn ɪz ðət ðər ə ˈmɛnɪ gəd ˈweɪz əv ˈspikɪŋ ɪt. ˈɛvrɪbɒdɪ bəlivz ɪz ˈoʊn tə bɪ ðə ˈbɛst, ən ˈætɪtjud ðət, ɪn ˈʌðə ˈsfɪəz əv ˈlaɪf, sɪvəlaɪ ˈzeɪʃn əz ˈtɔt əs tə dɪs ˈpaɪz.

6   Transcribe the following words using the IPA alphabet. Justify your choices, whenever necessary, in terms of the variety of English to which you are referring.

knee, wrought, lamb, table, wooing, debt, button, wart, chill, psyche, ghost, sure.

7   Make a phonetic transcription of the following passage in IPA symbols, first as it would correspond to RP pronunciation (newscasters can provide a useful model here) and then as it would sound in your own variety of English.

I think that anyone's political ideas or their ideas of social organisation must be rooted ultimately in some concept of human nature and human needs. Now my own feeling is that the fundamental human capacity is the capacity and the need for creative self-expression, for free control of all aspects of one's life and thought. One particularly crucial realisation of this capacity is the creative use of language as a free instrument of thought and expression. Now having this view of human nature and human needs, one tries to think about the modes of social organisation that would permit one to be fully human in the sense of having the greatest possible scope for one's freedom and initiative. Moving along in this direction, one might actually develop a social science in which a concept of social organisation is related to a concept of human nature which is empirically well-founded and which in some fashion leads even to value judgements about what form society should take, how it should change and how it should be reconstructed.

8   For each of the groups of vowels and glides below, specify what dimension of what parameter has been used in the grouping.

1 [i, y, u, ɯ]   2 [w, ø, œ, u, ɒ]
3 [a, ɑ, ɒ]   4 [ʌ, ɤ, u, ɑ, ɔ]
5 [j, ɪ, ɯ, ə, ɑ]   6 [ɛ, e, æ, j]

9   State which vowel corresponds to each of the following F1 and F2 patterns. Give your reasons for your choice with respect to articulation.

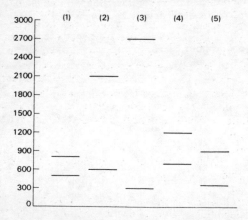

10 Find the odd man out in each set. State your reasons.

1 [ɹ, l, ɾ, x]   2 [ʃ, v, ð, r, χ, ʕ]
3 [k, d, b, ɣ, t, g]   4 [θ, β, q, ʒ, f, z]
5 [ç, m, h, ɬ, s, x]

11 One sound from group 0 can be added to each of the other sets. State which it is in each case and give reasons.

0 [n, q, c, g, b]   1 [ŋ, ɣ, k, x]
2 [v, m, p, f, β]   3 [χ, ʁ, ʀ, ɢ]
4 [ʎ, ç, ɟ, ɲ]   5 [s, t, l, d, z]

12 Specify in each of the groups below which is the voiceless and the nasal counterpart (if any) of the sound outside the brackets.

1 d (ð, N, n, p, t)   2 g (ɣ, θ, k, ɲ, m)
3 b (ɲ, t, q, m, p)   4 z (ð, n, ŋ, s, x)
5 ʤ (ʒ, d, ɣ, ʃ, h)

Bibliography: Chapter 3

Abercrombie, D., *English Phonetic Texts* (London: Faber, 1964). A very useful collection of (RP) English phonetic transcriptions using the IPA system; it includes a short general introduction on phonetic transcription.

Borden, G. J., and Harris, K. S., *Speech Science Primer* (Baltimore, Md: Williams & Wilkins, 1980). A useful, pedagogically oriented presentation of the fundamental aspects of speech at the levels of production, acoustics and perception, complemented by chapters on experimental techniques, speech and language origins, and language and thought; given the necessary amount of attention, it can probably be profitably attempted by the beginner.

Fry, D. B., *The Physics of Speech* (Cambridge: Cambridge University Press, 1979). A very clear introduction to this crucial area of phonetics, otherwise difficult to tackle for those without at least a rudimentary background in the 'hard' sciences; it will be read most profitably by all.

Fry, D. B. (ed.), *Acoustic Phonetics* (Cambridge: Heffer, 1960, 9th edn). A very handy, if by necessity advanced, collection of readings on aspects of speech acoustics, too varied to be given even a cursory description here; excellent for consultation purposes for the more advanced student.

Gimson, A. C., *An Introduction to the Pronunciation of English* (London: Edward Arnold, 1970). (3rd edn, 1980). It brings up-to-date and complements Jones's (1960) description of British English; undoubtedly the best of its kind.

Heffner, R.-M. S., *General Phonetics* (Madison, Wis.: University of Wisconsin Press, 1950). It usefully complements Ladefoged's (1982) treatment; it includes a thorough inventory of speech sounds represented in IPA notation.

Jones, D., *An Outline of English Phonetics* (Cambridge: Heffer, 1960, 9th ed). A thorough but traditional description of the English sound-system in

IPA transcription; it includes useful references to foreign sounds and to the problems faced by the foreign learner of English.

Ladefoged, P., *A Course in Phonetics* (New York: Harcourt Brace Jovanovich, 1982, 2nd edn). The most complete, up-to-date handbook of the discipline, dealing with all the important aspects of phonetics and including a variety of exercises, on both theory and performance.

Lehiste, I., *Suprasegmentals* (Cambridge, Mass.: MIT Press, 1970). A very useful, authoritative discussion focused on duration, tone and stress, not easy to read for the beginner, but of great value for consultation.

Minifie, F. D., Hixon, T. J., and Williams, F., *Normal Aspects of Speech, Learning and Language* (Englewood Cliffs, NJ: Prentice-Hall, 1973). An excellent collection of papers written by specialists presenting the areas of acoustics, respiration, phonation, articulation, psychoacoustics, auditory physiology, and language and speech; recommended.

Stubbs, M., *Language and Literacy* (London: Routledge & Kegan Paul, 1980). A useful discussion of the relationship between written and spoken language, including sections on English spelling, reading and educational failure, which relates to aspects of Chapter 12 in this book.

The Principles of the International Phonetic Association (London: University College, 1949). Lays down the principles of the IPA system of transcription; includes all the official IPA symbols, as well as phonetic transcriptions of the passage 'The North Wind and the Sun' in fifty different languages and three varieties of English.

Zemlin, W. R., *Speech and Hearing Science* (Englewood Cliffs, NJ: Prentice-Hall, 1968). An advanced but authoritative study of the biological aspects of linguistic sound; it includes chapters on respiration, phonation, the articulators and the nervous system.

Chapter 4

Phonology

4.1 Physical sound and linguistic sound

In the preceding chapter we introduced the basic notions of acoustics and the mechanics of the generation of sound, and speech sound was seen to be a special case of general physical sound. At the end of the chapter mention was made of suprasegmentals and of the role they play in differentiating words or sentences otherwise alike. As linguists, we are particularly interested in this linguistic function of the sound generated by the articulators. This concern is already implicit in Saussure's conception of the signifier as a *sound-image*, as distinct from the material substance of the sound which is its physical manifestation (see Chapter 1, p. 8). This chapter deals with such linguistic aspects of speech sound.

Inertia gives rise to coarticulation. In the word *me*, for instance, the transition from the initial nasal consonant to the vowel is not abrupt, the raising of the soft palate usually lagging behind the release of the labial closure, so that at least part of the vowel becomes nasalised (as mentioned in Chapter 3, nasalisation is particularly accentuated in certain dialects). *Coarticulation* is due to the dynamic and linear nature of speech. Physiologically, speech consists of a series of neural commands sent to the articulators through a network of nerves and of the movements of the articulators themselves. Neural messages travel fast, but the articulators are massive bodies and therefore possess inertia. Because of this, they may fail to keep up with the speed of the incoming commands, hence the nasalisation of the vowel in *me* through *delatory coarticulation*. Thus the situation common in speech is one where the articulatory movements involved in the production of individual sounds form an intricate linear network of overlapping gestures. But perceptual analysability is not hampered, and the somewhat nasalised vowel [ĩ] in *me* (NB the diacritic ˜ stands for nasalisation) is heard as distinct from the preceding nasal consonant, and it is identified with the oral vowels (i.e. in words like *pea*, *tea*, *key*, *fee*, *sea*, *she*, *he*, *lee*, etc.). Thus while objectively (i.e. acoustically) speech is non-discrete, subjectively (i.e. perceptually) it is felt as made up of discrete segments (the invention of alphabetic writing constitutes evidence for this intuition, as the invention of syllabic writing can be taken to suggest reality for the syllable).

Each phonetic context determines the configuration of the segments in it. But phonetic variation goes well beyond environmental conditioning and it has become a commonplace in phonetics manuals to affirm that no two utterances of a sound are ever the same. The important point to be emphasised here is that there is a gap between objective physical sound and perceived sound, such that all repetitions of a word like *lee* will be perceived as being the same, and also its vowel will be identified with that in *me*, despite the presence of nasalisation in the latter. Two distinct processes seem to be at work in interpreting physical sound into linguistic sound. First, the string of overlapping gestures is segmented into discrete perceptual units or *phones*. Secondly, the infinite variety of phones is organised into a finite number of units of linguistic sound, as stars in the sky are grouped into constellations. Note that it follows from the present discussion that each of the IPA symbols stands in reality for a constellation of sounds and, therefore, it already represents a certain level of analytical abstraction.

4.2 Contextual variation of sound

In Chapter 3 the vowels in *he* and *who* were defined as front and back respectively and the consonant [k] as a velar consonant. In a word like *key* one would, therefore, expect a phonetic sequence velar consonant plus front vowel, i.e. the string [ki] in IPA script. Self-observation will suffice to show that this expectation is not fulfilled, the initial plosive in *key* being in fact articulated on the hard palate, somewhere between the places of occlusion for [ɟ] (as in *chew*) and [k] (as in *coo*). A more accurate phonetic transcription for *key* for many speakers will in fact be [ci], where [c] represents the voiceless palatal stop (see Chapter 3, p. 84).

The alternation between [c] and [k] can best be understood if it is related to the nature of the following vowel regarding backness (and height, but this is constant in the examples at hand) – in *coo* a back consonant ([k]) co-occurs with a back vowel ([u]), while in *key* the front vowel ([i]) favours an advancement in the point of articulation of the preceding consonant, and therefore [k] gives way to [c]. This positioning of the articulators ahead of the sound to which they primarily relate characterises the second variety of coarticulation, *anticipatory coarticulation*. While the motivation for anticipatory coarticulation is still the overcoming of muscle inertia, it must be neurally programmed. It follows from this that it is repressible (by repressing the neural programming), and while most languages will be expected to have a similar alternation in plosives as the one in English *coo-key* (cf. French *cou* [ku], 'neck', and *qui* [ci], 'who'), it will not be surprising to find some languages where it is lacking – Basque, for instance, differentiates [coca] 'eau de vie' from [koka] 'smack'. Apart from a few exceptions like this, *regressive assimilation* of the type exemplified in [ci] is universal and stems from the general drive towards smoothness in the speech flow.

On the surface at least, the words *lee* and *eel* are made up of the same segments in opposite orders and ought to be transcribed as [li] and [il] respectively. On closer examination, however, an important systematic difference can be observed between the two liquids – in the articulation of *eel*, and simultaneously with the movements necessary for the alveolar articulation of *l*, the back of the tongue hunches up in the direction of the soft palate, thus giving a superimposed velar quality to the liquid. In keeping with normal IPA practice, velarised *l* is given a special sign that distinguishes it from ordinary *l*, thus differentiating *eel* ([iɫ]) from *lee* ([li]).

The two types of alternation [k] [c] and [l] [ɫ] are crucially distinct. The former, as has been seen, is automatic. The latter, on the other hand, is idiosyncratic to English (cf. French *lit* [li], 'bed', *il* [il], 'he', which show no alternation), and even here it is not present in all varieties of the language – Anglo-Irish and Anglo-Welsh, for instance, tend to use a plain [l] in all positions and Scottish English and many American dialects systematically utilise only velarised [ɫ].

It follows from the previous discussion that a very important distinction must be made between universal (unless actively repressed) sound variations which are *intrinsically* determined, like the alternation between [k] and [c] in the environment of back and front vowels respectively, and variations which are *extrinsically* determined and happen idiosyncratically in some languages without being directly attributable to *phonetic* contextual factors (e.g. the alternation between [l] and [ɫ] in RP English). Only the latter variations need be specified in the competence grammar of the language.

4.3 Criteria of analysis

As pointed out before, the infinite variety of physical sound corresponds to perceptual constellations of phones where abstraction is made from irrelevant physical properties. It is the linguist's task to replicate (albeit not necessarily isomorphically) such a procedure, so that the infinite number of phones is reduced to a finite set of linguistically significant sound units. In order to perform this operation, criteria must be laid down to guide the analyst in the delimitation of the different constellations. *Phonology* is the branch of linguistics that concerns itself with such an undertaking.

There are immediate difficulties, however. If the words *till* and *rill* are played simultaneously each through one earphone, listeners will identify the stimulus with the word *trill*, despite the fact that the spelling *tr* can represent a postalveolar affricate which is from many points of view phonetically closer to the [ɣ] in *chill* than to the sequence [t] plus [ɹ]. The linguist is thus faced with the dilemma of whether to trust his own intuitions and be liable to the charge of subjectivism, or to adhere to the physical evidence even when clearly counter-intuitive. Either course of action seems unsatisfactory and the linguist might try to resolve the dilemma by laying down *objective* criteria which would none the less accord with his intuitions both as a linguist and as a speaker of his native language. This solution to the problem has been popular with phonologists and will be expanded on now. In what follows we shall reserve the term 'phone' to refer to constellations of physical sound at the first level of abstraction, i.e. the level at which minute (albeit physically real) and imperceptible sound differences are glossed over.

One such criterion is provided by the principle of *complementary distribution*. The environments determining the phonetic occurrence of [k] and [c] in English are mutually exclusive (back versus front vowels), as are those governing the alternation [l], [ɫ] (onset versus offset of syllable). The phones [c] and [t], on the other hand, exhibit contextual overlap, as the words *key* and *tea* bear witness, and thus any possibility of their inclusion in the same constellation must be ruled out, even if phonetically the difference between [c] and [t] is not obviously greater than that between [c] and [k].

The sounds [h] and [ŋ] (both represented in *hang*) have the same distribution as [l] and [ɫ] respectively, and therefore a literal interpretation of the principle of complementary distribution will group them together in one constellation. Intuitively, however, phonetic distance makes the relationship between [h] and [ŋ] quite different from that between, say, [k] and [c], since the latter are both voiceless plosives, but the former pair is made up of a voiceless glottal fricative and a voiced velar nasal. In order to overcome this difficulty, the additional principle of *physical similarity* is invoked, according to which only phonetically similar sounds *can* be assigned to the same constellation (note, however, that they *need* not be; see the discussion on [c] and [t] in the previous paragraph). So stated, the principle is of necessity vague, since no rigorous criterion is specified to determine the *degree* of phonetic proximity which is necessary to warrant common membership for any two sounds – the decision is left to the linguist, thereby introducing an unwelcome element of arbitrariness into the procedure.

The principle of physical similarity is essentially a corrective to the possible excesses of the principle of complementary distribution, which therefore remains our major criterion of analysis so far. Both criteria would assign the *t* phones in *tar* and *star* to the same constellation, regardless of the fact that the *t* in *tar* (but not that of *star*) is aspirated – the time-lag between the release of the occlusive and the start of glottal vibration for the vowel allows a puff of air through the glottis (*aspiration* is normally represented in phonetic notation by a small ʰ superscript on the plosive: [tʰɑ:]; a colon following a vowel indicates a long vowel). In final position *t* can be aspirated or unaspirated – both variants can occur in a word like *tart* ([tʰɑ:tʰ] or [tʰɑ:t]), depending on speech tempo, style and other individual or social factors. The situation where two phonetically distinct (though similar) phones alternate freely (but subject to variables such as those just mentioned; for a more detailed discussion see Chapter 12, Section 6), known as *free variation*, is not at all uncommon in languages, and a new principle is needed which will allow the inclusion of *free variants* in the same constellation. Note that all the varieties of *t* mentioned above may well pass the test of physical similarity, but this is not necessarily the case (at least to the same degree) for all free variants. A common instance of this in English is the seemingly totally free alternation (i.e. not obviously subject to any variable constraints such as those mentioned above) of [ε] and [i] in words like *egotistic*, *equilibrium*, *economics*, etc. As will be seen below, [ε] and [i] are significantly distinct (they differ in height of tongue, tenseness, duration, etc.) and constitute two independent functional units within the sound system of English. Their status as free variants in the words mentioned (and that of the various *t*s in *tart* also) is captured by the principle of *word identity*, according to which freely substitutable phones which do not alter the identity of the word are grouped together. Note that the definition of word is not itself unproblematic (see Chapter 5, p. 134 ff.). More straightforward appears to be *utterance* identity – a behavioural test can be devised in which a speaker has to judge the identity or lack of identity of two utterances. But this is not without problems either. As has been emphasised throughout, at the physical level all utterances are strictly speaking different, and it is not far-fetched to imagine that, to some extent at least, the subject is basing his judgements on meaning. While this is not necessarily undesirable, it must be mentioned here that several schools of thought within the structuralist movement which developed in Europe and in America in the 1930s, 1940s and early 1950s would ban the use of more abstract criteria, such as meaning, in the analysis of more concrete linguistic levels, such as sound. Given this framework the phonological analysis of free variants seems highly problematic.

4.4 Daniel Jones and the phoneme

The most celebrated operational procedure in phonological analysis is the so-called *commutation* or *minimal pair test* which, along the lines of the test discussed in the previous section, presents a subject with two utterances which only differ by one segment in the same position, and questions him on the identity of the pair. Putting aside the problems mentioned above, the utterances [ɑːtʰ] and [ɑːt] (*art*) are expected to be judged identical, whereas [pʰɪɫ] and [tʰɪɫ] will be deemed different, as corresponding to the words *pill* and *till*. Note that the requirement of minimality in the test automatically disqualifies a pair such as [tʰɪɫ] and [pʰæɫ], which differ by two segments.

The result of the commutation test systematically applied to all significantly distinct phones of a particular language is an inventory of minimal units of distinctive linguistic sound for that language. These units are known as *phonemes*, and they constitute the most important elements in phonological analysis. While there has been agreement to regard the phoneme as the main unit of linguistic contrast at the level of the signifier, both the criteria used for the establishment of phonemes and the ontological status of the construct vary somewhat from author to author. It will be worth reviewing some of the principal theories of the phoneme here.

In his definition of the phoneme, the British phonetician Daniel Jones explicitly incorporates the principle of physical similarity, which is conspicuously absent from the commutation test as formulated above. For Jones (1950, p. 10) a phoneme is 'a family of sounds in a given language which are related in character and are used in such a way that no other member ever occurs in a word in the same phonetic context as any other member'. The above definition sets the word as the domain of phonemic contrast, and it uses the criteria of physical similarity ('a family of sounds . . . which are related in character') and of complementary distribution ('no other member ever occurs . . . in the same phonetic context as any other member'). Note the vagueness of the principle of physical similarity, mentioned earlier.

Jones's theory of the phoneme is imbued with practical considerations, his main motivation being the improvement of transcription systems to assist in collecting previously unrecorded languages, in devising orthographic conventions to help the development of the societies where they are spoken, and so on. A welcome side-effect of this orientation is that, in contrast to the structuralist trends referred to above, he freely admits to the semantic function of phonemes, and thus to the role of meaning in the principle of word identity and in the commutation test which operationalises it.

The correlation between degree of detail in the phonetic analysis and enrichment in the transcription system can be mentioned here. The number of symbols must keep pace with the progressive specification of phonetic detail in the sound wave (or, equivalently, in the complex of articulatory movements), and a reasonably precise phonetic transcription for English must, for instance, include the symbols [l] and [ɫ] for *l*, [tʰ], [t] and [t°], for *t* ([t°] stands for an unreleased or implosive [t], see Chapter 3, p. 79, which is common in a position of syllable offset, as in the word *art*). Pushed to the ultimate limit, a detailed transcription ought to include a different symbol for each different phonetic context, and even a different symbol for each new utterance! Most of these phonetic modifications are, however, imperceptible, and, in any case, they are too small to provide a sufficiently strong justification for the proliferation of symbols which would ensue from a too rigid adherence to phonetic realism. Moreover, for many practical purposes, even phonetically distant variants of the same phoneme can be subsumed under a common symbol. Consequently, there are two alternative types of phonetic transcription: *narrow transcription*, ideally geared to the reproduction of all non-random phones occurring in the speech chain, and *broad transcription*, which limits the inventory to elements with phonemic import. From this point of view, phonetics can be regarded as the art of narrow transcription and phonology as the art of broad transcription.

4.5 Sapir's psychological approach

So far we have enumerated three principles of phonemic analysis (physical similarity, complementary distribution and word identity) and have advanced the view that these criteria accord with the linguistic intuitions of the native speaker regarding the sound-structure of his language. The question now is to what extent the outcome of phonological analysis matches any mental reality in the speaker. Chomsky is, of course, mentalistically inclined and he often uses the word 'grammar' with systematic ambiguity, to refer both to the linguist's construct and to the set of rules internalised by the speaker. By and large, the initiators of phonemic theory were not so preoccupied with psychological concerns. There are two positions regarding the ontological status of linguistic analyses. According to the *hocus-pocus* position, the constructs arrived at only represent a particularly economical and revealing way of introducing order in the data, and are thus a matter of mere convenience for the analyst, whereas for those defending a *God's truth* position language has an inherent structure which it is the linguist's task to discover. Note that even within the latter approach it does not necessarily follow that the structure present in the mind is isomorphic with the grammar arrived at formally. Linguists sympathetic to Chomsky's position would undoubtedly try to narrow the gap between the two. A similar concern is present in the works of the American linguist and anthropologist Edward Sapir several decades before Chomsky.

Apart from random variation, the RP pronunciation of *sawed* is identical to that of *soared*, but they are often perceived or 'felt' as different. The same applies to *lead* (the name of a metal) and *led*, the vowel in the latter being felt, according to Sapir, as a deflected form of that of the verb *to lead*. More evidence for the disparity between objective sound and native speaker feeling comes from Sapir's fieldwork with Amerindian informants. One of them, for instance, a speaker of Sarsi (an Amerindian language of Alberta, in western Canada) perceived as different the seemingly identical forms [dinih], 'this one', and [dinih], 'it makes a sound', and ascribed the difference to the presence of (an inaudible) *t* in the second word. This suggestion can only be understood in the light of the structure of the language. When the so-called 'basic form' of a word ends in a vowel, this vowel is always followed by aspiration ([h]), but basic forms which ought to end in aspirated [tʰ] drop the [t] by a process of general application in the language, although the aspiration is kept. The result is the phonetic conflation of both 'this one' and 'it makes a sound' into [dinih], although phonologically they can be considered different and given the representations /dini/, /dinitʰ/, respectively (note that phonological forms are customarily enclosed within diagonal bars, as opposed to the use of square brackets in phonetic transcription). Table 4.1 may help to clarify this situation. Sapir's conclusion is that it is phonological patterns, rather than objective physical sound, that have psychological reality.

Table 4.1   *Phonemic and Phonetic Representations of the Sarsi Words for 'This One' and 'It Makes a Sound'*

Phonological Form	General Process	Phonetic Form
/dini/	V# $\downarrow$ Vh#	[dinih]
/dinitʰ/	tʰ# $\downarrow$ h#	[dinih]

Note: The phonetic merger is predictable from the phonemic forms, given the existence of these phonological processes (the symbol # indicates the boundary of the word).

Interestingly, at least some mentalistic hypotheses have received a measure of confirmation from psychological experimentation (see Chapter 9) and from findings in the fields of language pathology, language change, language games (e.g. so-called pig or hog Latin) and others. A case in point is Sapir's correlation of the English phone [ŋ] with the phonological sequence /ng/, from which it would derive via assimilation of place of articulation of the nasal to the following obstruent (a general process of English) and by deletion of *g* in word-final position when following [ŋ] (note that *g*-deletion can only take place if assimilation has already applied, thus introducing an element of ordering in the procedure). As it stands, the hypothesis is elegant but the supporting evidence is not very compelling. There are additional facts, however, which lend it more weight.

Sapir's argumentation on this point deserves close attention here. Sounds in any particular language show regularities in distribution, i.e. each language possesses its own specific *phonotactics*. The only sequences of two consonants allowed in word-initial position in English, for instance, are those where the second element is *l* or *r*, or where the first segment is *s*. Thus a string like [ts], which appears in final position in *cats* [kæts], cannot start a word in English (cf. German *Zimmer* [tsɪmɐ], 'room'). Distributional gaps can be *systematic* (i.e. related to the phonotactics of the language) or *accidental*, and only the latter can be filled without doing violence to the phonotactic rules. Thus a word with initial [ts] would be unnatural in English. The final segment in the French import [ɹuːʒ], on the other hand, although ordinarily absent from the word-initial slot in English, can be regarded as an accidental gap and native speakers of English, Sapir claims, find it quite feasible to utter foreign words starting with such a segment (cf. [ʒɪskɑːd] 'Giscard'). A German name with initial [ts], however, would be difficult to pronounce for an Englishman, according to this reasoning.

Now, according to Sapir, English speakers find it just as difficult to pronounce initial [ŋ] as initial [ts]. This fact deserves an explanation, since [ŋ] is a single segment and would be expected to behave rather like [ʒ]. But note that Sapir's correlation of phonetic [ŋ] with the phonological sequence /ng/ fits it into the same category as [ts]. This mode of reasoning, as already pointed out, was not congenial to the bulk of the American structuralists, one of whom, W. Freeman Twaddell, strongly objected to Sapir's analysis and suggested a behavioural test that would supposedly refute it. Recent evidence from speech errors, however, supports Sapir's approach. Victoria Fromkin mentions attested cases of speech errors involving segment re-ordering where the phonetic sequence [ŋk] is dislocated into [n] and [k], and likewise the single phonetic segment [ŋ] reappears as [n] and [g]. Thus parallel to the change from [ðə bæŋk wɪl peɪ] (*the bank will pay*) to [ðə bæn wɪl peɪk] (*the ban will payk*), the sentence [swɪŋ ənd sweɪ] (*swing and sway*) becomes [swɪn ənd sweɪg] *swin and swayg*), although [g] is not phonetically present in the target sentence.

The difference in phonotactic strength between initial [ŋ] and initial [ʒ] can therefore be related to the general patterns of the language. Sapir emphasises that besides its phonetic manifestation a phoneme carries in itself a trace of the whole phonological system, because of the speakers' intuitive feeling of its relationships with other sounds within the structure of the language. Thus, although the phonotactic status of initial [ŋ] within the system of English nasal consonants may appear similar to that of [ʒ] within the system of fricatives, as displayed in Tables 4.2 and 4.3, its interpretation as the phonological sequence /ng/ will place it under the same phonotactic constraint as exists for word-initial sequences of two consonants.

Table 4.2 *Classification in Terms of Place of Articulation and Voice of the English Fricatives Occurring in Word-Initial Position*

	Labiodental	Dental	Alveolar	Palatoalveolar
Voiceless	f	θ	s	ʃ
Voiced	v	ð	z	—

Note: The voiced palatoalveolar [ʒ] does not occur.

Table 4.3 *Phonetic Cross-Classification of English Nasals According to their Positional Distribution, Showing the Existence of the Distributional Gap for the Velar [ŋ] in Initial Position*

	Bilabial	Alveolar	Velar
Initial	m	n	—
Medial	m	n	ŋ
Final	m	n	ŋ

4.6 Discovery procedures

Sapir's emphasis on phonological pattern is reminiscent of Saussure's conception of language as a system of oppositions. A similar interpretation is found in Bloomfield, who defines the phoneme as 'a minimum unit of *distinctive* sound-feature' (1933, p. 79; our emphasis), underlining that 'the importance of a phoneme . . . lies not in the actual configuration of the sound-waves, but merely in the *difference* between this configuration and the configurations of all the other phonemes of the same language' (ibid., p. 128; our emphasis).

Probably the most elaborate theory of phonology within the structuralist tradition was worked out during the 1920s and 1930s by the so-called Prague Linguistic Circle, of which the Russian-born scholar

Prince Nicolai Sergeievich Trubetzkoy is arguably the outstanding representative. Trubetzkoy's phoneme is also based on the Saussurean idea of opposition; among the sound differences found in a language, only some serve to differentiate the lexical meanings of words and it is these oppositions that constitute the subject-matter of phonology. The additional requirement of minimality is imposed on the phoneme, which is accordingly defined as 'the *smallest distinctive* unit of a given language' (Trubetzkoy, [1939] 1969, p. 35; our emphasis). Thus phonemic analysis is confronted with two tasks – the determination of the distinctive status of sound chunks and the segmentation of such chunks into minimal units of distinctiveness. Before giving an account of Trubetzkoy's own procedure we must consider one methodological point.

Chomsky has summed up the goal of classical structuralist linguistics (particularly in its American version) as the construction of a set of procedures designed to yield an automatic analysis for a given corpus, such that, for example, at the level of phonology a collection of utterances could be mechanically and unambiguously analysed into phonemes, allophones, free variants, etc. Chomsky suggests that the aims of all other sciences are more modest and that linguists ought to lower their sights accordingly. The structuralist methodology follows from an inductive approach to scientific research, which consists essentially in the belief that a theoretical analysis can be obtained through processing the raw data, and Chomsky proposes a shift to a hypothetico-deductive method, where the actual mechanics of discovery are quite immaterial – a hypothesis may emerge on the basis of intuition, dreams, divine revelation, or any other hunch, and what matters is the elaboration of its implications and their submission to empirical testing. There are, of course, important differences between the type of evidence available in linguistics and that which is possible in, for example, the physical sciences, a fact that has led some to deny empirical status to linguistics; but this opinion is by no means universally accepted.

In keeping with the structuralist tradition, Trubetzkoy enumerates a set of discovery procedures for phonemes, summarised in Figure 4.1. In comparing two phones, the analyst applies the principles of complementary distribution, word identity and physical similarity in the normal way. In addition, Trubetzkoy suggests that two phonetically related segments S_1 and S_2 can only be granted allophonic status (i.e. viewed as contextual variants, or *allophones*, of the same phoneme) if a sequence $S_1 S_2$ or $S_2 S_1$ never contrasts with one of the segments (i.e. S_1 or S_2) in the given language. For instance, RP English [ɪ] and [ə] are phonetically related (both possess a vocalic feature, since free airflow is never perturbed, see Chapter 3, p. 78), and they also exhibit complementary distribution ([ɪ] must and [ə] cannot precede vowels), but they still do not qualify as allophonic variants of a single phoneme because of the existence of pairs like *perfusion* [pəfjuʒən], *profusion* [pɹəfjuʒən] which are only kept apart by the contrast between [ə] and [ɹə].

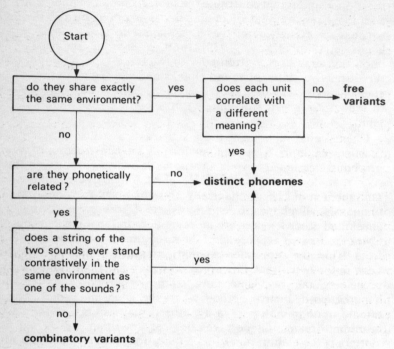

Figure 4.1   *Flowchart summarising Trubetzkoy's procedure for the establishment of the phonemic or non-phonemic nature of any two sounds in a given language.*

Regarding the requirement of minimality for the phoneme, Trubetzkoy first sets three phonetic prerequisites which must be met by the phonetic chunk before the phonological criteria for monophonematicity are applied, as follows:

(*a*) the chunk must belong to one syllable only;
(*b*) the chunk must be realised by means of a homogeneous articulatory movement or by the progressive dissolution of an articulation;
(*c*) the duration of the chunk must not be greater than that of the other phonemes of the language.

Let us apply these criteria to the English affricate [ʧ] in *chew*. First, the fact that it can occur in word-initial position suggests that the chunk belongs to one single syllable. Secondly, affricates are articulatorily distinguished from plosives (the monophonematic status of which is straightforward) in that the release of the occlusion is not instantaneous, but gradual, so that it goes through a fricative phase – [ʧ] is therefore realised by the progressive dissolution of a palatoalveolar stop. Thirdly, the duration of the chunk is not obviously greater than that of other phonemes of English, and therefore [ʧ] passes the phonetic test and must be next submitted to phonological examination.

The phonological conditions can be summarised as follows:

(a) there is no possibility of regarding any fraction of the chunk as an allophone of another phoneme;
(b) the chunk disobeys the phonotactic constraints on phoneme clusters;
(c) monophonematic treatment increases the symmetry of the phonemic pattern.

The fulfilment of at least one of these conditions leads to the granting of monophonematic status. Consider [ʧ] again. The first condition is not fulfilled, since [ʃ] belongs to an independent phoneme of English and the palatoalveolar stop may be considered a combinatory variant of the normally alveolar phoneme /t/. However, the fact that [ʧ] violates the phonotactic constraints regarding word-initial clusters and that its treatment as a single phoneme increases the symmetry of the phonemic pattern (it places [ʧ] in similar relation with [ʃ] as, for example, [t] has with [s], i.e. one of interruptedness versus non-interruptedness of the airflow) are sufficient arguments to give it monophonematic value. Note that this principle of *pattern congruity*, like the principle of physical similarity, is open to a variety of interpretations which may potentially lead to different phonemic inventories. A noted defender of *non-uniqueness* for phonological analysis is Yuen-Ren Chao, for whom the question is not the correctness or incorrectness of the system, but rather its suitability for the purpose it is designed for – phonetic accuracy (i.e. narrow transcription) would, for example, be favoured in dialectal and historical studies, whereas a more strict adherence to opposition (i.e. broad transcription) would be in order when there is a need for economy of symbols.

4.7 Classification of phonemes

In typical structuralist methodology segmentation is followed by classification and, having discussed some of the procedures used for the establishment of phonemes, we shall now look at the relations that can be hypothesised to exist between them. It must be remembered here that for Saussure all structural relationships in language are based on oppositions. These oppositions are of two kinds, depending on whether we take as our focus the speech chain or the actual language-system. In the former case we will oppose, for instance, *stars* to *shine*, in the expression *stars shine*, or, at the level of phonemes, /s/ to /t/, /t/ to /ɑ/, and so on. In the latter, *shine* can be opposed to *shone*, or, at a different level, *stars* to *planets*. Phonematically, /ʃ/ can be related to, for example, /s/ (cf. *shine* v. *sign*). This type of opposition is usually known as *paradigmatic*, whereas linear oppositions are called *syntagmatic*. Syntagmatic relations are characteristically based on the co-occurrence of elements in the speech chain, while paradigmatic oppositions only obtain within the total system, all elements of each network of relations but one being absent from the actual string of phonemes or words through which *langue* manifests itself in *parole*.

From the discussion above it follows that phonemes can be classified either syntagmatically or paradigmatically. According to its syntagmatic relations with other phonemes, each phoneme exhibits a certain pattern of distributional arrangements – in English, for instance, /r/, but not /l/, can appear after word-initial /t/ (see the discussion on phonotactics on p. 101). This criterion was followed by Bloomfield, who set up thirty-eight classes of English consonants based on their syntagmatic distribution and, interestingly, he pairs /ʒ/ with /ŋ/ (which, unlike Sapir, he treats as a single phoneme), because neither segment is found in word-initial position.

Phoneme classifications based on syntagmatic distribution are rather cumbersome and are not commonly used. The more frequent systems are paradigmatically oriented and are based on phonetic substance in as much as phonetic substance is instrumental in establishing and maintaining the phonological oppositions found in any language. Trubetzkoy's typology, for instance, in the main makes use of the traditional phonetic parameters. We have already referred to these in Chapter 3 and need not concern ourselves with the matter further. More innovatory is his taxonomy of the logical relations existing between distinctive oppositions and we shall look at this in some detail next.

There are three criteria for the logical classification of distinctive oppositions – the first concerns the type of relationship which exists between the two phonemes being considered; the second, the relationship between a phoneme pair and the rest of the system; and the third, the strength of any particular opposition. We shall examine each of these in turn.

Regarding the relation between two phonemes, oppositions can be privative, gradual, or equipollent. One of the members in a *privative* opposition possesses a property which the other member lacks (or is 'deprived of'), as with English /b/ (which has voice) and /p/ (which does not). The member with the property is said to be *marked* and the one without *unmarked*. Note that the phonetic complexity present in any phoneme can give rise to arbitrariness here. In the case at hand, if voice is taken to be the defining property /b/ will be marked and /p/ unmarked, but if we replace it with 'glottal opening' (i.e. aspiration), then the marking relationship is reversed. A *gradual* opposition exists when both members share the property in different degrees. For example, the tongue is raised to some degree in both English /i/ (a high vowel) and /ɛ/ (a mid-low vowel). Finally, oppositions which are neither privative nor gradual are termed *equipollent* (e.g. /k/ and /l/ in English). Members of equipollent oppositions are said to be logically equivalent because their relationship is indirect and remote – privative and gradual oppositions, on the contrary, give rise to close networks of relations, as will be seen below.

With respect to the second criterion (relationship between a phoneme pair and the rest of the system), oppositions can be *bilateral* or *multilateral*, depending on whether the *base* (the set of properties common to both members) is only present in the pair or is shared with some other phoneme, and *proportional* or *isolated*, depending on whether or not the particular relationship existing in the pair is found in some other pair. Thus English /b/, /p/ stand in bilateral opposition (they are the only oral bilabial plosives in the language), while /p/, /t/ are in multilateral opposition, since they share their base (voiceless-ness, oralness and plosiveness) with /k/. On the other hand, /b/, /p/ are in proportional opposition (cf. /d/-/t/, /g/-/k/, /v/-/f/, etc., all privative oppositions of voice), but the opposition /l/-/r/ (lateral v. non-lateral liquid) is isolated.

The final criterion refers to the strength of the opposition and according to it oppositions can be *constant* or *neutralisable*. An example will clarify this. The *p* in *spy* can be seen as being halfway between the *p* in *pie* and the *b* in *buy*, as illustrated in Table 4.4. Moreover, both

Table 4.4   *Phonetic Subclassification of Oral Bilabial Stops in English*

Aspirated		Voiced
pʰ	p	b

[pʰ] and [b] show a distributional gap after word-initial *s*. All this strongly suggests that the opposition between *p* and *b* is *neutralised* in this position, in which they are both represented by the *archiphoneme* /P/ (archiphonemes, i.e. representatives of neutralised phonemes, are often represented by capital letters), realised as [p]. Note that not all cases of *defective distribution* (failure of a segment to appear in a particular position) can be interpreted as neutralisations – for instance, the fact that in English /r/ but not /l/ can follow word-initial /t/ is not necessarily an indication that an archiphoneme /R/ is in existence there. Following from our discussion earlier on, defective distribution can be contingent on a phonotactic constraint or represent an accidental gap.

The phonetic substance of archiphonemes can be variously determined. As seen in the paragraph above, they can represent a middle term between the two neutralised phonemes. Also, they can be shaped by coarticulation effects, as happens with English intrasyllabic clusters of stops and fricatives, which must have the same voice value for both segments (e.g. *pots* [pɒts] v. *pods* [pɒdz]), or by the structural properties of the word (unstressed vowels usually weaken in English, but their phonetic quality depends on their position with respect to stress, on the type of neighbouring segments, etc.). Finally, if the phonetic content of an archiphoneme is not determined by the context or does not represent a compromise between the two neutralised phonemes, it will be determined by a universal tendency which favours unmarked as against marked segments, and also segments with the extreme degree of a property. Thus in German and Russian voiced and voiceless plosives neutralise in word-final position, the archiphoneme being represented by the unmarked term of the opposition, i.e. the voiceless phoneme. In Portuguese and Catalan there is neutralisation of *o* and *u* in unstressed position; *u* has extreme tongue height and therefore represents the archiphoneme.

A special label, *correlation pair*, is used by Trubetzkoy to designate oppositions which are privative, bilateral and proportional, because of the particularly close relationship exhibited by the members which enter such oppositions, as evidenced, for instance, in the frequency and regularity of their neutralisation processes. The phonological property which defines a correlation pair is given the name *correlation mark* (e.g. voice for /p/-/b/). Clusters of correlation pairs constitute *correlation bundles*, whose members may be said to possess a still stronger bond. One such correlation bundle corresponds to the vowel-system of Classical Arabic:

$$i \qquad \qquad u$$
$$a$$

and it is organised along the axes 'height' (open *a* v. closed *i*, *u*), and 'backness' (front *i* v. back *u*). Correlation bundles come in different shapes depending on the type of correlation networks in the system. Compare, for example, the simple vowel triangle of Arabic with the more complex cubic Turkish vowel-system given in Figure 4.2. Note that not all sound-systems can be reduced to correlations. The

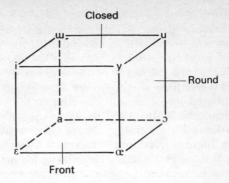

Figure 4.2 *Vowel-system of Turkish geometrically displayed showing how the correlation bundles organise themselves into a cubic shape. Note that the slot occupied by [a] in the diagram ought to be filled by [ʌ] to maintain a one-to-one correspondence between phonological function and phonetic substance. As it happens, however, languages often phonologise segments in ways which are not entirely isomorphic with their phonetic make-up.*

typologically predominant system for vowels, for instance, includes three degrees of height, as well as two classes of backness, as in Classical Latin and Modern Spanish:

$$\begin{array}{ll} i & u \\ e & o \\ a & \end{array}$$

The gradual nature of the height opposition in the non-back vowels entails a multilateral opposition for the phonemes partaking in it, which do not therefore qualify as correlation pairs and cannot form a correlation bundle.

The establishment of typologies of sound-systems was for Trubetzkoy one of the chief tasks of phonology. Later research has elaborated on the possible bases for the statistically attested differences in the frequency of phonological patterns across natural languages (for relevant discussion in a different context, see Chapter 11).

4.8 Distinctive features

Trubetzkoy's emphasis on the importance for phonology of correlations, minimally differentiated by correlation marks, points to the existence of units of opposition smaller than the phoneme. Phonological oppositions are in effect implemented by some (and not all) of the phonetic properties of the phonemes (e.g. by the correlation mark in the case of correlations). The words *pie* and *buy*, for instance, are kept apart by the feature 'voice' rather than by the phonemes /p/, /b/, which include many non-distinctive or redundant features.

The idea of *distinctive features* as basic phonological units received a definite impetus with the work of the Russian-born scholar Roman Jakobson, who redefines the phoneme derivatively as 'the distinctive features combined into one simultaneous or . . . concurrent bundle' (Jakobson, Fant and Halle, 1952, p. 3). Jakobson's theory is of paramount importance for phonology. Sets of distinctive features like that pioneered by Jakobson are put forward as hypotheses regarding the underlying parameters available to humans for making phonological differentiations either perceptually or articulatorily, or both. Evidence for these parameters is available from various areas of verbal behaviour, and Jakobson himself laid special emphasis on the temporal order in which phonemes are acquired by children as reflecting their progressive mastering of the distinctive feature system (see Chapter 10 for further discussion). On the other hand, Jakobson appears to have overstated the claim that the order of feature loss in pathological states mirrors that of child acquisition. Speech errors, rhyming conventions, various types of language games, perception experiments (see Chapter 9), all provide additional evidence as to the existence of distinctive features, as does the fact that historical sound changes often affect all phonemes sharing one or more particular feature – the existence of such *natural classes* can be formally captured by means of distinctive features. Data from these and other areas provide the empirical ground for the testing of alternative sets of features. Although many such sets have been proposed, we shall restrict ourselves here to those of Jakobson and of Chomsky and Halle, arguably the most widely used in the literature. A word of caution must be given to the reader concerning the technical nature of at least some of the phonetic descriptions of the features, and a full understanding of all the phonetic correlates, while useful, is not always an essential prerequisite for familiarisation with the phonological function of the distinctive features. We shall now proceed to the presentation of Jakobson's and Chomsky and Halle's models of distinctive features.

Jakobson carried out a drastic reduction in the inventory of phonological primes in relation to more traditional phonetic classifications (e.g. that of the IPA or the more phonologically oriented one of Trubetzkoy). The major motivation of Jakobson's approach is to establish a minimal set of distinctive phonological oppositions which would be capable of capturing all phonological contrasts in the world's languages. This set is justified in terms of the acoustic and articulatory properties of sounds (not always in a one-to-one correlation) and is put forward as a hypothesis concerning the phonological categories underlying the perception of language. This perceptual bias leads Jakobson to do away with Trubetzkoy's category of gradual opposition and to adhere strictly to a binary principle. Two arguments have been put forward to justify this move. The first relates to the supposed intrinsic binarism of language structure, taken over from the human mind, where the pattern of nerve fibre responses is organised in terms of all versus none. The second, advanced by Morris Halle, one of Jakobson's co-workers, makes appeal to simplicity, both at a general level and from the point of view of evaluating alternative descriptions of the same system (cf. Chao's view on non-uniqueness, referred to above).

As well as aiming at economy of inventory, Jakobson makes a determined attempt to use common features for subclassifying vowels and consonants. Interestingly, some fifteen years later, Halle, now collaborating with Noam Chomsky, deems this identification too radical a move and reverts to a more traditional approach where some of the parameters used are different for each category. Chomsky and Halle, in effect, put forward a set of features which, while keeping the binary principle, also diverges from Jakobson's in notably increasing the number of features in order to allow for a complete description of the phonetic capabilities of man, and not just of the phonological oppositions found in human languages. A final important discrepancy between these approaches is that, while Jakobson's features relate to perception and are, therefore, primarily defined on the basis of the acoustic properties of segments, Chomsky and Halle's, although supposedly neutral, are effectively defined on an articulatory basis. In what follows we shall try to review the complete inventory of Jakobson's distinctive features and to compare it with the alternatives advanced by Chomsky and Halle. A contrastive display of both sets is given in Table 4.5, the contents of which will become clear as the discussion proceeds.

In Chapter 3 we mentioned that free exit of air through the front of the mouth is a crucial feature which distinguishes vowels (with free airflow) from consonants (where the air passage is constricted to some degree). This dichotomy is central to human speech, and there is some evidence that there are two entirely separate neuro-muscular systems for vowels and consonants. Also, it has been suggested that the basic skeleton of speech consists of a series of movements for vowel articulation, upon which consonants are superimposed in the manner of secondary features that modify the fundamental vocalic stream. It is little wonder therefore that both Jakobson's (J) and Chomsky and Halle's (CH) systems include the features [±VOCALIC] and [±CONSONANTAL], defined articulatorily in the manner specified above (CH add the additional constraint that the constriction for vowels cannot exceed the one found in [i], [u]; consequently, the glides [j], [w] are [−VOCALIC] in their system), and acoustically in J as possessing a well-defined formant structure (for [+VOCALIC]) and having a low-

Table 4.5 *Cross-Comparison of Jakobson's and Chomsky and Halle's Distinctive Features*

JAKOBSON	CHOMSKY AND HALLE		
α vocalic	α vocalic		
α consonantal	CONSONANTS	α consonantal	VOWELS / α low
α compact		– α anterior	
α diffuse			α high
+grave		k p c t / – coronal	+back
–grave		/ +coronal	–back
	distributed		
	lateral		
α tense	α tense		
α flat	α round (labialisation)		
	α low (pharyngealisation)		
	α high/coronal (retroflection)		
α sharp	α high		
α interrupted	– α continuant		
strident	strident		
	delayed release (affricates)		
checked	various features		
+voice	+voice		
–voice	–voice		
	sonorant		
α nasal	α nasal		

Note: The table is to be read from left to right, since the reverse correspondences are not exhaustive. The variable α stands for the value + or –, such that two αs across the line indicate agreement in the specification of the feature, and one α in line with a –α, disagreement. Note that the correspondences between the two systems do not hold across vowels and consonants for the features COMPACT, DIFFUSE and GRAVE. Sometimes Chomsky and Halle's features have no correspondence in Jakobson's set, or several of their features correlate with just one of Jakobson's. In other cases the two taxonomies define different areas, and in these cases the horizontal lines do not meet in the middle.

ered first formant and less overall intensity (for [+CONSONAN-TAL]). These two features define the four fundamental categories of speech sound in the manner displayed in Table 4.6.

Table 4.6 *Specification of Some Traditional Phonetic Major Categories in Terms of the Features* [±VOCALIC] *and* [±CONSONANTAL]

	Vowels	Consonants Proper	Liquids	Glottals
Vocalic	+	−	+	−
Consonantal	−	+	+	−

Place of articulation for consonants and height and backness for vowels are defined in J's framework by means of the common features [±COMPACT] and [±GRAVE]. Compactness refers to the ratio between the volume of the resonator in front of the narrowing and that of the one behind, which relates acoustically to the presence of a central area of formant energy (high first formant for vowels and overall central location of the energy for consonants). The higher the ratio between the volumes of the resonators and the higher the degree of central energy, the more compact a segment is. It follows from this that the assignment of a plus or minus value for this feature must take account of the *relative* amount of compactness displayed by the sound in relation to other sounds. This relativity is an important characteristic of many of J's distinctive features, and it can be related to his concern for perception.

The feature [±COMPACT] can separate low vowels (e.g. [a]) from high vowels (e.g. [i], [u]), but it runs aground for mid vowels (e.g. [e], [o]), common in so many of the world's languages (cf. the vowel-system of Latin and general discussion on p. 109). In order to overcome this difficulty, J makes the move of giving independent feature status to the non-compact end of the scale of compactness, setting up the feature [±DIFFUSE]. Mid vowels can now be defined as [−COMPACT] *and* [−DIFFUSE].

As was mentioned before, CH are dissatisfied with the common treatment given to vowels and consonants in J's system, for reasons which will become more apparent as we proceed. They therefore replace the feature COMPACT for consonants with the feature ANTERIOR. Anterior consonants are articulated by means of an obstruction in front of the palatoalveolar area where English [ʃ] is produced (see Chapter 3, p. 81). It follows from this that there is an inverse correspondence between the values for COMPACT and for

ANTERIOR. On the other hand, vowels are all [−ANTERIOR], and two new features are brought in to substitute for their description in terms of compactness and diffuseness. These are the features [±HIGH] and [±LOW], which form with [±BACK] the set of features related to the body of the tongue. They are defined in terms of deviation (raising, lowering and retracting, respectively) of the tongue from the *neutral position* it occupies at the moment prior to speech (similar to that for the vowel in *bed* for English; it can be different in other languages because of the influence of the articulatory setting; see Chapter 12).

The other place of articulation feature (backness for vowels) in J's system is [±GRAVE], which is related to the size of the vocal cavities. Sounds which are [+GRAVE] are produced with a single large mouth cavity, and this shows spectrographically as having the second formant closer to the first than to the third formant, so that the lower end of the spectrum predominates. Sounds which are [−GRAVE] involve a division of the mouth into two smaller cavities. We now display the cross-classification of both vowels and consonants in terms of the features COMPACT, DIFFUSE and GRAVE in Table 4.7.

Table 4.7   *Specification of the Traditional Place of Articulation for Consonants and of Height and Backness for Vowels, in Terms of Jakobson's Features* [±GRAVE], [±COM-PACT] *and* [±DIFFUSE]

		Grave	Compact	Diffuse
Consonants	Labials	+	−	
	Dentals/ alveolars	−	−	
	Palatals	−	+	
	Velars	+	+	
Vowels	High front	−	−	+
	High back	+	−	+
	Mid front	−	−	−
	Mid back	+	−	−
	Low front	−	+	−
	Low back	+	+	−

Note: Redundant values for DIFFUSE in consonants have been left blank.

In CH's system, BACK replaces GRAVE for vowels, with the same value. The situation is more complex for consonants, and none of the new features corresponds exactly with the old one. As shown in Table

4.5 [±CORONAL] can be partially related to GRAVE. The feature [+CORONAL] corresponds to the raising of the tongue blade from its neutral position. The diagram in Figure 4.3 shows the five articulatory regions defined by CH's features HIGH, LOW, BACK, ANTERIOR and CORONAL. Additional places of articulation for consonants are specified by the feature [±DISTRIBUTED], which relates to degree of length of the tongue constriction in the direction of the airflow. The reason for this feature is that differences in place of articulation besides the four basic ones are accompanied by differences in the length of the constriction, and need not therefore be directly specified. Also, CH use [+LATERAL] to differentiate *l*-like sounds from other coronal liquids such as [ɾ]. As already discussed in Chapter 3 (p. 77), lateral sounds allow free airflow on the sides of the tongue. Depending on the size of the passage, laterals can be vocalic (e.g. English [l]) or non-vocalic (e.g. Welsh [ɬ]).

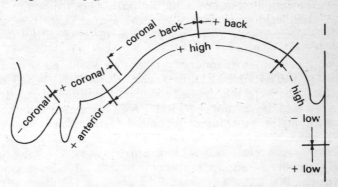

Figure 4.3 *Chomsky and Halle's place of articulation features plotted on a diagram of the vocal tract, showing the various areas they define.*

Source: Derived from Ladefoged, 1971, p. 101.

It must be apparent from the discussion in Chapter 3 (see, for example, Table 3.1 on p. 74) that the features COMPACT, DIFFUSE and GRAVE are insufficient to describe the vowel-system of English, and two further features must be now introduced. The feature [+TENSE] is associated with a greater deviation of the articulators from the neutral position and with a greater muscular effort and air pressure, which acoustically corresponds to a longer duration and a sharper delimitation of the formants. The second feature is [+FLAT], associated with a narrowed slit in the articulators and a lowering in the frequency of some or even all the formants. While TENSE is maintained in CH's system, FLAT presents the problem of conflating a variety of articulatory processes such as lip-rounding, pharyngealisation and retroflexion. CH use the new feature [+ROUND] for lip rounding, [+LOW] for pharnygealisation and [+HIGH], [+CO-RONAL] for retroflexion. Other *secondary articulations* (articulations which are simultaneous with the main stricture or primary articulation) are palatalisation and velarisation. J captures palatalisation with the feature [+SHARP] correlated with a dilation of the pharynx and with tongue-raising against the palate, which results in a slight rise in formant frequency (especially the second formant). CH, on the other hand, use [+HIGH] for palatalisation and [+BACK] for velarisation. Note that the CH treatment brings out the assimilatory nature of the characteristic palatalisation of consonants in front of non-back vowels and their velarisation in front of back vowels, which is missed out in J's approach. Also, the expression of processes of secondary articulation by means of tongue body features explains the fact that palatalisation, velarisation and pharyngealisation cannot co-occur, since the tongue cannot be simultaneously raised and lowered, etc. Finally, these secondary articulations (but not labialisation) do not happen with consonants articulated with the body of the tongue (e.g. there are no pharyngealised velars), a fact which is predictable within the new model, but not in J's.

We must next turn to manner of articulation. Stops and affricates are specified [+INTERRUPTED] in J, and [−CONTINUANT] in CH, while fricatives have the opposite values. J differentiates affricates from stops with the feature [+STRIDENT], correlated with the presence of a complex impediment at the articulatory point which causes air turbulence, shown in the spectrogram as a weakening in the lower frequencies and a reinforcement in the higher ones, which is evidence of high-intensity noise. J's prediction is that all affricates will be strident, but this is not necessarily the case (non-strident affricates have been reported in Chipewyan, an Amerindian language spoken in Alberta, western Canada) and CH introduce the feature [±DELAYED RELEASE] to keep stops apart from affricates and fricatives, while maintaining [+STRIDENT] to indicate greater acoustic noise.

The final group of features are associated with major processes relating to airstream mechanisms, voicing, or resonance. J's feature [+CHECKED] is used for a heterogeneous group made up of ejectives, implosives and clicks (see the discussion in Chapter 3, p. 71), and is articulatorily correlated with glottal (or, also, velaric) checking, and acoustically with higher energy and lower damping within a shorter time-interval. CH use different features for the two opposing motions of suction (clicks, implosives) and pressure (ejectives), as well as for the two different closure points – the glottis (implosives, ejectives) or the velum (clicks). These various airstream features are not directly relevant to English and need not concern us here.

More important are features related to voicing. Voicing is expressed by the feature [+VOICE] in J. The same label appears in CH's set, but its phonetic content is crucially different and deserves close attention. All sounds with a glottal opening sufficiently narrow for the Bernoulli effect (see Chapter 3, p. 70) to take place are defined as [+VOICE]. But because, for example, vocal fold tension can prevent voicing, not all sounds which are [+VOICE] are in fact voiced. Also related to voicing is CH's feature [+SONORANT], which is defined as correlating with a vocal tract configuration which permits the operation of the Bernoulli effect, and thus spontaneous voicing. It follows that sounds with too radical a stricture (e.g. greater than that in the glides [j], [w]) do not allow for an adequate degree of difference between supraglottal and subglottal pressure and are therefore nonsonorant.

The final feature in J's framework, also included in CH, is [+NASAL], and it is associated with the supplementary nasal resonator, whose articulatory and acoustic aspects have already been discussed in Chapter 3 (p. 84). Tables 4.8 and 4.9 display the distinctive feature matrix for English segments in J's and CH's models, respectively.

It is important to note by way of conclusion that, while CH's modifications are supposed to supersede J's set, the issue is far from settled. Problems in the area of distinctive features abound, including the empirical status of the binary principle (which is opposed for vowel height and consonant place of articulation by the phonetician Peter Ladefoged, among others), the interrelation between articulation and perception in the establishment of units of sound opposition, the amount of phonetic detail to be allowed in phonological description, the total number of features and the closed or open nature of the list, etc. Familiarisation with both sets of features and with the phonetic properties associated with them is therefore to be encouraged.

4.9 Rules and formalism

In the previous section it was mentioned that one of the advantages of CH's tongue body features over the corresponding ones in J is that the former reveal the assimilatory nature of processes like palatalisation and velarisation in front of nonback and back vowels, respectively. We shall now present the rudiments of a formalism which allows us to capture these differences in an obvious way.

The mechanism of coarticulation (see Sections 1 and 2 above) is responsible for the raising of the body of the tongue during the articulation of the consonant in anticipation of the following front vowel, and palatalisation is common in many of the world's languages, both present and past (e.g. Russian, Brazilian Portuguese, etc.). It is also frequent in fast colloquial speech in English, where there is often *sandhi*

Table 4.8 *Matrix Containing the Specification for RP English Phonemes According to Jakobson, Fant and Halle's Set of Distinctive Features*

	i	u	e	o	a	ə	l	p	b	f	v	m	t	d	θ	ð	n	s	z	ʒ	ʤ	ʃ	ʒ	k	g	ŋ	h
Vocalic	+	+	+	+	+	+	+	−	−	−	−	−	−	−	−	−	−	−	−	−	−	−	−	−	−	−	−
Consonantal	−	!	−	−	−	−	+	÷	+	+	+	+	+	+	+	+	+	+	+	+	+	+	+	+	+	+	−
Compact	−	−	+	+	+	−	−	−	−	−	−	−	−	−	−	−	−	−	−	+	+	+	+	+	+	+	+
Grave	−	+	−	+	+	+	−	+	+	+	+	+	−	−	−	−	−	−	−	−	−	−	−	+	+	+	+
Flat	−	+	−	+	−	−	−	−	−	−	−	−	−	−	−	−	−	−	−	−	−	−	−	−	−	−	!
Nasal	−	−	−	−	−	−	−	−	−	−	−	+	−	−	−	−	+	−	−	−	−	−	−	−	−	+	−
Tense	±	±	±	±	±	±	−	+	−	+	−	−	+	−	+	−	−	+	−	+	−	+	−	+	−	−	+
Interrupted	−	−	−	−	−	−	−	+	+	−	−	+	+	+	−	−	+	−	−	+	+	−	−	+	+	+	−
Strident	−	−	−	−	−	−	−	−	−	−	+	−	−	−	−	−	−	+	+	+	+	+	+	−	−	−	−

Note: Irrelevant features have been omitted.

Table 4.9 Specifications of the Main English Segments in Chomsky and Halle's Distinctive Feature Model

	i	u	ɑ	o	ə	ɛ	ɔ	æ	ɒ	ʌ	ɨ	j	w	r	l	p	b	f	v	m	t	d	θ	ð	n	s	z	y	ʤ	ʃ	ʒ	k	g	ŋ	h
Vocalic	+	+	+	+	+	+	+	+	+	+	+	−	−	+	+	−	−	−	−	−	−	−	−	−	−	−	−	−	−	−	−	−	−	−	−
Consonantal	−	−	−	−	−	−	−	−	−	−	−	−	−	+	+	+	+	+	+	+	+	+	+	+	+	+	+	+	+	+	+	+	+	+	+
Sonorant	+	+	+	+	+	+	+	+	+	+	+	+	+	+	+	−	−	−	−	+	−	−	−	−	+	−	−	−	−	−	−	−	−	+	+
High	+	+	−	−	−	−	−	−	−	−	+	+	+	−	−	−	−	−	−	−	−	−	−	−	−	−	−	+	+	+	+	+	+	+	−
Back	−	+	+	+	+	−	+	−	+	+	+	−	+	−	−	−	−	−	−	−	−	−	−	−	−	−	−	−	−	−	−	+	+	+	−
Low	−	−	+	−	−	−	−	+	+	−	−	−	−	−	−	−	−	−	−	−	−	−	−	−	−	−	−	−	−	−	−	−	−	−	+
Anterior	−	−	−	−	−	−	−	−	−	−	−	−	−	−	+	+	+	+	+	+	+	+	+	+	+	+	+	−	−	−	−	−	−	−	−
Coronal	−	−	−	−	−	−	−	−	−	−	−	−	−	+	+	−	−	−	−	−	+	+	+	+	+	+	+	+	+	+	+	−	−	−	−
Round	−	+	−	+	−	−	+	−	+	−	−	−	+	−	−	−	−	−	−	−	−	−	−	−	−	−	−	−	−	−	−	−	−	−	−
Tense	+	+	+	+	−	−	−	−	−	−	+	+	+	+	+	+	−	+	−	−	+	−	+	−	−	+	−	+	−	+	−	+	−	−	−
Voice	+	+	+	+	+	+	+	+	+	+	+	+	+	+	+	−	+	−	+	+	−	+	−	+	+	−	+	−	+	−	+	−	+	+	−
Continuant	+	+	+	+	+	+	+	+	+	+	+	+	+	+	+	−	−	+	+	−	−	−	+	+	−	+	+	+	−	+	+	−	−	−	+
Nasal	−	−	−	−	−	−	−	−	−	−	−	−	−	−	−	−	−	−	−	+	−	−	−	−	+	−	−	−	−	−	−	−	−	+	−
Strident	−	−	−	−	−	−	−	−	−	−	−	−	−	−	−	−	−	+	+	−	−	−	−	−	−	+	+	+	+	+	+	−	−	−	−

Note: Predictable features are not included.

(phonological conditioning across word boundaries) between, say, a final [d] and a following [j], the former becoming [ʤ]. For instance, the vowel in *do* is commonly dropped in the expression *do you* (*d'you like it?*), and the glide [j] in *you* often induces palatalisation of [d] into [ʤ] through regressive assimilation ([ʤjɒ]; note that in even more casual or faster speech the glide is dropped altogether and the vowel in *you* reduced to [ə] : [ʤə]). If we were to express this process by means of phonemes we could write a rule like:

(1) d → ʤ / ___ j

which is to be read 'a /d/ becomes a /ʤ/ when it immediately precedes a /j/' (the arrow, therefore, reads 'becomes' and the slash 'in the environment of'; the scoring represents the slot where the change occurs). Palatalisation, however, also occurs with other consonants, such as [t] (*I know what you think*), [z] (*where's your hat?*), etc. We will then need rules (2) and (3), and probably an additional number of similar ones.

(2) t → ʧ / ___ j
(3) z → ʒ / ___ j

The problem with this proliferation of rules is not only that we are using too much space on the page, but, more importantly, that what is a general process of English is being presented in a piecemeal manner. In other words, rules (1), (2), (3) fail to capture the generality of English palatalisation and it will not follow from them that the process will apply to other segments as well (e.g. [s]).

This difficulty is overcome if distinctive features are used in the place of phonemes. Rules (1) to (3) can now be rewritten as follows.

$$(4) \begin{bmatrix} +\text{coronal} \\ -\text{sonorant} \end{bmatrix} \rightarrow \begin{bmatrix} +\text{high} \\ -\text{anterior} \end{bmatrix} / \underline{\quad} \begin{bmatrix} +\text{high} \\ -\text{consonantal} \end{bmatrix}$$

The arrow in (4) is to be interpreted as indicating that the output features change to the given value in the input segment. Because the minimum number of features is used to define the change and the segments involved in it, rule (4) has predictive value, i.e. any other segment specified [+coronal, −sonorant] (e.g. *s*) will also undergo the process in the given environment. Also, notice that there has been an important gain in economy – while any addition to rule (1) (i.e. rules (2), (3), etc.) subtracts simplicity from the system, even if they all express a similar process, rules formulated in terms of features, like (4), are in fact simpler (shorter, i.e. they contain fewer features) the more general the process is. Thus the simplicity of a phonological system (for example, its symmetry; see the discussion on pattern congruity on p. 105 above) can now be related to the simplicity (i.e. the brevity) of the rules necessary to describe it. This is particularly important if we consider that the main purpose of linguistic description is to capture the generalities present in the system (an additional, as yet unresolved, question is whether these generalities possess any psychological correlate in the speaker's mind).

Rule (4) also makes explicit the phonetic nature of the process of palatalisation, as suggested at the outset of the section, since part of the change consists in the addition of the feature [+HIGH], which is present in the segment which immediately follows. Note that formulations like that in (1) are entirely opaque with regard to evaluation of alternative distinctive feature systems, while the one in (4) permits the assessment of J's and CH's frameworks in the light of the underlying phonetic nature of the process they formalise, as becomes evident when we compare rule (4) with rule (5) which uses J's features.

$$(5) \quad \begin{bmatrix} -\text{grave} \\ +\text{consonantal} \\ (-\text{nasal}) \end{bmatrix} \quad \rightarrow \quad [+\text{sharp}] \quad / \underline{\quad\quad} \begin{bmatrix} -\text{grave} \\ -\text{consonantal} \end{bmatrix}$$

All the rules used so far express a process for the reality of which there is external evidence in the language, since palatalisation does not take place in slow or formal speech, and thus the input segments ($d, t,$ etc.) can thereby be empirically attested. But the same type of rule is also used in cases where the process is automatic and, therefore, there is no trace of the input segment formalised in the rule. For example, it was mentioned at the beginning of the chapter that (at least in some dialects) the vowel in *me* undergoes nasalisation as a result of delatory coarticulation, a situation captured in rule (6).

$$(6) \quad [+\text{vocalic}] \rightarrow [+\text{nasal}] \quad / \quad \begin{bmatrix} +\text{consonantal} \\ +\text{nasal} \end{bmatrix} \underline{\quad\quad}$$

Notice once more that the assimilatory motivation of the process is elegantly captured in the formalisation (including the set of distinctive features). But the rule format seems to imply a change from a nonnasal vowel to a nasal vowel, and the dialects being discussed do not allow for a nonnasal vowel after a nasal consonant. Is the rule therefore wrong? Before answering this question, it must be noted that this type of situation is common for the rules usually included in the phonological descriptions of languages, a fact that indicates that they are readily accepted by practising theorists. On what basis are they accepted?

A total answer to this question would take us into areas where disagreement and, sometimes, heated discussion are not uncommon, but we can none the less attempt to justify such a practice. Remember that, in accordance with what was said earlier, native speakers of English are usually quite unaware of the nasalised character of the vowel in *me* and they identify it with the oral vowels in *pea*, *tea*, etc. Remember also that such intuitions play a major role in Sapir's phonological description. Whatever our personal inclination may be regarding the issue of psychological reality, it is necessary that facts like those just mentioned be the object of phonological description, which as a consequence of this is different from a purely phonetic one. So the idea is that in a word like *me* the vowel is phonologically oral, and phonetically nasal, and this disparity is expressed by means of a rule like (6). Phonological rules can, therefore, be seen as a formal device which maps a phonemic level on to a phonetic level, and they do this regardless of the putative physical or psychological reality of the process.

The degree of abstractness which ought to be allowed into phonological rules is as yet an unresolved question. We shall finally examine two cases of more abstract rules than those proposed so far. First, Sapir's derivation of [ŋ] from /ng/ now can be expressed by means of the following two ordered rules.

$$(7) \quad [+\text{nasal}] \quad \rightarrow \quad \begin{bmatrix} \alpha\text{anterior} \\ \beta\text{coronal} \end{bmatrix} \quad / \underline{\hspace{1em}} \begin{bmatrix} \alpha\text{anterior} \\ \beta\text{coronal} \\ -\text{sonorant} \end{bmatrix}$$

$$(8) \quad g \rightarrow \emptyset \, / \, \eta \underline{\hspace{1em}} \#$$

Rule (7) is an assimilation rule and makes use of the Greek-letter variables α, β (each of which can take the values + or −) to indicate that there is agreement in point of articulation between the output segment and the following obstruent. Rule (8) is a deletion rule (the output is zero) and it has been stated in phonemic terms because of its idiosyncratic nature, in contrast with (7) which is a general assimilation rule for nasals. Whatever their psychological status, rules (7) and (8) do capture the phonological relations observed by Sapir. Secondly, and more arguably, a word like *oppression* ([əpɹɛʃən]) could be related to *oppress* ([əpɹɛs]) (after all, *oppression* is the effect of *oppressing*), and the consonant [ʃ] could be derived by rule (4) above on the assumption that at the input level *oppression* can be analysed as a combination of *oppress* and the ending *ion* (as in, for instance *champion*). This would be convenient in that it would be consistent with both meaning and the palatalisation process discussed above. Note, however, that while this analysis does reflect a historical reality palatalisation in the case at hand is automatic, and the pronunciation of *oppression* with [s] in place of [ʃ] is definitively non-English. There is, therefore, an important difference between optional changes such as those discussed earlier in connection with sandhi palatalisation and obligatory processes which can be regarded as an artefact of the analysis itself. To what extent any kind of reality (psychological or even phonological) can be claimed for this type of *morphophonemic* process is an open question. Word analysis of the kind just suggested takes us into the area of *morphology*, which deals with such questions as the nature and delimitation of words and their internal structure, and is the topic of the next chapter.

Exercises: Chapter 4

1   The following phenomena are attested for (at least some variety of) English. State which are likely to be intrinsically determined (e.g. by delatory or anticipatory coarticulation) and which are more plausibly viewed as extrinsically determined:

(a) word-initial voiceless stops are aspirated (as in *tie*);
(b) nasals assimilate to the place of articulation of the following obstruent (cf. *ankle* v. *ample*);
(c) stressed vowels are longer (cf. *to invite* v. *an invite*);
(d) consonants take on lip-rounding when preceding *u* (as in *too*);
(e) liquids and glides devoice when following aspirated stops (as in *clear* and *queer*);
(f) words like *due* are homophonous with *Jew*;
(g) words like *mince* are homophonous with *mints*;
(h) words like *ask* are homophonous with *axe*.

2   State which of the following phones are complementary variants in RP English. Justify your decisions on the basis of distribution and of physical similarity.
   (NB ɦ = voiced *h*; ţ = retroflex *t*; superscript ʲ = palatalisation; subscript ₒ = devoicing; subscript ̩ = syllabic; bar - = centralisation.)

ɐ (*hotter*), pʲ (*spew*), ņ (*beacon*), ɦ (*ahead*), b̥ (*rob*), ʉ (*music*), ŋ (*longest*), ç (*humour*), ţ (*try*), p° (*ape*)

3   List as many free variants as you can think of for the following English phonemes (cues: phonetic environment, style, speed of speech, dialect):

/m/, /t/, /r/, /l/, /h/, /ʃ/, /θ/, /n/, /k/, /æ/

4   Using the minimal pair test work out the phonemes for the subset of RP English represented by the words below.

cot, call, pip, get, kill, bet, dip, bill, doll, pop, let, pill, putt, debt, bull, pot, bit, cut, pet, pull, pit, got, cull, lit, dot, but, lot, gut.

5   Work out the phonemic inventory for vowels and diphthongs in RP English by means of the commutation test. The following words will be of assistance (you may find it useful to refer to Daniel Jones's *An English Pronouncing Dictionary*).

rope, loud, cut, head, card, sown, dock, pull, coat, need, cool, by, law, tack, sore, heard, chip, taut, burn, moor, toy, fuse, pair, sheer, mare, late, wreck, sir, hoard.

6   If your pronunciation of English is other than RP, establish your own system of vowel and diphthong phonemes with the help of the words provided in Exercise 5.

7   Change the broad transcription below into a narrower one for conversational style, first in RP pronunciation and then in your own variety of English.

'mɛnɪ əv ðɪ 'ædvəkəts əv 'spɛlɪŋ rɪfɔm ər ɪn ðə 'hæbɪt əv ə 'sɜtɪŋ, əz ɪf ɪt wər ən 'æksɪəm əd'mɪtɪŋ əv 'noʊ dɪs'pjut, ðət ðə 'soʊl 'fʌŋkʃən əv 'raɪtɪŋ ɪz tə 'rɛprɪzɛnt 'saʊndz. ɪt ə'plɛz tə 'mɪ ðət ðɪs ɪz 'wʌn əv ðoʊz 'spjɔərɪəs 'truɪzəmz ðət 'ʌnt ɪn'tɛlɪʤəntlɪ bə'livd baɪ 'ɛnɪwʌn, bət wɪʧ kən'tɪnjə tə bi rɪ'pitɪd bɪkɒz 'noʊbədɪ tɛɪks ðə 'trʌbl tə kən'sɪdə wɒt ðeɪ 'rɪəlɪ 'min. aɪ doʊnt 'mɪəlɪ dɪ'naɪ ðə 'truθ əv ðə prɪ'tɛndɪd 'æksɪəm əz ə dɪs'krɪpʃən əv ðə rɪ'leɪʃnz bɪtwin 'spiʧ ən 'raɪtɪŋ əz ðeɪ ɪg'zɪst ət ðə 'prɛznt 'deɪ 'ɪŋglɪʃ ənd 'ʌðə læŋgwɪʤɪz, aɪ ə'sɜt ðət, soʊ 'far əz 'piplz əv 'lɪtərərɪ 'kʌltʃər ə kən'sɜnd, ðə 'nɛvə 'wɒz ə 'taɪm wɛn 'ðɪs 'fɔmjələ wəd əv kə'rɛktlɪ ɪks'prɛst ðə 'fækts; ən ðət ɪt wəd 'stɪl rɪmeɪn 'fɔls, 'ivn ɪf ən 'ækjərətlɪ fə'nɛtɪk 'spɛlɪŋ həd bɪn ɪn junɪ'vɜsl 'jus fə 'hʌndrədz əv 'jɜz.

8   Carry out the following thought-experiment. Mark the word pairs below that you consider to be homophonous (i.e. to sound exactly the same). Then check your intuitions against a standard pronouncing dictionary and try to explain any disparities that might exist.

writ – wit, male – mail, dough – doe, dear – dare, groan – grown, hat – hut, roam – Rome, flaw – floor, here – hear, peel – peal, heir – hair, put – putt, source – sauce, pain – pine, flew – flu, kin – king.

9   State the type of opposition existing between the RP English phonemes in the pairs below in accordance with Trubetzkoy's logical classification of distinctive oppositions. Make sure that you take the whole phonemic system into account.

/t/ – /d/ /b/ – /k/ /n/ – /d/ /ɪ/ – /ɑ/ /ɑ/ – /ɒ/ /ɛ/ – /æ/ /f/ – /v/ /ʃ/ – /t/ /f/ – /h/ /j/ – /w/ /r/ – /l/ /ʌ/ – /ə/

10   State the distinctive features that differentiate the phonemes in each of the pairs below, first in terms of Jakobson's system and then of Chomsky and Halle's.

/p/ – /k/ /d/ – /t/ /u/ – /ɑ/ /i/ – /j/ /θ/ – /s/ /m/ – /n/ /z/ – /ʒ/ /ŋ/ – /k/ /ʌ/ – /ɔ/ /v/ – /ð/

11 Describe in ordinary English the phonetic changes likely to happen in the italicized words below as a result of sandhi in rapid speech. Then, state them formally and comment on any gain in degree of generalisation and/or explicitness of the naturalness of the process.

he *can* come

not *this* year

the cat *is* asleep

would you?

tell *them*

I *saw* it

doesn't she?

maybe *next* day

that cup?

that pen

12 Account for the following morphophonemic alternations by means of phonological rules. Present some arguments for or against their psychological reality:

keep – kept

elastic – elasticity

width – wide

artifice – artificial

appeal – appellative

rigid – rigour

criticism – criticise

plutocrat – plutocracy

inane – inanity

divine – divinity

regal – regicide

fact – factual

reduce – reduction

medicine – medical

13 Provide a plausible context for each of the following utterances of the expression *yes*, where the intonation has been impressionistically indicated in each case.

(*a*)   (*b*)   (*c*)   d)   (*e*)

yes   yes   yes   yes   yes

14 Find ten pairs of words with stress variations similar to those in per 'mit – 'permit. Give some possible reasons for the stress shift.

15 Syllabify the following uncommon English words. Check your results against a standard dictionary.

slubberdegullion, quincuncial, aquileigia, holoblastic, pergamereous, ratheripe, sterigma, lactifluous, mixolydian, catoptromancy, isospondylous, margaritiferous, pipinnatifid, iguanodon, tazaspedlan, holmgang, dyscrasite, ramentum, sertularia, stuppeous.

16 Rank the words in each of the following groups according to duration (say, from shortest to longest).

(*a*) cut, cat, cart

(*c*) but, boot, bud

(*e*) tot, taught, dot

(*b*) hard, had, hart

(*d*) hurt, heard, head

(*f*) bit, bead, bid

Bibliography: Chapter 4

Bloomfield, L., *Language* (London: Allen & Unwin, 1933). See also Chapter 11.

Chomsky, N., and Halle, M., *The Sound Pattern of English* (New York: Harper & Row, 1968). Ch. 7 gives a very precise account of their distinctive feature theory and its phonetic basis, definitely not to be read in a hurry, but extremely instructive if properly studied; the rest of the book relates to Chapter 8 in this book and is unquestionably too advanced for the beginner. See also Chapter 8.

Fischer-Jørgensen, E., *Trends in Phonological Theory* (Copenhagen: Akademisk Forlag, 1975). A very useful and accessible summary of phonological history, Prague phonology, Daniel Jones's phonology, American phonology and discovery procedures, and Jakobson's and Chomsky and Halle's distinctive features, and several chapters on other schools.

Fromkin, V (ed.), *Speech Errors as Linguistic Evidence* (The Hague: Mouton, 1973). Contains several papers, including one by the venerable Sigmund Freud, on the exciting evidence provided by slips of the tongue for the psycho-neurological reality of phonological patterns.

Fudge, E. (ed.), *Phonology* (Harmondsworth: Penguin, 1973). A useful selection including papers by, among others, Jones on the meaning of 'phoneme', Trubetzkoy on how to determine phonemes, Martinet on neutralisation, Sapir on sound-patterns in language, Jakobson and Halle on distinctive features, and Fudge on universal distinctive features.

Hempel, C. G., *Philosophy of Natural Science* (Englewood Cliffs, NJ: Prentice-Hall, 1966). A concise and clear, but highly to-the-point, presentation of scientific methodology, relevant to the discussion of the methodological differences between pre- and post-Chomskyan phonology and linguistics in general.

Hyman, L., *Phonology: Theory and Analysis* (New York: Holt, Rinehart & Winston, 1975). A useful and clear presentation of the topics of phonological rules, distinctive features and the phoneme; the second part of the book is more advanced and related to Chapter 8 in this book.

Jakobson, R., Fant, G., and Halle, M., *Preliminaries to Speech Analysis* (Cambridge, Mass.: MIT Press, 1952). The first general account of Jakobson's distinctive features, not easy to read through but useful for consultation.

Jakobson, R., and Halle, M., *Fundamentals of Language* (The Hague: Mouton, 1956). Contains a short summary of Jakobson *et al.*'s (1952) distinctive feature inventory, as well as a general discussion on features and phonemes, and on phonemic patterning.

Jakobson, R., and Waugh, L., *The Sound Shape of Language* (Hassocks, Sussex: Harvester, 1979). The latest of Jakobson's discussions on the topic of distinctive features, also including his personal reflections on various aspects of speech sounds and their functions. Packed with information and insights, it makes fascinating reading.

Jones, D., *The Phoneme: Its Nature and Use* (Cambridge: Heffer, 1950). It contains Jones's somewhat idiosyncratic approach to phonemic theory, easy to read but to be taken with some caution.

Joos, M. (ed.), *Readings in Linguistics* (Chicago: University of Chicago Press, 1957). A very complete sample of classical American phonology and linguistics in general, including papers by Sapir, Bloomfield, Chao, Swadesh, Twaddell, Bloch, Hockett, Harris and others; very useful for background reading and consultation.

Ladefoged, P., *Preliminaries to Linguistic Phonetics* (Chicago: University of Chicago Press, 1971). Gives the articulatory background underlying most phonological description and lists his own strictly phonetically oriented distinctive features.

Sapir, E., 'The psychological reality of phonemes', in D. G. Mandelbaum (ed.), *Selected Writings of Edward Sapir* (Berkeley, Calif.: University of California Press, 1949), pp. 46–60. Recounts Sapir's experiences with Amerindian and other informants and states his conclusion that phonemes are not just a theoretical construct.

Sommerstein, A. H., *Modern Phonology* (London: Edward Arnold, 1977). Contains a useful summary of classical phonemic theory and a discussion of distinctive features; other chapters, some related to Chapter 8 in this book, are definitely too advanced at this stage.

Trubetzkoy, N. S., *Principles of Phonology* (Berkeley, Calif.: University of California Press, 1969). A translation of Trubetzkoy's (1939) major work, arguably the most outstanding representative of Prague phonology and one of the milestones of European structuralist linguistics; some of the chapters, however, are now unquestionably out of date, and are of historical interest only.

Chapter 5

Morphology

5.1 The morpheme as a basic unit

In Chapter 1 'duality of structure' (also known as 'double articulation') was mentioned as one of Hockett's sixteen design features, expressing the fact that the laws governing the patterning of significant sounds, such as those explored in the last chapter, are independent of the laws governing the linear combinations of meaningful units. In (1), for instance, it is possible to segment the stream of sound into units of sound contrast, or phonemes, the combinations of which must obey the phonotactic constraints of English.

(1)   The farmer shot the trespasser

For instance, syllables of the form obstruent-liquid-vowel . . . (such as *tres* in *trespasser*) are well-formed in English but not syllables of the form liquid-obstruent-vowel . . . (e.g. **rtes*). At a higher level of segmentation, the constraints ruling the combination of meaningful units are quite independent of phonological constraints, as witness the possibility in English of a phrase such as *the farmer* in (1), but not **farmer the*. So also, if *shot* recurs in other sentences, it will still retain the same meaning and can be seen to be a word of the same type as in (1). On the contrary, if we segment *shot* into its component phonemes – /ʃ/, /ɒ/ and /t/ – there is no element of meaning which is liable to recur in other uses of the same elements. *Cat*, for instance, shares with *shot* a syllable-final occurrence of the phoneme /t/, but it could not be said that they share any aspect of meaning by virtue of that.

In order to arrive at the minimal meaningful units of a given language, one simply continues to segment until such time as there are no forms within the resulting segments which have a constant meaning in a variety of contexts. Take the word *farmer*: we may try to segment this in various ways – *far* and *mer* recur in various contexts (he'll go *far*', 'it was a *far*ce', 'give him the ham*mer*', 'add a com*ma*'), but it is impossible to discern any meaning in common between these forms. *Farm* and *er*, on the other hand, recur in a variety of contexts where the meaning remains constant ('he *farm*s thirty acres', 'he is a *farm*-hand', 'he is a labour*er*', 'writ*er*s write'). The meaning of *farmer* is a composite of the meaning of *farm* ('engage in agriculture') and *-er* ('one who'). Of course, not all instances of these sequences fit this pattern (cf. 'take off *arm*-bands', 'wat*er*'), but as long as a satisfactory analysis is available also for these forms, it does not matter that they overlap phonologically with units of a different meaning.

This relatively simple position allows us to define a *morpheme* as a minimal sequence of phonemes which is used in a variety of contexts with a constant meaning. The insistence that the sequence be minimal ensures that the morpheme cannot be divided into smaller units to which the same definition would apply. In other words, it is the smallest meaningful unit of language. In reality, things are not nearly as simple as this definition would suggest, and the history of the development of morphological analysis this century can be seen as an attempt to reconcile the notion of 'morpheme' with the host of problems which render its applicability dubious. The major set of problems relates to situations where there is a constant and easily identifiable meaning, but where the form varies or is difficult to specify for some reason. There is also a very restricted number of examples of the converse – where the form is constant but the meaning varies considerably, since single forms with distinct ranges of meaning will generally not be recognised as single morphemes simply by virtue of the fact that they differ in meaning. A case of this is provided by words of Latin origin in English which begin with a prefix such as *con-*, *per-*, *trans-*, *pro-*, etc., and end with an element such as *-fer*, *-tain*, *-vert*, *-gress*, etc. Apart from the fact that this process of combination is not fully productive (there is no **perfer*, **transtain*, **provert*), while there may be some constant meaning among the various uses of these forms when they are viewed in the light of their etymology, there is little possibility of finding a synchronic meaning for them. This is, in fact, true in varying degrees: it is easier to abstract the general meaning 'across' from the prefix *trans-* than it is to extract any single meaning from the prefix *con-* and, correspondingly, new words (especially technical words) are fairly readily formed with *trans-* (e.g. *transduce*, *transceive*, etc.), though not with the other prefixes.

5.2 Phonologically conditioned morphological variation

The simplest type of variation in form of morphemes relates to phonological conditioning. The English plural form of nouns provides a simple example of this. Although orthographically such forms as *dogs*, *rats* and *horses* are related to their corresponding singular forms merely by the addition of *s*, phonologically they are /ræts/, /dɒgz/ and /hɔsəz/ – the plural morpheme may either be the voiceless sibilant /s/, or the voiced sibilant /z/, or the voiced sibilant /z/ preceded by the neutral vowel /ə/. (A sibilant is [+ coronal] and [+ strident] in Chomsky and Halle's notation – see Chapter 4, Table 4.9.) Extending the examples makes the reason for this alternation quite clear: the vowel is inserted when the preceding morpheme ends in a sibilant (*masses*, *mazes*, *rushes*, *churches*, *badges*, *garages* – [gəɹɑʒəz] in some dialects – etc.). Otherwise the consonant is voiceless if the preceding segment is voiceless (*pits*, *rocks*, *taps*, *laughs*, etc.) and voiced if the preceding segment is voiced (*dogs*, *pads*, *ribs*, *bananas*, etc.). Exactly the same alternation occurs with the morpheme added to the verb to mark the subject as third person singular (e.g. *comes*, *hits*, *washes*). More generally still, English phonological structure does not permit two sibilants to occur next to each other in the same syllable, nor does it allow a voiced consonant to be immediately followed by a voiceless sibilant in the same syllable, or vice versa (see Chapter 4, p. 108). So this morpheme, and others like it, vary in form in order to fit in with the general phonological patterning of English (i.e. to comply with the phonotactic constraint just stated). These variants of the plural morpheme are, therefore, said to be 'phonologically conditioned'.

Phonological conditioning is one common factor determining the form that morphemes take in particular contexts. But morphemes can also be 'lexically conditioned'; this is also a very common phenomenon, and it needs a little more discussion. Exemplifying it first, we can again use the formation of plurals in English. The forms examined in the previous paragraph are the regular, productive means of forming plurals in English. But there is a not inconsiderable number of words which form plurals on one of a variety of different patterns, e.g. *ox* – *oxen*, *criterion* – *criteria*, *sheep* – *sheep*, *formula* – *formulae*, etc. These irregularities derive from the historical development of English, and may be fossilised forms of a once-regular pattern (e.g. *oxen*) or learned words retaining the plural form of their original language (e.g. *criteria*). Some of these words have an alternative plural form, based on the regular pattern of English plural formation – it is now as common to hear *formulas*, for instance, as it is to hear *formulae*. In terms of the synchronic pattern of the language, however, these irregular patterns appear entirely arbitrary – it is not possible to predict the plural *sheep* from the phonological structure of the singular *sheep*, and therefore we are clearly not dealing with phonological conditioning. The distinction between phonological and lexical conditioning is, of course, one made use of in dictionaries, which make no mention of the plural forms of nouns where these are formed on the regular pattern, but make special mention of lexically conditioned plural forms.

It can be seen that to talk of the plural morpheme in connection with the above is a departure from the notion of morpheme introduced earlier, since if a morpheme is a constant form paired with a constant meaning, then by definition the various means of forming plurals cannot involve a single morpheme by virtue of their different forms.

But there is a second criterion of morpheme identity which can override this strict correspondence between form and meaning. This criterion is based on the occurrence of forms in relation to each other in sentences (i.e. on their syntactic properties), where the form and meaning of words are of crucial importance in specifying their possible range of occurrence. This can be illustrated by the following examples.

(2) *a* The dog is barking   *b* The dogs are barking
(3) *a* The horse is jumping   *b* The horses are jumping
(4) *a* The ox is tired   *b* The oxen are tired
(5) *a* The formula is correct   *b* The formulae are correct

In the *a* sentences the singular form *is* reflects the singular form of the preceding noun, while in the *b* sentences the plural form *are* is used with preceding plural forms of nouns. Mixing of singular verb form with plural noun or vice versa would result in unacceptable sentences.

(2) *c* *The dogs is barking
(3) *c* *The horse are jumping
(4) *c* *The oxen is tired
(5) *c* *The formula are correct

This general principle holds whatever the specific plural marker on the noun. If we were obliged to recognise a number of different morphemes here, the statement of these regularities of occurrence would have to be considerably more complex, and so the greater abstractness of the notion of morpheme is compensated for by the greater simplicity of the syntactic description which is thereby made possible.

It is useful at this point to reintroduce the notions of 'free variation' and 'complementary distribution' (see Chapter 4, p. 96). Recall that two forms are in free variation if either may occur with no consequences at all for their co-occurrence with other elements in the utterance, or for the meaning of the utterance. At the morphological level, the plural of *formula* – formed either by changing the final vowel or by adding /z/ – is such a case. (There may, of course, be sociolinguistic or dialect factors affecting the choice of form, although these are not readily apparent. For related discussion see Chapters 11 and 12.) The notion of complementary distribution is a crucial one at all levels of linguistic structure; two morphological elements are said to be in complementary distribution if one occurs in a certain set of contexts (say, suffixed to the end of a certain set of words) while the other occurs in a set of contexts not overlapping with these. The significance of this notion is that, barring cases of free variation, complementary distribution is the most important test of whether two different forms can be analysed as belonging to the same morpheme or not. Take again the example of the plural in English: /z/ may be suffixed to words such as *dog*, *car*, *penny*, /s/ to words such as *hat*, *cup*, *elephant*, etc. Therefore, the set of words to which /z/ may be suffixed does not overlap with the set of words to which /s/ may be suffixed, or for that matter with the sets of words which have other plural forms. So /s/ and /z/ occur in distinct sets of contexts – they are in complementary distribution. It is usual to define as *allomorphs* of a single morpheme those forms which are in complementary distribution relative to each other, and which express the same meaning. It is this development which changes the status of 'morpheme' from that of a chunk of phonological material to that of an abstract unit of grammatical significance. The allomorphs of a particular morpheme are the forms which realise it in particular linguistic contexts.

5.3 Boundaries between morphemes – the morph

Up to this point we have been considering problems related to instances in which the form representing a particular meaning varies according to the context in which it occurs. Another problematic aspect of the form of morphological elements is the question of locating the boundaries between morphemes. Most of the examples we have discussed so far are quite straightforward in this respect, but it is fairly easy to find in English forms which do not admit of such simple segmentation. Take, for instance, singular-plural pairs such as *man–men*, *woman–women*, *sheep–sheep*. It is no longer possible to isolate a sequence of phonemes and describe them as the allomorph of the plural morpheme in these contexts. But from a grammatical point of view, such pairs of words behave just like any other singular-plural pair. Numerous different solutions for this sort of problem have been proposed, most of them sharing the common characteristic that the notion of morpheme becomes even more abstract; not only may a morpheme be realised by a number of different allomorphs, but these may include a lack of any form at all (*zero allomorphs*), as in *sheep*, or even the possibility that an allomorph is not a segment at all, but some more complex construct. Among the possibilities which have been suggested, we note two: the plural morpheme in the case of *man* is an instruction to change the vowel to /ɛ/; alternatively, the word-stem is taken to have a gap in the middle (m_n) and the singular and plural are formed by the insertion of vowel-allomorphs of their respective morphemes. All such suggestions remain contentious, but in general it is clear that if the notion of morpheme is to be extended to cover such cases, it will need to be made more abstract in some way.

Perhaps the easiest solution to this problem is to distinguish two levels of structure which usually correspond. This correspondence

does not always obtain, however. At one level, there will be *morp*
the smallest sequences of phonemes which correspond to some meaning – and at the other, more abstract level, morphemes, which are
meaningful units that need not be straightforwardly realised as a
sequence of phonemes (i.e. as a morph). In the simplest case,
sequences of morphs can be put in direct correspondence with sequences of morphemes. Other morphs will correspond to two morphemes simultaneously, without the possibility of segmentation – e.g.
men (a morph) will correspond to the pair of morphemes {man} and
{plural} (with conventional use of curly brackets to represent morphemes). It is also quite possible that there are morphs corresponding
to no morpheme (*empty morphs*) – examples of this are usually more
contentious than other types, but French provides one fairly simple
example: French subject pronouns usually precede their verbs, giving
sequences such as:

(6) *a* j'ai   'I have'   [ʒɛ]
   b tu as   'you have' [tya]
   c il a   'He has'   [ila].

To form a question, the subject pronoun and verb may be inverted.

(7) *a* ai-je   'have I'   [ɛʒ]
   b as-tu   'have you' [aty]
   c a-t-il   'has he' [atil]

The first two of these examples invert in a simple way; in the third,
however, /t/ is inserted between the verb and the pronoun. An analysis
of this sequence into morphs would yield the two which are characteristic of both declarative and interrogative, with a residue of /t/. This
latter may then be described as a morph with no corresponding morpheme.

This conception of the distinction between morpheme and morph
clearly involves a far more radical departure from the intuitively
natural notion that we started with. A direct connection between a
segment of an utterance and a meaningful unit is no longer necessary.
Furthermore, the precise relationship between morpheme and morph
is open to a wide variety of interpretations. It is no doubt for this reason
that it is conventional to impose all sorts of restrictions on the range of
admissible analyses along these lines.

The major restriction of this type permits the recognition of zero
morphs (not to be confused with empty morphs) only as exceptional
realisations of morphemes which are normally expressed with some
concrete morphological form, where consistency of patterning
requires us to maintain the parallel between a specific morphological

sence of such a form. Cases like *sheep* and *deer* in
ve the status of exceptions, and they occur in syntac-
h are characteristic both of singular and of plural
nouns (e.g. before *is* and before *are*), so it makes sense to talk of them
as having singular and plural forms which just happen to be identical.
By contrast, there are also instances where postulation of zero
allomorphs would be inappropriate. For instance, we can distinguish a
subject form of pronouns from an object form in English (e.g. *I* v. *me*,
he v. *him*) and, in line with tradition, we would call them nominative
and accusative respectively. These two forms occur in distinct contexts,
e.g. before a verb like *hit* and after it.

(8) I hit him
(9) He hit me
(10)*Him hit I

In principle we could claim that all nominal forms had an opposition of
nominative and accusative, but that it just happened not to be
expressed. The exceptionality restriction forbids such an analysis, as
the vast majority of nominal forms (all nouns in fact) fail to distinguish
nominative and accusative. Anything which requires an excess of zero
allomorphs is to be avoided, if only as a matter of common sense.

5.4 The word – definitional criteria

Any discussion of morphology would be incomplete without reference
to the question of how morphemes relate to words. In spite of the
apparently straightforward nature of the latter – native speakers of
English and other languages can identify words with a considerable
degree of consistency – attempts to define the word as a unit of
grammar are in many ways more problematic than similar attempts
with respect to the morpheme. And unlike the morpheme, which is the
smallest meaningful unit in any language at all, those elements which
have been identified as words in languages of different structure are
extremely heterogeneous. These difficulties notwithstanding, the word
can be defined in a reasonably satisfactory way across all languages,
and it is often a necessary part of grammatical statements.

Words are given orthographical prominence in English – they occur
between spaces – and while this fact cannot in any way fulfil the role of
a theoretically useful definition of the notion (see Chapter 3, Section 1,
for discussion), any definition which resulted in a radically different set
of units would be regarded with considerable, and justifiable, suspi-
cion. Bloomfield described the word as the 'minimal free form' (i.e. the
minimal expression which can occur as a complete utterance). This can

be illustrated by the fact that the minimal answer to a question is one word (as in 11–14 below): units smaller than the word may not function in this way (15–16).

(11) Who came? John
(12) What colour is his shirt? Red
(13) What did John do? Run
(14) How old is little Willie? Seven
(15) How happy is Larry? *Un (i.e. unhappy)
(16) Which man flew in? *Super (i.e. Superman)

Unfortunately for this criterion, many things which are recognised as words also fail to occur in this sort of context. Quite apart from such marginal cases as *the*, *mere*, etc., many nouns fail to occur as single-word answers.

(17) What did John stand on (*a)? *Table (a table)
(18) What is this? *Question (a question)

Many transitive verbs behave similarly.

(19) What did John do to Bill? *Hit (hit him)
(20) What is John's position in that firm? *Own(s) (he owns it)

(Contrast the use of an intransitive verb as an answer as in (13) above.)
    In other words, it is clear that many of the things which are normally counted as words do not fit in very well with this definition.
    The notion of relative freedom may, however, be defined in terms of two other concepts in a slightly different way. The first of these notions is that of positional mobility: an element is positionally mobile if it can occur in different positions in the sentence while retaining more or less the same relationship with other elements in the sentence. This notion is a matter of degree; it can be illustrated with reference to the following sentence:

(21) The book is interest-ing.

As we can see, this sentence consists of five morphemes: there is a variant in which the last two morphemes are positioned at the front:

(22) Interest-ing the book (certainly) is.

But the last two morphemes cannot be separated:

(23) *Interest the book is ing.

The criterion that words are the minimal positionally mobile elements is roughly equivalent to the criterion invoked in the previous paragraph in that expressions which serve as answers tend also to be positionally mobile; accordingly it has the same difficulties. The second notion – separability – supplements it. A form such as *interesting* contains two morphemes, and these two morphemes may on occasion be found separated from each other, as in:

(24) It is of *interest* that he is com*ing*.

But in such cases their relationship to each other is entirely destroyed, and nobody would seriously suggest that they still make up the same linguistic element. On the other hand, a form such as *the man*, which also consists of two morphemes which are not freely movable around a sentence, may have these two morphemes separated by almost any quantity of material and they will still stand in the same relation to each other, cf. (25).

(25) the large, pot-bellied, beer-swilling . . . man.

So if we refine Bloomfield's notion of 'minimality' to involve positional mobility and separability, the notion of 'word' which results is close to our intuitive conception.

A distinction rather similar to the morph-morpheme distinction may be made also with words (and unfortunately the term 'word' is commonly used with reference to both concepts resulting from this distinction). The form *words*, for example, is a word (or *word form*) – it is a chunk of linguistic material which occurs regularly in texts. On the other hand, it may be said that both *words* and its singular *word* are occurrences of the same word (or *lexeme*), in so far as the role played by both of these word forms is predictable from the grammatical and semantic properties common to both of them, and an appreciation of the grammatical notion of number. It is the second concept which is of practical importance in dictionaries, for instance. No dictionary would give separate entries to *box* and *boxes*, for example, although it is common practice to give separate entries to *box* and *boxer*.

This distinction between lexeme and word form is closely related to the distinction between *inflexional* and *derivational* morphology. A word such as *consider* in English may be followed by a variety of suffixes, such as *ing* or *ation*, yielding forms such as *considering*, *consideration*. The first of these words is commonly considered a word form of the same lexeme as *consider*, while *consideration* is analysed as a separate lexeme. There are several grounds for treating inflexionally derived word forms as part of the same lexeme, while derivationally derived forms constitute separate lexemes. Inflexional forms are typically productive, being characteristic of all semantically appropriate words. Thus, the 'progressive' form of the verb ending in *ing* applies to all verbs which can be considered as specifying processes; the reason for the oddity of a sentence such as *I am being here* is the semantic one that it does not specify a plausible process. By contrast, derivational forms are not productive as a rule; there are many verbs in English which fail to co-occur with a suffix such as *ation*, even though there is no semantic reason for this. A second means of differentiating inflexion and derivation is that a given inflexional form typically has a constant meaning, while derivational forms often have totally idiosyncratic meanings when applied to some lexemes; thus, *ing* consistently has the meaning of progressive action, while *ation* tends to take on totally idiosyncratic meanings – cf. *application* in the sense of 'diligence', *reparation* in the sense of 'making amends', etc. A further distinguishing feature is that inflexional categories are in general obligatorily expressed in a language – an English verbal form is either progressive or non-progressive, but never neutral between the two – while derivational categories are often merely one way of several of expressing a particular meaning. Finally, a further typical distinction is that inflexion relates word forms which can be considered to fall within the same syntactic category (see Chapter 6, Section 3), while derivation often relates forms of different categories: *consider* and *considering* are both verbal forms, but *consideration* is a noun.

The distinction between inflexional and derivational forms is an important and useful one, but this does not mean that it is always possible to distinguish them clearly. As a case in point, consider the category of aspect in Russian, similar in some ways to the progressive/non-progressive distinction of English. This is an obligatory category – every verbal form must be considered either imperfective (indicating progressive or habitual meaning) or perfective (indicating completed action) – although there are some verbs to which this distinction is inapplicable on semantic grounds (e.g. *ponimat'* 'understand'). But there are some subtle semantic differences between pairs of aspectually related verbs: *ubeždat'* means 'try to persuade' while its perfective counterpart *ubedit'* means 'to persuade'; *čitat'* means 'read', while its perfective counterpart *pročitat'* means 'finish reading'. It is a controversial question whether the differences between these pairs are the 'same' aspectual distinction or not, but there is certainly reason to doubt the straightforward applicability of this criterion. Moreover, while this aspectual distinction is characteristic of the vast majority of verbs in Russian, an increasing number of recent acquisitions, such as *telefonitrovat'* 'to phone', are neutral as to aspect – i.e. they occur in contexts which are appropriate for both perfective and imperfective verb forms. Russian aspectual forms are, therefore, an unclear case with respect to the distinction of inflexion and derivation.

Returning to the problem of defining words (in the sense of word forms), there also exist phonological features which characteristically distinguish words. The most common of these in the languages of the world are word-stress and vowel harmony. In English, for instance, each word contains a syllable which is particularly salient with respect to stress, e.g. *consider'ation*, *'confiscate* (using ' to indicate that the following syllable is salient). Any sequence of two (or more) words is likely to contain two (or more) such syllables, although these will differ in relative salience – e.g. *dis'cussion 'paper*, where the first stressed syllable is more salient than the second. Although not all words are independently stressed (a phrase such as *the 'news* would sound rather peculiar with two stressed syllables), unstressable words are also likely to be rather marginal in terms of the other word delimitation criteria. It can be seen, then, that there is an approximate correlation between the number of salient syllables in a sequence and the number of words in that sequence.

In other languages in which stress is more regular than in English, other sorts of information can also be derived from this delimitative function of stress. In Swahili, for instance, as in many other languages, words of more than one syllable are stressed on the penultimate syllable. Addition of a suffix to a word will, therefore, have the effect of changing the position of stress. In fact, Swahili has relatively few suffixes, but nouns may be associated with a suffix of location *-ni*, which has the stated effect.

'jiko 'kitchen'	*ji 'koni* 'in the kitchen'
'nyumba 'house'	*nyum 'bani* 'in the house'
ki 'tanda 'bed'	*kitan 'dani* 'in the bed'

In a language of this sort, therefore, the stress-pattern not only helps to identify the number of words in a sequence, but also identifies with some precision the boundaries between the words.

Vowel harmony, another common phonological reflex of the word as a unit, is a term used to describe restrictions on the co-occurrence of vowels within a word. In Turkish and other Turkic languages, for instance, a word may contain either back vowels or front vowels, but not both, and suffixes in Turkish, therefore, have back- and front-vowel variants, conditioned by the vocalic make-up of the word to which they are suffixed. For example, the plural suffix has the alternative forms *lar* and *ler*: a noun such as *ev* 'house' is pluralised as *evler* 'houses', while a noun such as *adam* 'man' is pluralised as *adamlar* 'men'. Neither of the other combinations is possible (**evlar*, **adamler*). But the constraint does not hold between adjacent words which are therefore not required to contain vowels of the same series.

(26) *kasap eti kesti* 'The butcher cut the meat'
     butcher meat cut

There are added complexities to Turkish vowel harmony, and in other languages it works on a rather different pattern, but this discussion is sufficient to show the function fulfilled by vowel harmony in distinguishing words from non-words.

5.5 Morphological classification of languages

Up to this point we have restricted our discussion largely to English, with the aim of clarifying certain basic concepts in morphology. But many other languages have much more highly developed systems of inflexional and derivational morphology; in fact there appears to be systematic variation between languages concerning the relationship of words and morphemes, both in terms of the typical 'size' of these units, and on the basis of ease of division of words into morphemes.

One of the traditional ways of classifying morphemes is into *bound* and *free* forms; a bound morpheme is one which is not capable of functioning as a word in its own right (e.g. *un-*, *-ing*, and also such elements of indeterminate status as *cran* in *cranberry*). A free morpheme, by contrast, may occur as an independent word form. The vast majority of English morphemes are free in this sense. But in other languages this may not be so: in Latin, for instance, the word for 'wolf' occurs in a variety of forms – *lupus*, *lupum*, *lupi*, etc. These forms are the different *cases* of the noun, expressing the relation that it bears to other elements in sentences. The three forms cited are respectively nominative, accusative and genitive singular cases, the central uses of which mark the nouns as subject of a verb, object of a verb and possessor, respectively. Clearly, on the basis of these three word forms, the morpheme for 'wolf' in Latin is *lup*, to which are added case forms such as *-us*, *-um* and *-i*. But since the form *lup* cannot be used without the addition of some case form in Latin, neither it nor the case markers are free morphemes in Latin, a situation which is typical for that language.

A language in which every morpheme was free would not have any morphology proper: such languages are called *isolating*, or *analytic*. A language where most words consist of more than one morpheme is known as a *synthetic* language, while a special term – *polysynthetic* – is reserved for languages which allow accumulations of large numbers of morphemes in a single word. This is not to be seen as a clear-cut distinction, but rather as a matter of degree: it has been suggested that languages may be placed on an analytic-synthetic scale by dividing the number of morphemes which occur in a text of that language by the number of words in the same text. Using such a method, Vietnamese comes out as a highly analytic language (yielding a result of 1·06); English is mildly analytic (with 1·68); synthetic and polysynthetic languages show higher ratios (Sanskrit 2·59, Eskimo 3·72). These figures entail that in a language such as Vietnamese a sentence such as (27) is fairly typical, whereas in Eskimo more complex words are typical, as in (28); in fact, Eskimo allows even such complex 'words' as (29).

(27) tôi sẽ làm cho ông 'I'll do it for you'
     I future do benefit man
(28) aʁnaʁ-aʁ-jāg-ət   qũx-saχtū-ma-lʁi-t
     woman-dim.-coll.-pl.   wood-fetch-past-report-pl.
     'Some girls went to fetch firewood'
(29) qanujaʁ-ruŋ-əsta-lʁu-taχ-aŋ-la-raxki-ʁa-ka-m-kən
     brass-thing-small-coll.-container-small-make-quickly-present-
     indicative-I-you
     'I am quickly making you a little box for percussion caps'

It follows from facts such as these that morphology, as the study of combinations of meaningful elements within the word, does not offer much scope for study in Vietnamese, while much of the syntax of other languages corresponds to what is the morphology of Eskimo.

A single language may have the option of expressing the same grammatical notion analytically or synthetically. An example of this occurs in English, where the comparative form of the adjective is expressed either analytically (with *more* – two separate words are used, e.g. *more lovely*) or synthetically (with *-er* – only one word results, e.g. *lovelier*). The same type of phenomenon is found in many other languages, where, for instance, synthetic equivalents of English prepositions may compete with analytic prepositional constructions, or synthetic equivalents of English verbal auxiliaries compete with analytic counterparts.

The second classificatory dimension along which languages differ involves the relative ease of divisibility of words into morphemes. There are two aspects of this, one regarding the divisibility of a sequence of sounds into morphs, the other relating to the correspondence between a morph and a specific semantic category. A language which enjoys ease of divisibility in both of these senses is known as an *agglutinative* language, while one which poses problems of analysis is known as an *inflecting* language. (Of course, all isolating languages are agglutinative.) As with the analytic–synthetic scale, this distinction is a matter of degree. Turkish and Latin are frequently cited as paradigm examples of these types respectively. We have already seen in the case of Turkish that nouns are made plural by adding a suffix *-ler/-lar:* if we wish to convey the meaning of location, a further suffix may be added (*-de/-da*). Therefore 'house' is *ev*, 'houses' *evler*, 'in a house' *evde* and 'in houses' *evlerde*. As can be seen, each morpheme is expressed with a clearly distinct morph, and each morpheme expresses a constant single meaning. Perhaps, the most startling contrast to this in Latin is the paradigm for the verb *esse* ('to be') in the present tense.

sum 'I am	*sumus* 'we are'
es 'you are' (sing.)	*estis* 'you are' (pl.)
est 'he/she/it is'	*sunt* 'they are'

From this list of forms it is possible to work out a division into morphs, such as *es*, *sum/n*, *t*, *us* and so on, but such a task is full of arbitrary decisions and special cases.

Having performed such a division, it would then be necessary to assign some meaning to the corresponding morphemes, and the result could hardly be satisfactory: *es* would have to be analysed as a morpheme meaning 'be', with suitable restrictions as to its occurrence in conjunction with first person meaning or with third person plural meaning. But it would also have to be analysed as expressing second person singular meaning when not occurring with any other morpheme in the same word (such as *t* or *tis*). The complexities and artificialities become worse as more and more verb forms are introduced, and it is this which has led many linguists to claim that the traditional paradigm notation is more successful as a representation of Latin inflexional morphology than an attempt to factor out morphs within such verb forms (see Section 8 below for further discussion).

There is a sense in which the English forms that we considered in Section 2 above represent an intermediate stage between the morphological transparency of Turkish and the opacity of Latin. The compromises that were reached in that section lead to the conclusion that the more abstract notion of the morpheme may still be maintained alike for languages such as Turkish and Latin; the term 'present tense morpheme', or 'dative case morpheme', makes sense whether the realisation of that notion is expressed in a determinate morph or not. But we maintain this abstract notion of 'morpheme' at a cost – in Latin and languages like it there may be very little correspondence between the level of abstract morphemes and the regularities of linear form which provided the initial intuitive plausibility for the notion.

These types of variation provide much of the complexity of morphological analysis and they have always been considered one of the major ways in which languages can differ from one another. But equally significant is the fact that this variation is essentially confined to the relationship of words and morphemes, while languages do not on the whole present us with comparable difficulties of isolating words within sentences This suggests that the notions of word and morpheme are not simply convenient fictions with which we may analyse English, but are to some degree the natural basic units of grammatical analysis.

5.6   The priority question − words *v.* morphemes

The next question to be addressed is whether words or morphemes are the basic building blocks of language. The answer is not straightforward, and arguments can be put forward either way. Starting with morphemes, they often have meaning, and the meaning of derived words is consequently composite. For instance, *farm + er* means something like 'one who habitually *farms*', *bak + er* 'one who habitually *bakes*', and so on. Even more clear are cases like *dogs*, which simply means 'more than one *dog*'. Since in English, as in many other languages, nouns can generally take a plural and verbs can be conjugated, it follows that, at least for these categories, composite meanings are the order of the day. In synthetic languages like Latin, as has already been mentioned, all stems are bound forms (a *stem* can be conceived of as the main part of a word which is not itself a word), and from this it seems to follow that the meaning of the resulting complex item will in all cases be composite, at least in some way.

Morphemes can be considered language primitives from at least another point of view. Consider the phrases in (30).

(30)   red rose
     blue rose
     yellow rose
     green rose
     large rose

     .

     .

It seems reasonable to approach these phrases as made up of two units, a noun (*rose*) and a preposed adjective (*red*, etc.), rather than as indecomposable units. Confirmation for this analysis comes from the fact that we can substitute, say, *carnation* for *rose* and get another set of well-formed phrases. But if this is so, why not carry over the argument into the word itself and propose, e.g. a primitive *-er*, which combines with (a certain class of) verbs to yield such words as *farmer*, etc.?

Equally persuasive arguments can however be made for the primitive status of the word. Thus, while any well-formed combination of English words is a good English sentence (remember for instance the absurd long sentence about the tortoise we gave in

Chapter 2, p. 35), it is not the case that any seemingly well-formed combination of English morphemes is a word of English, or that the structure of all English words is recognisably 'English', either morphologically or phonologically. Consider for instance the following words.

(31) *a* tirage   *b* arrivation
         luctuoso   gloriosity

(32) *a* mirage   *b* derivation
         virtuoso   curiosity

The four sets in (31) and (32) are cross-classifiable with respect to whether they 'feel' more English (the *b* sets) and whether they actually are part of the English vocabulary: only the words in (32) are. Why this should be so is however far from obvious, as (32) appears to contain at once too much (cf. (32)*a*) and too little (cf. (31)*b*). What is clear, however, is that possession of 'English structure' is neither a sufficient nor a necessary condition for a word to be considered English. Such facts and arguments carry over to other languages, thus pointing to a striking contrast between words and sentences, the structural vagaries of the former underscoring the case for full primitive status.

Turning back to the issue of compositionality of meaning broached at the beginning, there are serious difficulties for the view that the meaning of morphologically complex words is derived from the meaning of their component morphemes. Consider such words as *application*, meaning 'diligence', or *reparation*, 'making amends', mentioned above. While in the case of sentences idiosyncratic interpretation is relatively rare (specifically, it is restricted to the so-called *idioms*, i.e. phrases with unpredictable meaning, such as *to kick the bucket* for 'to die'), it is the norm with words, as a cursory glance at the dictionary will reveal. A small sample is provided in (33).

(33) *a* counter   *b* transmission
         reporter   admission
         chanter   extraction

Besides their obvious composite meanings, these words have other, unpredictable ones. For instance, *chanter* also refers to the blowing pipe of a bagpipes, *extraction* to 'lineage', *admission* to 'entrance fee', and so on. Thus, unlike sentences, words seem to act as a sort of 'magnet for meaning', irrespective of history or internal structure. The sceptic could perhaps retort that such words as those in (33) are morphologically unanalysable in their specialised meanings. But notice that, besides being clearly unparsimonious, this stance provides no explanation for the fact that the two members of each such homophonous doublet are identical in all but meaning. For instance, it would leave it to chance that, if one such word ends in *-er* or *-ion*, then it is predictably a noun, rather than, for example, an adjective. Naturally, if *-er* and *-ion* are construed as nominalising suffixes, this fact follows automatically (NB a *suffix* is a morpheme bound on the right-hand side of the word).

The capacity of words for idiosyncrasies does not end with meaning, and they can for example also display peculiar or deviant pronunciations. For instance, it is a characteristic of English that words ending in *-ion* or *-ity* have a short or lax vowel preceding the suffix where their base has a long or tense vowel, or a diphthong.

(34) decide   decision
      expedite   expedition
      extreme   extremity
      obscene   obscenity
      profane   profanity
      opaque   opacity

The across-the-board nature of this alternation, parallel to that of, e.g., [s] v. [ʃ] discussed in Chapter 4, Section 9 (*oppress* v. *oppression*), favours the postulation of a rule predicting one of the variants from the other. Suppose for instance that we dictate that the addition of these suffixes entails, among other things, the shortening of the last root vowel (exactly how this is done need not concern us here). The establishment of such generalisations of course constitutes the primary goal of a grammar, because it results in the minimisation of unpredictability. Note now that our present prediction fails for the word *obesity*, which keeps the long or tense vowel of its base *obese*. It would seem parsimonious to encode this fact by means of a direct statement to the effect that *obesity* contains a long [i:] in the antepenultimate syllable. But this seems to presuppose that words, rather than morphemes, are the primitive entities of the mental lexicon. According to this line of reasoning, morphemes will have only derivative status, being arrived at from words by analysis.

5.7 Lexical productivity – the creation of words

If pre-eminence is accorded to words, the paradox regarding the 'Englishness' of the words in (31) and (32) above can be resolved; the reason why only the forms in (32) are English words would ultimately be tautological, namely, because they are. This answer will appear less suspect if we take the listing of full words in the lexicon seriously, since list membership is by its very nature open to arbitrariness.

Note once more the difference with syntax, where (rule-governed) creativity reigns supreme (cf. our discussion in Chapters 1 and 2). In the case of words, the very existence of such labels as 'barbarism' and 'neologism' is indicative of the social curtailment of the speaker's creative freedom − unlike sentences, words must ultimately be given the seal of approval by the community. This is of course not to say that creation does not take place, as indeed it must if the inventory of words is to be increased or simply renewed, and we shall now review some of the most common strategies speakers follow for this purpose.

The easiest procedure (but, for the language, perhaps the least gratifying) consists in simply adopting a foreign word. Much of the richness of the English lexicon is accountable for by the particular liberal-mindedness of English-speaking communities with regard to such adoptions or 'loans' (the reader might be unaware that *bungalow* is originally a Hindi word, *veranda* Portuguese, and *patio* Spanish, although he or she might have been in close daily contact with the objects since birth!). Also typical of English borrowings is their minimal *nativisation* (i.e. structural adaptation), perhaps relatable to the lack of an institution in the English-speaking world aimed at maintaining the purity of the language (cf. for instance the French Academy, founded as long ago as 1635). In this, English contrasts with, say, Japanese, where foreign words are recast almost beyond recognition to accord with the phonotactic constraints of the language:

(35) extra ⟶ ekisutora
    eccentric ⟶ ekisentorikku
    boxing ⟶ bokusingu
    strike ⟶ sutoraiki
    truck ⟶ torakku
    table ⟶ teeburu

An extreme form of nativisation is *calque*, i.e. literal translation from the source language. German is well endowed with such words:

(36) Einführung ⟵ ein Führung GERMAN
                      intro ductionem LATIN
     'introduction'   'in' 'leading' GLOSS

     B + armherzigheit ⟵ arm herz + ig heit GERMAN
                         miseri cord ia LATIN
     'pity'   'poor' 'heart' suffix GLOSS

Jungfernrede	←	Jungfer Rede	GERMAN
		maiden speech	ENGLISH
'maiden speech'		— —	GLOSS

The next two avenues to word creation are closely related to the socioeconomic circumstances of contemporary advanced societies. First, words can be formed by stringing together the initial letters of the words in a phrase typically designating some technical apparatus or some institution. What is interesting about such formations, known as *acronyms*, is that consciousness of the phrasal origin is gradually lost (as reflected in the orthographic changes from dotted capitals to ordinary small case characters), as the reader can test with the following sample.

(37) radar (radio detecting and ranging)
laser (light amplication by stimulated emission of radiation)
wasp (white Anglo-Saxon protestant)
quango (quasi-autonomous national government organisation)
aids (acquired immune deficiency syndrome)
yuppie (young urban professional + *ie*)

Second, trade names can simply be adopted generically to designate the object, as with the British use of *Hoover* for 'vacuum cleaner' or the generalised one of *Xerox* for 'photocopy' (cf. also *Biro, Kleenex*, etc.).

So far no mention has been made of any grammatical means of word creation, and we must turn our attention to these next. We have already seen that the apparent regularity of affixation can be used as an argument to assign priority to the morpheme over the word, although, as pointed out, matters are far from being so simple. Focusing on unproblematic cases here, we give in (38) and (39) examples of prefixes and suffixes of seemingly unrestricted productivity within their respective syntactico-semantic classes (note that a *prefix* is the mirror image of a suffix, i.e. a bound morpheme concatenated on the left-hand side).

(38)	mini-	anti-	pro-	sub-	inter-
	para-	hyper-	super-	co-	counter-
	pre-	ante-	neo-	crypto-	post-
	pseudo-	semi-	ultra-	vice-	tele-

(39)	-ful	-less	-ish	-let	-ly
	-ness	-ship	-ise	-ee	-er
	-most	-like	-wards	-wise	-worthy

Interestingly, the prefixes of (38) appear to allow recursion (*she's my ex-ex-wife, because I married her again*), only limited by considerations of performance: ?*I refer to him as the ex-ex-ex-ex-ex-ex-president, because he lost office three times but finally recovered it once more!* v. the attested journalese *re-re-re-repeat* (cf. the discussion in Chapter 2).

A third affixal category is that of *infixes*, which, as the label itself suggests, are inserted in the word. Although English does not have specific infixes, the process of infixation itself does exist, as certain evaluative adjectives (*bloody, bleeding, fucking*, etc.) can indeed be used to break words. Interestingly, as the data in (40) indicate, this process is rule-governed as regards the place where the insertion takes place.

(40) uni-bleeding-versity
    *u-bleeding-niversity
    *univer-bleeding-sity

Sometimes a word looks like a derivative from a non-existent base. For instance, *transgression* can be related to *transgress*, but there is no *aggress* corresponding to *aggression* (cf. also *aggressive, aggressor*), at least in the standard common language. None the less, a tendency can be observed to supply the missing base, and some use of *aggress* can already be attested. In many cases, the resulting word has been fully accepted into the language, e.g. *burgle*, a *back formation* from *burglar*, with an apparent suffix *-er* (in America it is however more common to hear *burglarise*).

Particularly productive in English is *compounding*, i.e. the juxtaposition of two words to form a new, composite one, with distinct properties of its own. For instance, white *blackboards* are now a common occurrence, and *wetbacks* need not have been in the water. *Greenhorns* are neither green nor horns, like *shoehorns*, usually made of plastic, or *greenhouses*, which are seldom, if ever, green (admittedly, though, they do sometimes house greens). This situation is of course reminiscent of the one with morphemes mentioned above. The high frequency of compounding in English makes further exemplification idle.

A further step towards the integration of the component words is represented by the procedure called *blending*, whereby two words simply merge into each other, by cutting off the adjoining edges:

(41) motel (motor + hotel)
    smog (smoke + fog)
    brunch (breakfast + lunch)

We are now in a position to understand why there are differences in the synchronic productivity of affixes (as the reader will have gathered by now, the term *affix* is used generically to designate prefixes, suffixes and infixes), or, equivalently, in the number of possible derivatives which actually make their way into the lexicon. The reason is really not linguistic at all. Since words must be listed, and listing presupposes social acceptance, it follows that, for any one particular linguistic context, the more words there are with a particular affix, the more socially acceptable this affix is. Now, like any other aspects of human behaviour, affixes are subject to the dictates of fashion. Accordingly, when an affix goes out of favour, the formation of new words with the affix will be less frequent. Clearly, then, what appears as the synchronic productivity index of an affix is simply a relic of the vagaries of social history.

Even very productive affixes are liable to be restrained. Consider, for instance, *-ness*, which at first sight can be added to any adjective to form a noun (*blueness, silliness,* etc.). A moment's reflection will however suffice to reveal that there are many *-ness* formations which are at least dubious (?*intelligentness*, etc.). Why should this be so? Note that a similar situation obtains in inflexional morphology, which is commonly thought of as totally productive. Consider such a verb as *go*, to which the rule of *-ed* suffixation in the past tense does not apply: **goed*. In fact, the past of *go* is, irregularly, *went*, and this form must of course be listed in the lexicon alongside *go*. The question however still remains of what prevents *-ed* from being added to *go*, perhaps at random, giving rise to a situation of free variation similar to the plural *formulae–formulas* discussed above. The solution proposed in the literature uses a device called *blocking*. Very simply, it is assumed that, parallel to the morphological paradigm, there runs a semantic paradigm, where each canonical meaning is assigned one slot. For verbs, one such canonical meaning is of course 'past'. Notice now the difference between *go* and, say, *mow*. For the latter, there is no morphological form listed corresponding to the meaning 'mow in the past'. For *go*, on the other hand, there is: *went*. We can accordingly say that the morphosemantic slot for the canonical meaning 'go in the past' is already filled, and that the morphological formation of **goed* according to rule is consequently blocked. Similar considerations apply to **intelligentness*, with *intelligence* already in the lexicon.

Despite its obvious usefulness, the idea of blocking is not free of problems. First, it does not prevent doublets like the two plurals of *formula*. This is not a serious obstacle, however, as it can simply be said that the irregular plural *formulae* is optional. Correspondingly, the morphosemantic slot for 'more than one formula' need not be filled, and this allows for the regular formation *formulas*. More puzzling is the existence of morphological gaps in otherwise extremely productive inflexional paradigms. In Russian, for instance, there are about 100 verbs lacking the first person present indicative, for no apparent semantic or phonological reason (they are simply listed in the dictionary as not existing in that form): *lažu 'I climb', *muču 'I stir up', etc. The other side of the coin is represented by cases where simultaneity of morphological realisation is indeed possible (as if, say, English had the plural *formulaes*). For instance, in Hopi (a native language of the American South-West) the plural of *wu'ti* 'woman' is *momoyam*, where the idea 'plural' is marked twice, once in the suppletive (i.e. phonologically unpredictable; cf. Chapter 8, p. 249) plural stem *moya* and once in the prefix *mo-* (in addition, the suffix *-m* indicates that this word is not a singular, but a plural or a dual!). Also, as we shall see in Chapter 8, Arabic forms its plural by means of two *combined* morphemes, one related to the quality of the vowels, and the other to the linear patterning between consonants and vowels. A trace of this phenomenon can be found even in English; compare the ordinary past tense *loved*, with a *-d* marker, to the irregular *told*, where the idea 'past' is additionally conveyed by the change [ɛ] → [əʊ] in the vowel.

There are of course disagreements on practically all of the issues presented here, and we certainly do not wish to create the impression that a monolithic solution has been achieved. One thing appears to be clear, however; there is much information about words which cannot be meaningfully transferred to the morpheme, and this includes the existence of the word itself, i.e. its inclusion in the lexical list. Notice however that, even if words were to be universally accepted as morphological primes, it would still be undeniable that most words are structurally analysable into smaller units or morphemes, and that such an analysis is advantageous to linguists and learners alike. In the next section we will address the question of how this analysis is best carried out.

5.8 Approaches to morphological description

So far in this chapter we have been concerned with a fairly basic level of morphological concepts; but it is important to be aware of the fact that morphological variation can be approached from a number of different angles. Following the classic article of Charles Hockett (1954), three such different approaches are known as 'item-and-arrangement' (IA), 'item-and-process' (IP) and 'word-and-paradigm' (WP). Hockett himself was only dimly aware of the major features of this latter approach, even though this is the framework in which much of the Western grammatical tradition has been couched. IP also has a long tradition, derived, according to Hockett, from the predominantly historical nineteenth-century approach to language, while IA was at the time felt to be relatively novel.

As opposed to the historical precedence of these models of description, IA is the most parsimonious in terms of the theoretical apparatus which it brings to the task of morphological description. It involves only the assumption that there exist morphs, and that these morphs are arranged in particular ways in accordance with the 'tactical' rules of the language. For example, in Turkish there is a large set of nominal stems, including *ev* 'house' and *el* 'hand', and a much smaller set of case affixes, including *de* 'in' and *den* 'from'; the case affixes always occur immediately following a noun stem – e.g. *evde* 'in the house', *elden* 'from the hand', etc. (We deliberately simplify here: considerations of vowel harmony, considered earlier, p. 138, complicate the picture somewhat.) IP, on the other hand, recognises not just the existence of elements and linear arrangements of these (at levels higher than the word), but also (within the word) grammatical processes which 'operate on' a stem to produce a form of that stem. In such an approach, we would recognise the same class of noun stems as before. However, corresponding to IA 'tactical rules', grammatical processes such as 'locative formation' or 'ablative formation' would apply to noun stems such as *ev* and *el* to change them into word forms such as *evde* and *elden*. Combinations of word forms in higher syntactic units would still be couched in terms of elements being arranged in particular ways (e.g. adjectives precede nouns in Turkish); the difference relates to the internal composition of word forms. Finally, WP is couched entirely in terms of word forms, such notions as 'stem' and 'affix' being abstractions from sets of word forms. We would, therefore, recognise a number of Turkish word forms, which can be tabulated according to their points of similarity.

ev	*el*	. . . . .
evde	*elde*	. . . . .
evden	*elden*	. . . . .
.	.	
.	.	
.	.	

Such tabulations are known as *paradigms*.

There is little doubt that, were all languages like Turkish, IA would be the most satisfactory form of morphological description. As we shall see in the next chapter, the statement of the occurrence of elements relative to each other is a crucial part of syntax, and IA as a method of morphological description treats morphology essentially as if it were syntax. But we have already seen in Section 5 of this chapter that all languages are *not* like Turkish. Two types of evidence argue against the adequacy of IA for all languages – and argue for different alternatives.

One such piece of evidence involves *reduplication*; in Tagalog, for instance, a verbal form roughly equivalent to the future tense is formed by reduplicating the initial consonant and vowel of the verb form – e.g. *bigyan* ('give') *bibigyan* ('will give'), *tapusin* ('finish') *tatapusin* ('will finish'). This phenomenon is very simply formulated as a process. But to formulate it in IA terms, it would be necessary to have every consonant-vowel sequence as an allomorph of the future morpheme, and to have conditions on the occurrence of each of these allomorphs. More seriously, however, it appears that reduplicative constructions may interact with other affixal constructions in ways which would be difficult to break down into arrangements of morphemes. Bloomfield gives the example of another reduplicative construction in Tagalog, where the following two sequences of processes occur.

(42)	*tawa*	'a laugh'	reduplication gives
	tatawa	'one who will laugh'	infixation (insertion of an affix within the word – in Tagalog, after the initial consonant) gives
	tumatawa	'one who is laughing'	
(43)	*pilit*	'effort'	infixation gives
	pumilit	'one who compelled'	reduplication gives
	(nag)/ pupumilit	'one who makes an extreme effort'	

These two cases are naturally described in terms of the same processes occurring in different orders. It is quite unclear how an IA approach could deal with this sort of case.

The other type of evidence we have already looked at in some detail – with the example of the verb 'to be' in Latin in Section 5 above. Here, both arrangement and process seem inapplicable, as both require regularity of form as a prerequisite for their application. Other words of Latin, although not irregular to the same degree, pose essentially the same kind of problems, and IA/IP approaches to Latin are characterised by a considerable degree of artificiality. The traditional solution, and still the most adequate, is simply to list the various forms of verbs (or other parts of speech) in paradigms, and to classify together all those verbs which operate in the same pattern. In the case of the verb 'be' there are no other such verbs, but there are verb classes in Latin which are quite regular, even though stating them in terms of arrangement of morphemes or processes is quite unsatisfactory.

We may wish to draw a variety of conclusions from considerations such as these. If we require that a single morphological model should encompass all languages then we would be forced to the conclusion that WP was 'best', in that word forms can always be stated in a paradigm, but not necessarily in terms of processes or arrangement of elements. But in other ways, it seems sensible to recognise that different languages pattern differently, and that different approaches to them may be separately valid. It is on the whole contemporary practice to use IA descriptions in strongly agglutinative languages where a representation of morphemes as occurring in a specific sequence, with only small and predictable variations of form, is possible. IP and WP frameworks are brought in when IA is not a natural description of what goes on in a language.

At various points throughout this chapter, we have made reference to the ways in which morphology links up with syntax. The more abstract notion of the morpheme which we arrived at (p. 133) is largely motivated by the use of morphological forms in syntactic constructions, while the 'item-and-arrangement' approach to morphological description derives much of its intuitive appeal from its relationship to syntactic analysis. We therefore turn now to the nature of syntax.

Exercises: Chapter 5

1   The following pairs of English words illustrate a variety of morphological forms. Show
(*a*) how they might be divided into morphemes,
(*b*) how productive these variations are (e.g. do they apply to all words of a particular form?, is there any way to specify the set of words which vary in this way?),
(*c*) what conditioning factors exist for allomorphic variation.

A   *reduce – reduction, except – exception, contend – contention*
B   *deport – deportation, derive – derivation, condemn – condemnation*
C   *contemplate – contemplation, tabulate – tabulation, retaliate – retaliation*
D   *fat – fatter, lovely – lovelier, funny – funnier, good – better*
E   *spectacle – spectacular, single – singular, vehicle – vehicular, title – titular, mandible – mandibular*

2   The English prefixes *anti-*, *pre-*, *un-*, etc., occur in a wide range of novel forms (*anti-nuclear*, *pre-independence*, *un-Chomskyan*). There are also certain combinations in which they seem inappropriate as novel formations (*anti-crab-like*, *pre-suitable*, *un-Chomsky*). For each of these prefixes, attempt to show which type of words it can be prefixed to, and which it cannot.

3 The prefixes of Exercise 2 are something of an intermediate case for our definitions of words as opposed to morphemes, e.g. they occur before phrases as well as simple words (*in pre-heart-transplant days*) and, to a limited degree, they occur as independent forms (*I'm anti*). Consider their status in the light of a wider range of data. Are there other such ambivalent elements?

4 Does English contain any morphological elements which might be considered empty morphs? You might like to begin by considering the status of -*o* in e.g. *Franco-Belgian*, *politico-economic*.

5 Russian has a number of apparently irregular contrasts in the formation of case forms in nouns where the nominative singular case form ends in -*ok*.

nominative form	genitive form
glotok 'mouthful'	*glotka*
potok 'stream'	*potoka*
kon'ok 'hobbyhorse'	*kon'ka*
prorok 'prophet'	*proroka*

In the light of the following additional data, analyse these words morphologically, and decide whether they really are irregular.

glotat' 'to swallow'	*poglotit'* 'to swallow up'
tok '(electric) current'	*teč* 'to flow'
kon' 'steed'	
proročit' 'to prophesy'	*reč* 'speech'

6 In Eskimo the following forms occur as derivatives of *qikmiq* ('dog'), *atkuk* ('parka') and *pana* ('spear') – words which are fairly representative of large classes of other words with similar endings in the language. Establish morph divisions, and specify allomorphy, where possible.

qikmim	'dog's'	*atkugəm*	'parka's'	*panam*	'spear's'
qikmit	'dogs'	*atkugət*	'parkas'	*panat*	'spears'
qikmimun	'to (a) dog'	*atkugmun*	'to (a) parka'	*panamun*	'to (a) spear'
qikminun	'to dogs'	*atkugnun*	'to parkas'	*pananun*	'to spears'
qikmiqa	'my dog'	*atkuka*	'my parka'	*panaka*	'my spear'
qikminka	'my dogs'	*utkunka*	'my parkas'	*pananka*	'my spears'
qikmiχput	'our dog'	*atkuxput*	'our parka'	*panavut*	'our spear'
qikmiput	'our dogs'	*atkuput*	'our parkas'	*panaput*	'our spears'
qikmimnun	'to my dog'	*atkumnun*	'to my parka'	*panamnun*	'to my spear'

7 On the basis of the data in Exercise 6, decide the extent to which Eskimo is agglutinative and the extent to which it is synthetic in its morphology.

Bibliography: Chapter 5

Greenberg, J. H., 'A quantitative approach to the morphological typology of language', *International Journal of American Linguistics*, 26 (1960), pp. 178–94. A treatment of typological distinctions as involving scalar variation, and a quantification of these.

Harris, Z. S., *Structural Linguistics* (Chicago: University of Chicago Press, 1960). The earliest (1951) edition is known as *Methods in Structural Linguistics*. Chs 12–19 are a rigorous – and very difficult – formulation of what is needed to establish morphemic status. See also Chapter 2.

Hockett, C. F., 'Two models of grammatical description', *Word*, 10 (1954), pp. 210–31. The source for the terms 'item-and-arrangement', 'item-and-process', and a comparison of what these involve.

Lyons, J., *Introduction to Theoretical Linguistics* (Cambridge: Cambridge University Press, 1968). Ch. 5, on linguistic units, is a good discussion of the status of words.

Matthews, P. H., *Morphology* (Cambridge: Cambridge University Press, 1974). A detailed introduction to the basic concepts of morphology. It contains, among other things, the most explicit comparison of the 'word-and-paradigm' approach to morphology with other approaches.

Sapir, E., *Language* (New York: Harcourt, Brace & World, 1921). Ch. 6 is one of the classic accounts of morphological typology of languages, and still makes very useful reading.

Chapter 6

Syntax

6.1 The domain of syntax

There is some diversity of opinion among linguists about the range of phenomena which may be considered syntactic, and about the ways in which a syntactic description of a language might relate to the phonology and semantics of that language. Nevertheless, within this argument there is a large measure of agreement on the subject-matter of syntax; it is concerned with the organisation of meaningful elements within the sentence. At its most general, such a view implies that a large part of morphology should be considered part of syntax, and there is indeed a body of opinion which holds that this is so. For our purposes, however, in line with tradition, we may take the word as the minimal unit of syntactic analysis. In the context of this book, this has the advantage of providing convenient chapter divisions, but more seriously, there are also genuine differences between the internal and external organisation of words, as can be seen from our discussion of the word–morpheme distinction in Chapter 5.

The upper limit of syntax is the sentence. It is true that larger units than this are quite conceivable − paragraphs, texts, etc. (these terms usually being taken to include units of the spoken language) − but the principles of organisation that operate at these levels are quite different from those that operate within the sentence. To see this, it is sufficient to consider data of the following sort.

(1) *a* The dog chased the rabbit
    b *Rabbit the chased dog the
(2)   John hopes to dissolve

Sentence (1)*a* is a normal English sentence; both (1)*b* and (2) are odd, although in different ways. (2) says something peculiar; outside science fiction we cannot make sense of the situation it purports to describe. (1)*b* does not describe an odd situation; it is odd simply by virtue of the fact that it violates rules of English syntax. The constraints on juxtaposition of sentences to make up a discourse are more akin to the constraints which make (2) odd than they are to the syntactic constraints that exclude (1)*b*. (3) is an odd thing to say, although it could no doubt be contextualised in such a way as to make it possible.

(3) John looked out the window. Two and two are four.

But there is no aspect of the structure of either sentence which renders them incompatible with each other. So the study of the connection of sentences, interesting though it is, is not part of syntax.

While every native-speaker of English would agree that (1)*a* is a well-formed English sentence and that (1)*b* is ill formed, the nature of the well- or ill-formedness of these strings may not be immediately apparent. In particular, it would be open to someone to maintain that whereas (1)*a* is meaningful, (1)*b* cannot be interpreted, and that these semantic properties are what we refer to when we say that (1)*a* is well formed and (1)*b* ill formed. Such a view, if it could be defended, would lead to the conclusion that syntactic well-formedness or grammaticality cannot be distinguished from meaningfulness, and would force us to consider the possibility that there is no syntactic domain for linguists to study independently of semantic considerations. In order to resist these conclusions, we have to display phenomena which appear to require autonomous syntactic concepts for their explication, and this is fairly easy to do.

First, we can argue that meaningfulness is not a necessary condition for syntactic well-formedness, i.e. we can produce strings of words which are meaningless but syntactically well formed. Chomsky's famous example to illustrate this is (4).

(4) Colourless green ideas sleep furiously

which can be contrasted with an ill-formed string using the same words, as in (5).

(5) *Sleep ideas green furiously colourless

Of course, it is open to the sceptic to maintain that Chomsky's view that (4) is meaningless is questionable. Certainly, a little ingenuity can produce a metaphorical interpretation for this string, e.g. books which contain boring and naïve ideas are rarely removed from library shelves. But if this avenue is pursued, a fundamental question must be raised; is the metaphorical interpretation alluded to above *the*, or even *a*, meaning of (4), or is it an interpretation that we have imposed on (4) which, in itself, is meaningless? Note that it is open to different individuals to offer different, perhaps equally plausible, interpretations for (4). Are we to say that (4) is multiply ambiguous? It is surely more prudent at this stage to agree that (4) is meaningless, while recognising that speakers of a language have the ability to impose interpretations on such meaningless strings (see Chapter 7, Section 6, for discussion relevant to how this might be done). Note that this stance commits us to the view that there is a valid distinction between the *meaning* associated with a particular string of words, a property of the linguistic system, and the *interpretation* that a hearer can impose upon a string of words, something which may require more than the properties of the linguistic system for its explication.

Second, we can show that meaningfulness is not a sufficient condition for syntactic well-formedness, i.e. we can give examples of strings of words which, while readily interpretable by native-speakers in a way which is constrained by the linguistic system, are not syntactically well formed. Chomsky's original example to make this point is (6).

(6)   *The child seems sleeping

Other examples have played an important role in more recent linguistic theorising:

(7)   Each of the men believes that Mary kissed the others
(8)   *The men believed that Mary kissed each other
(9)   *John believes that Mary kissed himself

Presumably, if confronted with (8), we would be able to interpret it, and the interprctation we would assign to it would be the interpretation of (7); the hearer would not have the freedom of interpretation we have suggested for (4). But this does not destroy the difference between (7) and (8); the former is syntactically well formed, and the latter is ill formed. Furthermore, (9), while clearly ungrammatical in English, can be translated into Japanese, the result being a perfectly grammatical Japanese sentence with the meaning that John believes that Mary kissed John, i.e. precisely the meaning that native-speakers of English will assign to (9). This suggests that the fact that (9) is ill formed in English is a fact about the *syntax* of English and cannot be reduced to semantic considerations. We seem, then, to be justified in concluding that some aspects of any human language are going to be irreducibly syntactic in nature, but note that this does not imply that there will be *no* interaction between the syntactic and semantic properties of the sentences in a language, a proposition which is certainly false (cf. Chapter 7, Section 1).

Returning now to (1)*a* and (1)*b*, the crucial difference between them is the linear order in which the words occur. Alongside (1)*a*, we have the well-formed (10).

(10)   The rabbit chased the dog

All other permutations of the words in (1)*a* yield ill-formed strings. Thus, one of the phenomena a syntactic account of English is going to have to come to terms with is the relatively fixed word order in English sentences.

The fact that the words in (1)*a* appear in a particular linear order is not all we need to note about this sentence. It is readily apparent that certain words in the sentence 'belong together' in a way in which others do not. Awaiting a more explicit justification for this 'feeling' in Section 3 below, we shall here content ourselves with noting that, for example, the first *the* and *dog* appear to form some sort of unit, *the dog*, and the same is true for the second *the* and *rabbit*, *the rabbit*. Compare, in this respect, *chased* and the second *the* which, while adjacent in the sentence, do not display any intuitive coherence (note here the reliance on intuition argued for in Chapter 2). Linguists refer to such sequences as *the dog* and *the rabbit* in (1)*a* as *constituents*, and we can propose that a second requirement on a syntactic account of a language is that it makes explicit the constituent structure of the sentences of the language.

Recall now our discussion in Chapter 2, Section 2, where it was argued that the number of well-formed sentences in any language is infinite. We can illustrate this same point here with the following sentences.

(11)   John believes Mary hates linguistics
(12)   John believes Bill believes Mary hates linguistics
(13)   John believes Bill believes Harry believes Mary hates linguistics

Of course, we can extend this set of sentences as far as we like and, given the considerations of Chapter 2, Section 2, and those above on the autonomy of syntax from semantics, it follows that our syntactic account of a language will have to be an account of an infinite set of well-formed sentences. Accordingly, a *list* of the well-formed sentences with their syntactic properties (e.g. constituency) displayed would be never ending. Clearly, what we have to develop is a finitely stable theory which accounts for the grammatical properties of the infinite set of sentences in the language under study. The consequences of such a theory must be capable of being explicitly formulated (an explicitly formulated theory of this type is technically known as a *generative grammar*) and tested against further data of the type we shall now discuss.

If we consider the following pair of sentences, our first response to them might be that they are syntactically organised in similar ways.

(14)   Linguists are keen to learn
(15)   Linguists are difficult to employ

Although superficially similar in that they contain the same grammatical categories strung together in the same way, these sentences are clearly different, as will become apparent if we think for a moment about the relationship between *linguists* and *learn/employ*. In (14) it makes some sense to say that *linguists* is the subject of *learn* (more properly, of the subordinate clause in which *learn* appears); after all, linguists are doing the learning. In (15), however, it seems more appropriate to view *linguists* as the direct object of *employ*; linguists are being employed, not doing the employing. We might begin to feel that such observations are more significant when we note that the parallelism between (14) and (15) breaks down in sentences which are clearly closely related to them.

(16) It is difficult to employ linguists
(17) *It is keen to learn linguists
(18) Employing linguists is difficult
(19) *Learning linguists is keen

We can require that a grammar will make explicit the appropriate grammatical relations between expressions in sentences, even when these are obscured, as in the pair (14) and (15).

The next phenomenon to be accounted for by the theory is *structural* ambiguity. We are all familiar with examples of *lexical* ambiguity as displayed in the following sentences.

(20) I'll meet you at the *bank* in twenty minutes
(21) Has the *post* come yet?
(22) When will the *case* be opened?

Each of these sentences contains an italicised word which has two distinct meanings — it is traditional to list these meanings in a dictionary — and these differences are what accounts for the fact that the sentences themselves are ambiguous. Probably less familiar is the type of ambiguity displayed by the following sentences.

(23) The stout teacher's wife is exciting
(24) John likes linguistics more than Mary
(25) What John became was horrible

(The ambiguity in (25) might not be immediately obvious; one interpretation is simply that John became horrible; the other interpretation is that John became something, say a werewolf, and that this werewolf was horrible.) In each of these sentences there is no word to which we can point and say that it has two meanings; rather, the ambiguity appears to arise from the possibility of construing the words as 'going together' in different ways. This is most obvious in the case of (23), where we would talk of *stout* modifying *teacher* or *teacher's wife*. It follows, then, that this sort of ambiguity is concerned with structural organisation.

Finally, from our introductory perspective, we might hope that a grammar will help to explicate our intuitions about structural relatedness between sets of sentences. In addition to some of the examples already used, there appears to be a regular syntactic (as well as semantic) relationship between the following pairs of sentences.

(26) *a* John concluded the argument
      b The argument was concluded by John
(27) *a* That linguistics is fun is obvious
      b It is obvious that linguistics is fun

To say that this syntactic relationship is 'regular' is merely to note that very many sentences of the form (26)*a* have analogues of the form (26)*b*, and the same goes for the sentences in (27).

Armed with these preliminary concepts, we shall now turn our attention to the task of formulating generative grammars that account for them.

6.2 Representing constituency: phrase structure grammar

In this section we shall formulate one variety of grammar to account for the fact that certain words in sentences 'belong together' (i.e. may be viewed as forming constituents). Consider a small set of simple sentences.

(28) The dog chased the rabbit
(29) The students can do this exercise rather easily
(30) John is extremely tall
(31) Mary walked in the park

For (28) we have already suggested that *the dog* and *the rabbit* are constituents. We might graphically represent this as in (32):

(32)

The dog chased the rabbit

or, equivalently, as in (33).

(33)   [The dog] chased [the rabbit]

Perhaps going beyond untutored intuition, we could extend these representations to include the claim that *chased* and *the rabbit* form a constituent to the exclusion of *the dog* (notice that this is tantamount to adopting the traditional subject–predicate distinction). Such an extension could be represented as in (34).

(34)

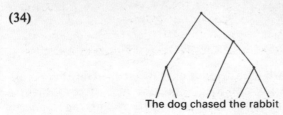

The dog chased the rabbit

where we have taken the liberty of regarding the whole sentence as a constituent, or, equivalently, as in (35).

(35)   [[The dog] [chased [the rabbit]]]

The object in (34) is known as an *unlabelled tree* and that in (35) as an *unlabelled bracketing*. Given either of these representations, a sequence of words is a constituent if the sequence can be traced back to a single *node* in the tree, with no other material under this node, or, correspondingly, if the sequence exhausts the contents of a pair of brackets. From now on, except briefly in Chapter 8, we shall use only trees, because they are visually easier to comprehend.

Consideration of (29)–(31) might yield the following unlabelled trees.

(36)

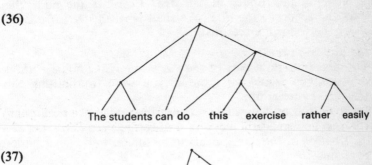

The students can do   this   exercise   rather   easily

(37)

John is extremely tall

(38)

Mary walked in the park

Such representations, while making it clear what the constituents of a sentence are, do not say anything about the *type* of constituents. Yet, we would wish to maintain that *the dog, the rabbit, the students*, etc. are a different type of constituent to, say, *rather easily* or *extremely tall*. A way to build this view into our representations is to attach labels to the various nodes in the trees.

At the lowest level of the trees we have words and we might simply consult a traditional grammar or even a dictionary for appropriate labels (justification for choice of labels is something to which we shall return in Section 3). Such a source might tell us that in (34) *the* is a determiner, *dog* and *rabbit* are nouns and *chased* is a verb. So we might propose (39) as a start in constructing a labelled tree from (34).

(39)

What about higher nodes in the tree? Consider the node that dominates the sequence *the dog*. We shall label this NP (for noun phrase) for the following reasons:

(i)   *the dog* is a phrase;
(ii) The most important part of *the dog* is surely the noun – think of what you would miss out if you were transmitting this sentence by telegram;
(iii) we could substitute a single noun (proper noun or plural noun) for *the dog* and still have a well-formed sentence, i.e. the *distribution* of *the dog* appears to be similar to the distribution of nouns.

By similar reasoning, the node dominating *the rabbit* will be labelled NP. Now, what about the node dominating *chased the rabbit*? It is readily apparent that the whole expression behaves rather like a verb, since we can substitute a simple verb for it and still have a well-formed sentence.

(40)   The dog ran

We cannot perform a similar substitution using a noun or a determiner, the other elements appearing in the sequence.

(41)   *The dog John
(42)   *The dog a

Therefore, on distributional grounds, we are justified in labelling this node VP (for verb phrase). Finally, the topmost node dominates the whole sentence and will accordingly be labelled S. Introducing all these labels into our tree for (28) yields the *labelled tree* (43).

(43)

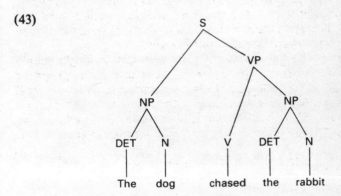

Similar considerations applied to (29) give us the following representation.

(44)

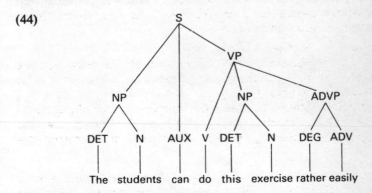

The new labels in this tree are ADVP for adverbial phrase, ADV for adverb, DEG for degree modifier and AUX for auxiliary verb. Of these, only the last is likely to be at all puzzling, but, in fact, there is a variety of reasons for recognising a special class of such verbs (*can, must, will*, etc.) in English. First, such verbs do not take the standard inflections to indicate person agreement, i.e. they are degenerate morphologically.

(45) *a* I can, he can, *he cans
     b I must, he must, *he musts
     c I will, he will, *he wills

Second, these verbs are crucially involved in the formation of English questions, taking up a position at the front of such structures. Ordinary verbs do not behave in this way.

(46) *a* He can answer the question
     b Can he answer the question?
     c *Answers he the question (cf. he answers the question)

Third, in negative sentences, the negative morpheme *not* or *n't* follows these verbs and it cannot follow ordinary verbs.

(47) *a* He cannot/can't answer the question
     b *He answern't the question (cf. he doesn't answer the question)

All of this suggests that it is necessary to recognise a distinct class of auxiliary verbs in the syntax of English.

Consideration of (30) and (31) suggests the following labelled trees for these sentences.

(48)

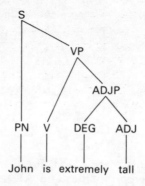

(49)

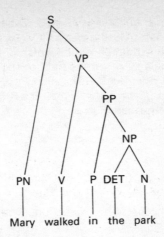

Here the new labels are PN for proper noun, ADJP for adjectival phrase, ADJ for adjective, PP for prepositional phrase and P for preposition.

Accepting that something along the lines of (43), (44), (48) and (49) is at least a part of the correct syntactic analysis of (28)–(31), two questions now arise.

(i) How can we formally construct objects like the above labelled trees, i.e. what is our grammar for English going to look like if we require it to produce representations such as these?

(ii) How can we justify the details of any one constituent structure analysis, particularly if it goes beyond our raw intuition?

As far as the first of these questions is concerned, the formal device most commonly used consists of a set of *phrase structure rules*, such a set constituting a *phrase structure grammar*. Such grammars were implicit in a great deal of the structuralist linguistics of the 1930s and 1940s (see Chapter 2, Section 1) but were made explicit only by Chomsky in his earliest work.

Consider again (28) with its associated structure (43). In order to *generate* this sentence with its appropriate structure, we might propose the following set of phrase structure rules.

(50)   S ⟶ NP – VP
        NP ⟶ DET – N
        VP ⟶ V – NP

Each line in (50) is a rule to be interpreted as an instruction to construct a sub-part of a tree in a particular way. The label appearing on the left of the rule will label a node which dominates one or more nodes bearing the labels given on the right of the rule, in precisely the order specified in the rule. Such rules, therefore, contain information about *dominance* and *linear order*. Thus, the first line of (50) enables us to construct the sub-tree:

(51)

and the second line licenses the expansion of this to:

(52)

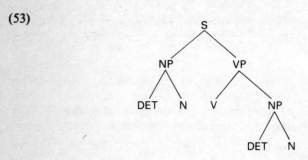

An application of the rule in the third line followed by a further application of that in the second line will yield:

(53)

This tree is identical to that in (43), except that it does not contain the words at the lowest level. An easy remedy for this omission is simply to expand the phrase structure rules in (50) by adding the rules in (54).

(54)   DET $\longrightarrow$ the
       N $\longrightarrow$ $\begin{bmatrix} \text{dog} \\ \text{rabbit} \end{bmatrix}$
       V $\longrightarrow$ chased

(The braces in the second line indicate that either *dog* or *rabbit* may be dominated by a node labelled N.) Note that even with this simple grammar consisting of the rules in (50) and (54) we also generate:

(55)   The rabbit chased the dog

An alternative way of entering words into structures like (53) will now be presented, the reasons for which will be more fully understood as we proceed. This alternative consists in adding to the rules of (50) a *lexicon* and a *single* rule of lexical insertion. At this point, the lexicon can be construed as simply a pairing of words with an appropriate grammatical category, as in (56).

(56)   *the* – DET   *chased* – V
       dog – N   *rabbit* – N

The rule of lexical insertion is now given.

(57)   Insert any word from the lexicon into a tree under label X if the word is paired with X in the lexicon.

As must be obvious, (56) and (57) have exactly the same effects as (54).

Our grammar fragment can now be extended in two ways: first, at the level of the lexicon, so as to be able to generate more sentences with the same structure; second, at the level of the phrase structure rules, so as to be able to generate the other simple sentences we started from. For instance, (29) requires that we complement the rules in (50) with those in (58).

(58)   S $\longrightarrow$ NP – AUX – VP
          VP $\longrightarrow$ V – NP – ADVP
       ADVP $\longrightarrow$ DEG – ADV

For (30) we need to add (59).

(59)   S $\longrightarrow$ PN – VP
          VP $\longrightarrow$ V – ADJP
       ADJP $\longrightarrow$ DEG – ADJ

And, correspondingly, for (31):

(60)   VP $\longrightarrow$ V – PP
           PP $\longrightarrow$ P – NP

While the rules in (50), (58), (59) and (60), together with an appropriately extended lexicon, correctly generate our four sentences along with many others, they can actually be tidied up considerably. PNs, such as *John* and *Mary*, have similar distributions to full NPs such as *the dog* and *the rabbit*, so we can remove the first rule of (59), letting the first rule of (50) do the work by allowing NPs to consist either of PNs or of sequences of determiner and noun:

(61) $\text{NP} \longrightarrow \begin{bmatrix} \text{DET} - \text{N} \\ \text{PN} \end{bmatrix}$

Here, again, the braces indicate optionality. On the other hand, the first rule in (58) includes AUX, but this element is clearly optional, as illustrated by (62).

(62) The students do this exercise rather easily

Indicating this optionality by parentheses, we can maintain a single rule for building trees dominated by S.

(63) $\text{S} \longrightarrow \text{NP} - (\text{AUX}) - \text{VP}$

Similar considerations for VP lead to:

(64) $\text{VP} \longrightarrow \text{V} - \begin{bmatrix} \text{NP} - (\text{ADVP}) \\ \text{ADJP} \\ \text{PP} \end{bmatrix}$

The full set of rules which, supplemented by a lexicon, will generate our four sentences and many others is therefore the following.

(65)
$$\text{S} \longrightarrow \text{NP} - (\text{AUX}) - \text{VP}$$
$$\text{NP} \longrightarrow \begin{bmatrix} \text{DET} - \text{N} \\ \text{PN} \end{bmatrix}$$
$$\text{VP} \longrightarrow \text{V} - \begin{bmatrix} \text{NP} - (\text{ADVP}) \\ \text{ADJP} \\ \text{PP} \end{bmatrix}$$
$$\text{ADJP} \longrightarrow \text{DEG} - \text{ADJ}$$
$$\text{ADVP} \longrightarrow \text{DEG} - \text{ADV}$$
$$\text{PP} \longrightarrow \text{P} - \text{NP}$$

It may be interesting at this point to look at where we have got to with respect to our initial set of syntactic phenomena. Obviously, phrase structure rules handle aspects of linear order, as the symbols on the right-hand side are stipulated to appear in the desired order.

Equally, they come to terms with constituent structure, having been introduced expressly to deal with this. It is also straightforward to be optimistic about their ability to deal with the fact that English sentences are infinite in number. Consider, for instance, the examples of (11)–(13). The rules of (66), two of which we have already formulated in (65), along with the appropriate lexicon, will give all of these sentences.

(66)   S $\longrightarrow$ NP – (AUX) – VP
     NP $\longrightarrow$ PN
     VP $\longrightarrow$ V – (S)

This set of rules generates not only (11)–(13) but also the infinite number of well-formed sentences which are constructed on this pattern, due to the property of *recursiveness*. What this means is that one application of the rules creates the conditions under which the rules can apply again and so on indefinitely. In this case, the first rule introduces a VP node, which, by the third rule, may dominate an S node, which may, in turn, dominate a further VP node and so on. Clearly, this process can be extended as far as we like.

    Some instances of structural ambiguity can also be taken care of within this framework. Recall (23), repeated here as (67).

(67)   The stout teacher's wife is exciting

Focusing on the initial NP and without committing ourselves on node labels, it should be clear that there are two constituent analyses for this phrase.

(68)

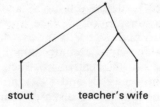

corresponds to 'teacher's wife who is stout', and

(69)

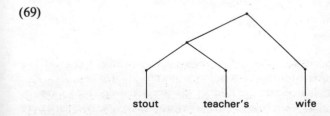

corresponds to 'wife of stout teacher'. It is far from obvious, however, that similar considerations can be brought to bear on (24) and (25), and, indeed, it was originally suggested by Chomsky that one of the major failings of phrase structure grammars was that they cannot deal adequately with many examples of structural ambiguity, the classic case being:

(70) Flying planes can be dangerous

Nothing we have said so far bears on the other phenomena we introduced in Section 1, i.e. grammatical relations and structurally related sentences. We shall return to these in Section 5.

6.3 Justifying constituency: empirical diagnostics

There are two questions we must consider in this section.

 (i) How are words assigned lexical categories (N, V, ADJ, etc.) in the lexicon? Earlier we suggested consultation of a traditional grammar or a dictionary, but how does the traditional grammarian or the lexicographer justify the assignment of words to syntactic classes?
(ii) On what basis do we split up a sentence into phrasal constituents, particularly where intuition deserts us?

We shall first attend briefly to the question of lexical categories.
   Traditional, notional definitions of the parts of speech are notoriously unreliable. To define a noun as a word which is used to refer to an object, a person, or a place appears to exclude such obvious nouns as *beauty* and *electricity*; and to define a verb as a word which is used to name an action excludes, among many others, *hear, contain* and *be*. As an alternative to such semantically based definitions, linguists in the 1940s and 1950s attempted to formulate distributional definitions, trying to discover diagnostic environments where only words from a particular category could occur. For example, we can consider the environments:

(71) is ⎯⎯ -ing
(72) forget to ⎯⎯

These appear to be diagnostic for verbs in that only verbs can be entered in the spaces to produce a well-formed English expression. But even in these environments certain verbs are excluded, e.g. *know, own*. The belief is that there are other diagnostic environments where such verbs can occur, perhaps to the exclusion of other verbs, but definitely to the exclusion of members of any other lexical category. In other words, occurrence in a certain environment can be seen as providing a sufficient condition for being a member of a particular lexical category though not as a necessary condition.

Moving on to the second question, a variety of tests are available which the linguist might find useful in motivating a specific constituent analysis. At one end of the spectrum there is of course intuition, perhaps backed up by psycholinguistic investigation (cf. Chapter 9, Section 3), while at the other, details of a certain analysis may be so embedded in abstract theoretical considerations that it would be truly difficult for the beginner to come to terms with it. Between these two extremes, however, there are avenues that the novice can fruitfully explore. These avenues are unlikely to provide definitive answers, particularly if the questions being asked are sophisticated, but they may at least add support to a tentative analysis. We have already alluded to the use of distributional evidence, both in our justification for assigning NP, VP, etc. status to certain strings of words and in our brief discussion of deciding questions of lexical category membership. We shall now mention three further considerations which are worth taking into account.

A. Movement

Often a pair of sentences appear to be related in that they are identical except for some sequence of words in one sentence, which turns up in a different position in the other, as with the sequence *in the park* in (73).

(73) *a* John kissed Mary in the park
      b In the park, John kissed Mary

The fact that *in the park* can be 'moved' between (73)*a* and (73)*b* adds weight to our earlier decision to treat it as a PP, since it appears to be the case that *only* constituents can be 'moved' in this way. If we attempt to 'move' the non-constituent *Mary in* in (73)*a* to any other location in the sentence, ungrammaticality results.

(74) *a* *Mary in John kissed the park
      b *John Mary in kissed the park
      c *John kissed the Mary in park
      d *John kissed the park Mary in

Note, however, that it is not always the case that constituents can be 'moved', nor that they can be 'moved' to any position in the sentence. The latter point is illustrated in (75).

(75)   *John kissed in the park Mary

With respect to the former, note that although *the park* would appear to be an uncontroversial constituent in (73)*a*, if we attempt to 'move' it to the front of the sentence, the result is just as bad as in the case of (74).

(76)   *The park John kissed Mary in

In conclusion, we can say that 'movement' is at best a sufficient condition for constituenthood; it is not a necessary condition.

B. Co-ordination
Consider (77).

(77)   The ship sailed down the river and up the canal

In this sentence *down the river and up the canal* is a co-ordinate structure involving the two conjuncts *down the river* and *up the canal*. What expressions can be conjoined in this manner in English? The answer appears to be: only constituents of the same type. Accordingly, this test provides us with information not only about what sequences are constituents but also about their type. Clearly, in (77) we have two PPs being conjoined; the co-ordination of other types of constituent is illustrated in (78)–(82).

(78)   *John and the man from Oldham* swept into the room (NP and NP)
(79)   John *likes linguistics and hates literature* (VP and VP)
(80)   John is *rather tall and extremely shy* (ADJP and ADJP)
(81)   John *quietly and secretly* swallowed the memo (ADVP and ADVP)
(82)   *John arrived and Mary left* (S and S)

What happens if we try to conjoin non-constituents? Consider (83).

(83)   The students can do *this exercise rather* easily and the students can do *that translation very* easily

Attempting to conjoin the italicised non-constituents yields:

(84)   *The students can do this exercise rather and that translation very easily

That the conjoined constituents must be of the same type is illustrated by:

(85)   Deng Xiao Ping wrote *a poem* and Deng Xiao Ping wrote *to Thatcher*

Attempting to conjoin the italicised NP and PP gives:

(86)   *Deng Xiao Ping wrote a poem and to Thatcher

So, if we are going to make correct statements about co-ordination, it is necessary to have information about constituency. Conversely, facts about co-ordination possibilities can be used to support constituent analyses.

It is important to point out here that this test sometimes gives what look like implausible results. For example, in (87) we appear to be conjoining sequences which intuitively are not constituents.

(87)   John *arrived at and left from* Victoria

There are at least two responses to the problem created by such examples. First, we could admit that our test is fallible and use it only with caution. Second, we could attempt to construct an analysis whereby the troublesome sequences *arrived at* and *left from* are after all constituents, despite what our intuitions say. Such an analysis would be an example of the theory-embedded considerations that we mentioned at the beginning of this section.

C. Pro-Forms

Pro-forms are expressions which 'stand for' other expressions in a sentence. Thus, in (88) *him* can be interpreted as referring to the same individual as *John*.

(88)   John came in and Bill tripped him up

Traditionally, *him* is called a pronoun, although it would be more accurate to refer to it as a pro-NP, as (89) shows.

(89)   *The king came in and Bill tripped the him up

Here the attempt to have *him* 'stand for' the noun *king* yields an ungrammatical string. The idea behind introducing pro-forms in the discussion is based on the claim that pro-forms stand only for constituents. Thus, in (88) *him* stands for *John* and, uncontroversially, *John* is a constituent in this sentence; it is an NP. Less intuitively obvious NPs can be identified using this criterion.

(90)   If the lady in the blue coat comes in, don't let her out

In (90) *her* can be seen as standing for *the lady in the blue coat*, suggesting that the whole of the latter expression is an NP. Again, in (91):

(91)   The fact that Bill is a fool worries his mother and it also worries his wife

it, a pro-NP, is standing for *the fact that Bill is a fool*, arguing that this is an NP. Other pro-forms stand for constituents other than NP. Consider (92) and (93).

(92)   John has never been to Hemel Hempstead but Bill has been there
(93)   John likes to eat caviare but Bill can't stand to do so

There is a pro-PP standing for the PP *to Hemel Hempstead*, and *do so* is a pro-VP standing for the VP *eat caviare*.

The tests we have described here are among the most common in linguistic argumentation. Along with distributional criteria, they should provide the beginner with an entry point into constituent structure, although, as noted, they are unlikely to lead to definitive analyses except in the simplest cases.

6.4   Subcategorisation restrictions

While a set of phrase structure rules along the lines introduced above is an essential component of an adequate syntactic theory of English, there appear to be compelling reasons for believing that it is not by itself sufficient. In this section, we shall examine why this is so and discuss, in an informal way, what additions are necessary in order to make the theory more adequate.

The attentive reader will have noted that the phrase structure grammar of (65), as well as generating a range of well-formed sentences, also generates the following.

(94)   *a* *The students can is this exercise
       b *John chased extremely tall
       c *Mary chased in the park

Quite simply, this is because, in the grammar of (65), there are no restrictions on the co-occurrences of verbs and the material following them.

Let us take a simple case to illustrate this. Consider the data in (95).

(95) *a* The fish sleeps
      b *The fish sleeps the frog
      c *The fish excites
      d The fish excites the frog

The machinery we have available so far might suggest a set of phrase structure rules as in (96).

(96) S $\longrightarrow$ NP – (AUX) – VP
      NP $\longrightarrow$ DET – N
      VP $\longrightarrow$ V – (NP)

The only novelty is the optionality of NP in the third rule, by which we intend to capture the traditional distinction between transitive and intransitive verbs. Along with (96), we might propose a set of lexical entries in the lexicon along the following lines.

(97) *the* – DET   *sleeps* – V
      fish – N   *excites* – V
      frog – N

Such a theory generates the well-formed sentences (95)*a* and (95)*d* and assigns them sensible structures. Unfortunately, however, it also predicts that (95)*b* and (95)*c* are well formed. The application of the phrase structure rules will allow us to produce trees like (98) and (99).

(98)

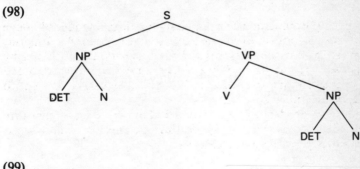

(99)

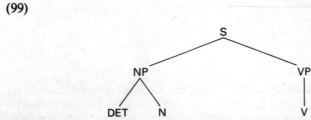

Now, our rule of lexical insertion (57) allows us to insert any verb under a node labelled V. So, we could insert *sleeps* under the V in (98) and *excites* under the V in (99), leading ultimately to the ill-formed (95)*b* and (95)*c*. It follows that our grammar is failing in a very obvious way; it is characterising some strings as grammatical which are not. We now rectify this inadequacy.

One possibility would be to build the transitive–intransitive distinction into our set of grammatical categories. Consider (100):

(100)   S $\longrightarrow$ NP – (AUX) – VP
         NP $\longrightarrow$ DET – N
         VP $\longrightarrow$ $\begin{bmatrix} V_I - NPT \\ V_I \end{bmatrix}$

along with a modification in the lexicon in (97) as in (101).

(101)   *sleeps* – V_I *excites* – V_T

Given the structure:

(102)

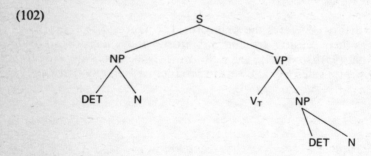

it will now be possible to insert only *excites* under V_T, since *sleeps* is paired in the lexicon with V_I. Equally, given the structure in (103):

(103)

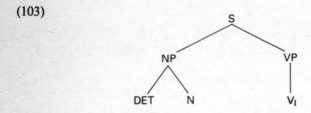

only *sleeps* can be inserted under V_I, since *excites* is paired with V_T in the lexicon. This manoeuvre, obviously, will enable our grammar to overcome the problem we are considering, but there is an important price to pay; V_T and V_I are quite distinct symbols in the grammar of (100), i.e. this grammar does not recognise a grammatical category of verbs (note that the fact that we have used the symbols V_T and V_I both containing the letter 'V' is due to mnemonic considerations; we could just as easily have used X and Y). If part of what a native-speaker of English knows about the language is that *sleeps* and *excites* belong to the same grammatical category, this solution must be rejected.

An alternative is to complicate the entries in the lexicon along with the rule of lexical insertion, by representing the fact that *excites* is a transitive verb directly in its lexical entry as follows.

(104)   *excites* – V, + [____ NP]

The second part of this entry indicates that *excites* is a verb, just as before, but, additionally, it says that it *must* (this is the force of the '+') be followed by an NP. The corresponding entry for *sleeps* may be as in (105):

(105)   *sleeps* – V, – [____ NP]

where *sleeps* is explicitly forbidden from occurring in structures where it is followed by an NP. Verbs which may or may not take a direct object, such as *cooks*, can be entered in the lexicon with an optional direct object, formalised by means of parentheses.

(106)   *cooks* – V, + [____ (NP)]

More complicated cases can be given a parallel treatment. For example, the verb *realise* must be followed by a sentence which may be preceded by the complementiser *that* (cf. Chapter 8, Section 3, for some discussion of complementisers).

(107)   *a* John realises that linguistics is fun
        b John realises linguistics is fun
        c *John realises Mary

Accordingly, the lexical entry for *realise* will be as follows.

(108)   *realise* – V, + [____ (*that*) – S]

The rule of lexical insertion must now be complicated along the lines of (109).

(109)   We can insert any word from the lexicon into a tree under the appropriate category label provided the environmental

conditions specified in the lexical entry for the word are satisfied in the tree.

It seems plausible that, as well as verbs, members of other lexical categories may require to have their lexical entries complicated in similar ways, but we shall not pursue this possibility here. What should now be clear is that with lexical entries for *excites* and *sleeps* as in (104) and (105) and the rule of lexical insertion (109), it is not possible to insert *sleeps* into (98) nor *excites* into (99). Furthermore, this solution preserves the integrity of the grammatical category verb. According to these proposals, both *sleep* and *excite* are verbs.

The device we have introduced above is known as *subcategorisation* and objects such as + [____ NP] as *subcategorisation frames*. It is a vitally important notion, not only for understanding the structure of the theory we are outlining here, but also in some recent developments in syntactic theory which will be discussed in some detail in Chapter 8, Section 1.

6.5   Transformations

On the assumption that the above proposal is well motivated and expresses correct generalisations about the syntactic properties of English words, we shall now raise a new problem. Consider (110).

(110)   Who(m) will the fish excite?

If we attempt to generate this sentence using phrase structure rules, our generalisation about *excite* requiring a following NP will run into trouble. In (110), however we decide to handle the first part of the sentence, *excite* is not followed by an NP. To be more specific, we might contemplate introducing a phrase structure rule as in (111).

(111)   S ⟶ NP – AUX – NP – V

Ensuring somehow that the first NP is a question word (*who(m)*, *what, why*, etc.) or *Wh*-word as they are anglocentrically known, we will get trees like (112).

(112)

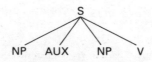

Consultation of the lexical entry for *excite* will now forbid insertion into this structure. Equally badly, consultation of our lexical entry for *sleep* will allow us to insert it into this structure, leading to the false prediction that (113) is well formed.

(113)   *Who(m) will the fish sleep?

The same point can be made using a verb with a more complex lexical entry such as *put*. In simple sentences, *put* is obligatorily followed by a direct object NP and a PP, as the following examples demonstrate.

(114)   *a*   John put a book on the table
     b   *John put
     c   *John put a book
     d   *John put on the table

These facts suggest that the lexical entry for *put* must be as in (115).

(115)   *put* – V, + [___ NP – PP]

This creates immediate problems with the well-formed questions in (116) and (117).

(116)   What did John put on the table?
(117)   Where did John put the book?

Specifically, in (116) *put* is not immediately followed by an NP, and in (117) *put* is followed by an NP not followed by a PP. Consequently, if we wished to generate such sentences using only phrase structure rules, we would not be able to insert *put* in the appropriate positions on the basis of the lexical entry (115).

Note now that, alongside these linguistic arguments, in (110) *who(m)* is intuitively the direct object of *excite* (hence its marking in written English and some varieties of spoken English as an accusative pronoun). All this suggests the following analysis. First, we allow the phrase structure rules to function as before and thus produce a structure in which *who(m)* follows the verb as in (118) (note that questions of the form *the fish will excite whom* are well formed in English and are in fact used as 'echo' questions).

(118)

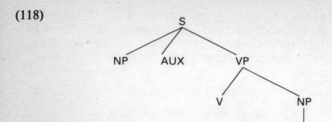

The verb *excite* will be insertable into such a structure on the basis of the lexical entry (104). Second, we formulate a rule to MOVE *who(m)* from its position at the end of the sentence to the position in which it actually appears at the beginning of the sentence. This rule is known as *Wh*-movement and is an example of a transformational rule. An intuitive feel for how a rule of this type differs from phrase structure rules may be obtained by noting that, unlike phrase structure rules, it is not a rule for *building* trees but for *changing* them after they have been built.

Informally, we are envisaging the following analysis for (110). First, the phrase structure rules in conjunction with the lexicon and the lexical insertion rule generate the structure in (119).

(119)

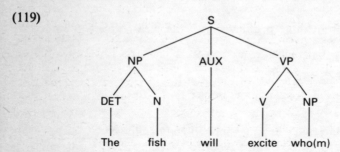

The rule of *Wh*-movement will convert (119) to something like (120).

(120)

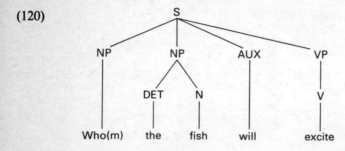

Now the *Wh*-word is in its correct position at the front of the sentence, but a further transformational rule of subject–auxiliary inversion has to apply to permute the positions of the subject NP *the fish* and the auxiliary verb *will*. Application of this rule gives (121).

(121)

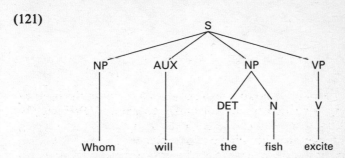

According to this way of looking at things, the grammatical structure of (110) is only partially elucidated by (121), which represents the *surface structure* of the sentence. (119) is referred to as the *deep structure* of the sentence and is related to the surface structure via one or more transformational rules. (The terms 'deep structure' and 'surface structure' have been replaced by *D-structure* and *S-structure* in more recent writings and have been given a rather more abstract character than that described here.)

The argument we have seen above can easily be extended to deal with the sentences involving *put*, and the reader will find it worthwhile to reflect on its structure. The obvious message is that, while in characterising the grammatical sentences in a language we have to get the words in the correct linear order, this linear order sometimes obscures important structural relations in the sentence (e.g. *who(m)* in (110) appears to be functioning as direct object of *excites*). So, in order to have our cake and eat it, we introduce another, more abstract level of structure at which the important relationships are transparent, and complicate our theory with rules linking these two levels of structure.

If we accept the need for transformational rules such as *Wh*-movement in the grammar of English, we can immediately be optimistic about the phenomena discussed in Section 1. The rule of *Wh*-movement involves the copying of some element of a sentence's structure into a new position and its deletion at the original site. But perhaps transformational rules can also perform other operations, e.g. permuting elements in trees or inserting material at some specified place in a structure. With these possibilities in mind, let us return to (26)*a* and (26)*b*, repeated here as (122)*a* and (122)*b*.

(122)   *a* John concluded the argument
      b The argument was concluded by John

The structure of (122)*a* is presumably (123):

(123)

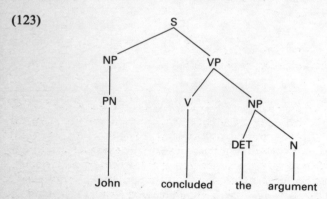

whereas that of (122)*b* is something along the lines of (124).

(124)

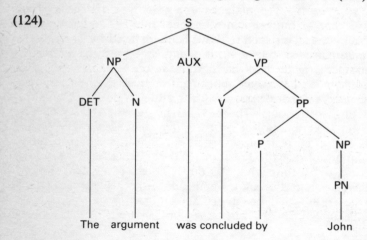

We could of course formulate phrase structure rules to generate
(123) and (124) directly, but an alternative is to let the phrase structure
rules generate (123) only and formulate a transformational rule of
Passive which will convert it into (124). Such a rule will be more
complicated than *Wh*-movement, involving switching the positions of
the two NPs and introducing the preposition *by* and the auxiliary verb
was, but among its benefits would be the formal representation of the
intuition of syntactic relatedness between active and passive sentences.
Similar arguments apply to (27)*a* and (27)*b* and many other sets of

related structures, the result being a plethora of transformational rules operating in tandem with a fairly simple set of phrase structure rules and a lexicon.

Again, the discussion of (14) and (15), repeated here as (124) and (125), is suggestive.

(124)   Linguists are keen to learn
(125)   Linguists are difficult to employ

In connection with (124), we observed that *linguists* is functioning as the subject of the embedded sentence. With the distinction between deep and surface structures now available, we can postulate that (124) has a deep structure in which *linguists* overtly appears as subject of the embedded clause, its appearance as apparent subject of the main clause being due to the operation of a transformational rule which moves it to its position in (124). Similar remarks can be offered in connection with (125).

Finally, the sentence ambiguities which are difficult for a phrase structure account, such as those exhibited by (24) and (25), may also be amenable to a transformational treatment. It could be suggested that such sentences have two distinct deep structures, the differences being obliterated by the operation of various transformational rules. Thus, (24), repeated here as (126), might be related to the two deep structures roughly represented in (127)*a* and (127)*b*.

(126)   John likes linguistics more than Mary
(127)   *a* John likes linguistics more than Mary likes linguistics
        b John likes linguistics more than John likes Mary

Various deletion transformations will operate on these structures to yield (126).

The view that a grammar consists of a *base* (i.e. a set of phrase structure rules and a lexicon) and a set of transformational rules performing a variety of operations (hence the label 'transformational generative grammar') stimulated a great deal of research in psycholinguistics (see Chapter 9) and child language acquisition (see Chapter 10). This notwithstanding, it has come under increasing pressure in the last fifteen years or so. We shall return to the question of why this is so and discussion of more recent approaches in Chapter 8.

Exercises: Chapter 6

1 For each of the following strings of English words, say whether it is ungrammatical, grammatical and unambiguous, or grammatical and ambiguous. Supplement your judgements with brief discussion. For example, if you decide that a string is ambiguous, describe the two meanings; if you decide that a string is ungrammatical, say something about what changes would make it grammatical, and so on.

(*a*) Everyone in the room knows two languages.
(*b*) The boy saw the girl with a telescope.
(*c*) The small plastic block is on the table.
(*d*) French language teachers are usually sexy.
(*e*) The blue bucket is green.
(*f*) Two languages are known by everyone in the room.
(*g*) Each of the men thought that Mary loved the others.
(*h*) The boy saw the girl with a wooden leg.
(*i*) John found the book on the table.
(*j*) John thought that Mary loved himself.
(*k*) The plastic small bucket is on the table.
(*l*) The men thought that Mary loved each other.
(*m*) John thought that Mary loved him.
(*n*) The boy pushed into the crowd was crushed.
(*o*) Mary wonders who John told what to do.
(*p*) Mary wonders who John told to do what.

2 The *cleft construction* is illustrated by the following sentence.

(*a*) It is Mary who John loves Ø

In (*a*) *Mary* is the clefted constituent and, in some sense, originates in the position marked Ø. Furthermore, *Mary* is an NP. That not all constituents can be clefted is illustrated by:

(*b*) *It is intelligent that Mary is Ø

Here, the attempt to cleft the ADJP *intelligent* results in an ungrammatical sentence. Investigate this construction by producing examples to illustrate which constituents can and cannot be clefted.
  The *pseudo-cleft construction* is illustrated by:

(*c*) What John saw Ø was a rat

In (*c*) *a rat* is the pseudo-clefted constituent and, again, in some sense, originates in the position marked Ø. Investigate which constituents can and cannot be pseudo-clefted. Are the possibilities for the cleft and pseudo-cleft constructions the same? What conclusions can be drawn about the autonomy of syntax from your discussion?

3 Provide labelled trees for each of the following sentences.

(*a*) John bought a big green car.
(*b*) The police ran in the park.
(*c*) The police ran in the criminal.
(*d*) John may have seen Mary.
(*e*) John is bigger than Mary.
(*f*) John is more enthusiastic than Mary.
(*g*) John found the book on the table in the cellar.
(*h*) John believes that the economy is in a mess.

Construct a set of phrase structure rules and a lexicon which will generate these sentences with their appropriate structures. What other sentences do your rules generate? Are any of these sentences ungrammatical? Can your rules be modified to prevent the generation of these sentences?

4 In the chapter we have referred to a transformational rule of subject–auxiliary inversion as involved in the derivation of *Wh*-questions. Such a rule is also involved in the derivation of questions which require the answer *yes* or *no*, so-called yes/no questions:

(*a*) Can Mary eat the cake?
(*b*) Will John go to school?
(*c*) May Mary drive the car?
(*d*) Will John have gone to school?

On the basis of data such as the above and any further data you care to consider, formulate the rule of subject–auxiliary inversion. Does your rule enable you to account for a yes/no question which corresponds to a declarative sentence lacking an auxiliary verb, as in (*e*) and (*f*)?

(*e*) John answered the question.
(*f*) Did John answer the question?

5 In English, simple adjectival phrases precede the noun, but complex adjectival phrases follow the noun.

(*a*) The old man
(*b*) *The man old
(*c*) The man angry at his brother
(*d*) *The angry at his brother man

There are at least two alternative ways of approaching such data:

(i) have the phrase structure rules:
     NP ⟶ . . . ADJP – N . . .
     ADJP ⟶ . . . ADJ . . .

     and a transformational rule to postpose complex ADJPs;

(ii)   have the phrase structure rules:
  NP ⟶ . . . N – ADJP . . .
  ADJP ⟶ . . . ADJ . . .

and a transformational rule to prepose simple ADJPs.

Evaluate (i) and (ii). Further data you may care to take into account are:

(e)   The bread on the table
(f)   *The on the table bread
(g)   The boy chasing Mary
(h)   *The chasing Mary boy

6   Produce subcategorisation frames for each of the following English verbs.

(a)   *wonder*, (b) *persuade*, (c) *ask*,
(d)   *believe*, (e) *prefer*, (f) *want*,
(g)   *place*, (h) *tell*, (i) *say*

7   The italicised words in the following examples are among those which pose problems in assigning words to lexical categories in English. Consult a dictionary to see how they are traditionally assigned and discuss whether the techniques introduced in the chapter suggest alternative analyses.

(a)   feet *apart*, (b) *metal* toys,
(c)   a *total* mess, (d) take, *say*, twenty
(e)   *even* an idiot could do that
(f)   I'd *rather* not do that
(g)   he knocked the lid *off*
(h)   the chair is *all* dirty

8   The chapter suggests that English might contain a rule of passivisation which converts the structure in (a) into the structure in (b).

(a)   John concluded the argument.
(b)   The argument was concluded by John.

Taking account of the fact that such a rule must switch the position of two NPs, and introduce the auxiliary verb *was* and the preposition *by*, formulate this rule.
  It seems likely that a similar process is involved in the relationship between the active and passive nominalisations in (c) and (d).

(c)   John's conclusion of the argument
(d)   The argument's conclusion by John

What are the difficulties in reformulating your rule to account for this?

Bibliography: Chapter 6

Chomsky, N., *Syntactic Structures* (The Hague: Mouton, 1957). Contains many examples where the use of transformational devices circumvents difficulties encountered in a constituency account. Hard, though, on first reading.

Harris, Z. S., 'From morpheme to utterance', *Language*, 22 (1946), pp. 161–83. A very dense, because explicit and rigorous, account of the use of distributional criteria in establishing syntactic units.

Jespersen, O., *The Philosophy of Grammar* (London: Allen & Unwin, 1929). Contains interesting discussion, and suggested modifications, of the traditional theory of the parts of speech.

Lyons, J., *Semantics*, Vol. 2 (Cambridge: Cambridge University Press, 1977). Ch. 11 is an outstanding, though difficult, discussion of the usefulness of notional definitions in establishing equivalence of parts of speech across languages. See also Chapter 7.

Matthews, P. H., *Syntax* (Cambridge: Cambridge University Press, 1981). Strong in pointing out areas which pose problems for theoretical approaches, and the shortcomings of many commonly-accepted analyses in syntax.

Perlmutter, D., and Soames, S., *Syntactic Argumentation and the Structure of English* (Berkeley, Calif.: University of California Press, 1979). One of the better introductions to transformational grammar, giving the general flavour of transformational solutions without indulging in excessive formalism. See also Chapter 8.

Quirk, R., Greenbaum, S., Leech, G., and Svartvik, J., *A Grammar of Contemporary English* (London: Longman, 1972). A standard modern reference grammar of English: chs 3–6 present the parts of speech in an essentially traditional way, albeit cautiously.

Radford, A., *Transformational Syntax* (Cambridge: Cambridge University Press, 1981). An excellent, clearly written introduction to Chomsky's syntactic theory. The early chapters are very valuable for an understanding of constituency and the motivation for transformational rules. Later chapters are relevant to the discussion of syntax in Chapter 8.

Wells, R. S., 'Immediate constituents', *Language*, 23 (1947), pp. 81–117. The first detailed account of how to establish immediate constituent structures, and still very useful, although later sections on juncture, etc., can safely be ignored.

Chapter 7

Semantics

7.1 Word-meaning and sentence-meaning

Semantics, that area of linguistics devoted to the study of meaning, enjoys a large set of fundamental and difficult problems. Whereas the subject-matter of phonetics, phonology, morphology and syntax is relatively clear, the domain of investigation met by the student of semantics is steeped in obscurity. The very nature of meaning is elusive and the principal question examined by semanticists has been that of how we are to conceptualise meanings rather than those arising from empirical and descriptive issues. Thus, while recognising the legitimacy of, say, asking whether French has a morpheme corresponding in meaning to English *yellow*, we can also admit that any answer we provide to such a question will be on a firmer basis if it assumes some general theory of meaning.

In studying semantics we quickly confront problems which strike us as philosophical and, indeed, in this chapter ideas first put forward by philosophers will occupy us to a greater extent than any emerging from linguistics. In addition, because it is not clear that any distinction can be drawn between a system of concepts or ideas and a system of meanings, we find psychologists making claims which have to be interpreted as having semantic relevance (see Chapter 9). Again, starting from an interest in systems of conceptualisation and their relationship to the culture in which they are embedded, some of the most detailed descriptive work in semantics has been carried out by anthropologists working on 'exotic' languages. It would be remarkable if, out of this diverse and far-ranging collection of intellectual enterprise, a common methodology and theoretical foundation for semantics had emerged. The fact that it has not should not occasion despair. Undoubtedly the system of meanings which our native language makes available to us is closely linked to the way in which we think and the way in which we perceive the world. That problems in these areas have concerned the greatest minds since Antiquity without yielding ready solutions should allow us to applaud what has been achieved.

Broadly speaking, in what follows we shall distinguish between views on the meanings of words and ideas which have been developed in connection with the meanings of *sentences*. This is not to suggest that other linguistic units, e.g. noun phrases or subordinate clauses, are not subject to semantic investigation. Indeed, we shall sometimes allude to such constructs in the course of the chapter. Our decision is simply a reflection of the fact that most semantic theories adopt either the word or the sentence as the primary object of investigation. Most important, it must be perfectly clear that the decision to begin with either words or sentences does not excuse a semantic theory from saying something about the unchosen alternative. A theory of the meanings of words which did not also contribute to our understanding of the meanings of sentences, while significant, would rightly be viewed as incomplete, and similarly for a theory of the meanings of sentences. This is because word-meanings and sentence-meanings, no matter how we construe them, are closely related.

To see this we have only to note that, if we replace a word in a sentence with another word having a different meaning, we thereby change the meaning of the sentence. That (1) and (2) have different meanings can be put down entirely to the fact that (1) contains *hate* where (2) contains *love*.

(1) Men hate gnomes
(2) Men love gnomes

In general, we shall require an adequate semantic theory to satisfy a *Principle of Compositionality* which insists that the meanings of sentences (and other linguistic expressions consisting of more than one word, such as noun phrases) are understood in terms of the meanings of their component words and, equivalently, the meanings of words are understood in terms of the contributions they make to the meanings of the sentences in which they occur.

The Principle of Compositionality demands that the meanings of sentences depend on the meanings of their component words, and we may immediately ask whether this is all they depend on. That this is not so is easily demonstrated by (3) and (4).

(3) The man in the garden despises the gnome
(4) The gnome in the garden despises the man

These sentences contain exactly the same words but they are clearly different in meaning. So, in addition to the meanings of the component words, the meanings of sentences are going to depend upon the way in which the words are put together, i.e. on the syntax of sentences. The example above illustrates the interaction of the syntactic device of word-order with sentence-meaning and further examples show that other, more abstract, aspects of syntactic structure also have a role to play. Thus (5) is ambiguous, and which meaning it has depends on whether we have the bracketing of (6) or (7) (see Chapter 6).

(5) Nineteenth-century philosophers and linguists are dull to read
(6) [[[Nineteenth-century] [philosophers]] and [linguists]] [are dull to read]
(7) [[Nineteenth-century] [[philosophers] and [linguists]]] [are dull to read]

This leads to the conclusion that the Principle of Compositionality must have access to the constituent structure of a sentence as well as to the linear order of its component words. That still more abstract aspects of syntactic structure must be taken into account directly follows from an inspection of the examples of ambiguity on p. 159 (Chapter 6), and it is clear that an approach to semantics developed in conjunction with an explicit syntactic theory will be the only one capable of meeting the requirement of relating the meanings of words to the meanings of the sentences in which they occur.

There are two reasons for wishing to keep theories of word-meaning and sentence-meaning apart, at least initially. The first is the purely exegetical one that the semantic properties of words and sentences are, with one or two exceptions, distinct and, correspondingly, there are distinct sets of technical terms for talking about them. The second reason is that theories of meaning starting from words have often taken seriously the question of what meanings *are* and have attempted to pair with each expression in the language something which is that expression's meaning. A more modest, and, some would say, more reasonable goal for a semantic theory is that of predicting the semantic properties of expressions without embracing anything in the theory which can be seen as the meaning of the expressions. This, although not without exception, has been the path chosen by those who have started their deliberations with sentences. That this task is non-trivial can easily be seen from the fact that there is an infinite number of expressions in a language which require semantic analysis (cf. the arguments in Chapter 2 on grammaticality). Therefore, such a theory must produce an infinite number of statements ascribing semantic properties to expressions, and, at the same time, it must, of course, be finitely statable (see p. 212 below).

7.2 Semantic properties and relations of words

There is one distinction which is often drawn in the literature which we shall not discuss in detail but which we mention here so that the reader is aware of it. This is the distinction between *descriptive*, *referential*, or *cognitive* meaning, on the one hand, and *emotive*, *expressive*, or *social* meaning on the other. It is best illustrated by an example. Our pre-theoretical intuitions might tell us that (8) and (9) are similar in meaning in certain respects, while differing in other respects.

(8) My friend likes Paris
(9) My mate likes Paris

This similarity and difference in meaning can be traced directly to the similarity and difference in the meanings of the words *friend* and *mate*, and it is this response to the sentences that the above distinction is designed to label. Accordingly, (8) and (9) are said to be identical in descriptive (referential, cognitive) meaning, hence our feeling of similarity, while differing in emotive (expressive, social) meaning, hence our feeling of difference. Exactly how to draw the line between descriptive and expressive meaning and, indeed, whether we are correct to try is a difficult question. The German philosopher G. Frege, manipulating what we can regard as an identical distinction between *sense* and *tone*, suggested that if an expression, recognisably different in meaning from another, could, nevertheless, be substituted for it in a sentence in which it occurred without changing the truth-value of the sentence, i.e. without turning a true sentence into a false sentence or vice versa, and if this substitution could be performed in this way for every sentence in which the first expression can occur, then the two expressions should be regarded as identical in sense and differing in tone. Thus, if (8) is true so is (9), and if (8) is false, (9) is also false. Furthermore, the same goes for any sentence-pairs differing only in that one contains *mate* where the other contains *friend*; by Frege's criterion, *friend* and *mate* are identical in sense but differ in tone.

Something like this criterion has been adopted by most writers on semantics and its appropriateness will not concern us further here. Without suggesting that expressive meaning is unimportant, we shall assume that the primary subject-matter of semantics is descriptive meaning and take it that *friend* and *mate*, along with similar pairs of words, have the same meaning.

A most obvious semantic property, which is taken for granted by the above discussion, is that of 'having meaning'. There are no words in a language which lack meaning and, of course, meaning has often entered crucially into the definition of the morpheme (Chapter 5). It might be immediately objected that 'function words' such as *a*, *the*, *of*, *for*, *if*, *although* have no meaning and certainly if we are attempting to identify something which could be the meaning of one of these words, it is difficult to see what this 'something' could be. However, once we take the Principle of Compositionality seriously, it becomes evident that such function words are meaningful, at least to the extent that they make distinctive semantic contributions to the expressions in which they occur. We only have to compare such phrases as *a book* and *the book*, or *jar of jam* and *jar for jam*, or the sentences, (10) and (11), and note that the members of each pair differ in meaning.

(10)   Although John went to London he would not have gone to Paris
(11)   If John went to London he would not have gone to Paris

This difference can only be put down to the choice of *a* or *the*, *for* or *of*
and *although* or *if*. It may well be that we cannot assign meanings to
these words when we consider them in isolation and we may wish to go
so far as to say that they lack significance under these conditions (the
technical term for this property is *syncategorematic*), but this is not to
say that they are exempt from semantic treatment. Having meaning,
then, can be seen as setting a lower bound for a comprehensive
semantic theory. Such a theory must treat everything which has meaning; all words have meaning and therefore the theory must, in principle, be applicable to all words. Where we set the upper bound for
semantic theory will be discussed in Section 6 below.
   A very general semantic relation is 'similarity of meaning'. Consider
the sets of words in (12)*a–e*.

(12)   a   *cow*, *horse*, *tiger*, *animal*, *dormouse*
       b   *vehicle*, *car*, *bus*, *tandem*, *van*
       c   *chemistry*, *science*, *meteorology*, *physics*, *astronomy*
       d   *tree*, *forest*, *bower*, *wood*, *copse*
       e   *yellow*, *red*, *puce*, *violet*, *green*

It is immediately apparent that each of these sets comprise part of a
natural grouping of English words and, to this extent, we might say that
the words in each set are similar in meaning. Some semanticists talk
about this idea of similarity in meaning in terms of *semantic fields*.
Thus, the words in each of (12)*a–e* are viewed as covering a distinct
semantic field: animals, vehicles, sciences, 'woody' things and colours.
   The notion of semantic field has proved particularly useful in
examining historical change in systems of meanings and in semantic
comparisons of different languages. An example provided by the
Danish linguist L. Hjelmslev will show how this is so. He considers the
semantic field of 'woody' things for Danish, German and French,
presenting the results of his deliberations as in Figure 7.1. From this it
is apparent that the three languages segment this semantic field in
different ways. German and French are similar in that they both have
forms used to refer to single trees, woods and forests. They differ in
that *Holz* in German will be used of bigger woods than will *bois* in
French. Danish differs from both French and German in having a
single form, *træ*, used for single trees and small woods.
   One immediate implication of this is that translation from one
language to another is often impossible without some knowledge of
what is being talked about. It is not enough for a translator of Danish to
German to know simply that his text contains an instance of *træ*; he

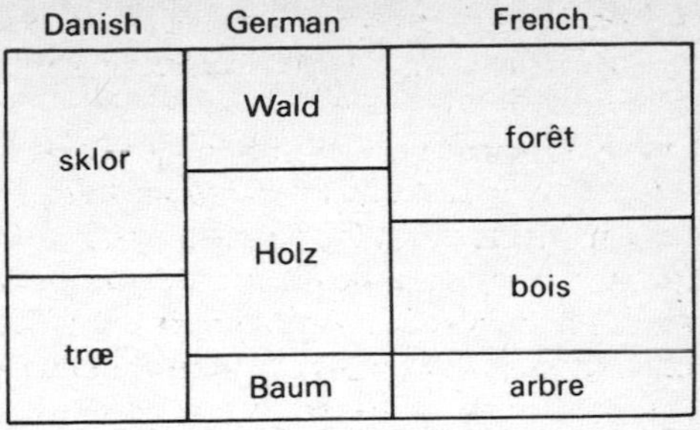

	Danish	German	French
		Wald	forêt
	sklor		
		Holz	bois
	træ	Baum	arbre

Figure 7.1 *The semantic field of 'woody' things in Danish, German and French.*

Source: L. Hjelmslev, *Prolegomena to a Theory of Language* (Madison, Wis.: University of Wisconsin Press, 1961), p. 54.

must also know whether, in using the word, the Danish speaker or writer was talking about a single tree or a small group of trees. An important question concerns whether languages can segment experience in an unconstrained way or whether there are universal principles governing this process (see Chapter 9, Section 10).

Two difficulties must be raised in connection with similarity of meaning and the associated notion of semantic field. The first is that similarity itself is a relative notion and, even if we consider the set of words in (13), it could be argued that their meanings are similar in certain respects.

(13) *cow, vehicle, tree*

We might, for example, maintain that they are each used in connection with concrete objects, contrasting, in this respect, with words such as *virtue, beauty* and *number*, and accordingly see them as constituting part of a semantic field. There is no obvious way in which we can counter this sort of suggestion and it seems necessary, therefore, to require that a semantic theory treat similarity of meaning as a relative notion, indicating that, for example, *cow* is more similar in meaning to *horse* than it is to *vehicle*. The second point, not unrelated to the first, is that there is no precise definition of the idea of semantic field. Worse, a quite different sort of semantic relationship from that of similarity of meaning has been seen by some authors as defining semantic fields. The reader may have noticed that in (12)*a–e* the words in each set come from the same syntactic class; the examples in (12)*a–d* are all nouns and those in (12)*e*, adjectives (ignoring the fact that the colour words can also be used as nouns). Now, membership in the same syntactic class partly depends upon substitutability in sentence-frames and, because of this, we can say that the semantic fields we have discussed so far are generated by *paradigmatic* semantic relations between words (see Chapter 4, p. 106, for a discussion of the notions 'paradigmatic' and 'syntagmatic'). But now consider the sets of words in (14).

(14) a *bark*, *dog*
　　 b *mew*, *cat*
　　 c *rancid*, *butter*

Once again, it seems reasonable to say that they are semantically related, although not, in this case, semantically similar. To appreciate the semantic relatedness we need only contemplate giving the meaning of *bark* verbally without using *dog* or giving the meaning of *rancid* without mentioning *butter*. In these cases, though, the words do not belong to the same syntactic class and the relationship between them is a *syntagmatic* one. The pairs of words in (14) typically co-occur in syntactic constructions (*dogs bark*, *rancid butter*) rather than entering into paradigmatic oppositions with each other. To say that the sets of words in (14) also define semantic fields removes what little precise content this latter notion has, and so, while recognising the existence of syntagmatic semantic relations, we shall confine our attention to paradigmatic relations in what follows.

Synonymy is, perhaps, the best-known paradigmatic semantic relation and can be seen as a limiting case of similarity of meaning. Two words are synonymous if and only if they are identical in descriptive meaning (see p. 191). Following from our earlier discussion we can say that *friend* and *mate* are synonymous as well as better-known examples such as *nag*, *horse* and *steed*, or *liberty* and *freedom*.

Pairs of words which are opposite in meaning are a pervasive feature of the semantic structure of any language. In English there are many clear cases of a word having a single opposite, e.g. *wide* and *narrow*, *male* and *female*, as well as words with two opposites, e.g. *married* has the two synonymous opposites *unmarried* and *single*, of which the first is morphologically complex. In addition, there are cases of words which have two senses and there is an opposite corresponding to each sense. For example, *old* has the opposites *young* and *new* which, of course, are not synonymous.

Oppositeness of meaning has been extensively analysed and shown to admit a number of subtypes, just two of which we shall mention here. Consider the pairs of opposites, *married* and *single* and *wide* and *narrow*. Assume that there is a set of objects to which the adjectives *married* and *single* can be applied without absurdity. These adjectives cannot be applied to stones, numbers, or kangaroos but they can be applied to a class of human beings belonging to cultures which recognise an institution of marriage. For objects in the set to which the adjectives can be applied, we say that the adjectives are *predicable* of the objects. Similarly, for *wide* and *narrow*, we can consider the set of things of which they are predicable. In this case, we can talk about rectangles, buses and tree-trunks as being wide or narrow, but such talk in connection with virtues or numbers strikes us as bizarre. It is with reference to these sets of predicables that the differences between our two pairs of opposites emerge. In the case of the set of which *married* and *single* are predicable, it is true to say that *every* member of the set is either married or single. There is no appropriate member (i.e. excluding children up to a certain age) of a human society recognising marriage who is neither married nor single. However, for the set of which *wide* and *narrow* are predicable, there are objects which are neither wide nor narrow. Diagrammatically, the situation can be represented as in Figure 7.2 where the left-hand circle represents the set of objects of which *married* and *single* are predicable and the right-hand circle does the same thing for *wide* and *narrow*.

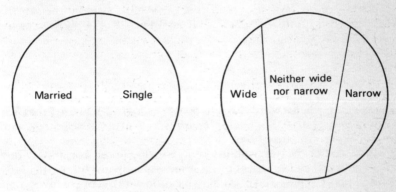

Figure 7.2 *Different types of oppositeness.*

There are further facts concerning our adjective pairs which follow from the above distinction. *Wide* and *narrow* can be used in explicit comparisons as in (15).

(15) *a* The bridge is wider than the river
      b The sofa is narrower than three fat ladies

However, a comparison involving *married* and *single* requires a special interpretation. Thus, if someone were to utter (16), they would be taken to mean that Peter showed more of the behaviour typically associated with being married than Paul did and not that Peter was further through the marriage ceremony than Paul.

(16) Peter is more married than Paul

Because these pairs of opposites behave in such different ways, it is desirable to introduce special terminology for them and the British linguist John Lyons refers to pairs like *married* and *single* as *complementaries*, while pairs like *wide* and *narrow*, he calls *antonyms*. The corresponding semantic relations are *complementarity* and *antonymy* and we should note that this latter term is used by many authors as a cover term for all cases of oppositeness of meaning.

The semantic relation of *hyponymy* can be seen as imposing a hierarchical structure on sections of the vocabulary of a language. If we consider the domain of fish, we say that *trout*, *shark*, *eel*, etc., are hyponyms of *fish*; we can represent this in the form of a tree.

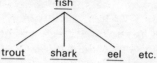

Similarly, for the domain of 'getting', we can say that *buy*, *borrow*, *steal*, etc., are hyponyms of *get*, representing this as follows.

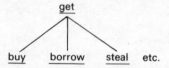

In general, when a word X is a hyponym of a word Y, we say that Y is a *superordinate* of X. For example, *fish* is a superordinate of *trout* and *get* is a superordinate of *buy*.

The extent of the applicability of hyponymy in the vocabulary of a language is difficult to assess but it is undoubtedly useful, particularly in the areas of animal and plant classification, and of course taxonomic structures such as we find here need not be restricted to two levels. As well as *trout* being a hyponym of *fish*, the latter is itself a hyponym of *animal*, and we can construct a three-level taxonomy.

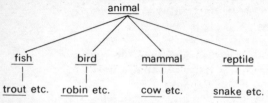

The list of semantic properties and relations for words which must be taken account of by a semantic theory could be extended considerably, but the ones we have introduced here provide a useful yard-stick against which we can evaluate theoretical proposals.

7.3 Semantic properties and relations of sentences

There is a number of interrelated properties and relations concerning the semantics of sentences which depend crucially on our understanding something about when a sentence is true or false, i.e. something about the *truth-conditions* of a sentence.

A property which has received a great deal of attention in the philosophical literature is that of *analyticity*. A sentence is said to be analytic if it is true by virtue of the meanings of the words which comprise it (and, of course, the syntax of the sentence). It follows from this that, no matter what the world happens to be like, so long as words have their usual significance, an analytic sentence will be true. Arguments have been advanced, most notably by the American philosopher W. V. Quine, against the cogency of the distinction between analytic and *synthetic* (true or false by virtue of the meanings of words, syntax of the sentence *and* the way the world is) sentences, but it is not our purpose to review these here. Rather, we can simply note that a sentence like (17), while true of the world as we know it, might not have been.

(17) London is the biggest city in England

In this respect, it contrasts with the putatively analytic sentences in (18).

(18) *a* Bachelors are unmarried men
      b Bachelors are unmarried
      c Bachelors are men

Entailment is, perhaps, the most important relation between sentences. Given two sentences, S_1 and S_2, we say that S_1 entails S_2 if and only if, whenever S_1 is true, S_2 is also true. According to this definition, it is impossible for S_1 to be true and S_2 false. Examples of entailment are provided in (19)–(22) where, in each case, the *a* sentence entails the *b* sentence.

(19) *a* John has an elm in his garden
      b John has a tree in his garden
(20) *a* John is not married
      b John is single
(21) *a* John managed to close the door
      b John closed the door
(22) *a* John failed to close the door
      b John did not close the door

Two remarks can be made in connection with these examples. First, in some cases, the relation of entailment holding between the sentences clearly depends upon a semantic relation holding between words which appear in the sentences. The fact that (19)*a* entails (19)*b* is a reflex of the fact that *elm* is a hyponym of *tree* and the complementarity of *married* and *single* underlies the relation between (20)*a* and (20)*b*. That such a reduction is not always possible, however, is shown by (21) and (22). The second point is that, again only in some cases, e.g. (20), we can reverse the entailment relation: (20)*b* entails (20)*a* just as (20)*a* entails (20)*b*. In such cases we say that the two mutually entailing sentences are *logically equivalent*. In (19), of course, we cannot reverse the entailment and the fact that our intuitions do not always provide ready answers for us in this area is demonstrated by (21) and (22). If John closed the door must it also be true that he *managed* to close the door (assume that he did it without much effort)? There is a temptation to identify logical equivalence with *synonymy* between sentences, and certainly for (20) this would appear to be an appropriate step. However, in general, our pre-theoretical intuitions about synonymy would argue against this move, as the pairs of sentences in (23) and (24) are logically equivalent but not, many would say, synonymous.

(23) *a* John bought a parrot from Nancy
      b Nancy sold John a parrot
(24) *a* The biscuit is under the tin
      b The tin is on top of the biscuit

The alternative, of course, is to reject our pre-theoretical intuitions and say that, for example, (23)*a* and (23)*b* are synonymous; but we will not explore this possibility further here.

A further relation between sentences which is definable in terms of entailment is *presupposition*. S_1 presupposes S_2 if and only if, whenever S_1 is either true or false, then S_2 is true. Equivalently, we can say that S_1 presupposes S_2 if and only if both S_1 and its negation entail S_2 or, and again equivalently, S_1 presupposes S_2 if and only if S_2 being true is a necessary condition for S_1 having a truth-value (i.e. being either true or false). To illustrate this, consider the sentences in (25).

(25) *a* It bothers John that garden gnomes are ghastly
      b Garden gnomes are ghastly

Assume that (25)*a* is true. It seems to follow immediately that (25)*b* is also true. One cannot be bothered by something which is false. Now assume that (25)*a* is false. Arguably, and this is much more controversial, it again follows that (25)*b* is true. So, (25)*a* presupposes (25)*b* according to the first definition. Equivalently, we can say that (25)*a* entails (25)*b* from our definition of entailment and, again arguably, that the negation of (25)*a*, i.e. (26), also entails (25)*b*.

(26) It doesn't bother John that garden gnomes are ghastly

Furthermore, if (25)*b* is false, there seems to be some force to the view that (25)*a* is neither true nor false but somehow out of place. This amounts to saying that the truth of (25)*b* is a necessary condition for (25)*a* having a truth-value. Further examples which have been taken to demonstrate presupposition as a semantic phenomenon appear in (27)–(30) where, in each case, the claim is that the *a* sentence presupposes the *b* sentence.

(27) *a* The book is on the table
      b There is a book
(28) *a* The book is on the table
      b There is a table
(29) *a* John walks slowly
      b John walks
(30) *a* The gnome you saw in the shop is a garden gnome
      b You saw a gnome in the shop

Presupposition is a controversial notion (although its definition is impeccable) and there is a great deal of disagreement as to its status within a comprehensive linguistic theory. The definitions we have given above are often contrasted with an alternative view of presupposition where it is seen, not as a relation between sentences, but as a relation between *speakers* and sentences (see Section 6 below).

It is our claim that a semantic theory, whether it be primarily addressed to words or sentences, will ultimately be judged in its recognition of the Principle of Compositionality and in its treatment of semantic properties and relations of words, sets of words, sentences and sets of sentences, including those we have briefly introduced here.

7.4 Theories of word-meaning

If we ask what the meaning of a word is, one initially plausible answer might be that it is that object or objects in the world to which the word is used to refer, an answer which has the virtue of relating meanings to relatively familiar things, namely, objects. Thus, restricting our attention for the moment to proper names, for which the most plausible case can be made, we might suggest that the meaning of *Everest* is simply that lump of rock which happens to be the highest mountain in the world and the meaning of *London* is that city which is the capital of the United Kingdom. Such a suggestion is not immediately unattractive and we can contemplate extending it to other grammatical classes along the following lines. If we take a common noun, say, *cow*, there is no single object to which the word refers. Nevertheless, there is a set of objects which are cows and we might try equating the meaning of *cow* with this set. Similarly for an adjective like *yellow* or *beautiful*, we could postulate abstract objects, yellowness and beauty, as their meanings, or, more comfortably, we can equate the meaning of *yellow* with the set of things which happen to be yellow and the meaning of *beautiful* with the set of beautiful 'things'. A similar tactic could be used for intransitive verbs like *walk*, and for transitive verbs we can take as the meaning the set of all *pairs* of objects such that the first is the subject and the second a direct object in a true sentence using the transitive verb. Thus, the pair of objects (John, Mary) will belong to the meaning of *love* just in case John loves Mary.

A first objection to this proposal is that, despite being attractive in reducing the problematic notion of meaning to the familiar idea of object, it appears to be wrong in a very basic way. Taking proper names as our model, we merely note that mountains can be climbed and cities lived in. It seems a serious conceptual confusion to suggest that the same is true of meanings; yet this is what the meaning-as-object view demands. Lack of pre-theoretical plausibility has rarely been a deterrent in philosophy but, in this case, it is not difficult to find several equally compelling reasons for wanting to reject our first theory.

Consider the class of syncategorematic words we have already introduced (p. 192). As there is no object and no set of objects corresponding to, say, *of* or *for*, the only conclusion we can draw from this theory is that they are meaningless; but we have seen that such a conclusion is intolerable. A response which says that they *are* syncategorematic, only contributing to the meanings of expressions in which they occur and not having meaning in isolation, will have to face up to the Principle of Compositionality, and, to see the general problem this raises, consider the noun phrase *the present Prime Minister of the United Kingdom*. The meaning of this phrase, according to the theory, at the time of writing, will be Mrs Thatcher (the woman), and this meaning must be somehow dependent on the meanings of the component words and their syntax. The meanings of the component words will include the meanings of *Prime Minister* (a set of individuals) and of *United Kingdom* (a land and sea mass), treating these as simple words, which will be operated on in some way by *the*, *present* and *of* to yield Mrs Thatcher. But all of this is impossibly vague and the necessary machinery has never been spelled out. Note further, in connection with this example, that the theory would appear to demand that the meaning of the phrase changes whenever there is a change in the holder of the office. But this is incorrect.

With some semantic relations such as hyponymy the theory fares reasonably well, the relation being explicated by a subset relation between the meanings of the words which are in the hyponymy relation. Taking our earlier observation that *cow* is a hyponym of *animal*, we can see that this corresponds to the fact that the meaning of *cow* (the set of all cows) is a subset of the meaning of *animal* (the set of all animals). However, the theory's failure with regard to synonymy is well known. Frege used the examples of *Venus* and *the morning star* to demonstrate that two expressions might refer to the same object (in this case, the planet Venus) without being identical in meaning. The point raised above that the meaning of *the present Prime Minister of the United Kingdom* does not change with a change in the person holding office indicates, in conjunction with Frege's argument, that sameness of reference is neither a necessary nor a sufficient condition for sameness of meaning.

The conclusion Frege himself drew from such arguments was that it is necessary to distinguish between *sense* (already contrasted with *tone*, p. 191) and *reference*. According to this distinction, *Venus* and *the morning star*, while identical in reference, differ in sense. Thus, the study of meaning becomes the study of sense, but of course our understanding of the latter has not been advanced at this stage beyond our realising that it cannot be identified with the study of reference.

An approach to word-meanings which does not suffer from the problem raised by Frege is that which identifies the meaning of a word or a longer expression with an *idea* or *concept*. It seems intuitively correct to say that someone who has mastered the meaning of a word has become acquainted with some sort of idea or mental construct. Nor does it follow from the fact that *Venus* and *the morning star* refer to the same object that the ideas corresponding to these expressions are identical. The problem is not that a theory of meanings-as-ideas is clearly wrong, but rather that such a theory does not seem to take us anywhere. To illustrate: if two words are synonymous, we shall require that the ideas which are their meanings be identical. But how can we know that this is so without some independent hold on the ideas we are manipulating? Unfortunately, unlike objects, ideas are just as mysterious as meanings. Again, for oppositeness of meaning (of any variety) we can say that two words are opposite in meaning just in case the ideas which are their meanings are suitably opposed. But what is this opposition between ideas and how could we know that two ideas were opposed in this way? Identical considerations apply for hyponymy, and it rapidly becomes clear that the view that meanings are ideas has hardly deepened our understanding of semantic relations. Further difficult problems arise for syncategorematic words and for the Principle of Compositionality. To say that there is a difficult-to-define idea associated with *of* is to say no more than that the meaning of *of* is difficult to define; to say that component ideas are somehow associated to yield complex ideas is to say nothing more than that the meanings of words are somehow combined to give the meanings of sentences.

The meaning-as-object view can be seen as one attempt to get away from talk of ideas in this connection. Another such attempt was promoted by Leonard Bloomfield in his book *Language*. Couched in the language of behaviourist psychology (see Chapter 2), Bloomfield's position is best illustrated by his own example. We are asked to imagine Jack and Jill walking down a road and Jill is hungry. She sees an apple on a tree and utters *I'm hungry*. Jack climbs the tree, gets the apple, gives it to Jill and she eats it. Bloomfield is concerned with the meaning of *I'm hungry* and argues that this should be identified with the stimulus conditions existing before the utterance – these will include light reflected from the apple impinging on Jill's retinae and gastric secretions in her stomach, and the responses following the utterance – these will include Jack's climbing the tree and giving the apple to Jill, and Jill's eating the apple. In general, if an utterance is flanked by certain relevant stimuli and responses, these are seen as the meaning of the utterance.

Bloomfield's example uses a syntactically structured utterance but, as he says nothing about how different aspects of the stimulus situation and ensuing responses are to be assigned to the meanings of the different parts of the utterance, it seems fair to see him as treating it as an unanalysed semantic whole and, in a sense, equivalent to a single word. This, of course, immediately amounts to a criticism from the point of view of the Principle of Compositionality, but there are several other grounds for seeing the theory as hopelessly confused. Intolerable vagueness surrounds the question as to what stimuli and responses qualify for entry into the meaning of the utterance. In the Jack and Jill story we can imagine that, as well as seeing the apple and feeling hungry, Jill has a toothache and that, as well as climbing the tree and giving the apple to Jill, Jack scratches his ear. No criteria are presented for ruling out these possible aspects of the situation from the meaning of *I'm hungry*. Turning to synonymy, it is difficult to see that two synonymous expressions will always be accompanied by the same stimulus situation and ensuing responses. The limiting case of this is exhibited if we consider two distinct utterances of *I'm hungry* in different circumstances which have different consequences: Jack does not have to climb the tree in order for Jill's utterance to mean that Jill is hungry, nor does the sentence mean something else if Jack does not climb the tree. Oppositeness of meaning and hyponymy offer little comfort to this position. It is simply not clear what aspects of stimuli and responses could reliably be associated with these semantic relations. This is because it is not clear that *any* aspect of situation or ensuing behaviour is reliably associated with any but the most stereotyped utterances such as greetings.

Each of the positions we have discussed so far originated outside linguistics. Meanings-as-objects and meanings-as-ideas have been examined by philosophers, while Bloomfield's views have their origins in the writings of the behaviourist psychologist A. P. Weiss. The theory with which we conclude this section, however, is firmly anchored in linguistics and holds that the meaning of a word can be broken down into components, variously referred to as *semantic components*, *semantic features*, *semantic primes*, or *semantic markers*. These constructs are expressions in a theoretical vocabulary and so, according to this view, the meanings of words are complex expressions in a theoretical language which uses this vocabulary.

We have already seen (Chapter 4) that one of Trubetzkoy's important insights in phonology was the recognition of *proportional oppositions*, which provided one of the foundations for the theory of phonological distinctive features. In some areas of the vocabulary of English it is possible to examine proportional 'equations' which have a semantic basis, as in (31).

(31) *man : woman : child = bull : cow : calf = stallion : mare : foal*

Evidently, a native speaker of English 'knows' that the semantic relationship between *man* and *woman* is the same as that between *bull* and *cow* and as that between *stallion* and *mare*. It seems reasonable to suggest that this is because the pairs of words contrast along the same semantic dimension and we can implement this suggestion by saying that, whereas the meanings of *man*, *bull* and *stallion* include a component +MALE (or −FEMALE), the meanings of *woman*, *cow* and *mare* include −MALE (or +FEMALE). Pursuing this line of thought for the nine words in (31) might yield the results of Table 7.1, where

Table 7.1   *Componential Analysis of Some English Vocabulary*

man:	+MALE	+HUMAN,	+ADULT	
woman:	−MALE,	+HUMAN,	+ADULT	
child:		+HUMAN,	−ADULT	
bull:	+MALE,	−HUMAN,	+ADULT,	+BOVINE
cow:	−MALE,	−HUMAN,	+ADULT,	+BOVINE
calf:		−HUMAN,	−ADULT,	+BOVINE
stallion:	+MALE,	−HUMAN,	+ADULT,	−BOVINE
mare:	−MALE,	−HUMAN,	+ADULT,	−BOVINE
foal:		−HUMAN,	−ADULT,	−BOVINE

each of the features has the function of distinguishing the meanings of at least two words.

One obvious question we can ask in connection with the above procedure concerns its generality. It is readily apparent that the sort of proportional 'equations' we have used in (31) are not available for most areas of the vocabulary of English. Consider the set of words in (32) drawn from the 'furniture vocabulary' of English.

(32) *table, chair, bed, drawers, carpet, sofa*

There is no obvious way in which we can approach the components of meaning of these words. To some extent, this is also true in the analysis of kinship terminology, where *componential analysis*, as the approach we are discussing is known, has found its widest application. To overcome this problem, anthropologists working in this area have resorted to a different methodology, which involves listing all instances of the applicability of a term and then trying to *infer* a set of semantic dimensions which can be seen as underlying the system under analysis. For English kinship vocabulary, such a procedure might yield the listing of Table 7.2. Note that this method assumes that we can identify the basic biological relationships involved in specifying the set of instances and, while Table 7.2 gives us some fairly unspectacular

Table 7.2 *The Applicability of English Kinship Terms*

Term	Domain of Applicability	Term	Domain of Applicability
father	Fa	*husband*	Hu
mother	Mo	*wife*	Wi
grandfather	FaFa, MoFa	*uncle*	FaBr, MoBr, FaSiHu, MoSiHu
grandmother	FaMo, MoMo	*aunt*	FaSi, MoSi, FaBrWi, MoBrWi
son	So	*nephew*	BrSo, SiSo, WiBrSo, WiSiSo, HuBrSo, HuSiSo
daughter	Da	*niece*	BrDa, SiDa, WiBrDa, WiSiDa, HuBrDa, HuSiDa
grandson	SoSo, DaSo	*cousin*	MoBrSo, MoBrDa, MoSiSo
grand-daughter	SoDa, DaDa		MoSiDa, FaBrSo, FaSiSo
brother	Br		FaBrDa, FaSiDa
sister	Si		

Note: 'XY' is read as X's Y, 'XYZ' as X's Y's Z.

Key: Fa = father, Mo = mother, So = son, Da = daughter, Br = brother, Si = sister, Hu = husband, Wi = wife.

results, more surprising kinship-systems are quite common (see Exercise 8 to this chapter for an example).

Inspection of Table 7.2 rapidly reveals that sex is an important semantic dimension in the English kinship-system, distinguishing *father* from *mother*, *son* from *daughter*, etc., and so we are justified in postulating a feature ±MALE. Generation is also important, as in the distinction between *father* and *grandfather* and between *nephew* and *uncle*. To accommodate this we might introduce a five-valued feature, $-2G, -1G, 0G, +1G, +2G$, such that the meaning of *father* includes $+1G$, that of *sister*, $0G$, that of *grandson*, $-2G$, and so on. Alternatively, we could introduce a three-valued feature, $0G, 1G, 2G$, such that the words for both grandparents and grandchildren would include $2G$ in their meanings, those for parents, immediate offspring, uncles, aunts, nephews and nieces, $1G$, and those for siblings, spouses and cousins, $0G$. If we adopt this move, we still have to distinguish, say, *grandson* from *grandfather*, by introducing a binary feature ±OLDER-THAN-SELF, with *grandfather* being +OLDER-THAN-SELF and *grandson* being −OLDER-THAN-SELF. Thus, part of the work of one five-valued feature is being carried out by one three-valued feature and one binary feature. Now, although neither of the above analyses is intended to be complete, they do pose an important question: as far as they go, which of them is correct?

This question has been seen by some anthropologists as constituting a methodological crisis for componential analysis. One way to deal with it is to dispute its legitimacy, arguing that correctness is not at issue but merely elegance of description, with the features lacking any significance outside the system in which they are employed. This position, already introduced in Chapter 4, is known as the *hocus-pocus* view and opposed to it is the view which glamorises the features with the label 'psychologically real', a variant of the *God's truth* view, and attempts to get some independent leverage on the status of the features via psychological experimentation. The use of proportional 'equations' with which we introduced this discussion could be seen as providing some informal evidence of this nature. Some anthropologists have taken this route with modest success, although linguists such as J. Katz and M. Bierwisch, attempting to develop comprehensive semantic theories using semantic features, have contented themselves with expressing the belief that such features will ultimately be grounded in a theory of human cognition.

Putting these questions aside for the moment, we can ask how semantic feature theory fares as a theory of word-meaning for the properties and relations of Section 2 above. As far as the general notion of relatedness of meaning is concerned, we would simply anticipate some overlap in the sets of features comprising the meanings of the related words and this is clearly the case in Table 7.1. Also similarity of meaning would emerge as a relative notion, as there could be more or less overlap between sets of features. Synonymy would be explicated by identity of feature sets, and for oppositeness of meaning it seems plausible to suggest that, if two words are opposite in meaning, then there will be a feature such that it appears positively specified in the meaning of one of the words and negatively specified in the meaning of the other. Additional machinery would, of course, be necessary in order to distinguish between the different sorts of oppositeness of meaning discussed in Section 2 above. Hyponymy too has a straightforward interpretation, whereby we can say that one word is a hyponym of another if and only if the set of features associated with the superordinate is a subset of the set of features associated with the hyponym. Thus, we would predict that *trout* would have included in its meaning all the features associated with *fish* plus some additional ones – we can only speculate on the nature of these – which give the 'specialised' part of the meaning of *trout*.

On the whole, the theory of semantic features does well, but we would like to close this section by raising a problem for such a theory and examining some of the implications of this problem.

Taking the view that a set of semantic features constitutes the meaning of each word in a language, we can inquire about the relationship between the set of features and the *extension* of words, i.e. the class of objects of which the word can be truly predicated. It seems reasonable to suggest that the set of features provides necessary and sufficient conditions for an object falling in this extension. If we go back to our analysis of *man* as [+MALE, +HUMAN, +ADULT], this amounts to claiming that if anything is a man, then it is also male, human and adult, i.e. the features are singly necessary, and failure to satisfy any one of them will discount something from being a man. Furthermore, if something is male, human and adult, that suffices for it to be a man, i.e. the features are jointly sufficient. It is debatable whether this connection between meaning and extension is one all componential semanticists would subscribe to, but certainly the anthropological linguists, with their methodology of beginning from a set of instances in the extension of a word and attempting to infer properties which are true of just those instances, would appear to be committed to this position. So assume, adopting the tone of Chapter 2 and the God's truth view of componential analysis, that what we are interested in capturing is what the native speaker *knows* when he knows the meaning of a word. It is easy to see that, in general, this knowledge is not sufficient to fix the extension of the word and that, therefore, it cannot consist in a set of features fixing this extension. For consider the example of *gold*. This has as its extension all gold stuff, but most native speakers of English do not have access to a set of properties which can be seen as providing an appropriate test for whether a piece of stuff is gold or not. In particular, most native speakers of English do not even know the atomic number of gold, which a scientist might see as providing the basis of such a test. Yet we would not wish to say that most native speakers of English do not know the meaning of *gold*. Again, consider *beech*. The majority of English speakers would know that a beech is a kind of tree and have some approximate idea of its size and shape. But many would not have criteria for identifying instances of beech trees and we would not conclude from this that such people did not know the meaning of *beech*.

At this point it may be objected that what is at issue here is a distinction between competence and performance in the semantic domain (see Chapter 2) and that we ought to ignore individual differences, focusing on the ideal case. However, we would point out that this discussion was introduced by a question about a native speaker's *knowledge*, a question about his competence, which would appear to indicate that non-determination of extensions by meanings is an *intrinsic* feature of the latter. In addition, it is far from clear that the ideal case can be studied in any systematic way, as this would involve us in producing necessary and sufficient conditions for the applicability, not only of those terms which have been the subject of scientific inquiry, e.g. *gold*, *water*, *electron*, but also of abstract words such as *virtue*, *justice* and *anger*.

Two further points can be made here. The first is that the indeterminacy of extensions entails that, if we are interested in knowing whether an instance is an instance of a particular category, we shall often have to consult an expert. Simply knowing the meaning of the relevant term will not do. The philosopher Hilary Putnam has talked about this in terms of a Division of Linguistic Labour, and it indicates a point where semantics and sociolinguistics make contact. The second point concerns the nature of the meanings available to the native speaker, if they are not such as to fix extensions. Putnam has suggested that some idea of *stereotype* will be useful here. The average English-speaker's stereotype for gold will include the information that it is a yellow metal with a certain commercial value, but this is insufficient to determine the term's extension. Similarly, a stereotype for *beech* will include the information that it is a tree of a certain approximate size and, of course, we can intuit similar stereotypes for abstract terms like *justice*. As a final comment, we might note that the plausibility of a stereotype approach within a psychologically interpreted framework has been increased by recent work in experimental psycholinguistics (Chapter 9, Sections 9 and 10).

7.5 Theories of sentence-meaning

Perhaps the best-known theory of sentence-meaning in linguistics is that developed by J. Katz and his associates, which views sentence-meanings (like word-meanings in the previous section) as a complex of semantic features. There are several versions of this theory, reflecting the changing emphases and directions of linguistic research, but they all share the view that the meaning of a sentence (and, indeed, of any expression containing more than one word) is built up by the systematic application of rules to the component words. It is, therefore, a 'words-first' theory, and the meanings of words are given, as sets of semantic features, in a *dictionary* or *lexicon*. This dictionary constitutes one component of the theory, and the other is the set of rules (rules of semantic interpretation) which yield the meanings of complex expressions by reference to the dictionary and syntactic properties of the expressions. One very attractive aspect of the theory has been the attention paid to the interaction between syntactic rules governing the formation of well-formed sentences and rules of semantic interpretation. The simplest view that one might adopt on this is that, corresponding to each syntactic rule, there will be a semantic rule which will, as it were, 'mirror' the operation of the syntactic rule. To illustrate, consider (33).

(33) Dogs chase cats

Syntactically, this consists of a subject (*dogs*) and a predicate phrase (*chase cats*). In its turn, the predicate phrase consists of a verb (*chase*) and a direct object (*cats*). This hierarchical structure is represented in Figure 7.3. Lines 1 and 2 in Figure 7.3 are related by the syntactic rule

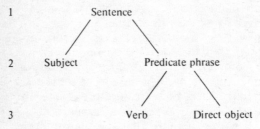

Figure 7.3 *The syntactic structure of (33).*

which says that a sentence may consist of a subject and a predicate phrase and lines 2 and 3 by the rule which says that a predicate phrase may consist of a verb and a direct object. *Semantically*, the proposal under consideration would suggest a rule for amalgamating the meanings of a verb and a direct object to give the meaning of a predicate phrase and a further rule amalgamating the meaning of the predicate phrase with the meaning of the subject to give the meaning of the whole sentence. In Figure 7.4 these two rules relate lines 3 and 2 and lines 2 and 1 respectively.

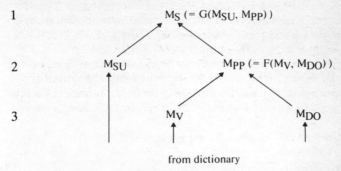

from dictionary

Figure 7.4 *Semantic rules of amalgamation for a simple sentence structure. M_X represents the meaning of X. F and G represent whatever operations are specified in the semantic rules, so $F(M_V, M_{DO})$ is the result of combining the meaning of the verb with the meaning of the direct object in the way allowed by the relevant rule.*

Concrete examples of this sort of procedure would involve us in a much fuller exposition of the theory than we have space for here but its general principles should be clear from the above. The relationship between syntactic and semantic rules has undergone a number of modifications from this simple possibility in the last few years and these too are beyond the scope of an introductory chapter. The points which we go on to consider now are, we believe, independent of these modifications and apply equally to any version of a theory employing semantic features.

The theory can cope with synonymy for sentences in exactly the same way as it does with synonymy for words. Two sentences will be synonymous only if their *semantic representations* (the set of semantic markers giving their meanings) are identical. For analyticity, we can follow tradition and restrict attention to sentences which, syntactically, consist of a subject, a form of the verb to *be* and a predicate nominal. Putative analytic sentences of this form appear in (18), repeated here as (34).

(34) *a* Bachelors are unmarried men
    b Bachelors are unmarried
    c Bachelors are men

Assume that *bachelor* has as its semantic representation [+ UNMARRIED, +MALE, +HUMAN, +ADULT], that *unmarried* has the semantic representation [+UNMARRIED], and that *man* has the representation [+MALE, +HUMAN, +ADULT]. Ignoring two occurrences of the plural morpheme, assume further that the semantic rule determining the interpretation of an adjective-noun construction (e.g. *unmarried man*) simply lumps together the features from the adjective and the noun. Accordingly, the semantic representation of *unmarried man* will be [+UNMARRIED, +MALE, +HUMAN, +ADULT], and for each of the sentences in (34) we have the generalisation that the meaning of the predicate nominal is contained in the meaning of the subject (this is, in fact, not far from the definition of analytic sentence given by Kant). This relation of containment on sets of features can then be used to explicate analyticity for sentences of this form.

It is possible that entailment can be given a similar interpretation. For consider (35) and (36).

(35) John managed to sell three garden gnomes
(36) John sold three garden gnomes

Sentence (35) entails (36) and, *a priori*, there is no clear objection to the suggestion that the set of features giving the meaning of (35) will include all those giving the meaning of (36), with some additional ones to cope with the sense of *manage*. Of course, the details need to be worked out, but all this coupled with attention to syntax puts the theory in a strong position. We must now turn to two searching criticisms of semantic feature theory, the second of which will lead us into an alternative.

The first criticism simply expresses disquiet over the set of semantic features and their manners of combination by the semantic rules. As we have seen, there is no ready procedure for establishing an inventory of semantic features and this means that, to a large extent, the consumer is at the mercy of the whim of the theorist. We are probably happy to admit, say, ±HUMAN or ±ANIMATE, as being basic in human conceptual structures, but what are we to make of (something with legs) (equivalently, ±LEGGED!), to take an example from Katz's dictionary entry for *chair*? This, coupled with the fact that the formal nature of the rules of semantic interpretation has remained obscure, casts doubt on the basic machinery of the theory.

More pressing, however, is the complaint from logicians and philosophers that, whatever semantic feature theory is, it is not a *semantic* theory, if this latter is construed, as Katz would urge, in terms of a theory of what the native speaker knows in order to understand expressions in his language. For what semantic feature theory does at best is provide a *translation* from the language being analysed to the theoretical language of semantic features and, it is claimed, one could have perfect knowledge of this translation without understanding any expressions in the language under analysis, the *object language*. Let us try to approach the significance of this point by considering translation from one natural language to another.

Assume that a native speaker of English, knowing no French and no German, is provided with a translation procedure from French to German such that, given any French expression, he is able to produce the German equivalent. Having knowledge of this translation procedure does not enable our English native speaker to understand French; he is not, thereby, semantically competent in French. Of course, if we change the situation and allow our native speaker of English to also understand German, then equipping him with the translation procedure *will* enable him to understand French. But his semantic competence now has two components: the translation procedure and knowledge of the language being translated into. Consider now a native speaker of English equipped with a procedure for translating English expressions into the theoretical language of semantic features (Markerese, as the philosopher D. Lewis has so aptly termed it). Such a translation procedure will not constitute a theory of semantic competence by the above argument, *unless* the native speaker understands Markerese. There is no evidence that the native speaker does understand Markerese and the position collapses. What is to be done?

Take as our task that of beginning to construct a theory of meaning for German and consider (37) and (38).

(37) 'Schnee ist weiss' means 'Snow is white'
(38) 'Schnee ist weiss' means that snow is white

Both of these sentences are true, but, reinforcing the point of the previous paragraph, it does not follow that someone who knows that (37) is true knows anything about the meaning of the German sentence *Schnee ist weiss*. In order for this to follow, the English sentence *Snow is white* must be understood, and it is nonsense to suggest that competence in German demands competence in English – (37) forms part of a translational theory of meaning. For (38), however, this criticism does not obtain, as what we have on the right of 'means that' is not an expression being *mentioned* as in (37) (indicated by the quotation marks) but an expression being *used* in its standard fashion to describe a state of affairs. Sentence (37) establishes a correspondence between expressions in two languages, (38) establishes a correspondence between an expression in German and a state of affairs. The fact that some language, in this case English, has to be used in order to state what (38) says is a reflection of the fact that any semantic theory must be stated in some language, the *metalanguage*.

To attempt to get this vital distinction perfectly clear, note that (37) and (38) translate into French as (39) and (40).

(39) 'Schnee ist weiss' signifie 'Snow is white'
(40) 'Schnee ist weiss' signifie que la neige est blanche

Consider a native speaker of French, who does not understand English, wishing to come to terms with the German sentence *Schnee ist weiss*. Neither (37) or (38) as stated will be of any use to him, but, if he knows what (38) says, he will be able to understand the German sentence, whereas this is not true for (37). Sentence (37) says what (39) says and (39) is no more use to him than is (37). Sentence (40) says what (38) says and knowledge of (40) suffices for interpretation of the German sentence. It is possible to know *what* (38) (and 40) says without understanding English (or French), although, of course, one cannot know *that* (38) says it without such understanding. It should also now be apparent that, while (41) expresses a trivial truth, (42) does no such thing.

(41) 'Snow is white' means 'Snow is white'
(42) 'Snow is white' means that snow is white

This can be seen by again translating these sentences into French as (43) and (44).

(43) 'Snow is white' signifie 'Snow is white'
(44) 'Snow is white' signifie que la neige est blanche

The *apparent* triviality of (42) is a reflex of the fact that the metalanguage, the language in which we are stating the theory, contains the object language, the language the theory is concerned with.

We can, in the light of the above, define a goal for a semantic theory of a language L. The theory must, for every sentence of L, provide us with a sentence according to the schema in (45).

(45) X means that p

In (45), X is the *name* of a sentence in the object language (we have formed names using quotation marks in 37–44) and p is an appropriate sentence in the metalanguage. But now note that there is an infinite number of sentences in the object language (if it is a natural language) and that, therefore, one thing we cannot do is simply *list* an appropriate sentence of the form of (45) for each object language sentence. Instead, we have to take seriously the problem of specifying a finite number of *axioms* and *rules* from which instances of (45) can be derived for each of the infinite number of sentences in the language. Because of this, Donald Davidson and many others have suggested that (45) is inappropriate, as it employs the logically problematic 'means that', which is likely to lead to major difficulties when we attempt to produce a deductive theory. As an alternative, Davidson suggests (46) as a general schema, with its instances (47)–(49).

(46) X is true if and only if p
(47) 'Schnee ist weiss' is true if and only if snow is white
(48) 'La neige est blanche' is true if and only if snow is white
(49) 'Snow is white' is true if and only if snow is white

Here, (49) is not trivial for exactly the same reason as (42) is not, and in these examples, the English sentence *snow is white* is being *used* to give *truth-conditions* for the corresponding German and French sentences and for itself. The claim then becomes that an adequate semantic theory of L will, from a finite set of axioms and rules, give us an infinite number of true instances of (46), one for each sentence in the object language. We would like to conclude this discussion of Davidson's position with a demonstration that this is an extremely difficult exercise.
   Consider (50)–(53).

(50) Tweety-Pie is a yellow canary
(51) Rover is a hungry dog
(52) Edinburgh is a beautiful city
(53) Bessie is a fat girl

Each of these sentences is an instance of the grammatical schema in (54).

(54) Proper Name *is a* Adjective Noun

Furthermore, we can make a generalisation about the truth-conditions of these sentences. For instance, it seems to be the case that 'Tweety-Pie is a yellow canary' is true if and only if 'Tweety-Pie is yellow' is true and 'Tweety-Pie is a canary' is true, and it appears that here we have a situation where we can define the truth-conditions for a set of sentences in terms of truth-conditions for more simple sentences, exactly what we want if we are looking for a finite set of axioms. So, we can now imagine a semantic theory of the sort Davidson envisages, including the axioms of (55) and the rule of (56).

(55) *a* 'Tweety-Pie is yellow' is true if and only if Tweety-Pie is yellow
    b 'Tweety-Pie is a canary' is true if and only if Tweety-Pie is a canary
    c 'Rover is hungry' is true if and only if Rover is hungry

    d 'Rover is a dog' is true if and only if Rover is a dog
       etc.

(56) 'Proper Name *is a* Adjective Noun' is true if and only if 'Proper Name *is* Adjective' is true and 'Proper Name *is a* Noun' is true

Giving this partial theory (50), analysed syntactically as (54), (56) will apply, yielding (57).

(57) 'Tweety-Pie is a yellow canary' is true if and only if 'Tweety-Pie is yellow' is true and 'Tweety-Pie is a canary' is true

Axioms (55)*a* and (55)*b* can now be applied to (57), finally giving (58).

(58) 'Tweety-Pie is a yellow canary' is true if and only if Tweety-Pie is yellow and Tweety-Pie is a canary

All of this is quite straightforward, but now consider (59).

(59) *a* Sid is a fake policeman
     b Robert is a toy rabbit
     c Mrs Thatcher is a good housewife

Each of these sentences fits the schema of (54). Accordingly, the rule in (56) ought to apply. But it is immediately apparent that this leads to the wrong results. In particular, the analysis of (59)*a* leads to (60).

(60) 'Sid is a fake policeman' is true if and only if Sid is fake and Sid is a policeman

If Sid is a policeman, one thing he is not is a *fake* policeman. There is no ready solution to this and many similar problems and we present it here merely to attempt to give some idea about how such a theory might be constructed and to demonstrate that this is a non-trivial task.

    In general, a theory involving truth-conditions is strong in that it avoids a translation position. It is also a 'sentence-first' theory, taking the truth of sentences as the primitive semantic notion and, on the whole, saying little about the meanings of words. In Davidson's theory there is nothing which corresponds to the meanings of sentences or the meanings of words (see Section 1 above). These meanings are in some sense *given* by the instances of (46) but there is nothing in, say, (47) that one could point to and say that *it* is the meaning of *Schnee ist weiss*. As for analyticity and entailment, although it is possible to see them being adequately dealt with in this framework, this would involve us in a rather longer discussion of the relationship between object language and metalanguage than we have space for here. We shall therefore close this section by turning to a facet of sentence-meaning which is not readily accommodated to a truth-based approach.

If we consider (61) and (62) it is immediately obvious that they differ in meaning, yet nothing in our discussion so far provides us with the concepts we need to approach this difference.

(61) Garden gnomes are ghastly
(62) Are garden gnomes ghastly?

It might be our first reaction to say that there is something quite wrong with a theory taking truth as its basic semantic concept, as this immediately excludes (62) from the theory's compass, and the Oxford philosopher J. L. Austin, starting from this position, drew a distinction between *constative* and *performative* utterances, the latter, in contrast to the former, not being analysable in terms of truth/falsity. Austin was subsequently led to extended discussion of the acts which are associated with using language (*speech acts*) and by far the most important category of such acts is that of *illocutionary acts*. These were defined by Austin as those acts which were performed *in* the uttering of sentences. Thus, typically, an utterance of (61) would constitute an act of stating, and an utterance of (62), an act of questioning. Sometimes the nature of the associated illocutionary act is explicit as in (63) (a promise) and (64) (an order).

(63) I promise to buy you a garden gnome
(64) I order you to return that garden gnome

However, in cases like (61) and (62) this is not so. How are these observations to be accommodated in a semantic theory?

It has been suggested that illocutionary acts be given the central role in semantics, the meaning of a sentence being equated with the set of illocutionary acts the sentence *could* be used to perform, the sentence's *illocutionary act potential*, but this suggestion has two weaknesses. The first is that it throws little light on the semantic difference between (65) and (66).

(65) I promise to buy you a pint of beer
(66) I promise to buy you a pound of beans

The illocutionary act potential of (65) will include promises to buy pints of beer and that of (66), promises to buy pounds of beans, but it is in the *content* of the different promises that the distinction between (65) and (66) lies and, of course, it is exactly this content that the theory of semantic features and the truth-based theory attempt to explicate. The second point can be illustrated by (67).

(67) Can you light the fire?

The illocutionary act potential of this sentence will include *requests* to light the fire (the most common use of 67) and also *questions* concerning the ability of the addressee. But it is far from clear that such requests and questions should have the same status in a semantic theory. This point is, perhaps, made more vividly by (68).

(68) It's hot in here!

Sentence (68) might be used to make a statement about the temperature, to request that a window be opened, to request that the heating be turned off, to order that a window be opened, and so on. Little is gained by assembling a long list of acts and assigning them to (68) as its meaning. This would amount to saying that (68) is multiply ambiguous, which is surely incorrect.

In response to both of these points, the most fruitful direction appears to be that which combines some marker of *illocutionary force* with a semantic analysis of the 'content' of the sentence, this latter being achieved in terms of the approaches we have already considered. The marker of illocutionary force will be that corresponding to the *literal* meaning of the sentence in question. For (67) it will be a marker of interrogation, not request, and for (68) a marker of statement, not request and not command. This leaves open the question of how to deal with the additional interpretations of (67) and (68). This belongs to the field of *pragmatics*, to which we now turn.

7.6 Semantics and pragmatics

According to one powerful intellectual tradition, syntax is concerned with signs and relations between signs, semantics with the relations between signs and the world and pragmatics with the relations between signs and their users. According to this definition, as soon as reference to speaker and addressee becomes vital to an analysis, that analysis properly belongs to pragmatics, and there are two broad areas in which there has been a good deal of research in the last few years.

The first of these concerns the interpretation of sentences which include *indexical* expressions. These are expressions which depend on the context of utterance, if they are to be fully understood, and include such things as personal pronouns (*I, you, he,* etc.), demonstrative pronouns and adjectives (*this, that,* etc.), locative adverbs (*here, there*), temporal adverbs (*now, then*) and such morphological categories as tense. Clearly, with the inclusion of this latter category, pragmatic factors infect the analysis of all sentences which have tense. On the whole, these expressions have been handled using methods incorporated into linguistics from logic and it would take us too far afield to discuss them here. More important, in the context of problems we have already met, is work which has been done on the analysis of conversation and on the distinction between what a speaker's words (literally) mean and what that speaker might mean by his words.

We have seen, at the end of the previous section, that a particular sentence can be used with a range of illocutionary forces. This sort of variability is not confined to illocutionary aspects of meaning, however. Consider (69).

(69) The way you fell over that chair was extremely elegant

This sentence *could* be used in a contest to see who can fall over chairs elegantly. In such a situation it would have its literal meaning, and there would be no distinction between what (69) means and what the speaker of (69) on that occasion means. It is much more likely, though, that (69) is used in circumstances of the addressee coming to grief with little or no grace – we would talk about the speaker using (69) *ironically* – and then the speaker does not mean what (69) means, but the exact opposite. In these circumstances, H. P. Grice has talked about a speaker *implicating* something distinct from the literal meaning of his words and the phenomenon is referred to as *conversational implicature*. How do conversational implicatures arise and how do we locate the study of this concept with respect to semantics?

Grice has suggested that conversations are typically regulated by a number of *conversational maxims*, several of which are listed in (70).

(70) a *Maxim of Quantity*: Make your contribution to the conversation as informative as is required
b *Maxim of Quality*: Be truthful
c *Maxim of Relation*: Be relevant

Being conventions, it is possible for these maxims to be violated, and Grice claims that when they are violated blatantly so that the addressee knows that they are being violated and the speaker intends the addressee to know that they are being violated, then conversational implicatures arise. Going back to the non-literal interpretation of (69), the addressee will know that the speaker's utterance is false, and blatantly false. This violates the Maxim of Quality and, since there is no indication that the speaker is opting out of the conversation, he must be trying to say something distinct from the literal meaning of (69). The obvious candidate, in this case, is seen as the opposite of what he in fact said.

Consider another example. You are asked your opinion of your linguistics teacher and reply with (71).

(71) He walks well

This can be seen either as a violation of the Maxim of Quantity or of the Maxim of Relation (or both – there is a good deal of vagueness in the formulation of the maxims) and, again, if there is no indication that you wish to opt out of the conversation, your addressee will take the violation as blatant and assume that you were trying to say something distinct from (or, perhaps, in this case, in addition to) what your words literally mean – something along the lines of the person in question not being any good as a linguistics teacher.

Examples of this sort can be multiplied and analyses have been offered for the illocutionary force variation that we discussed earlier. What it is important to be clear about in all this is that one must keep a sharp distinction between conversational implicature and the semantic relation of entailment. One way in which one can check which of these relations is at issue is to examine whether the conjunction of a pair of sentences amounts to a contradiction. Thus, (72) is a contradiction but (73), uttered in the context we described for (71), while odd, does not commit the speaker to absurdity.

(72) John managed to close the door but didn't close it
(73) He walks well and he's an excellent teacher

If we take this test seriously, we can see that the examples of presupposition discussed in Section 3 above are more appropriately treated as involving implicature or some other non-semantic notion. It was argued there that (25)*a* (repeated as 74*a*) entails (25)*b* (repeated as 74*b*), but that the entailment relation between (26) (repeated as 74*c*) and (25)*b* is more contentious.

(74) *a* It bothers John that garden gnomes are ghastly
       b Garden gnomes are ghastly
       c It doesn't bother John that garden gnomes are ghastly

This issue hinges on whether (75) is a contradiction or not and our view on this is that, while it is misleading or odd, it is not contradictory.

(75) It doesn't bother John that garden gnomes are ghastly and they're not.

One is left with a pragmatic notion of presupposition, whereby presupposing is something that speakers do. Anyone uttering (74)*c* would normally be taking the truth of (74)*b* for granted and often assuming that his addressee was doing likewise, but nothing follows for the *logical* relationship between (74)*c* and (74)*b* on this basis. Whether a unified framework can be developed for dealing with conversational implicatures and pragmatic presuppositions remains to be seen.

Exercises: Chapter 7

1   Look at the following list of words and for each word write down its opposite, e.g. for *hard* write *soft* (and *easy*), for *big*, *small*, etc. See how many different sorts of 'opposite' you can find in the list and attempt to describe how they differ.

parent	bad	fat	above	short
north	male	left	husband	massive
front	strong	black	buy	top
married	come	old	open	flat

2   Words like *long*, *wide*, *high*, *thick*, *broad*, *deep*, etc., and their opposites are used to describe properties of three-dimensional objects. Examine how they are used with the following nouns and try to formulate a set of principles which will predict which terms will be used in connection with which objects.

bus	door	cupboard	man
cigarette	room	tunnel	skirt

Bring up more examples to show that your 'rules' work (or do not work).

3   Consider the following sentences, many of which you will feel to be strange in some way.
(a)   *John arrived but he's no longer here*
(b)   *John has arrived but he's no longer here*
(c)   *John arrived but was never here*
(d)   *John has arrived but was never here*
(e)   *John killed the cat but it's not dead*
(f)   *John has killed the cat but it's not dead*
(g)   *John killed the cat but it was never dead*
(h)   *John has killed the cat but it was never dead*
(i)   *John bought a bike from Fred but hasn't got it now*
(j)   *John bought a bike from Fred but has never had it*
(k)   *John bought a bike from Fred but didn't give him anything for it*
(l)   *John bought a bike from Fred but Fred didn't sell the bike to John*
(m) *John bought a bike from Fred but it was never Fred's*
(n)   *Jumbo is an elephant and he's not got four legs*
(o)   *Jumbo is an elephant and he's not got tusks*
(p)   *Jumbo is an elephant and he's not got a trunk*
(q)   *Jumbo is an elephant and he's not an animal*
(r)   *Fred has a bicycle with only one wheel*
(s)   *Fred has a unicycle with two wheels*
(t)   *Fred has a bike with only one wheel*

The *Concise Oxford Dictionary* entry for *elephant* begins 'Huge four-footed pachyderm with proboscis and long curved ivory tusks'. One way to interpret this definition is to assume that something is an elephant if and only if it is huge, it is a pachyderm, it has a proboscis and it has long curved ivory tusks. If this interpretation were correct, all of (*n*)–(*q*) should be contradictory, i.e. it should be impossible for them to be true. Are they contradictory? If they are not, what is the status of our dictionary definition? Bring similar sorts of consideration to bear on the other sentences in the set.

4 For each of the following pairs of sentences say whether *a* entails *b*, *b* entails *a* or neither entails the other. In this last case attempt to describe the relationship that holds between the sentences.

(1) a *John persuaded Mary to leave*
    b *Mary left*

(2) a *Cyril the swan is white*
    b *All swans are white*

(3) a *John remembered his name*
    b *John was suffering from amnesia*

(4) a *Most fish have scales*
    b *Barry the goldfish has scales*

(5) a *This chalk looks white to me*
    b *The light is bad*

(6) a *Mary intended to hit Bill*
    b *John persuaded Mary to hit Bill*

(7) a *John dissuaded Mary from leaving*
    b *Mary didn't leave*

(8) a *Mary intended not to leave*
    b *Mary did not intend to leave*

(9) a *I invited some of my friends to my party*
    b *I did not invite all of my friends to my party*

(10) a *John got 10 per cent on all his papers*
    b *John failed his exams*

5 Attempt to devise a small set of semantic features with which you can analyse the following systems of personal pronouns.

	Ibo		Gilyak
mo	'I'	*ni*	'I'
e	'you' (sing.)	*ci*	'you' (sing.)
ya	'he, she, it'	*ja*	'he, she, it'
ane	'we'	*nin*	'we' (excluding hearer)
unu	'you' (plur.)	*mim*	'we' (including hearer)
ha	'they'	*cin*	'you' (plur.)
		irn	'they'

Hint: think of whether the speaker and/or hearer is included in the reference of the pronoun and whether the pronoun's reference can be extended to include more and more people.

Why would familiar languages such as English, French and German demand that you increase your set of features if you were to analyse their systems of personal pronouns?

6 The list below gives the set of Njamal kinship terms together with a specification of the kin-types to which each term refers; ' *s* ' means that the

speaker is a man and '₊' that the speaker is a woman. Attempt to produce a componential analysis for these data.

maili	FaFa, FaFaBr, MoMoBr, MoFaWiBr, FaMoHu, FaMoSiHu, FaMoBrWiBr, ₃SoSo, ₃SoDa, ₃BrSoSo, ₃BrSoDa, ₃DaDaHu, ₃DaSoWi, ₃DaSoWiSi, etc.
mabidi	MoFa, MoFaBr, MoMoHu, FaFaSiHu, FaMoBr, ₃DaSo, ₃DaDa, ₃SoSoWi, ₃SoDaHu, etc.
kandari	MoMo, MoMoSi, MoFaWi, FaFaSi, FaMoBrWi, ₊DaSo, ₊DaDa, ₊SoDaHu, etc.
kabali	FaMo, FaMoSi, FaFaBrWi, MoFaSi, MoMoBrWi, ₊SoSo, ₊SoDa, ₊DaSoWi, ₊DaDaHu, etc.
mama	Fa, FaBr, MoSiHu, FaFaBrSo, FaMoSiSo, MoMoBrSo, etc.
karna	MoBr, FaSiHu, MoFaBrSo, FaFaSiSo, ₃WiFa, SiHuFa, ₊HuFa, BrWiFa, etc.
midari	FaSi, MoBrWi, FaFaDa, MoMoBrDa, ₃WiMo, ₃WiMoSi, SiHuMo, ₊HuMo, ₊HuMoSi, BrWiMo, etc.
ngardi	Mo, MoSi, FaBrWi, MoMoSiDa, MoFaBrDa, FaFaSiDa, etc.
kurda	E(lder)Br, FaBrESo, MoSiESo, etc.
turda	ESi, FaBrEDa, MoSiEDa, etc.
maraga	Y(ounger)Si, YBr, FaBrYSo, FaBrYDa, MoSiYSo, MoSiYDa, etc.
njuba	₃Wi, ₃MoBrDa, ₃FaSiDa, ₃MoMoSoDa, ₃FaFaSiSoDa, ₃MoMoBrDaDa, ₃BrWi, ₃FaBrSoWi, ₃SiHuSi, ₊Hu, ₊MoBrSo, ₊FaSiSo, ₊MoMoBrDaSo, ₊FaFaSiSoSo, ₊SiHu, ₊BrWiBr, ₊FaBrDaHu, etc.
ngabari	₃WiBr, ₃SiHu, ₃MoBrSo, ₃FaSiSo, ₃MoMoSiSoSo, ₃FaFaSiSo-So, etc.
julburu	₊HuSi, ₊BrWi, ₊MoBrDa, ₊FaSiDa, ₊MoMoSiSoDa, ₊FaFaSiSoDa, etc.
ngaraija	₃SiDa, ₃WiBrDa, ₃SoWi, ₃DaHuSi, ₊BrDa, ₊HuSiDa, ₊SoWi, ₊DaHuSi, etc.
tjuja	So, Da, DaHu, BrSo, SiSo, ₃BrDa, ₊SiDa, ₃WiBrSo, ₊BrDaHu, SoWiBr, HuSiSo, DaHu, etc.

Hint: Njamal society is structured in terms of two *moieties* and everyone belongs to one or other moiety. When Njamal marry they must marry into the opposite moiety. Children inherit the moiety of their father.

7 Imagine that you are an anthropologist and that you discover a tribe which is acquainted with cats, dogs and cows but only has two words for them, X and Y, where English has three. You are to guess whether X is used for cats *and* dogs with Y reserved for cows or whether one of the other possibilities is likely to obtain. What do you think is informing your guess? Do the same thought-experiment for:

(a) flowers, bushes and trees,
(b) aunts, uncles and fathers,
(c) milk, water and steam,
(d) chairs, tables and tree-stumps.

8   Reconsider the question posed in Exercise 7 with the additional assumption that cats are sacred animals in the culture of the tribe in question.

9   Consider the following clause which might form part of a theory of meaning for English:

For any sentences S_1 and S_2, 'S_1 *and* S_2' is true if and only if 'S_1' is true and 'S_2' is true

Do you think this clause is true?
Hint: note that the clause claims that the truth of 'S_1 *and* S_2' depends *merely* on the truth of the component sentences. In this light consider sentences including *and* where S_1 and S_2 appear to be temporally or causally linked, e.g. *I got out of bed and got dressed*, *He swallowed poison and became ill*. What conclusions do you draw about the meaning of *and* in English?

Bibliography: Chapter 7

Alston, W. P., *Philosophy of Language* (Englewood Cliffs, NJ: Prentice-Hall, 1964). Somewhat dated now but does include useful discussion of 'meanings as objects', 'meanings as ideas' and behaviourist semantics.

Austin, J. L., 'Performative-constative', in J. R. Searle (ed.), *Philosophy of Language* (London: Oxford University Press, 1971), pp. 13–22. The original statement of the need to distinguish performative and constative utterances. Speech-act theory developed from this. Clearly written.

Burling, R., *Man's Many Voices* (New York: Holt, Rinehart & Winston, 1970). The best introduction to the problems of using componential analysis in connection with kinship and other domains. Lively in style and very readable. Contains discussion of the Njamal data presented as Exercise 6 above.

Davidson, D., 'Truth and meaning', *Synthèse*, 17 (1967), pp. 304–23; reprinted in J. F. Rosenberg and C. Travis (eds), *Readings in the Philosophy of Language* (Englewood Cliffs, NJ: Prentice-Hall, 1974). The author's first formulation of a theory of meaning as a theory of truth. Obscure and difficult for the most part.

Fodor, J. D., *Semantics: Theories of Meaning in Generative Grammar* (New York: Crowell, 1977). Surveys attempts to integrate semantic theories with syntactic theories as briefly discussed in Chapter 8 here. Contains a useful discussion of philosophical theories of meaning. See also Chapter 8.

Frege, G., 'On sense and reference', translation from German original dated 1892 in P. Geach and M. Black (eds), *Translations from the Philosophical Writings of Gottlob Frege* (Oxford: Blackwell, 1952), pp. 56–78. The classic statement of the need to distinguish sense and reference. Difficult in places.

Grice, H. P., 'Logic and conversation', in P. Cole and J. Morgan (eds), *Syntax and Semantics, Vol. 3: Speech Acts* (New York: Academic Press, 1975), pp. 41–58. A section of Grice's 1968 William James Lectures introducing conversational maxims and conversational implicature. Not always easy but informal enough to read selectively.

Katz, J. J., and Fodor, J. A., 'The structure of a semantic theory', *Language*, 39 (1963), pp. 170–210; reprinted in J. A. Fodor and J. J. Katz (eds), *The Structure of Language: Readings in the Philosophy of Language* (Englewood Cliffs, NJ: Prentice-Hall, 1964), pp. 479–518. The first attempt to integrate syntax and semantics. Introduces semantic markers and rules of semantic interpretation. Difficult. See also Chapter 8.

Kempson, R. M., *Semantic Theory* (Cambridge: Cambridge University Press, 1977). An excellent survey of many of the topics introduced in this chapter. Particularly recommended are Ch. 3 on 'Meaning and truth' and Ch. 5 on 'Speech act semantics v. truth-conditional semantics'. Chs 2, 4, 6 and 9 are also of central relevance.

Leech, G., *Semantics* (Harmondsworth: Penguin, 1974). A somewhat idiosyncratic treatment of a wide range of issues. Componential analysis is treated in some detail, but beware of non-standard notation throughout the book.

Lyons, J., *Semantics* (Cambridge: Cambridge University Press, 1977). The most comprehensive survey of the whole field in two volumes. Vol. I is mostly review and criticism and in Vol. II the author is more concerned to develop his own views. Chs 8 and 9 contain a very full treatment of the range of semantic relations between words. See also Chapter 6.

Platts, M., *Ways of Meaning* (London: Routledge & Kegan Paul, 1979). The only attempt to introduce truth-based theories of meaning in a way that is accessible to beginners. Reviews the motivation for and development of Davidson's ideas. Despite being introductory it is still rather formidable.

Putnam, H., 'Is semantics possible?', *Metaphilosophy*, 1 (1970), pp. 187–201; reprinted in H. Putnam, *Philosophical Papers: Mind, Language and Reality* (Cambridge: Cambridge University Press, 1975), pp. 139–152. A critical examination of the view that meaning determines reference and a consequent introduction of 'sociolinguistic' considerations into semantics. Difficult in places.

Chapter 8

Rules and Principles in the Theory of Grammar

8.1 Restricting the base

In this chapter we shall be exploring a style of argument which has become particularly important in linguistic theory in the last fifteen years or so. The broad outlines of this style of argument can be appreciated by noting a certain tension which confronts linguists. On the one hand, there is the need to develop systems enabling the adequate description of a variety of phenomena in a range of languages, and the various theoretical proposals we have developed in Chapters 4 and 6 could be seen as responding to this need. Obviously, languages are different and this might be seen as requiring that the linguist describe different languages in significantly different ways and develop formalisms which are sufficiently powerful to allow for such a variety of descriptions. On the other hand, we have the fact that all human languages are acquired by normal children in a remarkably efficient way, and this would appear to entail that the child is not confronted with a bewilderingly large range of choices as he or she acquires a native language. This can be seen as producing pressure from a different direction for the linguist to restrict the options that his or her formalisms make available, correspondingly restricting the choices that confront the child in language acquisition. The arguments that we shall see in this chapter are motivated by the belief that this fine balance between formalisms which allow for adequate description but which do not render the child's task unmanageable is worth striving for. These arguments will sometimes require assumptions for which we shall be able to provide only minimal justification. Extensive argumentation for these assumptions does exist and may be followed up by consultation of some of the items in the bibliography to the chapter. We begin by returning to our discussion of the base in Chapter 6, Section 4.

The reader will recall that there are various possibilities for constructing trees dominated by the phrasal category labels, NP, VP, ADJP, etc. For instance, for VP we have presented the rules in (1).

(1) VP ⟶ V – NP – ADVP
     VP ⟶ V – ADJP
     VP ⟶ V – PP
     VP ⟶ V – (S)
     VP ⟶ V – (NP)

This set of rules must of course be extended when a wider variety of English sentences is considered. For example, (2) and (3) seem to require the rules of (4).

(2) John promised Mary that she would win
(3) John persuaded Mary to go
(4) VP ⟶ V – NP – *that* – S
     VP ⟶ V – NP – *to* – VP

Now, all of the rules in (1) and (4) are of the form:

(5) VP ⟶ . . . V . . .

i.e. every tree dominated by the symbol VP contains a V at the next lower level. Obvious as this may seem, there is nothing in the theory of phrase structure rules, as presented so far, which requires it. Indeed, from the theoretical perspective of Chapter 6, the following are impeccable phrase structure rules.

(6) VP ⟶ NP – PP
     NP ⟶ ADJP – V – PP
     PP ⟶ V – N – N – V

This becomes important if we now consider the task which confronts a child acquiring a language. If the child is viewed as formulating hypotheses concerning the structure of his native language, and if the only constraint on these hypotheses is that the grammar of his language contains phrase structure rules, then he will have to consider, and somehow rule out, the technically correct but empirically bizarre rules of (6) along with many other similar possibilities. If, however, he comes to language acquisition already equipped with the information that all VPs contain Vs, all NPs contain Ns, etc., perhaps in the form of the schema in (7):

(7) XP ⟶ . . . X . . .

where X ranges over the lexical categories of the language (i.e. N, V, etc.), his task would be considerably simplified, a vast number of logically possible but empirically impossible options being ruled out by such a priori knowledge. The schema of (7) would then be postulated as one part of Universal Grammar, i.e. as being true of all languages.

Let us take these considerations a step further. Consider the NPs in (8).

(8) *a* a nose
     b a big nose
     c an extremely big nose

The systems we have developed so far would suggest the structures of (9) for these NPs.

(9) *a*   *b*

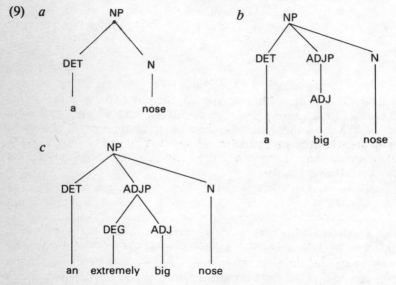

c

Notice that in (9)*b* and (9)*c* the ADJP and the N do not form a constituent. Yet there is some evidence that they ought to. For instance, such sequences can be conjoined.

(10) *a* John has a *big nose* and *large paunch*
      b John has an *extremely big nose* and *rather large paunch*

Remember that one of our tests for constituency was that only constituents can be conjoined, and thus the grammaticality of the sentences in (10) suggests that *big nose* and *extremely big nose* are in fact constituents. Furthermore, it appears that such sequences can serve as antecedents for the pro-form *one*.

(11)   John bought this extremely big nose and I bought that one

Certainly, one interpretation of (11) is that I also bought an extremely big nose, in which case *one* appears to 'stand for' the sequence *extremely big nose*. Thus, two of our tests for constituency point to the same conclusion, a consistency we cannot reasonably ignore. This conclusion is that (9)*c* is the wrong representation for (8)*c*. What we need is, instead, (12).

(12)

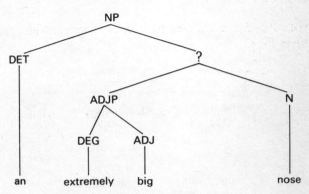

The question this raises is that of the identity of the '?', i.e. what sort of constituent is *extremely big nose*? The following conditions must be fulfilled:

(i)   it is a nominal-type constituent;
(ii) it is not a simple N;
(iii) it is not an NP because it does not have the distribution of an NP as (13) shows.

(13)   *Extremely big nose loomed on the screen

Accordingly, it is a nominal-type sequence lying somewhere between N and NP. To represent this, let us introduce a system of primes, replace NP (the 'largest' nominal category) by N'', use the label N' for the troublesome intermediate category and retain N (with no primes) for simple nouns. In fact, the approach we are developing here is known as *X-bar syntax*, since the linguists who introduced it used one or more bars over the category label instead of primes. For typographical convenience, we use primes, but retain the label 'X-bar syntax'. With these notational changes, the structure for (9)*c* will be:

(14)

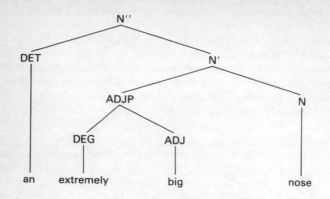

Similar considerations can be extended to the other phrasal categories, and so we end up with a set of labels N'', N', N, V'', V', V, ADJ'', ADJ', ADJ, etc. and a schema to replace (7).

(15) $X^n \longrightarrow \ldots X^m \ldots$

In this schema, n and m correspond to the number of primes on a category, and we impose the restriction that either $m = n-1$ or $m = n$. Where $m = n-1$, we produce such structures as (16):

(16)

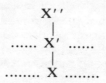

as in (14) above. Clearly, we must also allow for the possibility that $m = n$ to take account of recursion within some phrasal constituents. Thus, alongside the data in (8), we also have such NPs as (17).

(17) *a* an extremely big pointed nose
      b an extremely big pointed red nose

And, as the reader can quickly verify by considering co-ordination and pronominalisation possibilities, there are reasons for treating *big pointed red nose*, *pointed red nose* and *red nose* as N's alongside *extremely big pointed red nose*, i.e. the structure for (17)*a* is (18).

(18)

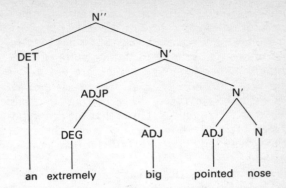

an extremely big pointed nose

(Here we omit extending the formalism to the adjectival phrase.) In this structure, we need N′ to dominate N′, and this is possible only if we allow m and n to be identical in the schema.

Taking the schema of (15) as part of the child's innate endowment supplied by Universal Grammar clearly reduces the learning load as far as phrase structure is concerned, but the child still has to learn the position of X^m in each instance of the schema, e.g. whether the N′ is initial, medial, or final in the N′′ in English, and also what categories can appear in the positions of the dots in the schema, e.g. what categories, if any, can follow the N in the English NP. Is there anything we can do to make these tasks more approachable?

Consider first the position of X^m on the right-hand side of the schema. In Japanese the word order in the major phrases is as in (19).

(19) (*a*) The N comes in final position in the NP.
  (*b*) The ADJ comes in final position in the ADJP.
  (*c*) The V comes in final position in the VP.
  (*d*) There are postpositions as opposed to prepositions, i.e. *in London* would translate into Japanese as the equivalent of *London in*.

The consistency displayed in (19) is quite striking. Moreover, languages *tend* to exhibit this sort of consistency or, as in the case of Welsh, its mirror image, with the lexical categories appearing initially in their phrasal categories. What we might now suggest is that children come to language acquisition 'expecting' to be confronted with a language like Japanese or Welsh and that Universal Grammar supplies the child with a choice.

(20) *a* $X^n \longrightarrow \ldots X^m$ (Japanese type)
  b $X^n \longrightarrow X^m \ldots$ (Welsh type)

For a child confronted with Japanese or Welsh, the problem of acquiring the information about where the lexical category appears in the phrase becomes now rather trivial, as he has only to figure out what goes on in one phrase type to 'know' automatically what goes on in the others. Other languages which are not as systematic as Japanese and Welsh in these respects are seen as *marked*, and thus rather more will be involved in acquiring the basic phrasal organisations of these languages. Given that the properties in (19) do tend to cluster together, however, to equip the child with the *unmarked* choice between (20)*a* and (20)*b* is to give him a considerable learning advantage.

Consider now what categories can appear in the position of the dots in (15) and recall the view of the lexicon we have adopted. Some lexical entries for verbs are as follows.

(21) *put*   – V, + [——NP — PP]
    persuade – V, + [——NP — *that* — S]
    excite   – V, + [——NP]

A moment's thought should persuade the reader that the information contained in these lexical entries is being duplicated in the phrase structure rules, since it is precisely because we have a verb like *persuade* in English which requires a direct object and a *that* – S complement that we feel we need the rule in (22).

(22) VP ——►V – NP – *that* – S

Now, if a child has learned the lexical entries of (21), then he has automatically acquired the information contained in the relevant rules for the expansion of the VP. Accordingly, the problem of learning the intricacies of phrase structure rules largely disappears, and it is replaced by that of learning the idiosyncratic properties of lexical items, an unavoidable task.

The above suggestion moves us towards a position where *rules* no longer play a very important role in the grammar. Rather, what we have is a set of general *principles*, such as that embodied in the schema in (15) and in the choice between (20)*a* and (20)*b*, rendering the need for complex rule systems superfluous.

8.2 Constraining transformational rules

Our discussion of transformational rules in Chapter 6, Section 5, was very schematic, simply amounting to an observation of the necessity for such rules and pointing out that an informal construal of what such rules can do enabled us to be optimistic about handling a variety of problems which resist solution within a phrase structure framework. In the next two sections of this chapter we shall bring the style of argument of the previous section to bear on the transformational component of the grammar. We begin by focusing on the rule of *Wh*-movement and noting that the operation of this rule must be constrained in a number of ways if our grammar is not to generate a range of ill-formed sentences. We must begin with a rather more precise discussion of *Wh*-movement than we have provided so far.

Recall the data that led us to suggest the rule of *Wh*-movement.

(23)   Who(m) will the fish excite?

We suggested that we analyse this sentence as having the deep structure in (24).

(24)

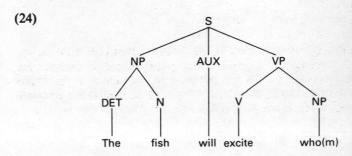

This deep structure is converted by the rule of *Wh*-movement into the structure in (25).

(25)

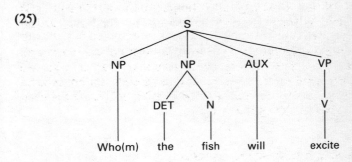

Subsequent application of the transformational rule of subject–auxiliary inversion will convert (25) to the surface structure for (23). We shall not concern ourselves further with this rule here, merely presupposing it in our examples.

The rule of *Wh*-movement must accept a structure like that in (24) and convert it to a structure like that in (25). How is such a rule to be formulated?

Notice, first of all, that the material preceding *who(m)* in (24) seems to be irrelevant to the functioning of the rule. Alongside (23), we have the following well-formed questions.

(26)   *a*   Whom did John chase?
      b   Whom was Mary chased by?
      c   What did John give Mary?
      d   Whom did John give a book to?
      e   Where did John learn linguistics?

Furthermore, material can follow the position from which the *Wh*-word is moved.

(27)   *a*   Whom did John see Ø yesterday?
      b   What did John give Ø to Mary?
      c   Where did John go Ø for his summer holiday?

(In these examples, Ø marks the position in the sentence where the *Wh*-word is assumed to originate.) It seems, then, that *Wh*-movement applies to structures in which a *Wh*-word occurs, and this word may be preceded or followed by arbitrary material. We can represent this class of structures in the following way.

(28)   X − *wh* − Y

(28) says that *Wh*-movement can apply to any structure which is a structure for a string made up of anything at all (X), a *Wh*-word (*wh*) and anything at all (Y). In such a representation, X and Y are *variables*. Thus, the rule will apply to (24), as represented in (29), with the Y term empty, an option which is always available.

(29)

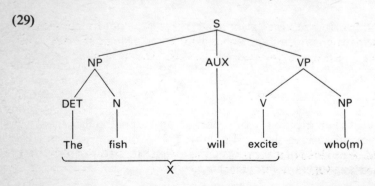

Equally, it will apply to (30), where the Y term is not empty.

(30)

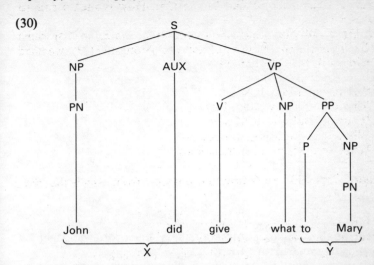

What we have in (28) is referred to as the *structural analysis* of the rule. The other part of a transformational rule is the *structural change* which provides information on what changes the rule performs on the input structure. It is evident in the case of *Wh*-movement that we want the rule to move the *Wh*-word to the front of the sentence. The full details of what is involved here are quite complicated, and here we shall simplify the question by proposing that the structural change for *Wh*-movement is as in (31), merely indicating that the *Wh*-word moves to the front and not being concerned with exactly what happens to it when it gets there.

(31) $wh - X - Y$

The complete rule is now formulated as in (32), the double-shafted arrow being the conventional symbol for transformational rules and the digits indexing the various terms in the structural analysis.

(32) $X - wh - Y \Longrightarrow 2\ 1\ 3$
　　　　$1 \quad 2 \quad\ 3$

It should be obvious that the result of applying (32) to (24) will be (25). If applied to (30), (33) will result.

(33)

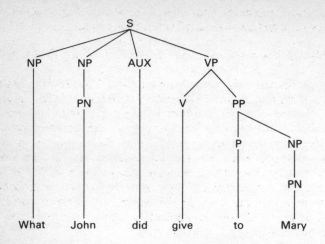

Subsequent application of subject–auxiliary inversion will yield an appropriate surface structure for (27)*b*.

Complications begin to arise when we consider more complex structures, and these complications have had profound implications for more recent work in syntax. On the basis of what we have seen so far, it might be thought that *Wh*-movement can always apply to move the *Wh*-word to its appropriate site, but in fact this turns out not to be the case. Our survey of *Wh*-movement has been thus far limited to simple sentences. What happens, however, when we consider examples in which the *Wh*-word originates in a subordinate clause? Consider (34).

(34)   What does Fred believe that John likes Ø?

Here as before Ø marks the original site of *what* as the direct object of *likes*, the verb in the subordinate clause, and so the deep structure for (34), on our current assumptions, is the structure corresponding to (35).

(35)   Fred believes that John likes what?

(35) is of course well formed in English as an echo-question. The rule of *Wh*-movement, as formulated in (32), will be applicable to this structure, with X = *Fred believes that John likes* and Y empty. If the *Wh*-word originates in a more deeply embedded subordinate clause, a grammatical sentence will again result.

(36)   *a* Bill hopes that Fred believes that John likes what?
       b What does Bill hope that Fred believes that John likes Ø?

Let us now, however, consider a case in which the *Wh*-word originates in a different kind of subordinate clause, as in (37).

(37)   Bill will know the politician who lost who(m) in the desert?

In order to discuss this example, we need a little terminology. The sequence of words *the politician who lost who(m) in the desert* is a relative clause, consisting of the determiner *the*, a head noun *politician* and a clause which serves to restrict the referential possibilities for the head noun. In this clause *who* is a relative pronoun, but the word we are interested in is the interrogative pronoun *who(m)*. Everything we have seen so far would suggest that *Wh*-movement can apply to (37), with X = *Bill will know the politician who lost* and Y = *in the desert*. But such an application, followed by an application of subject–auxiliary inversion, gives (38), an ill-formed sentence.

(38)   *Who(m) will Bill know the politician who lost Ø in the desert?

The following example makes exactly the same point.

(39)   *a* The people whom Mary betrayed will not elect her again
       b The people whom who betrayed will not elect her again?

Thus, we have an echo-question corresponding to the declarative (39)*a*. In (39)*a* the sequence *the people whom Mary betrayed* consists of the determiner *the*, the head noun *people* and the clause *whom Mary betrayed, Mary* being replaced by the interrogative pronoun *who* in (39)*b*. If we attempt to move this interrogative pronoun by *Wh*-movement and then have an application of subject–auxiliary inversion, we get:

(40)   *Who will the people whom Ø betrayed not elect her again?

This is clearly ill formed, and in fact, as the reader can readily check by constructing more examples, a *Wh*-word can never be moved out of a relative clause to produce a well-formed question. The rather charming terminology used by linguists to describe this phenomenon is that relative clauses are *islands* with respect to *Wh*-movement; once a *Wh*-word is in (or, perhaps, on) a relative clause, it cannot get off.

These observations about the island status of relative clauses with respect to *Wh*-movement immediately give rise to two complementary questions.

(i)   Are relative clauses the only structures which do not allow the extraction of an included *Wh*-word?

(ii) Is *Wh*-movement the only transformational rule which is subject to this restriction?

Both these questions must be answered in the negative. First, consider complex NPs which are headed by such nouns as *claim, fact, discovery,* and *observation* as in (41).

(41) *a* the claim that John loves Mary
     b the fact that 2 + 2 = 4
     c the discovery that Venus is the Morning Star
     d the observation that the country is in a mess

These structures may strike the reader as identical to the relative clauses we have already considered, but, in point of fact, there are important differences between them. The word following the head noun in the examples of (41) must be *that*.

(42) *a* *the claim which John loves Mary
     b *the fact which 2 + 2 = 4

Compare the free variation between *that* and *which* in relative clauses as in (43) and (44).

(43) *a* The claim that John made is outrageous
     b The fact that led to John's downfall must be well known
(44) *a* The claim which John made is outrageous
     b The fact which led to John's downfall must be well known

Additionally, relative clauses seem to involve a 'gap' parallel to that in the *Wh*-questions we have already looked at. Thus, in (44)*a made* is a transitive verb which is not immediately followed by a direct object. It appears likely, therefore, that *Wh*-movement may well be involved in the structure of relative clauses, with (44)*a* being derived from a deep structure as in (45).

(45) The claim John made which is outrageous

There is no reason to believe that similar 'gaps' occur in the complex NPs in (41). In (41)*a*, for example, *loves* is a transitive verb, but it is immediately followed by its direct object *Mary*. Accordingly, we conclude that these complex NPs are quite different constructions from relative clauses.

Now, it can be quite easily seen that, while *Wh*-words can occur in these complex NPs in echo-questions, they cannot be moved to the front of a sentence in which the NP occurs.

(46)   *a* The fact that who loves Mary will upset Bill?
       b *Who will the fact that Ø loves Mary upset Bill
(47)   *a* Bill has circulated the rumour that John loves who?
       b *Who has Bill circulated the rumour that John loves Ø

So, *Wh*-movement must be constrained not only to be prevented from extracting material from relative clauses, but also to disallow the movement of *Wh*-words from these complex NPs.

Turning now to question (ii) above, let us consider a second transformational rule which also has the effect of moving a particular expression, in this case a full NP, to the front of the sentence. This is the rule of Topicalisation, which can be seen to apply in the derivation of the structure of (48)*b* from the structure of (48)*a*.

(48)   *a* The fish excites the frog
       b The frog, the fish excites

Note that we have exactly parallel arguments for the existence of this rule as we had in Chapter 6, Section 5, for *Wh*-movement. Given our view of the lexicon, *excites* can be entered only into structures in which it is followed by an NP. But in (48)*b* *excites* is not followed by an NP, and therefore we treat the structure of (48)*a* as the deep structure of (48)*b* and formulate a transformational rule of the form (49) to move the NP *the frog* to the front of the sentence.

(49) $\text{X} - \text{NP} - \text{Y} \Longrightarrow 2\ 1\ 3$
       $\phantom{\text{X}}123$

Similar arguments to those we presented in connection with (32) can be offered for the presence of the variables X and Y in this rule.

Just as for *Wh*-movement, it turns out that NPs in some subordinate clauses can be moved to the front of the sentence by Topicalisation.

(50)   *a* John believes that Ron likes sardines
       b Sardines, John believes that Ron likes Ø
(51)   *a* John hopes that Bill believes that Ron likes sardines
       b Sardines, John hopes that Bill believes that Ron likes Ø

But when we turn to relative clauses, we find that the same constraint as for *Wh*-movement appears to be operative.

(52)   *a* I've met the student who never wants to do linguistics again
       b *Linguistics, I've met the student who never wants to do Ø again

(53)   *a* The man who Mary sacked thinks she's crazy
       b *Mary, the man who Ø sacked thinks she's crazy

So, neither *Wh*-movement nor Topicalisation can move material out of a relative clause, i.e. relative clauses are islands with respect to the operation of both of these rules. What is the situation with complex NPs headed by *claim, fact,* etc.? Predictably, perhaps, Topicalisation cannot move an NP out of such structures either.

(54)   *a* The fact that John loves Mary worries Bill
       b *John, the fact that Ø loves Mary worries Bill
(55)   *a* John was upset by the claim that he didn't like linguistics
       b *Linguistics, John was upset by the claim that he didn't like Ø

Having thus concluded that both of the rules in question are subject to exactly the same constraints we must now go on and attempt somehow to build these constraints into the statement of each individual rule. Thus, for example, (32) could be replaced by (56).

(56) $X - wh - Y \Longrightarrow 2\ 1\ 3$
       1   2   3
       so long as *wh* does not occur in a relative clause or in a complex NP headed by *fact, claim,* etc.

More interestingly, however, we might investigate a series of rules which involve the movement of some material in a sentence and discover that all such rules are blocked by the two structures we have examined here, so that we would not have to state the constraints individually for each rule, but simply suggest that the grammar contains a single statement constraining the operation of *all* rules of a certain type. And, of course, if cross-linguistic investigation revealed that such constraints were operative for similar rules in other languages, we would be moving in the direction of saying that the constraint was part of Universal Grammar and thus not something that the child had to learn. The rules to be learned could then be left in their maximally simple form.

An alternative way to proceed is to look at the characteristics of the *structures* which appear to block the operation of the rules. So far, we have suggested merely listing these in the statement of the constraint, and such a list, while perhaps empirically adequate, is not likely to prove to be particularly insightful. Perhaps it will be possible to formulate certain generalisations across this class of structures and thereby considerably simplify the statement of the constraint. This is the avenue we shall briefly explore in the next section.

8.3 Abstract principles in syntax

So far, we have assumed that *Wh*-movement has the effect of moving a *Wh*-word to the front of a sentence. However, the notion 'front of a sentence' is not particularly precise, and it is imperative to be clear on exactly what position the *Wh*-word gets moved to. It is quite common for certain types of subordinate clauses in English to be introduced by a word such as *that* or *whether*.

(57) John believes that Ron likes sardines
(58) John wonders whether Ron likes sardines

So far, we have said nothing about the grammatical status of such words, traditionally referred to as complementisers, their obvious role being that of introducing complement clauses. Now, in (57), it is clear that the sequence *Ron likes sardines* is an S, but what are we to make of the sequence *that Ron likes sardines*? Suppose we extend the X-bar system which we introduced in Section 1 and regard such sequences as members of the category S'. We can now postulate the following rule as part of the base of English.

(59) S' $\longrightarrow$ COMP – S

Unless such a rule were to be complicated in its statement, it will be involved in the generation of all sentences, and the structure of (57) will thus look like (60) (parts of the structure irrelevant to the discussion are dominated by an undifferentiated triangle).

(60)

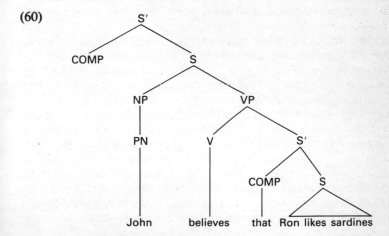

The proposal embodied in (60) may initially strike the reader as rather implausible, since, in English, main clauses are never introduced by complementisers. However, in many other languages, the equivalent of *whether* is common in this position in questions requiring a yes/no answer. Quite independently, but propitiously, the COMP position at the front of every clause provides an ideal site for the *Wh*-word to finish up in after *Wh*-movement has applied to it. To implement this suggestion, it is necessary to reformulate *Wh*-movement along the lines of (61) where the Ø indicates that the *Wh*-word has been deleted in its original site and has, in fact, moved into the position indexed by 1 in the structural analysis.

(61)   COMP – X – *wh* – Y $\Longrightarrow$ 3 2 Ø 4
      1   2   3   4

A simple sentence such as (62) will now have a deep structure like (63) and the intermediate structure (64), before the application of subject–auxiliary inversion.

(62)   What will John eat?

(63)

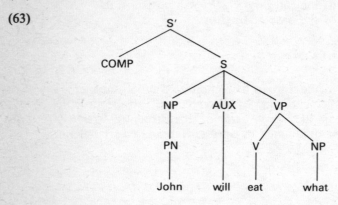

(64)

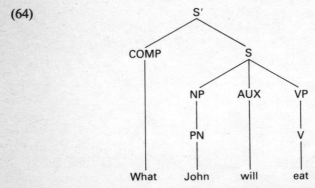

Consider now a more complex case.

(65)   John is hoping Ron likes what?

(66)   What is John hoping Ron likes?

The structure for (65) will be (67), which is also the deep structure for (66).

(67)

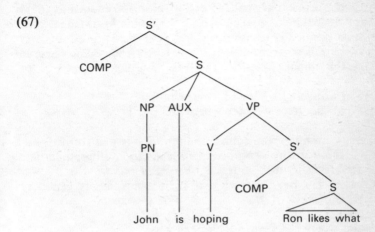

We still have not explained how the *Wh*-word in (67) gets from its position in the embedded clause to the COMP position in the main clause. There are clearly two alternatives which might be considered. According to the first, it moves by virtue of *one* application of *Wh*-movement; and according to the second, it gets to its target in *two* steps via the intermediate COMP. We shall adopt the second of these alternatives here, and the remainder of this section is largely concerned with the justification of this move.

To follow the first alternative would amount to recognising *unbounded* movement, since *Wh*-words can originate arbitrarily far down a structure including embedded clauses of the appropriate type. Now, clearly, the domain of some rules is *bounded*. For example, in Chapter 6, Section 5, we alluded to a rule involved in the generation of passive sentences and pointed out that, among other things, this rule has to exchange the positions of two NPs.

(68)   *a* John kissed Mary
       b Mary was kissed by John

But the two NPs in question cannot be arbitrarily far apart in a structure. If they were, we ought to be able to derive (69)*b* from the structure (69)*a*.

(69)   *a* Bill believes that John kissed Mary
       b *Mary is believed that John kissed by Bill

So, with the unbounded approach to *Wh*-movement, it would be necessary to recognise at least two kinds of transformational rules in the grammar, and the learner would be confronted with the task of having to work out which type each transformational rule belonged to. While this may not be a totally unmanageable task, if it were the sort of task that learners are confronted with, mistakes such as (69)*b* might be anticipated in language acquisition. To our knowledge, such mistakes never occur. Let us assume, then, that the bounded analysis of *Wh*-movement is correct and see if any further advantages accrue from taking this stance. Consider the following data.

(70)   *a* John wondered where Bill put what?
       b *What did John wonder where Bill put Ø

As in previous examples, the echo-question (70)*a* is well formed, but fronting the *Wh*-word by *Wh*-movement leads to an ungrammatical sentence. Referring to the sequence *where Bill put what* as a *Wh*-complement, it can be observed that such complements generally disallow the extraction of *Wh*-words by *Wh*-movement.

(71)   *a* John wonders whether Ron likes what?
       b *What does John wonder whether Ron likes Ø
(72)   *a* John asked where who hid the sardines?
       b *Who did John ask where Ø hid the sardines

Similar restrictions obviously apply to the rule of Topicalisation.

(73)   *a* John wonders whether Ron likes Margaret
       b *Margaret, John wonders whether Ron likes Ø
       c *Ron, John wonders whether O likes Margaret

What such data show is that *Wh*-complements can be added to relative clauses and complex NPs headed by such nouns as *claim* and *fact* as islands. Now, note that with our present machinery, we will have to list these constructions in a statement of the constraint, and even in the statement of individual rules. As we shall now see, the view of *Wh*-movement we are currently working with enables us to offer a more satisfying generalisation.

Consider again (70)*a* and (70)*b*. An appropriate deep structure for (70)*a* will be the structure (74).

(74)   John wondered Bill put what where

We have already seen that *put* subcategorises for a following sequence of NP and PP (in this case *where* is a pro-PP), and so we have to postulate (74) to be in a position to insert *put* into the structure. Next, in the formation of the *Wh*-complement *where Bill put what*, *Wh*-movement will move *where* into the COMP position at the front of its clause, yielding a structure along the lines of (75).

(75)

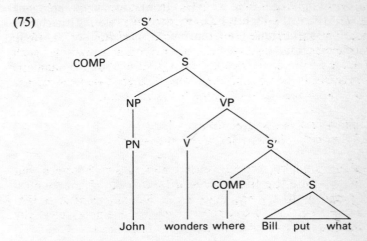

Now, in order to generate the ill-formed (70)*b*, we have to move *what*. Given the restriction on *Wh*-movement that it can move a *Wh*-word only to the next higher COMP, *what* cannot be moved directly into the COMP position at the front of the main clause. The alternative is to move it into the COMP position of the embedded clause, but this is already filled by *where*, and there is ample evidence to suggest that it is not possible to have two *Wh*-words in a COMP.

(76)   *a* John put what where?
       b What did John put where?
       c Where did John put what?
       d *What where did John put
       e *Where what did John put

(76)*a*, *b* and *c* are well-formed multiple questions which require, as well-formed answers, two pieces of information. (76)*b* comes from (76)*a* by moving *what* into COMP, and (76)*c* comes from (76)*a* by moving *where* into COMP. However, attempts to move *both* *Wh*-words into COMP by *Wh*-movement, as in (76)*d* and *e*, result in obviously ungrammatical strings.

From these observations, it would appear that we have a good explanation for why (70)*b* is ungrammatical. The two routes which the

Wh-word might have followed to get into the initial COMP position are both blocked. However, the ungrammaticality of (77) suggests that further considerations are necessary.

(77)   *Where did John wonder what Bill put

This string ought to be derivable from (75) by first moving *where* from the lower COMP to the higher COMP, thereby vacating the lower COMP position for the subsequent movement of *what*, i.e. (75) is first transformed into (78).

(78)

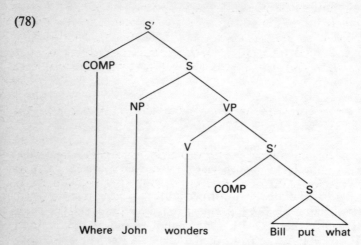

(78), in turn, can be transformed into (79).

(79)

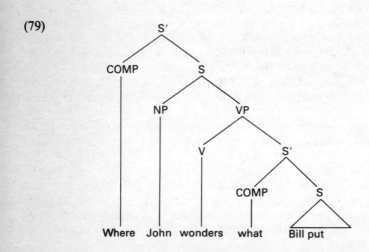

In order to rule this derivation out, it is necessary to formulate a principle which has the effect of making the operation of transformational rules cyclic in a very strong sense. In this particular case, this principle will not allow us to apply rules to the embedded sentence (the first movement of *where*), then apply rules to the main clause (the second movement of *where*) and then *return* to the embedded clause and apply further rules to it (the movement of *what*). Again, it is important to be clear that in addition to the descriptive motivation for this *Principle of the Strict Cycle*, as it is known, restricting the operation of transformational rules in this way cuts down the options available to the language learner.

Let us now return to the problems we were raising at the end of the previous section. We are now operating with the assumption that *Wh*-movement is bounded. Taking account of the structures we are assuming, one way in which we could state this boundedness is as follows.

(80) No rule of grammar may move material across more than one S-node.

This way of putting things is more readily appreciated by using labelled bracketings rather than labelled trees. Thus, consider (80) in the light of the following representation of (70)*a*, equivalent to (75).

(81) [s' [comp   ] [sJohn wondered[s' [compwhere] [sBill put what]]]]

In order to get *what* into the initial COMP position by one application of *Wh*-movement, *what* would have to cross *two* S-nodes, and this would be in violation of (80). For obvious reasons, S is referred to as a *bounding node*. Recall now that we demonstrated in the previous section that relative clauses will not permit the extraction of a *Wh*-word, as illustrated by (37) and (38), repeated here as (82)*a* and *b*.

(82) *a* Bill will know the politician who lost who(m) in the desert?
      b *Who(m) will Bill know the politician who lost Ø in the desert

The same is true for complex NPs headed by *claim*, *fact*, etc. as was illustrated by (46)*a* and (46)*b*, repeated here as (83)*a* and *b*.

(83) *a* The fact that who loves Mary will upset Bill
      b Who will the fact that Ø loves Mary upset Bill

Both relative clauses and complex NPs of the type under discussion have structures which we could schematise as (84) with the relevant *Wh*-word appearing in the embedded S.

(84)

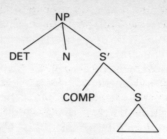

Consider (83)*a* in rather more detail. The deep structure for this sentence will be:

(85)

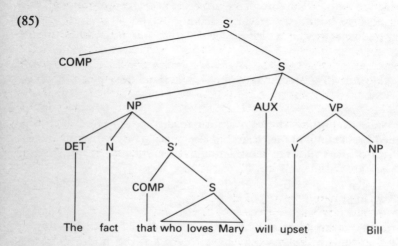

Equivalently, using labelled bracketings, we have:

(86) $[_{S'} [_{COMP} \quad] \; [_S [_{NP}$ the fact $[_{S'} [_{COMP}$ that$] \; [_S$ who loves Mary$]] \;$ will upset Bill$]]]$

Now, if *who* is first moved by *Wh*-movement to the COMP position of the embedded clause (nothing we have said forbids us to do this so long as the COMP is not already occupied by a *Wh*-word), what is to prevent it being moved by a subsequent application of *Wh*-movement so as to end up in the highest COMP leading to the prediction that (83)*b* is well formed? Clearly, (80) will not help here, since neither of the proposed applications of *Wh*-movement involves the *Wh*-word in crossing more than one S-node. The standard solution is to extend the class of bounding nodes to include NP. Thus, (80) is now replaced by (87).

(87)   No rule of grammar may move material across more than one
       bounding node, where the bounding nodes for English are S and
       NP.

With this modification, let us consider again (86).

The first movement of *who* into the embedded COMP remains
possible, but the second movement, into the higher COMP now
involves the *Wh*-word in crossing both an NP-node and an S-node,
and by (87) this is not allowed. Exactly parallel considerations
apply to instances where we attempt to extract a *Wh*-word from a
relative clause, so with (87) we now have a formulation of a general
principle which will apply to the three island constructions we have
considered and to the two movement rules of *Wh*-movement and
Topicalisation. Crucially, this constraint does not need to be stated
for each rule separately, nor are the structural characteristics of the
island constructions listed in the rule; instead, it constitutes a
generalisation across the structures of these islands. The principle
formulated in (87) is known as the *Subjacency Principle*.

It would be useful if we had additional reasons for assimilating the
behaviour of NPs and Ss, because this would make their coming
together in (87) less mysterious. One such reason is that whatever rules
are involved in relating active and passive sentence structures must
also relate active and passive nominalisations, which are, of course,
NPs. Consider the data in (88) and (89).

(88)   *a* The enemy destroyed the city
       b The city was destroyed by the enemy
(89)   *a* the enemy's destruction of the city
       b the city's destruction by the enemy

The parallels between (88) and (89) are obvious, and it would be
perverse to suggest that the grammatical rules involved in generating
these constructions do not share important characteristics. We shall
not examine these characteristics here, but it is sufficient for our
purposes to note that, whereas in (88) the rules are operating in the
domain of S, in (89) they are operating in the domain of NP.

Finally, the reader will have noted that in our formulation of (87)
we have explicitly referred to English. This is important and it relates
to our discussion of X-bar principles in Section 1. There we noted that
languages might differ with respect to their choice of basic phrasal
organisation, a choice which came down to whether lexical categories
occurred initially or finally in their phrasal categories. Careful
investigation of other languages has shown that there is also cross-
linguistic variation with respect to the Subjacency Principle. In
particular, it has been claimed that in Italian the appropriate

bounding nodes are NP and S', not NP and S. We are not in a position to pursue this here, but the reader should be clear that such variation does not conflict with the spirit of the arguments we have considered. If the child is confronted with a choice between S and S' as bounding nodes, there is indeed something he must learn: whether S or S' is a bounding node in the language to which he is being exposed. S and S' are referred to as values of a *parameter* within this approach, which is known as the *parameter-setting* model of first language acquisition. The consequences of a child learning which of these two options is operative are enormous. Indeed, all the complex properties of the data we have been considering in this section can be seen to follow from the choice of NP and S as bounding nodes and some fairly simple rules, and it is not at all plausible to suggest that the child is explicitly provided with information on these properties. For example, there is no reason to believe that at some stage in his linguistic apprenticeship every child has been instructed that (70)*b* and (71)*b* are ungrammatical in English. However, mature native-speakers of English are unanimous in their judgements with respect to these sentences. The aim of much modern syntactic research is to unravel the puzzle created by such observations. This is achieved by the discovery of abstract general principles such as (87) and the Principle of the Strict Cycle which may specify certain parameters of variation. In this section we have formulated only two such principles, and only one of these (the Subjacency Principle) allows for parametric variation. However, the choice between (20)*a* and (20)*b* in Section 1 can be seen in the same light, and there are many other principles, some parameterised and others not, which are currently the subject of very intensive research in syntactic theory.

8.4   Generative phonology

Just as in syntax a regular relationship between two surface forms may be represented in terms of a single underlying form they share (cf. Chapter 6, Section 5), so regular allomorphic variation can be formalised by postulating a unique underlying phonological representation for the morpheme and relating it to the surface allomorphs by means of one or more phonological rules.

A particularly simple illustration is provided by the alternation of [s], [z] and [əz] as the regular marker of plural nouns in English, briefly discussed in Chapter 5, Section 2. Specifically, the form [s] occurs immediately following voiceless segments (e.g. *cats* and *cuffs*), [z] combines with preceding voiced segments (e.g. *bags* and *hives*), and [əz] shows up when the last consonant of the singular belongs in the group of *sibilants* (the hissing and hushing sounds basically defined by the specifications [+ coronal, + strident] in Chomsky and Halle's feature system), as in *buses, ashes* and *prizes*. Two questions must be asked in relation to these alternations: what is the underlying form, and what are the rules which provide the link between this form and its surface manifestations?

We have however gone a little too quickly, as we have simply assumed that there is indeed a unique underlying representation for the three allomorphs. But this is an empirical matter, to be decided only by the facts. At stake is the status of the allomorphs, that is, whether they are really such, because they are reducible in underlying representation, or whether they must be considered 'suppletive' variants, as with the Hopi plural stem *moya* mentioned in Chapter 5 (the label *suppletion* is used to indicate phonological irreducibility of morphologically related surface forms).

We shall now show that a common underlying form can in fact be constructed. Consider first the English phonotactic constraint mentioned in Chapter 4 (p. 108) requiring that syllable-final obstruent clusters must have the same specification for voice throughout. This immediately accounts for the ill-formedness of, e.g., **ca*[tz] or **ba*[gs]. It is obvious that the voice specification of the plural suffix 'accommodates' to that of the preceding obstruent, thus suggesting a rule like (90).

$$(90) \quad \begin{bmatrix} +\text{coronal} \\ +\text{anterior} \\ +\text{strident} \end{bmatrix} \longrightarrow [\,\alpha\,\text{voice}\,] \ / \ \begin{bmatrix} -\text{sonorant} \\ \alpha\,\text{voice} \end{bmatrix} \underline{\hspace{2cm}}$$

The input of (90) represents that which is common to [s] and [z]. In particular, no value for voice is given. Instead, it is assigned by the rule on the basis of the voice specification of the obstruent. Thus, (90), like (6) in Chapter 4, is a rule of assimilation.

There is one important difficulty with (90) which must be tackled next, namely, the rule says nothing about the voice value of the plural allomorph in contexts where the preceding segment is not an obstruent. In these contexts we invariably find [z]. Now, at first sight this might suggest simplification of the environment of (90) by removing the [− sonorant] requirement altogether, since sonorants (and this includes vowels) are voiced, and thus their co-occurrence with the allomorph [z] could also be subsumed under assimilation. Further reflection will however reveal that this move cannot be right, because the segments [s] and [z] are contrastive after vowels (cf. e.g. *dice* v. *dyes, bus* v. *buzz, race* v. *raze* or *rays*), a situation which would be prevented by rule (90), which neutralises the opposition between the two segments in the given environment.

An alternative is readily available by postulating /z/ as the underlying representation of the plural morpheme (underlying forms are customarily enclosed in diagonal bars (/ . . . /) and surface forms in square brackets ([. . .]), cf. p. 100) and reformulating the assimilation process in terms of devoicing.

(91)　　$z \rightarrow s$ / [$-$ voice] _____

As regards the third allomorph, [əz], it is now derivable from /z/ via *epenthesis* (the technical term for the insertion of segments).

$$(92)\quad \emptyset \rightarrow \vartheta \ / \ \begin{bmatrix} +\text{coronal} \\ +\text{strident} \end{bmatrix} _____ \begin{bmatrix} +\text{coronal} \\ +\text{strident} \end{bmatrix}$$

The null input of (92) is mapped on to *schwa* (as the 'neutral' central vowel [ə] is known) in the given environment, giving the desired result. This is shown in some detail in (93), which gives the derivations of *cats, bags* and *ashes*. A *derivation* is a set of mappings from an input string where variation has been factored out to an output string corresponding to the surface allomorphs or allophones.

(93)

	/kæt + z/	/bæg + z/	/æʃ + z/
Epenthesis (92)	NA	NA	ə
Devoicing (91)	s	NA	NA
	[kæts]	[bægz]	[æʃəz]

This simple derivation contains only two steps. First, [ə] is epenthesised in *ash*, as the rule is not applicable ('NA') in the other environments. Then, devoicing occurs in *cats*.

A few observations on this derivation are apposite. First, the two rules interact with each other. In point of fact, they must apply in a sequence, i.e. not simultaneously. This procedure is not an a priori ruling, but, rather, it is empirically motivated. Consider for instance the derivation of *ashes*. Now, it is obvious that the underlying form /æʃz/ meets the environment of both Epenthesis and Devoicing. Therefore, if these rules were allowed to apply simultaneously, the incorrect output *[æʃəs] would result. Similar situations have been found again and again across the world's languages.

Not only do phonological rules apply sequentially, but also their particular order of application is not random. Consider once more *ashes*. Clearly, a reversal in the linear order of the rules would again yield the incorrect *[æʃəs]. Accordingly, the grammar of the language must include statements regarding the order of application of its phonological rules, although there are also some universal principles of rule application, as we shall see in Section 5. In the case at hand, we want Epenthesis to precede Devoicing so as to destroy the environment for the latter rule, which consequently cannot apply. This type of ordering situation is commonly given the name *bleeding*.

It is fairly clear, therefore, that our rules (91) and (92) give the desired results as regards plural allomorphy. As they stand, however, these rules are little more than a restatement of the facts, if a rather elegant one. We shall however next adduce some further facts that strongly support this type of formalisation.

Consider first the so-called 'Saxon genitive', exemplified in (94).

(94)　*a* The *bag's* handle is broken
　　　b The *rack's* net is torn
　　　c The *sash's* colour is fading

As can be seen, the approach adopted for plurals carries over verbatim here. Likewise as regards the third person singular in the present tense of verbs, as already pointed out in Chapter 5.

(95)　*a* He rides
　　　b He writes
　　　c He rushes

These extensions naturally lend support to the rule-based analysis, as they suggest that the alternation in question is not a property of the plural morpheme *per se*, but, rather, the automatic consequence of phonological processes of some generality.

At this point, we must reconsider our proposed model and ask whether we could not just as easily adopt /əz/ as the underlying form by replacing Epenthesis (92) with its converse, i.e. a rule deleting /ə/ when followed by /z/ and preceded by a non-sibilant segment. As should be obvious, this change will in no way affect the output of derivation (93).

It is important to realise that the type of analysis we are engaged in, which is typical of generative phonology and of generative linguistics in general, is exclusively based on linguistic facts, not on the whim or the preconceptions of the investigator. Accordingly, when confronted with alternatives, we must look around for additional facts which might help us reach a principled decision. If these facts are not available, and if neither solution is superior as regards the simplicity of the formal apparatus, choice will simply not be possible.

In the case at hand, there is some evidence that our initial proposal is the correct one. Consider first the Saxon genitive gap in the plural: the bags' handles (*the bags's handles). The reason for this gap is of course not purely phonological, as normally a sequence of two z's is simply broken up by the rule of Epenthesis (92), as in *rises* (cf. *rides*). This obviously does not happen in the sequence plural + Saxon genitive, which, instead, is subject to degemination (a string of two identical sounds, particularly consonants, is usually known as a *geminate*). Fortunately, we can give formal status to the difference between /bʌz + z/ → [bʌzəz] and /bʌg + z + z/ → [bʌgz], as only in the latter case are both z's full morphemes. Accordingly, we formulate a rule of Degemination as follows ('+' indicates the *boundary* of a morpheme).

(96)   z → Ø / + z + ____ +

While the occurrence of the process thus formalised is far from being universal, rule (96) is adequate for our present purposes, since it captures the special behaviour in English of the sequences under scrutiny. Note now that if /əz/ was chosen as the underlying representation of the morpheme the analysis would be complicated by the addition of a rule deleting the schwa in precisely the environment of (96). This duplication is avoided by the Epenthesis approach.

A second argument for this approach can be built on the basis of the behaviour of the third person singular of the present tense of the verb *to be*, which in rapid speech undergoes vowel deletion: *the train is late* → *the train's late* (similarly for the past tense with *has*: *he (h)as been seen* → *he's been seen*). Now, note that, interestingly, the resulting (orthographic) *'s* corresponds to the same type of allomorphy as the one we have been studying, and can thus be subsumed under the same analysis. In particular, in the context of a sibilant a schwa will be supplied by the regular Epenthesis rule (92): *the bu*[səz] *late*. Were we to do away with this rule for the general analysis (by postulating /əz/ as the underlying form of the plural and the Saxon genitive), it would have to be reintroduced to account for the variant [əz] for the reduced form of *is* after sibilants, thus complicating the model. Some illustrative derivations are now provided.

(97)

	bags' /bæg + z + z/	bus is /bʌs ɪz/
Degemination (96)	Ø	NA
is-Reduction	NA	Ø
Epenthesis (92)	NA	ə
Devoicing (91)	NA	NA

Once more, the order must be as given. In particular, we want Degemination (96) to bleed Epenthesis (92). We also want *is-*

Reduction to 'feed' Epenthesis (a rule is said to *feed* another when the application of the former creates the input for the latter), but not Degemination, as the reader can verify. Note also that, while Epenthesis and Devoicing apply across the board to the designated morpheme /ɪz/, the scope of both Degemination and *is*-Reduction is more restricted, the former being limited to the second of two z's, and the latter being specific to the verbal form /z/ (and, correspondingly, /hæz/) and being moreover contingent on the style of speech.

Returning now to our two basic rules Devoicing (91) and Epenthesis (92), we shall next show that the processes they capture are in fact more general than their formulation above gives credit for. In (91), Devoicing is presented as the change of *z* into *s* when following any voiceless segment. We must first note that the generality of the environment is confirmed by the facts. Thus consider a voiceless sound such as [x], which is not part of the inventory of English phonemes. Given (91), it is predicted that a (foreign) word containing this segment would be pluralised with [s] rather than [z]. One such word is the name Bach, as in the well-known family of composers, readily pluralised as [baxs] (similarly for its Saxon genitive). It goes without saying that, were the environment instead to be limited to the individual segments which do exist in English (i.e. *k, t, p,* etc.), this behaviour would remain unexplained.

As a matter of fact, such generality must be extended to the input and the output of (91) and (92). In order to understand why, consider the alternations in the past tense of regular verbs.

(98)   *a* wandered, mooed
       b killed, rubbed
       c tapped, sucked
       d padded, patted

In (98) *a* and *b* the presumably basic form /d/ is maintained, while in (98)*c* it undergoes Devoicing, and in (98)*d* Epenthesis breaks the homorganic sequence. Thus the situation is precisely parallel to that with /z/, and this warrants the reformulation of (91) and (92) as (99) and (100), respectively.

(99) $\begin{bmatrix} +\text{consonantal} \\ -\text{sonorant} \end{bmatrix} \rightarrow [-\text{voice}] \ / \ [-\text{voice}]_____$

(100)

$\varnothing \rightarrow \vartheta \ / \ \begin{bmatrix} +\text{coronal} \\ \alpha\text{strident} \\ \alpha\text{continuant} \end{bmatrix} \_\_\_\_ \begin{bmatrix} +\text{coronal} \\ \alpha\text{strident} \\ \alpha\text{continuant} \end{bmatrix}$

This covers precisely the desired ground.

The foregoing discussion is illustrative of the mechanics of generative phonology, where surface facts which may appear unrelated are brought together by the action of appropriately general rules. The input morphophonemic forms are accordingly freed of all the information which is predictable by rule. Equivalently, we can regard the *lexicon* as the repository of all and only the idiosyncratic properties. Rules therefore serve the purpose of mapping such maximally economic lexical representations on to the surface forms, which characteristically include much phonological and phonetic redundancy.

8.5   Autosegmental representations

In our discussion of the behaviour of sibilants as regards Epenthesis we have systematically omitted mention of the affricates [ʧ] and [ʤ], defined in Chomsky and Halle's framework by means of the specification [+ DELAYED RELEASE]. These sounds are however quite interesting. Consider the data in (101).

(101)   *a* clutches, judges
        b clutched, judged

Note that Epenthesis (100) applies before /z/, but not before /d/. This is peculiar, because the only relevant difference between, say, [ʃ] or [t] and [ʧ] appears to be precisely [DELAYED RELEASE]. Now, why should the specification of this feature (not included in our formulation of the rule) influence the application of (100)?

The feature [DELAYED RELEASE] itself is in fact not very satisfactory, because it refers to a dubious phonetic parameter, one which is at any rate confined to a handful of segments. Remember also that in Chapter 4, Section 6, there was some discussion about the mono- or biphonemic nature of [ʧ], and we finally decided for the former. Note, however, that the criteria given are to a large extent arbitrary, and must, at any rate, be stipulated, that is, they do not fall out of the formal representation of the segment itself, which in no way differs from that of other, less problematic segments.

The nature of the solution we shall advance for the problems just raised will best be understood if we first make a short digression into some facts of the Nigerian language Ogori. Specifically, in this language the last vowel of a noun deletes in front of the first vowel of an adjective which follows the noun in the noun phrase (ǰ = [ʤ]).

(102)   *a* igila 'yam' + okeke 'small' → igilokeke 'small yam'
      b ebi 'water' + oboro 'good' → eboboro 'good water'
      c ija 'woman' + osuda 'old' → iǰosuda 'old woman'
      d ɔbɛlɛ 'mat' + ɔnɛ 'this' → ɔbɛlɔnɛ 'this mat'

Now, as mentioned briefly in Chapter 3, Section 11, languages characteristically make linguistic use of voice pitch, either as 'intonation' (as in English) or as 'tone' (as in Ogori). Naturally, pitch changes represent a continuum, but, as in other areas of linguistic sound, it has been found that only some value ranges are invested with linguistic significance. In order to keep the discussion simple, we shall assume that there are only two phonological realisations of pitch: H(igh) and L(ow).

In (102) there is no indication of the tone carried by each vowel. What happens however to the tone on the vowel which is deleted? Let us consider the forms in (102)*c*, for instance.

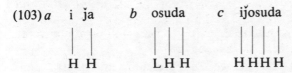

(103) *a*   i   ǰa   *b*   osuda   *c*   iǰosuda

           H   H   L H H   H H H H

In (103) we have represented the tone implemented on each vowel by means of a linking to the letters H or L, and we will soon see that such a graphic device goes beyond being an expository convenience and is in fact invested with crucial theoretical significance. Focusing now on the tone changes between (103)*a*, *b* and *c*, we observe that the tone of the deleted vowel remains unaffected, since the output (103)*c* exhibits four H tones, exactly the same number as the composite input, despite the fact that the vowel bearing one of the input H tones is no longer present in the output. On the other hand, the L on the first vowel of (103)*b* has disappeared, thus suggesting that Ogori has a second deletion rule with the focus on the internal boundary of the noun phrase, one which affects the first tone of the adjective.

Such facts are by no means anomalous and suggest that tones and segments are to some degree linguistically independent of each other, since the processes affecting one class do not necessarily affect the other. Accordingly, we grant full theoretical status to such representations as in (103). Specifically, phonological forms will be construed as consisting of a number of layers or *tiers*, the elements of which are linked or *associated* to each other in accordance with certain principles, largely universal, to be discussed later. On the one hand, the linkage represents the simultaneity of phonetic implementation. On the other, the fact that the elements or *autosegments* in each tier are given full independent status allows them operational autonomy, as dictated by the facts. A useful analogy is that of singing to played music, both aspects of the event being co-ordinated and yet separate. This new approach to phonology is known as 'nonlinear' or *autosegmental*, and contrasts with the traditional 'linear' one, where all phonological elements are bundled together into 'segments', which strictly follow each other like beads on a string.

We can now return to our problems concerning affricates. Suppose that, in addition to the two tiers in (101), namely, the 'tonal' tier made up of Hs and Ls and the 'melodic' tier corresponding roughly to the traditional segments, we set up a further tier indicating the phonological timing of the various component elements in any one structure. Strong evidence for this *timing tier* (also called the 'skeleton') will build up as we go along. According to this construal of phonological forms, the word *bell*, for instance, will have the following structure.

(104)

Following established practice, we are representing the skeletal units (or 'slots') as a succession of Cs (for 'consonant') and Vs (for 'vowel') (hence the alternative label 'CV-tier' for the skeleton). Consider now the effects of this approach for the issues at hand. Briefly, it provides the formal machinery for solving the paradox contained in affricates, at once one and two phonemes.

(105)

What (105) says is that the affricate [ʧ] is in effect one consonant with two distinct articulatory phases.

The advantages of this type of formalisation are overwhelming. besides resolving the classical phonemic paradox of affricates, it gives an elegant and intuitively satisfactory solution to the problem posed by their behaviour *vis-à-vis* the Epenthesis rule in (100). Consider the consequences of the independent status now granted to [t] and [ʃ] in the segmental tier. Simply, the feature specifications of these two articulatory units are now allowed to differ. Relevantly to the present issue, [ʃ] will be marked as [+ strident, + continuant]. Observe now the (simplified) underlying representation of *clutches* in (106).

(106)

```
C  C  V   C      C
|  |  |    \  /   |
k  l  ʌ t    ʃ    z
```

It is obvious that the structural description of (100) will be met, since [ʃ] and [z] agree in the specifications for [STRIDENT] and [CONTINUANT], as required by the rule, and therefore Epenthesis will take place. This is not the case for *clutched*, however, as illustrated in (107).

(107)

```
C  C  V   C      C
|  |  |    \  /   |
k  l  ʌ t    ʃ    d
```

Here [d], which is minus for both features, is adjacent to [ʃ] (NB not to [t]), which is plus. Accordingly, the rule will not apply. Parallel facts in the behaviour of affricates have been observed in many languages.

We must now make a more precise statement of the general autosegmental formalism, and will use a somewhat idealised version of English intonation to this end. Consider the simple word *no*, which can be said as a statement or as a question, normally corresponding to a 'falling' and a 'rising' intonation respectively. In our terms here, we shall relate the former to a tonal melody HL, and the latter to LH. The two layers entering into the composition of an intonated word must of course be related. Specifically, we shall assume that tones are realised on vowels. In the case at hand, there is only one vowel, and thus each of the two tone sequences will stand in a many-to-one relationship to it. We shall represent the linkage between tones and segments as mediated by the skeleton, which is assigned a central, pivotal role in autosegmental phonology, as befits its timing function.

(108)   *a*   *b*

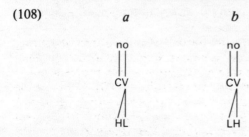

Let us now replace the monosyllabic word in (108) with a longer form, such as *never*. Do we now need a longer tonal melody to obtain the same effect? The answer is in the negative; simply, the outcome of the association procedure will be different, because there is now the same number of relevant elements in both tiers, namely, two vowels and two tones.

(109)

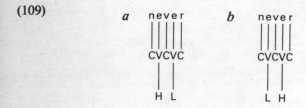

Finally, in (110) we exemplify a case where there are more vowels than tonal melodies.

(110)

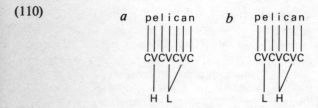

(It must be noted that the last vowel associated with H in such structures will be pronounced at an even higher pitch). Assuming, as is reasonable, that the associations in these representations are not given, but, rather, are effected by rule, we must now state the basic principles of autosegmental association, as follows.

(111)   (i)   Melodic elements associate to (the relevant) skeletal slots one-to-one.

      (ii)   Associations are carried out from left to right.

     (iii)   Any remaining unassociated elements may enter into multiple (one-to-many or many-to-one) associations.

The effect of these principles on the forms at hand is now shown for the tone melody HL.

(112)   (i)/(ii)

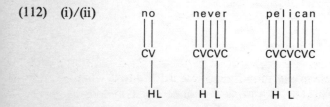

(iii)

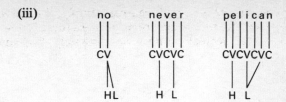

Importantly, the principles in (111) obey the following constraint.

(113) Association lines may not cross

This universal constraint lies at the heart of autosegmental phonology.

We can now see that in all the examples the linking of the elements in the tone tier has taken place strictly in accordance with the autosegmental principles in (111). As expected, this happens automatically, regardless of the number of syllables.

(114)

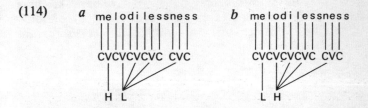

Similar results are observed in properly tonal languages. For instance, in Etung, a language spoken along the Nigeria–Cameroon border, a single tonal melody spreads over all the vowels of the word (y = [j]).

(115)

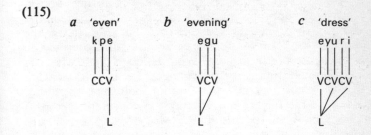

Two-tone sequences associate to the lone vowel of a monosyllabic word and show the expected spreading on the right edge, rather than the left, in trisyllables.

(116)   *a* 'how'   *b* 'leg'   *c* 'spoon'

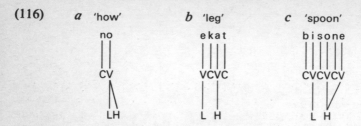

Thus, in all these cases, while the type of tonal melody corresponding to each word is a lexical or grammatical matter, exactly as is the identity of the segmental melodies, once these two objects are given, their pattern of interaction is predicted by general principles of autosegmental association.

8.6   Template-based morphology

We shall now apply the autosegmental model we have been sketching to the analysis of certain aspects of Arabic morphology of long-standing difficulty. Consider first the plurals in (117)*b* for the singulars in (117)*a* (*ǰ* = [ʤ]).

(117)   *a* manzil   'home'   *b* manaazil
         maktab   'office'   makaatib
         ǰundab   'locust'   ǰanaadib
         ǰudǰud   'cricket'   ǰadaaǰid

From the point of view of English, these plurals are very strange. Thus, while in English the plural is formed by the simple concatenation of the morpheme /z/ to the singular, as we saw in Section 4, in Arabic several processes appear to be occurring at once. Specifically, whenever appropriate, the first vowel of the singular is seemingly changed to *a*, and the last one to *i*. Simultaneously, the sequence *aa* is inserted between the second and the third consonants.

The stated facts are not in dispute. What is less clear is what the most adequate formalisation is for the changes. Let us establish that there are two different general types of morphological operation: concatenative, as in the English plural, and non-concatenative, as in the Arabic plural. Now, notice that another way of viewing the latter is as the insertion of a sequence *aaai* into the singular template emptied of its vowels. This makes sense in as much as the idea 'plural' seems to be conveyed in Arabic by precisely this vowel sequence, similarly to /z/ in English. Accordingly, we tentatively set up a plural morpheme as in (118) (*μ* = morpheme).

(118)

From this, it is only a short step to claiming that the singular vowels also have morphemic status, that is, that they are morphemically separate from the consonants, which in turn constitute the morpheme associated with the basic meaning of the word, i.e. the 'root' (there are compelling language-internal reasons for this analysis anyway). If so, we can view both singular and plural formation as a process of 'dovetailing' the two different segmental sequences. Now, as (117) shows, this dovetailing has very specific characteristics; the first *a* must go between the first and the second consonant, the next two *a*'s between the second and the third consonant, and so on. In other words, the landing place of each segment is determined beforehand. A simple autosegmental formalisation of this situation which makes use of the machinery presented above goes as follows.

First, in the lexicon the phonological representation of the 'neutral' semantic meaning of the word does not include any skeletal information, i.e. it is purely 'melodic'; in fact, it contains only consonantal melodies. Second, each realisation of the word requires the provision of a particular type of CV sequence or 'template'. Third, the morphemes for 'plural', etc. are also lexically given only as a melodic sequence, in this case one made up of vowels. We represent these various elements in (119) for the plural 'locusts'.

(119) *a*   *b*   *c*

These different objects will of course eventually be related via the skeletal template (119)*b*.

Implementing the associations, it follows from the no-crossing-of-lines prohibition in (113) that the representation to be constructed must be three-dimensional, since a purely two-dimensional one cannot guarantee that (113) will be respected. That is to say, the relationship between the skeleton and the elements of each of the other tiers must be construed as occupying a different spatial plane. The reader can easily verify that, unless this convention is adopted, crossing of lines will be unavoidable. Accordingly, an autosegmental representation can be thought of as analogous to a book suspended in space with open pages, the spine of the book corresponding to the skeleton, and each of the pages to a different *autosegmental plane* (planes thus replace the previous two-dimensional tiers). The result for the case at hand is displayed in (120) (three-dimensional figures are of course hard to fit on to the two dimensions of a page!).

(120)

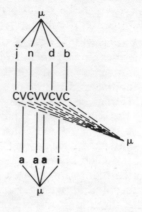

This analysis must now be refined somewhat. Consider the singular–plural alternants in (121) (š = [ʃ]; y = [j]; a subscripted dot indicates pharyngealisation).

(121)   *a* sulṭaan   'sultan'   *b* salaaṭiin
        šayṭaan   'devil'   šayaaṭiin
        miftaaḥ   'key'   mafaatiiḥ
        šuʔbuub   'rain shower'   šaʔaabiib

The difference between (121) and (117) resides in their respective last vowel, which is single in (117) but double in (121). Now, while this difference is unpredictable in the singular, in the plural it is derivable from the singular. This suggests that the plural template is best construed as the result of an operation on the singular template, rather than as an independent lexical morpheme, as we have been assuming so far (cf. (119)*b*). Rule (122) derives the plural template.

(122)   CVCCV⟨V⟩C → CVCVVCV⟨V⟩ C

The *angled brackets* are used to express the fact that if the material thus defined is present on the left of the arrow, it must also be present on the right. Rule (122) is therefore the Arabic rule of plural formation, the direct counterpart of the concatenation of /z/ in English.

Except, of course, that in Arabic (122) does not tell the whole story, and we must still associate the plural melody to the template provided by (122). Above we gave this plural melody as *aaai* (cf. (119)*c*), and it now appears that we must add a (conditional) extra *i*. In point of fact, however, we are going to suggest a streamlining of the representation. Notice particularly that the additional V in (121) is associated with *i*, as is its tautosyllabic mate (NB *tautosyllabic* is used to mean 'in the same syllable'). Perhaps this is no coincidence, nor is it that the rest of the V slots are linked to *a*. This generalisation can be captured by proposing the following lexical representation for the plural morpheme.

(123)

$$
\begin{array}{c}
\mu \\
\wedge \\
a \ \ i
\end{array}
$$

There is now a mismatch between the number of melodic units in (123) and the number of V skeletal slots provided by (122). But this is only a problem if the association between melodic elements and skeletal elements were required to be one-to-one. Instead, as we have already seen, multiple associations are allowed.

In the case under discussion, however, literal application of the principles in (111) will clearly yield incorrect results, as they predict, e.g., **saliiṭiin* from *sulṭaan*. What we need is a language-specific rule to correct this particular development of the derivation. Simply, we stipulate that the second of the two vowels in the plural melody must associate to the final syllable before the application of the general principles of autosegmental association (111). The rule in (124) formalises this procedure.

(124)

$$
\text{CVCVVCV} \langle V \rangle \text{C}
$$

$$
\begin{array}{c}
a \ \ i \\
\vee \\
\mu \\
\text{[Plural]}
\end{array}
$$

The dotted line simply stands for the command 'associate'. Naturally, as indicated, when this association takes place, the *a* is still unassociated. After (124), the general principles in (111) will apply, completing the derivation as desired.

One of the general consequences of the adopted procedure is that the representation of segment length (cf. Chapter 3, Section 11) may now be kept apart from the specific melodic realisation of the segment. Thus the long *i* in *salaaṭiin*, for instance, is formalised as in (125)*a*.

(125)

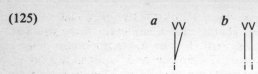

This configuration is of course the mirror image of that adopted above for affricates (and, similarly, other such complex segments). In fact, it has been suggested that the doubling of the melody in such structures, as represented in (125)*b*, is ruled out (or at least disfavoured) by Universal Grammar, a generalisation which has come to be known as the *Obligatory Contour Principle*.

8.7 Metrical structures

In our summary presentation of English intonation we deliberately chose forms with stress on the first syllable (*pelican, melodilessness*), and we must now consider the case where stress is not initial. One particularly long word is given in (126).

(126)

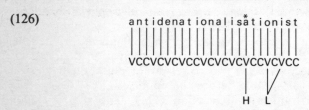

As before, the tone melody in (126) represents the falling intonation typical of statements. The star on the *a* indicates the locus of this word's primary stress, i.e. the place where the greatest prominence is felt (cf. Chapter 3, Section 11, for some discussion of the phonetics of stress). What is interesting for our purposes here is that such a mark clearly signals the starting point for the operation of our association algorithm (111). This situation is by no means atypical, and the free play of the algorithm is often constrained by the presence of such diacritic or 'accentual' marks.

Two questions now arise. The first refers to the tonal realisation of the unassociated syllables. Without going into details (simpler melodies are in fact associated with these syllables), it is clear that they fall outside the domain of the HL melody represented in (126). The second question, directly relevant to the concerns of this section, relates to the source of the stress mark itself. In other words, how does this mark come to be where it is?

Some discussion of English stress directly relevant to this question is included later in the chapter. First, however, we must examine some cases of simpler stress assignment.

Put at its crudest, stress can phonologically be equated with prominence within a domain. Thus, within the domain of the word in (126) the most prominent syllable is the one indicated by the star.

A useful contrast is provided by French and Hungarian, where stress falls right on the edge of the word. These languages choose however opposing edges: last and first, respectively (stress is again represented by a star; note in particular that the orthographic accents are unrelated to stress).

(127) *a* dése*rt   'desert'   *b* lányok   'girls'

    suffis*ant   'sufficient'   De*brecen   a town

    Romorantin* a town   bútorüzlet*   'furniture shop'

    personnalité* 'personality' mo*torkerékpár 'motor cycle'

We shall now adopt a more perspicuous formalism. Specifically, we shall define the stress domain by means of a metrical tree. A *metrical tree* is a device indicating common constituency and marking one of the elements as hierarchically prominent, i.e. as the head of the tree, represented here as a vertical branch. The metrical trees corresponding to (127) are consequently as follows.

(128)

As is implicit in (128), metrical structures are endowed with their own autosegmental plane. The motivation for introducing a new type of formalism is however still not clear and must be attended to next.

Simply, while the autosegmental configurations considered in the previous sections consist solely of one layer in any one plane, the metrical fabric allows for multilayered hierarchical structures. For instance, although in Weri and Maranungku (two native languages of New Guinea and Australia, respectively) the most prominent syllable is final and initial, respectively, thus paralleling French and Hungarian, other syllables also show some degree of salience. In particular, even-numbered syllables counting away from the locus of primary stress bear 'secondary' stress, less prominent than its primary counterpart but more pronounced than total stresslessness. This stress hierarchy is readily represented by means of a two-layered configuration.

(129)

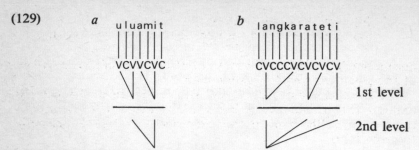

Notice that the second-level trees have been built on the roots of their first-layer counterparts (equivalently, on the Vs which are first-level heads), rather than on the full string of skeletal Vs. In (129) the first-layer (or 'foot-level') trees happen to have binary branching, while in those of the second layer, at the level of the word, the branching is unbounded. Also, in Weri the trees are right-headed at both levels (129)*a*, while in Maranungku they are left-headed (129)*b*. Finally, because the appropriate domain must be exhaustively parsed by the tree-construction algorithm, 'degenerate' (i.e. incomplete) trees are allowed (cf. e.g. the last tree in (129)*b*, which has only the head, the minimal component of a tree).

The algorithms required to construct the metrical structures in (129)*a* and (129)*b* are now all but obvious. We give them in (130)*a* and (130)*b*, respectively.

(130) *a* (i) In the first level, construct right-headed binary trees from right to left.
      (ii) In the second level, construct a right-headed unbounded tree.
    b (i) In the first level, construct left-headed binary trees from left to right.
      (ii) In the second level, construct a left-headed unbounded tree.

Notice that in the case of binary trees the direction of construction must be specified. This happens to be redundant for (129)*a*, where the same result would be obtained in any case, but it clearly is not for (129)*b*, where reverse directionality would incorrectly change the headedness of the first-level trees.

For greater clarity, (131) spells out the various parameters which play a role in the construction of metrical trees.

(131) (i) Level (foot level, word level, etc.).
     (ii) Number of branches (binary, unbounded).

(iii) Head location (right, left).
(iv) Direction of construction (right to left, left to right).

Such a simple model is sufficiently rich to account for a great variety of stress patterns found the world over.

The stress pattern of Latin is well known, and we shall now use it to illustrate two additional devices which interact with the algorithms constructed on the basis of the parameters in (131). Consider the forms in (132).

(132)   *a* refĕctus   *b* refēecit   *c* rēficit
      'made again'   'he made again'   'he makes again'

Stress falls on the penultimate syllable in (132)*a* and (132)*b*, and on the antepenultimate in (132)*c*. These contours exhaust the Latin inventory.

The question now is, what algorithm will give us these, and only these, patterns? Some simple observations are in order. First, stress never falls on the last of a sequence of syllables. Second, whenever stress is penultimate, either the penultimate syllable is closed by a consonant, as in (132)*a*, or it contains a long vowel, as in (132)*b*. Otherwise, stress is antepenultimate.

Suppose then that in Latin we construe antepenultimate stress as basic (there are languages, e.g. Macedonian, where this is indeed the only pattern). Given the parameters in (131), however, it is far from obvious what the formalisation of this pattern will be. In fact, we need to introduce an additional device, as in (133).

(133)   Make a peripheral syllable invisible to the stress algorithm.

This device is commonly known as *extrametricality*. Notice that, importantly, the possibility of extrametricality is confined to peripheral syllables, a constraint referred to as the *Peripherality Condition*.

We can now readily derive the Latin contour in (132)*c*.

(134)

The first step introduces extrametricality, graphically represented by means of parentheses. Then, in the last stage, a left-headed binary tree is built from the right. This procedure is summarised in (135).

(135) LATIN STRESS (FIRST VERSION):
    (i)   Make the last syllable extrametrical.
    (ii) Build a left-headed binary tree from the right.

We still have not accounted for the penultimate stress pattern in (132)*a* and (132)*b*. Clearly what these two cases have in common is that the penultimate syllable is complex or 'heavy', that is, it contains either a long vowel, as in (132)*b*, or a final consonant, as in (132)*a*. This leads us to the final device we will introduce in relation to stress assignment, which we will dub *metrical accent*. Simply, a vowel marked as a carrier of metrical accent is conceptually assigned some extra weight which attracts a tree head upon the operation of the tree-building algorithm (importantly, the diacritic *accent* is logically independent of the main stress in the surface). Accordingly, we complete (135) as follows.

(135) (cont.)

    (iii) Assign metrical accent to heavy syllables.

Logically, of course, (135) (iii) must precede (135) (ii).
The contrastive derivations of *refectus* and *reficit* are now given.

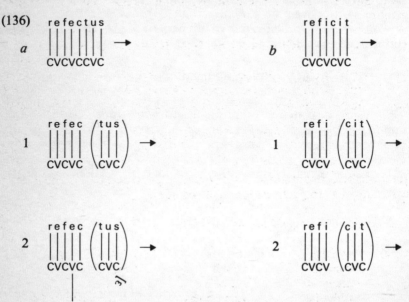

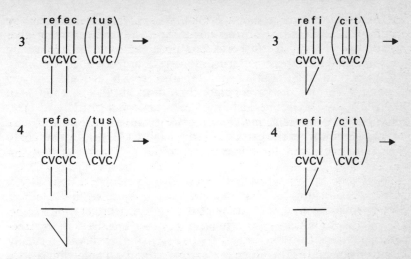

We have numbered the steps 1 to 4 for ease of exposition. In 1 the last syllable is made extrametrical. In 2 the heavy syllable *fec* in *a* is assigned metrical accent, represented here by a premature tree head. In 3 the tree-construction algorithm operates as predicted. Note in particular that in *a* the head carried over from step 2 prevents ordinary construction, as in *b*, forcing instead a doubling of tree structures. Finally, in 4 a second-level unbounded right-headed tree is built, to give the final contour. The complete Latin Stress Algorithm is now given.

(137)   LATIN STRESS ALGORITHM (FINAL VERSION):

    (i)   Make the last syllable extrametrical.
    (ii)   Assign metrical accent to heavy syllables.
    (iii) In the first level build left-headed binary trees from right to left.
    (iv) In the second level build an unbounded right-headed tree.

Interestingly, this algorithm plays an important role in the stress assignment of English, as we shall see next.

Consider the English nouns in (138).

(138) *a* asterisk   *b* horizon   *c* utensil
       cinema   aroma   agenda
       analysis   arena   synopsis
       Canada   thrombosis   conundrum

Clearly, they are parallel to the Latin forms in (132), and can thus be readily described by the same algorithm (we are assuming that diphthongs in English can be treated on a par with the Latin long vowels). English stress patterns, however, are considerably more complex than their Latin counterparts, which are exhaustively accounted for by the given algorithm. For instance, although in English derived adjectives exhibit similar contours to those in (138) (*municipal, complacent, indignant*), primary adjectives and verbs are usually exempt from the extrametricality clause (137)(i). Instead, only their final consonant is made extrametrical.

(139) *a* exquisi(te)   *b* extre(me)   *c* inten(se)
          astoni(sh)   maintai(n)   tormen(t)
          embarra(ss)   surmi(se)   collap(se)

Also, in nouns, (137)(i) does not excuse a final syllable with a long vowel from receiving stress.

(140)   monsoon   police   bazaar   brocade
         baroque   engineer   questionnaire   employee

Note that some of these nouns (especially those with more than two syllables) carry a secondary stress on their first syllable.

8.8 Stress in syntax

Rather than getting involved in the intricacies of English word stress, we shall turn our attention to units above the word, where tree constituency is directly taken over from syntactic constituency, thus providing an opportune link with some of the matters discussed in the opening sections of this chapter, the cycle in particular (cf. p. 245). Consider the difference between the two structures in (141), where the word carrying the greatest prominence has been capitalised (below the two components of *wildlife* are consistently separated to highlight their word status).

(141) *a* wild LIFE
       b WILD life

This stress contrast corresponds to a categorial difference between an ordinary noun phrase with the meaning 'life which is wild', as in 'the wild life of Hollywood socialites', and the compound noun meaning 'species living in the wild without man's interference', as in 'endangered wild life'. (142) provides two longer instances of the same basic patterns.

(142)   *a* Probe into the nefarious consequences of his wild LIFE
        b WILD life preservation lobby supporters survey

These phrases can be conceived of as, e.g., newspaper headlines. What is perhaps most interesting about them is the radical difference in stress contours, which apparently parallel those of simple words in French and Hungarian respectively. As stated, however, such structures originate in the syntactic component of the grammar (at least in the interpretation of morphology which limits its scope to the structure of the word), and we shall now explore the possibility that the rules which assign stress simply make use of the given hierarchies, displayed in (143).

(143)   *a* [$_{NP}$ Probe [$_{PP}$ into the nefarious consequences [$_{PP}$ of his wild LIFE]]]
        b [[[[[WILD life]$_N$ preservation]$_N$ lobby]$_N$ supporters]$_N$ survey]$_N$

In order to account for the difference in stress pattern we need different rules for the structures exemplified in (143)*a* and (143)*b*. Notice again that the former is a phrasal structure (a noun phrase, in fact; cf. p. 162 for some discussion of this category), while the latter, although also complex, is syntactically assigned the basic categorial label N(oun). This crucial labelling difference triggers off separate stress rules, as informally stated in (144), where it is understood that 'function words' such as prepositions or pronouns are in any event excluded from the domain of stress (they typically become parasitic to the adjacent 'content word', a phenomenon known as *cliticisation*).

(144)   *a* Enhance the stress of the last word of a *phrasal* structure (including the sentence).
        b Enhance the stress of the first word of a *compound* structure.

In the absence of any special emphasis in any other word, the predictions of the algorithm in (144) are basically correct, and we shall now bring it into line with the metrical model being presented.

(145)   *a* In a phrasal structure build an unbounded right-headed tree.
        b In a compound structure build an unbounded left-headed tree.

Now note that there are phrases superficially similar to (142)*b* but where the main stress is no longer initial.

(146) *a* Wild life preservation lobby ENTRY requirements
  b Wild life preservation SUMMER activities frenzy

Clearly, (145)*b* is incorrect as it stands and must be refined.

The answer requires two separate steps. First, the arboreal structures are built in layers, one for each syntactic constituent, in accordance with the principle of the cycle (cf. Section 3 above). Specifically, the rules will be applied to each syntactically defined structure 'bottom up', i.e. starting with the most deeply embedded constituent(s) and proceeding outwards until the outermost structure is reached. Second, we modify the rule for compound stress along the lines of (147).

(147) *a* In a compound constituent, build an unbounded right-headed tree,
  b provided the metrical material dominated by the head is branching;
  c otherwise, build a left-headed tree.

For greater clarity, we have presented the rule in three parts. Notice that the most general part, (147)*a*, is now identical with (145)*a*, a welcome development, since now all instances of stress above the word are treated as essentially one phenomenon. The difference between the phrasal stress in (145) and the compound stress in (147) now resides in the condition (147)*b* and the 'elsewhere' clause (147)*c*. The former imposes a condition on the operation of (147)*a*, namely, that the right-located head dominate a branching structure. If this condition is not fulfilled, the tree cannot be built (i.e. (147)*a* is rendered inoperative), thus paving the way for the default procedure in (147)*c*, which reverses the location of the head, without any conditions.

Before exemplifying the application of (145) and (147) it will be well to reflect on the ordering of the two rules in (147): (147)*a, b* and (147)*c*. Clearly, if the order were reversed, left-headed trees would be constructed in all cases, an incorrect result. Thus, as suggested by the English word 'otherwise' in (147)*c*, this rule must apply last. Interestingly, there is a way of predicting this order without a language-specific stipulation. The prediction uses the relative generality of overlapping rules; the more specific rule must apply first, a logical requirement, since otherwise it would invariably be pre-empted by the more general branch. This principle is known as the *Elsewhere Condition*, and, as stated, it has universal scope.

We now illustrate the action of (145) and (147) in (148), where horizontal lines separate different cycles corresponding to different degrees of embedding. For greater visual clarity, number subscripts indicating depth of embedding relate such lines to the structural brackets. As noted, the terminal elements of the algorithm are all and only content words, which in (148) have been abbreviated to their capitalised first letter. Cycles not containing new content words are therefore vacuous, and have accordingly been omitted.

(148)   *a*

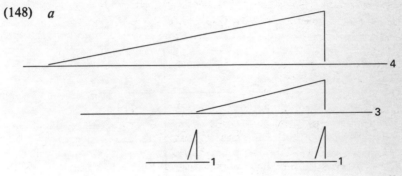

$[_4$ $[_1$ P$]_1$ $[_3$ $[_2$ into $[_1$ the N C $]_1$ $]_2$ $[_2$ of $[_1$ his W L $]_1$ $]_2$ $]_3$ $]_4$

b

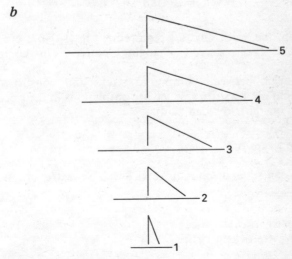

$[_5$ $[_4$ $[_3$ $[_2$ $[_1$ W L $]_1$ P $]_2$ L $]_3$ S $]_4$ S $]_5$

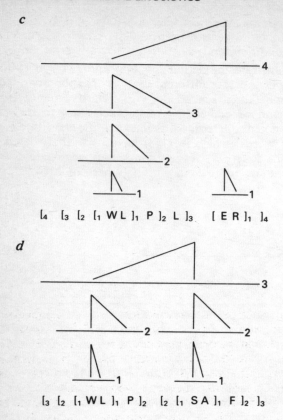

c

[₄ [₃ [₂ [₁ W L]₁ P]₂ L]₃ [E R]₁]₄

d

[₃ [₂ [₁ W L]₁ P]₂ [₂ [₁ S A]₁ F]₂]₃

As can be seen, the branchingness requirement in (147)*b* is crucial in accounting for the observed changing patterns in compound structures.

The correlation between compound stress and constituency is strongly brought out by strings which are ambiguous in their ordinary written form, but not so when said.

(149)   theatre ticket office

This sequence can either mean 'a ticket office at a theatre' or 'an office for theatre tickets'.

(150)   *a* [theatre [ticket office]]
         b [[theatre ticket] office]

Correspondingly, *ticket* or *theatre* will bear the main stress.

(151) *a*

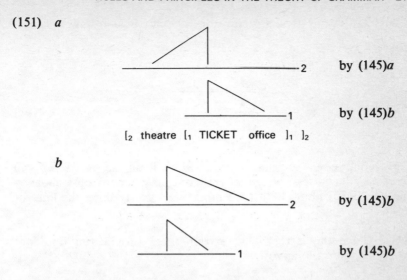

by (145)*a*

by (145)*b*

[₂ theatre [₁ TICKET office]₁]₂

b

by (145)*b*

by (145)*b*

[₂ [₁ THEATRE ticket]₁ office]₂

One important aspect of these derivations is to be noted. Although the syntactic and metrical constituencies are coextensive, the hierarchial relations in them need not be isomorphic. For instance, in *WILD life*, *wild* is the metrical head, but *life* is the syntactic (and semantic) head (after all, WILD life is a subset of all life, just as wild LIFE is). This means that, although our compound stress rule (145)*b* uses syntactic structures, it does not simply copy them, but rather performs a metrical head assignment operation on them. So, the syntactic and metrical structures are independent, although the construction of the latter makes use of information from the former. Within the context of the three-dimensional model we have adopted, metrical structures can thus be construed as pertaining to an independent metrical plane.

The final phenomenon we shall consider concerns the displacement of word stress exemplified in (152).

(152) *a* jăm for Japanĕse

b Jăpanese jăm

We are interested in the differences in the location of the main word stress in the word *Japanese*. Note that in our discussion of compound and phrasal stress the location of word stress was assumed to remain constant. The fact that this is not always so is however unrelated to structural or categorial considerations, but rather is brought about by rhythmic pressure.

In isolation the stress structure of *Japanese* is as follows.

(153)

Correspondingly, the primary stress will fall on *ese*, while *Jap* will bear secondary stress. Note that this contour is readily obtainable by our Latin algorithm (137) if we modify clause (i) along the lines of (154).

(154) Make the last syllable extrametrical provided it does not contain a long vowel.

Let us now represent the prominence relations in (153) by means of an array of asterisks.

(155) Japanese
    *   *
        *

Such representations are known as *metrical grids*. The grid in (155) includes the following information: (i) the word *Japanese* contains two degrees or levels of prominence; (ii) first-level prominence is assigned to the syllables *Jap* and *ese*; (iii) second-level prominence is assigned to the syllable *ese* only.

We shall now give the full grid representation for (152) the additional asterisk level corresponds to the application of rule (144)*a*.

(156) *a* jam for Japanese
      *   *   *
      *   *
              *

    b Japanese jam
      *   *   *
      *   *
           *

Assuming that (155) is indeed the correct lexical representation for the metrical structure of *Japanese*, we must account for the difference between (156)*b* and the intermediate structure in (157).

(157)   Japanese jam
     * *   *
       *   *
          *

Manifestly, the second-level asterisk of *Japanese* has moved from the last to the first syllable in (156)*b*, but not in (156)*a*. The following facts must therefore be accounted for: (i) why stress shifts in (157); (ii) why stress does not shift in (156)*a*; (iii) why the shifted stress lands on *Jap* rather than *an* (cf. (156)*b*).

The answers to (i) and (ii) are very straightforward and can be directly inferred from the grid's visual design. Specifically, in (157) there is a *stress clash* because the second-level asterisks are adjacent to each other without there being an intervening asterisk one level down, i.e. in the first level. This situation has obviously been corrected in (156)*a*. Such stress clash exercises rhythmic pressure for stress (i.e. asterisk) movement, hence (156)*b*. Note that movement is level-internal, and that it is confined to the minimal distance, as defined by the line of asterisks immediately below those subject to shift. This answers our three questions and enables us to bring the present chapter to a close.

Exercises: Chapter 8

1   The chapter provides reasons for developing the X-bar system with respect to nominal constituents. Discuss how the following well-formed conjoined structures suggest extending this system to adjectival and prepositional constituents.

(*a*)   Mary is more stunningly beautiful and disturbingly intelligent than ever.
(*b*)   Mary is less lovely to behold and pleasant to be near than she was last year.
(*c*)   Mary is more into therapy and out of common sense than she was last week.
(*d*)   The boat is further up the river and into the jungle than last time we heard from it.

Provide an X-bar analysis for the conjoined phrases in the above sentences.

2   The following is a well-formed echo-question.

(*a*)   John likes fish and what?

However, application of *Wh*-movement to this structure yields an ungrammatical string.

(b) *What does John like fish and Ø

Investigate the hypothesis that structures of the form X *and* Y and X *or* Y are islands with respect to the movement rules of *Wh*-movement and Topicalisation.

3 In (*a*) and (*b*), the italicised constituents are referred to as *sentential subjects*.

(*a*) *For John to love Mary* is a tragedy.
(*b*) *That John loves Mary* is obvious.

Furthermore, there exist well-formed echo-questions resulting from replacing one of the NPs in the sentential subject by a *Wh*-word.

(*c*) For who(m) to love Mary is a tragedy?
(*d*) For John to love whom is a tragedy?
(*e*) That who loves Mary is obvious?
(*f*) That John loves whom is obvious?

Investigate the status of Sentential Subjects with respect to *Wh*-movement and Topicalisation. Can their properties be subsumed under the Subjacency Principle?

4 If the Subjacency Principle is correct, it ought to follow that no part of an NP can be extracted by *Wh*-movement and moved into the COMP position. Such an extraction would involve the part of the NP in crossing two bounding nodes, NP and S. In the light of this consider the following sentences.

(*a*) John's cry to his mother went unheard.
(*b*) Who did John's cry to go unheard?
(*c*) John's passionate interest in Mary dismayed his mother.
(*d*) Who did John's passionate interest in dismay his mother?
(*e*) Bill heard John's cry to his mother.
(*f*) Who did Bill hear John's cry to?
(*g*) A picture of Mary was on the dresser.
(*h*) Who was a picture of on the dresser?
(*i*) John took a picture of Mary.
(*j*) Who did John take a picture of?
(*k*) A book about fossils is in John's pocket.
(*l*) What is a book about in John's pocket?
(*m*) John is writing a book about fossils.
(*n*) What is John writing a book about?

Go through these sentences deciding whether they are grammatical. What are the implications of your judgements for the validity of the Subjacency Principle?

5   In the chapter, it is suggested that relative clauses share important properties with *Wh*-questions and that the rule of *Wh*-movement is probably involved in the derivation of both. However, there are important differences between these structures, most obviously to do with the type of constituent that can be moved by *Wh*-movement. NPs do not differentiate between the structures.

(*a*)   COMP Mary will excite whom?
(*b*)   Whom will Mary excite?
(*c*)   The man COMP Mary will excite whom.
(*d*)   The man whom Mary will excite.

Consider other constituent types (ADJP, PP, ADVP) and give examples of how they behave under *Wh*-movement in *Wh*-questions and in relative clauses. Can you think of any reason for the differences you discover?

6   Consider the following data from French.

(*a*)   [bɔ̃fis]   'good son'
        [bɔnfij]   'good daughter'
        [bɔnɔm]   'good man'
        [bɔnfam]   'good woman'

(*b*)   [ptigaRsɔ̃]   'small boy'
        [ptitfij]   'small girl'
        [ptitɔm]   'small man'
        [ptitfam]   'small woman'

(*c*)   [gRɑ̃fis]   'grandson'
        [gRɑ̃dfij]   'granddaughter'
        [grɑ̃dmɛR]   'grandmother'
        [grɑ̃tɔm]   'tall man'

Carry out the following tasks.

  (i)   Divide each of the phrases above into its component morphemes.
 (ii)   List the allomorphs of each morpheme.
(iii)   Point out the phonetic differences within each group.
 (iv)   Proceeding from (*a*) to (*c*), postulate a unique underlying form for each adjective and a set of rules to account for its surface manifestations. (HINTS: French is a gendered language, males being usually masculine and females feminine; many feminine words are spelled with a final *e*, which was pronounced in old French and still survives as a schwa in certain styles of speech.)

7   (i)   As pointed out in Chapter 4, coronals in English palatalise when preceding the sequence *iV*, where the *i* is pronounced [j], i.e. it is not the main element in the syllable. According to this, the *t* in the following ought to be pronounced [ʧ], contrary to fact.

(a) gravitaţion   creaţion   excreţion
  repetiţion   instituţion   interjecţion
  hesitaţion   promoţion   conscripţion

Formulate a rule accounting for these facts. Test it out against further data.
  (ii) The following words appear to constitute an exception to the generalisation in (a).

(b) digesţion   exhausţion   basţion
  suggesţion   quesţion   Chrisţian

Do such forms have to be idiosyncratically marked in the lexicon or can a generalisation be achieved? If so, give it the appropriate formalisation.
  (iii) Assuming a phonological representation /jVs/ for the orthographic ending *-eous*, how can you account for the palatalisation of the *t* in *righteous* into [y]? Could the orthography conceivably give a clue? (HINT: compare the way *right* is pronounced in some dialects.)

8   Consider the following tonal alternations in Nzema (´ = H, ` = L, ^ = HL; *y* = [j]).

(a)   èbònú?   èbònú nɛ̀   èbònú yé
      'forest'   'the forest'   'this forest'

      àkùtú   àkùtú nɛ̀   àkùtú yé
      'orange'   'the orange'   'this orange'

      àkɔ́lɛ́   àkɔ́lɛ́ nɛ̀   àkɔ́lɛ́ yé
      'chicken'   'the chicken'   'this chicken'

      èzèká?   èzèká nɛ̀   èzèká yé
      'comb'   'the comb'   'this comb'

      ègyádé   ègyádé nɛ̀   ègyádé yé
      'kitchen'   'the kitchen'   'this kitchen'

(b)   bùlàlɛ́   bùlàlɛ́ nɛ̀   bùlàlɛ̂ yé
      'iron'   'the iron'   'this iron'

      èlùé?   èlùé nɛ̀   èlùê yé
      'yam'   'the yam'   'this yam'

      sàmìlá?   sàmìlá nɛ̀   sàmìlâ yé
      'soap'   'the soap'   'this soap'

      àdɛ̀lɛ́   àdɛ̀lɛ́ nɛ̀   àdɛ̀lɛ̂ yé
      'spoon'   'the spoon'   'this spoon'

(c)   àgòlè?   àgòlé nɛ̀   àgòlè yé
      'dance'   'the dance'   'this dance'

      àzùlè   àzùlé nɛ̀   àzùlè yé
      'river'   'the river'   'this river'

      àbɛ̀lɛ̀   àbɛ̀lɛ́ nɛ̀   àbɛ̀lɛ̀ yé
      'corn'   'the corn'   'this corn'

      àlùgbà   àlùgbá nɛ̀   àlùgbà yé
      'beans'   'the beans'   'these beans'

On the assumption that tones in Nzema must be given in the lexicon, what will be the underlying representations and, if necessary, the rules which account for these alternations? (NB represent each tonal entry as a *sequence* of tones, i.e. assume that the Obligatory Contour Principle does not apply here.)

9 (i) Consider the following table, which contains some words in three closely related Bantu languages (the following graphic representations have been adopted for tones: ´ = H, ` = L, ˇ = LH).

THARAKA	MWIMBI	KIKUYU	
mòràngí	mòlàngí	mòràngĭ	'bamboo'
ŋkíngɔ́	ŋkíngɔ́	ŋgìngɔ́	'neck'
moěrɛ̀kángériɛ́	moělɛ́kángéliɛ́	moèrɛ́kàngériɛ́	'way of releasing oneself quickly'
mòté	mòté	mòtĕ	'tree'
kèðàká	kèðàká	γèðàkǎ	'bush land'

Assuming that tones are lexically given in all three languages, must Kikuyu be provided with its own tonal melodies or can its divergences be accounted for by rule? Compare the tonal derivations of the three languages.

(ii) In the following words Kikuyu exhibits the phenomenon known as *downstep* (represented here as '!'), whereby an underlying high tone is phonetically lowered in pitch.

THARAKA	MWIMBI	KIKUYU	
èkárà	èkálà	ìkàrá!	'charcoal'
-nɛ́nɛ̀	-nɛ́nɛ̀	-nɛ̀nɛ́!	'big'
ròkó	ròkó	ròkǒ!	'firewood'

In the light of your findings in (i), is there any way of accounting for this behaviour of the high tone? (HINT: tonal rules are in principle allowed to perform all ki·ʰds of operations on tones.)

10 (i) Consider the following Arabic diminutives (i.e. the affectionate form of words, as in the English *Johnny* for *John*) in (*b*) from their base in (*a*) (cf. main text for orthographic conventions).

(*a*)		(*b*)
masjid	'mosque'	musayjid
ʕankabuut	'spider'	ʕanaakib
dirham	'dirham'	durayhim
jaḥmariš	'lazy old woman'	jaḥaamir
safarjal	'quince'	safaarij
miftaaḥ	'key'	mufaytiiḥ
ʕušfuur	'sparrow'	ʕušayfiir
fuqqaaʕat	'bubble'	faqaaqiiʕ

Will it be possible to formulate an account of these forms parallel to that suggested in the text for plurals? In particular, focus on the possible separation between the melodic and the skeletal tiers.

(ii) Assuming that you have been successful in formulating an autosegmental model of Arabic diminutives, is the diminutive template lexically given or is it possible to derive it from a perhaps more basic structure? (HINT: the theory allows for rule-based operations on the skeletal units; it is also possible to represent autosegmental elements as pre-associated to each other in the lexicon.)

11 Formalise the following patterns of primary stress making use of the metrical model in the text.

(i) Swahili: penultimate syllable.
(ii) Alyawarra: initial syllable if it begins with a consonant; otherwise, second syllable.
(iii) Hopi: first syllable if it is heavy; otherwise, second syllable, except in disyllables, which are stressed initially.
(iv) Macedonian: antepenultimate syllable.
(v) Damascene Arabic: last syllable if it is 'superheavy' (a heavy syllable followed by a consonant is known as 'superheavy'); otherwise, penultimate syllable if it is heavy; otherwise, antepenultimate syllable.
(vi) Hindi: last syllable if it is superheavy (cf. (v)); otherwise, the rightmost heavy syllable, provided it is not final; otherwise, the initial syllable.

12 (i) The following prose statement basically captures the distribution of secondary stresses in Garawa and Warao:

even-numbered syllables counting from the end of the word receive secondary stress.

Show how the analysis is underdetermined by these data as regards the use of extrametricality.

(ii) These languages differ however as regards the location of primary stress, which is penultimate in Warao but initial in Garawa. Does this affect the analysis of secondary stress carried out in (i)? Give the complete stress algorithm for both languages.

13 (i) Give metrical rules to account for the following stress data from Guajiro (symbols are as in IPA, excepting $\check{s}$ = [ʃ], $\check{c}$ = [ɟ], r = [ɾ], and $\ddot{u}$ = [y]; adjacent vowels are tautosyllabic; the stress bearer has been capitalised in each case).

(*a*)

ipA	'stone'
eʔrahAa	'to watch'
miʔirA	'party'
išI	'a well'
aʔlanAa	'to fell'
seʔE	'parasite'

	išli	'be sour'
	so?U	'her eye'
	ke?rÜ	'armadillo'
	ha?rAi	'five'
	ko?Oi	'beehive'
	he?rA	'how much/many?'
	sa?anÜin	'she weaves'
(b)	tačE?e	'my ear'
	atÜhaa	'to know'
	a?jatAasü	'she works'
	o?jotOwaa	'to cut'
	irAma	'deer'
	o?ünÜsü	'she goes'
	a?wanAahaa	'to change'
	tapÜna	'my way'
	arEepa	'corn bread'
	a?jalAhaa	'to cry'
	če?uh Aasü	'it is needed'
(c)	sapAatapü	'shoelace'
	akAmahaa	'to smoke'
	Ousahaa	'to kiss'
	Atpanaa	'rabbit'
	epEhüši	'he lights a fire'
	Ottahaa	'to distribute'
	ta?atO?uhee	'from my side'
	tOusahüin	'I kiss'
	ha?jumUlerü	'a fly'
(d)	pa?atO?upünaa	'by your side'
	Aasahawaa	'to speak'
	Eemerawaa	'to rest'
	Iipünaahee	'from above'
	Eirakawaa	'to turn one's eyes to something'
	šIinalu?u	'at the bottom'
	šEemeraain	'she rests'

(ii) Do the rules you formulated in (i) account for the alternations that follow? If not, reformulate your rules so as to take account of them.

mi?irA	'plaything'	temI?ira	'my plaything'
če?esA	'earrings'	tačE?esa	'my earrings'
ja͞?lA	'purchase'	ajA?lahaa	'to buy'
ka?I	'sun'	so?ukA?i	'today'
čü?Ü	'excrement'	tačA?a	'my excrement'
sa?atA	'its piece'	ipA?ata	'piece of stone'
čü?lAa	'to be wet'	ačÜ?lahawaa	'to get soaked'

Bibliography: Chapter 8

Botha, R. P., 'The phonological component', in E. Fudge (ed.), *Phonology* (Harmondsworth: Penguin, 1973), pp. 213–31. An excellent summary of the generative phonology model as stated in Chomsky and Halle (1968).

Chomsky, N., *Lectures on Government and Binding* (Dordrecht: Foris, 1981). The work from which most of the Chomskyan linguistics of the 1980s springs. It is an extremely demanding and technical treatment of most of the issues which have been central in recent syntactic work. Difficulties for the beginner are compounded by the style of presentation. It is becoming valuable as a reference work for those familiar with the field.

Chomsky, N., and Halle, M., *The Sound Pattern of English* (New York: Harper & Row, 1968). This is the standard exposition of classical generative phonology, superseded in parts by recent developments, but still valid in general and arguably one of the most outstanding works in linguistics ever. Unfortunately, most of the book will be rather formidable for the beginner, but chs 1 and 2 can be read profitably after completing this book. A must for those intending to take up a serious study of phonology. See also Chapter 4.

Dell, F., *Generative Phonology* (Cambridge: Cambridge University Press, 1980). A thoughtful and well-argued presentation of the classical model of generative phonology as in Chomsky and Halle (1968). Rather than summarising this work, Dell takes the reader by the hand in progressively exploring the main issues of linguistic sound. Most useful are the discussions of fragments of real phonologies, that of Zoque (a native language of Mexico) in particular. Also commendable is the emphasis placed throughout the book on mode of argumentation, within the general framework of philosophy of science.

Emonds, J., *A Transformational Approach to English Syntax* (New York: Academic Press, 1976). Difficult for a beginner, but a good survey of a wide range of claimed transformations, as well as a credible theory of how the constituent structure of the output of transformations should be specified.

Fischer-Jørgensen, E., *Trends in Phonological Theory* (Copenhagen: Akademisk Forlag, 1975). Ch. 9, pp. 174–296, gives a thorough outline of the standard model of generative phonology, also including discussions on features, phonological change, Chomsky's attack on the phoneme and several other areas. See also Chapter 4.

Halle, M., and Clements, G. N., *Problem Book in Phonology* (Cambridge, Mass.: MIT Press, 1983). This most useful book contains a succinct but most pointed introduction summarising the state of the art in generative phonology at the time of publication (the reader must note that progress in this field is particularly brisk at present). The bulk of the book consists of a carefully designed collection of phonology problems, most of them bearing on the classical linear model, but with a handful introducing the more recent autosegmental and metrical developments.

Hogg, R., and McCully, C. B., *Metrical Phonology* (Cambridge: Cambridge University Press, 1987). Conveniently summarises much of the primary literature. Not easy for the beginner, though, because of its excessive attention to detail, both as regards the data and the conflicting theories. Its closeness to the sources also impairs the clarity of the exposition, and some readers may find that the pedagogically-motivated question-answer structure hinders the smooth flow of ideas and arguments.

Kenstowicz, M., and Kisseberth, C., *Generative Phonology* (London: Academic Press, 1979). The most complete textbook on the model of phonology which developed from Chomsky and Halle's 1968 major work. It takes the reader through a decade of advances and changes in the formulation of the standard theory of generative phonology. A useful set of exercises accompanies each chapter.

Kimball, J., *The Formal Theory of Grammar* (Englewood Cliffs, NJ: Prentice-Hall, 1973). Supplies the technical detail for those interested in it.

Perlmutter, D., and Soames, S., *Syntactic Argumentation and the Structure of English* (Berkeley, Calif.: University of California Press, 1979). A good introduction to the rationale behind transformational grammar without much technical detail. See also Chapter 6.

Sampson, G., *The Form of Language* (London: Weidenfeld & Nicolson, 1975). A stimulating attempt to evaluate the significance of transformational grammar. See also Chapter 2.

Sampson, G., *Schools of Linguistics* (London: Hutchinson, 1980). A worthwhile reminder that there exist other approaches to linguistics too. All of them, including transformational grammar, come in for harsh criticism.

Schane, S., *Generative Phonology* (Englewood Cliffs, NJ: Prentice-Hall, 1973). A useful introduction to some of the types of phonological formalism used here.

Sloat, C., Taylor, S. H., and Hoard, J. E., *Introduction to Phonology* (Englewood-Cliffs, NJ: Prentice-Hall, 1978). A very useful concise presentation of (classical) generative phonology. The authors didactically take the reader from the basic facts of articulation and sound inventorying to the more abstract aspects of the model. Examples and rules are abundant, and each chapter is complemented by a set of exercises. Much recommended as a preliminary to Kenstowicz and Kisseberth (1979).

Van der Hulst, H., and Smith, N. (eds), *The Structure of Phonological Representations* (Part I) (Dordrecht: Foris, 1982). A collection of papers on several aspects of nonlinear phonology, both autosegmental and metrical, likely to be too advanced for the beginner. The introduction, 'An Overview of Autosegmental and Metrical Phonology', contains however a very accessible summary of the rationale, tenets and basic formalism of both areas, which the reader of this book could tackle profitably. An update of this overview is to be found in the collection *Advances in Nonlinear Phonology* (Foris, 1984), by the same editors, otherwise too specialised for the reader of this book.

Van Riemsdijk, H., and Williams, E., *Introduction to the Theory of Grammar* (Cambridge, Mass.: MIT Press, 1986). An excellent introduction to Chomsky's most recent views on syntactic theory. Not to be tackled by a beginner, but essential reading for anyone who has digested Radford (1981) (see bibliography in Chapter 6).

Part THREE

The Use of Language

Chapter 9

Psycholinguistics

9.1 Linguistics, psycholinguistics and cognitive psychology

Psycholinguistics is concerned primarily with investigating the psychological reality of linguistic structures. Less modestly, it sometimes also produces findings which make their own mark on linguistic research, leading to the modification of theoretical ideas.

If we view the task of psycholinguistics in the light of the general paradigm of cognitive psychology introduced in Chapter 2, it becomes identified with the search for behavioural manifestations of linguistic constructs. As psychology, in its modern guise, uses an experimental methodology, it also follows that such behavioural manifestations will be studied under experimental conditions, and it is reasonable to see the last twenty years or so of psycholinguistics in terms of the construction of ingenious laboratory techniques for pursuing this goal. In this chapter we shall be concerned with introducing and discussing a wide range of these techniques.

Before we embark on this course, however, it is useful to remark again on Chomsky's claim that linguistics (as opposed to psycholinguistics) is a branch of cognitive psychology. Linguistic analyses, as we have seen in previous chapters, are not usually the result of experimental investigation. Rather, the transformational linguist typically confronts his own intuitions with a set of data and attempts to produce an analysis consistent with these intuitions. Of course, if he is conscientious, he is likely to test informally any judgements he feels to be problematic with other native speakers, but this procedure is certainly not used systematically and is rarely reported in the literature. Chomsky's position is that the activity of consulting one's own intuitions can be more valuable in the construction and evaluation of psychological hypotheses than following a more traditional psychological paradigm. This amounts to a criticism of the restriction which all variants of modern psychology place upon their data and, correspondingly, leads to the formulation of a new and, some would say, regressive paradigm for psychological investigation, that which we have called neo-rationalism in Table 2.1.

It is not our purpose here to attempt to evaluate Chomsky's position on this issue. A supporter would point to the rich linguistic analyses which have emerged from the transformational approach and which have led to the formulation of questions concerning mental structures of a new and exciting kind. Such a supporter would also invoke the fact that, to some extent under the influence of linguistics, much more detailed and sophisticated models have found their way into traditional areas of psychological inquiry such as memory and visual perception. The detractor, however, might well respond that the reason for Chomsky's attempting to formulate a new paradigm is that many of the linguistic constructs uncovered by the transformational analysis have proved intransigent to traditional psychological inquiry; if views are not consistent with what the traditional approach reveals, change the traditional approach! To a large extent, the rest of this book, as it is concerned with linguistics, might also be seen as dealing with psychological questions in Chomsky's sense. In this chapter, without restricting ourselves entirely to transformational constructs, we focus on some of the successes and difficulties which have arisen in an experimental context.

9.2 Psychological reality of distinctive features

Chapters 4 and 8 (Section 4) introduced a number of constructs which have been advanced by linguists in trying to account for the phonological structure of different languages: phonemes, phonotactic constraints, underlying representations, phonological rules and distinctive features. Although there has been psychological experimentation involving all of these, it is probably true to say that distinctive features have attracted more attention than the other constructs. Because of this, we shall focus on them here, citing evidence from studies investigating *memory* for linguistic materials, experiments on the *perception* of such materials, and informal observations on the *production* of language.

Suppose that a subject (S) in an experiment is asked to remember a set of syllables in the order in which they are presented – a *serial memory task*. Each of the syllables consists of a consonant and a vowel (a CV syllable) and the vowel is constant throughout the set. Thus, a typical stimulus set for one trial for S might be *ba, ra, ma, ta, ka, sa*. The stimuli are presented auditorily and, after a short time, S is tested for recall. What is of particular interest is the pattern of errors that Ss produce under these conditions.

Assume, first, that people store, in their short-term memories, *phonemic* representations of the syllables (/ba/, etc.). From the point of view of phoneme theory, every phoneme differs from every other phoneme to the same extent. If, therefore, S is to forget something about, say, /b/, the information he loses must amount to the *identity* of the phoneme; there is no internal structure to the phoneme such that S can lose *part* of the information stored. Consequently, if S guesses at recall, any phoneme should be as likely as any other as a substitute for /b/ (obviously, given the structure of the stimulus materials, S will know that the segment in question is a C). But now assume that S stores a distinctive feature representation for *ba*, according to which the first segment will be specified as [+ cons, − voc, + ant, − cor, + voice, − cont, . . .], using Chomsky and Halle's system. On this assumption, if S forgets something, it may only be the value of one feature and so, at recall, he is only guessing whether the presented segment was, say, [±voice]. Now, supposing that Ss are more likely to forget one feature-value than two or more, we have the prediction that a certain type of error should predominate in memorising *ba*, those involving a switch in value for just one feature. Common errors should be *pa* (differs from *ba* only with respect to voicing), *ga*, *da*, etc. Such errors as *sa* and *ka* (differing from *ba* with respect to more than one feature) should be less common. This was discovered to be the case, thus providing behavioural evidence for the psychological status of distinctive features.

A rather different technique which leads to similar conclusions uses a *proactive inhibition* paradigm. If Ss are asked to remember a small number of similar items (say, letters of the alphabet) on successive tests, their performance deteriorates as the tests proceed. This is impressionistically viewed in terms of the earlier test items interfering with the recall of later materials, a process which is referred to as a build-up of proactive inhibition. If, after a number of tests involving items of a particular kind, items of a different kind are used (e.g. digits following letters), there is a release from proactive inhibition and performance returns to the level it was at the start of the experiment. We can represent this graphically as in Figure 9.1 where letters might have been used on tests 1−4 and digits on test 5. The trick now is to use

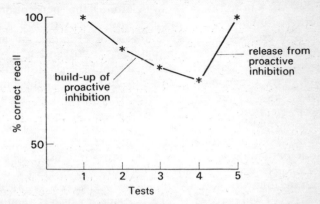

Figure 9.1   *The effect of proactive inhibition in recall tests.*

the pattern of Figure 9.1 to diagnose psychologically relevant differences between classes of stimuli. That we get this pattern when we switch from letters to digits is hardly surprising: letters and digits are obviously psychologically distinct. But what if we switch from phonological segments having one value of a distinctive feature to segments having the other value? Intuition does not provide a ready answer here.

To pursue this, two groups of subjects are presented with sets of CV syllables to memorise, all of the consonants being, say, [+voice]. The two groups are treated identically for four tests but on the fifth test the *experimental group* is asked to memorise a set of CV syllables with unvoiced Cs, while the *control group* receives another set of syllables including a voiced C. The experimental group shows a release from proactive inhibition on the fifth test and the performance of the control group continues to deteriorate. This demonstrates the psychological salience of [±voice] and, using this technique, other features relating to nasalisation and place of articulation have received support.

Turning to perception, one of the earliest relevant experiments involved the presentation of CV syllables against a background of white noise (see Chapter 3, p. 66). The task for an S in this study was simply to identify the syllable he had heard and the main interest in the results was in the pattern of errors Ss produced. It transpired that these errors grouped consonants into a number of sets including the following

/m/–/n/; /f/–/θ/; /v/–/ð/; /p/–/t/–/k/; /d/–/g/; /s/–/ʃ/; /z/–/dʒ/

with errors *within* these sets being particularly common. Of course, if the volume of background noise was increased, errors *across* the sets also began to appear but we shall not go into the details of this here. What is important is that the sets we have listed above are not random in their make-up – note that a theory claiming that perception took place in terms of unanalysed phonemes would have to predict a random pattern of errors with no groupings. For example, /m/ and /n/ differ in distinctive features only in that /m/ is [−cor] and /n/ is [+cor]. Without going into a detailed discussion, it should be clear that the sets are shown to have a certain degree of 'naturalness' if we have distinctive features available, and thus we have evidence for the role of such features in perception.

A rather more elaborate example is provided by examining the interaction between 'voice onset time' (VOT) and [±voice]. VOT is a continuous phonetic parameter and refers to the temporal interval between the release of a closure (say, for [p] or [b]) and the onset of vocal fold vibration for the following vowel. If this interval is less than 0·03 seconds, an English listener will perceive [b], i.e. a segment which is phonologically specified as [+voice]; if greater than this, he will perceive [p] (specified as [−voice]). In this way it makes sense to talk about the relationship between the continuous phonetic parameter of VOT and the discrete classificatory feature [±voice]. An ingenious technique attempted to 'tire out' the positive value of the [±voice] feature by repeatedly presenting Ss with instances of *ba* (the technical term is *adaptation* of the feature-value). That this adaptation was successfully achieved was then demonstrated by showing that the critical VOT for distinguishing [b] from [p] had moved in the direction of 0 seconds, i.e. stimuli which were perceived as *ba* before adaptation were now perceived as *pa*. But, of course, at this point we cannot discriminate between adaptation of [+voice] and adaptation of [b], and this is the difference between a theory of speech perception using distinctive features and one using unanalysed phonemes. To get around this problem we examine the effect of adaptation of *ba* on the critical VOT for discriminating between *ta* and *da* and between *ka* and *ga*. We find that these VOTs are also moved in the direction of 0 seconds, and now we have evidence for the psychological reality of [+voice] in perception: you cannot adapt what is not psychologically real.

Finally, there are a number of attested examples of slips of the tongue which involve the transposition of units smaller than full segments. Victoria Fromkin has offered the following examples: *Terry and Julia* pronounced as *Derry and Chulia* and *clear blue sky* emerging as *glear plue sky*. In both of these cases a [+voice] specification appears where a [−voice] should and vice versa.

This evidence that distinctive features are involved in various psychological processes should not be interpreted as showing that constructs 'above' the distinctive feature have no role to play. Speech perception and production are extraordinarily complex processes with units of different sorts being involved at different levels. Psychological evidence for the phoneme and the syllable also exists but, for lack of space, we cannot discuss it here. Instead, we immediately climb several rungs of the linguistic ladder to constituent-structure.

9.3 Psychological reality of constituent-structure

In this and the next section we shall be concerned with evidence for the psychological reality of grammatical structures and we might first ask whether such structure affects behaviour, in a quite general sense. If it does, we might, for example, anticipate that grammatically structured materials are easier to remember or perceive than materials that are not appropriately structured. That these anticipations are well-founded is demonstrated by the following two studies.

In the first, Ss are asked to remember sets of strings of nonsense materials. The strings can be of two types, illustrated in (1) and (2).

(1) The zigs wur vumly rixing hum in jegest miv
(2) The zig wur vum rix hum in jeg miv

The important difference between these strings is that (1), as well as being nonsense, incorporates some English morphology (the suffixes *-s*, *-ly*, *-ing* and *-est*), whereas (2) contains no such clues. A native speaker of English can begin to impose a syntactic structure on (1) – there would be a good deal of agreement, for example, that *the zigs* is the subject of (1) – but (2) is just a list of nonsense words including two English words, *the* and *in*. It turns out that, despite the fact that (2) is shorter than (1), strings of type (1) are much easier to remember than strings of type (2). Since both (1) and (2) are nonsense and equally unfamiliar, one can hardly invoke semantic or familiarity criteria to explain this result. The alternative is that Ss are implementing their knowledge of English syntactic structure, which is enabling them to store a more easily memorised representation of (1). Exactly how this is achieved is not, of course, answered by this particular study.

The second experiment on this theme uses a technique we have already met: the presentation of linguistic materials against a background of white noise. Under these conditions, Ss are simply asked to repeat what they hear and the materials can be of three types: normal English sentences, strings which are syntactically well formed but semantically deviant, and random strings of words. These last two categories are illustrated by (3) and (4).

(3) The virtuous rock threw honesty upstairs
(4) Rock upstairs the honesty virtuous threw

The result of the study was quite clear. Ss were much more accurate in their perceptions of grammatically and semantically well-formed strings than they were for the other two categories. Additionally, syntactically well formed, but semantically anomalous, strings were perceived more accurately than random strings of words. The first of these results indicates that Ss use their knowledge of the semantic properties of words and sentences in their perception, the second that, when semantic constraints are violated, knowledge of syntactic structure can still facilitate perception.

The question we must now consider is whether we can be more detailed about the nature of the syntactic knowledge that Ss use in memory and perception tasks. In Chapter 6 we introduced the idea of constituent structure and in Chapter 8 we saw how this notion has been developed within recent syntactic theory. So far, it has only been justified as a *linguistic* construct by using linguistic argumentation to do with substitutability, generality, etc. Is there any evidence for native speakers using this level of structure when they memorise or perceive sentences?

As far as memory is concerned, the following study is suggestive. Ss are simply asked to memorise a set of short English sentences, and the novelty of this experiment arises in the treatment of the results. Consider (5).

(5) The house across the street is burning

When people attempt to recall this, as one of a set of sentences, some will make mistakes. What we are interested in here is the probability that we get a mistake on a particular word given that the previous word in the sentence is recalled correctly. This is referred to as the *transition error probability* (TEP) for a position in the sentence. To illustrate, imagine that we have (5) recalled as (6) by an S.

(6) The house *down* the street is burning

The S is incorrect in his recall of *down* but correct on the preceding word. Therefore, this response will count positively in computing the TEP for the position between *house* and *across* in (5). No other aspect of (6) will count positively in computing TEPs for the other positions in (5). Assume, now, that on the basis of a set of experimental results we compute the TEPs for all possible positions in (5) (there are six of them). What we find, in general, is that TEP is highest between *street* and *is* and second highest between *house* and *across*. But note that these positions are those where the largest number of constituents coterminate in a constituent-structure analysis of the sentence. This is illustrated in (5′).

[[[The] [house]] [[across] [[the] [street]]]] [[is] [burning]]

This, then, is consistent with the suggestion that, when Ss remember sentences under these conditions, they break the sentence down into its constituents and store the constituents. If a particular constituent is recalled, the chances are that it will *all* be recalled (i.e. we shall get low TEPs within constituents). However, we shall be most prone to errors at boundaries of constituents when we have to begin to recall a new constituent (hence, higher TEPs across constituent boundaries). We are careful here to use the word 'consistent' because, as we shall see, there are several other views on what is stored when we remember sentences, and it would be foolhardy to say that the above interpretation is demonstrably correct.

Perception studies too suggest the involvement of constituent-structure in psychological processes. One such study involves the inducement of an expectation (the psychologist's term is *set*) for a certain structure in a group of subjects. By definition, if it is possible to induce an expectation for P, P is psychologically real. How do we induce the expectation? Consider (7) and (8), which have the relevant parts of their constituent-structures indicated by parentheses.

(7) [They] [[are] [[recurring] [events]]]
(8) [They] [[[are] [forecasting]] [cyclones]]

There are four groups of Ss asked to listen to and repeat sentences presented in noisy conditions. Two control groups hear either ten sentences of type (7) followed by an eleventh of type (7) or ten sentences of type (8) followed by an eleventh of type (8). Two experimental groups also hear either ten sentences of type (7) or ten of type (8), but for them the eleventh trial involves a switch of sentence-type (to type (8) for those who have heard ten type (7) and vice versa). What transpires is that the experimental groups do much worse on the crucial eleventh trial than do their corresponding control groups. Furthermore, their errors are in the direction of the structures to which they have been exposed on the previous ten trials, i.e. they have come to expect these structures. This is consistent with the claim that the perceptual mechanisms have access to the structures.

We would like to close this section by introducing one of the best-known experimental paradigms in psycholinguistics. This experimental technique involves presenting an S with a sentence through one ear (the S is wearing headphones) and, at some point in the sentence, transmitting an extraneous noise (usually a click) to S's other ear. Having heard the sentence S's task is to indicate where in the sentence the click occurred. The earliest study using this method employed complex sentences similar to (9).

(9) That he was happy was evident from the way he smiled
         * * * * 0 * ** *

Objectively, the click could occur in any of the positions marked by * or 0. The first result of note is that Ss do make errors on this sort of task. More important, however, the errors appear to be systematic in that the majority of them involve shifting the click in the direction of 0 in (9). Clicks located before 0 move from left to right, but not beyond 0, and those located after 0 move in the opposite direction. But now note that 0 marks the main constituent-structure break in (9); it appears that *this* is what attracts the click.

All of this is consistent (see above) with the view that our perception is guided by a constituent analysis and that, when we are perceiving a major constituent, an extraneous stimulus cannot gain access to our perception. Accordingly, the extraneous stimulus is 'heard' at the end of the processing unit. One objection that might be raised at this point is that the abstractness of constituent-structure is not required to explain click migration. Instead, Ss are mislocating the click on the basis of pausal and intonational phenomena. This possibility has been dismissed using sentences like (10) and (11).

(10) [In her *haste to marry*] [*the girl is stupid*]
         0   X
(11) [His *haste to marry the girl*] [*is stupid*]
              0   X

Tokens of (10) and (11) are recorded on tape. The trick then, using tape-splicing, is to replace the italicised portion of (11) with the italicised portion of (10). As a result, we have tokens of (10) and (11) which their italicised portions are phonetically identical, and, if we then perform an experiment of the sort described, using these 'doctored' sentences as stimuli, we find that the click migrates to 0, but not X, in (10) and to X, but not 0, in (11). Given the nature of the materials, this cannot be explained by superficial intonational or pausal phenomena and it seems that Ss must be credited with having available an abstract syntactic analysis of the sentences.

At this point we can ask how abstract the syntactic knowledge Ss use in this sort of task is and, of course, it is one of the claims of transformational grammar that a traditional constituent-structure analysis is not sufficient for explicating many aspects of syntactic structure (see Chapters 6 and 8). Transformational grammar recognises more abstract levels of structure (deep structures) and it makes sense to inquire whether these have any psychological validity.

9.4 Psychological reality of deep structures

It may occur to the reader at this point to wonder why we should seek evidence for the psychological reality of more abstract structures. After all, the previous section has persuaded us that constituent-structure plays a role in sentence memory and sentence perception. Cannot that be the end of the story? There are two responses to this query which are equally important for understanding the development of psycholinguistics.

The first of these has already been alluded to when we pointed out that alternative interpretations may be consistent with a set of experimental results. For example, if we use very simple sentences as stimulus materials, the chances are that the constituents recognised by a traditional analysis will coincide with the postulated constituents at the more abstract level, i.e. there will be no significant differences between surface structures and deep structures for these sentences. Thus, results indicating the involvement of surface structures in psychological processes could equally be taken as providing support for a psychologically real deep structure.

The second reason is, perhaps, more important and relies on the assumption that psychological processes involving language are extraordinarily complex, requiring a number of levels of analysis. If this assumption is correct, the way is open to investigate the possibility that apparently inconsistent results arise because different stages in these processes are being assessed by different tasks. Of course, in order to make this sort of suggestion convincing, it would be necessary to go into considerable detail on experimental design and task demands, detail which, on the whole, we do not have space for here (but see Section 7 below). However, we hope that enough has been said to persuade the reader that there is no necessary inconsistency between experimental results which appear to psychologically substantiate different linguistic levels.

Claims for the psychological reality of deep structures can again be seen as falling into two sets: those arising from studies of memory and those suggested by studies of sentence perception.

For the former, consider (12) and (13).

(12) Gloves were made by tailors
(13) Gloves were made by hand

These two sentences have identical surface structures. In particular, the NPs *tailors* and *hand* play identical syntactic roles in them – they are both prepositional objects. The deep structures of the two sentences, however, according to the analysis sketched in Chapter 6, will be quite different. That for (12) will approximate to the structure of (14), while (13) will be based on a structure like that of (15) (we ignore detailed structures here, as the point at issue does not require them).

(14) Tailors made gloves
(15) Someone made gloves by hand

Sentence (12) will be derived from (14) by an application of the passive transformation and (13) from (15) by a similar process supplemented by the application of a rule which deletes *someone*. Sentence (12) can therefore be referred to as a standard passive (SP) and (13) as a deleted agent passive (DAP). The important thing to note now is that the two NPs to which we drew attention above, *tailors* and *hand*, play quite distinct roles in the deep structures underlying (12) and (13). *Tailors* is, in fact, the subject of the sentence at this level, whereas *hand* maintains its surface role of prepositional object. With this in mind, consider the following experiment.

Ss are presented with a list of ten sentences to memorise. The sentences are either all SPs or all DAPs. At the time of recall Ss are *prompted* using words from the sentences they have to produce, and what we are interested in is the relative efficacy of *tailors* as a prompt for (12) and *hand* as a prompt for (13). It turns out that surface prepositional objects are much better prompts for sentences like (12) than they are for sentences like (13), with Ss remembering, on average, over seven of their ten SPs correctly, compared with less than four of their DAPs. There is an obvious objection: could it not be that SPs are simply easier to remember than DAPs and that the difference in correct recall has got nothing to do with prompt words? To counter this, each of the experimental groups in this study has a control group which is prompted by the surface subject, i.e. *gloves* in the case of both (12) and (13). For these two groups there was no difference in accuracy of recall and the objection is dispensed with. We are left with the conclusion that two words, which play identical surface structure roles, facilitate recall to differing extents. If we assume that Ss store deep structures and that the subject is more salient in these structures than is a prepositional object, we have an explanation for this result.

Let us now return to the click location paradigm introduced in the previous section. The original hypothesis which gave rise to this work was that any constituent boundary would attract clicks but this was rapidly shown to be false and evidence was accumulated to suggest that only *clausal* boundaries have this property (note that in (9)–(11) the position marked 0 is such a boundary). Later experimentation revealed that, in fact, click attraction only occurred at a position where the termination of a *deep structure* clause occurred. To see what is involved here, consider (16) and (17).

(16) John expected Bill to leave
$$0$$
(17) John persuaded Bill to leave
$$0$$

These have identical surface structures but their standard deep structure analyses differ, as suggested by:

(16a) John expected [$_S$Bill leave]$_S$
(17a) John persuaded Bill [$_S$Bill leave]$_S$

The justification for this difference is too complicated to go into here, but the reader might find some comfort in the intuition that in (17) Bill does get persuaded (i.e. it makes sense to regard *Bill* as the direct object of *persuade*) and in (16) Bill does not get expected (i.e. the direct object of *expert* is not *Bill* but *Bill to leave*). Sentences (16a) and (17a) are making this intuition explicit.

Now note that the positions marked 0 in (16) and (17) have different statuses with regard to deep structure clause boundaries. The boundary in (16a) occurs at 0 in (16), but the boundary in (17a) does not correspond unambiguously to any position in (17) (it occurs between two *Bills* in (17a) and there is only one *Bill* in (17)). It should come as no surprise, given the above, that the position marked 0 in (16) attracts clicks, whereas that similarly marked in (17) does not. This result can not be predicted by a surface constituent analysis, as, in this respect, (16) and (17) are usually taken to be identical. It can be approached if we assume that Ss have available information about deep clause structure, information which they use in their sentence perception.

Further evidence on the importance of deep structure clauses in sentence perception is provided by a technique known as *rapid serial visual presentation* (RSVP). This involves projecting the successive words of a sentence on to a screen, one by one and rapidly (rates of twenty words/sec. are commonly used); if the speed of presentation is sufficiently high, subjects, when asked to write down the visually presented sentence, will make mistakes. The technique can thus be used to investigate perceptual complexity – the more complex material is, the more mistakes it will induce under RSVP conditions. The major conclusion of immediate interest is that, of two sentences balanced for length, one involving two deep clauses will lead to more RSVP errors than one involving only one. Again, although admittedly the perceptual task is strange, it seems that deep structures are playing a role in sentence perception.

In the linguistic model, of course, deep structures and surface structures are linked by transformational rules. This and the previous section have reviewed evidence for the psychological reality of these two levels of structure in a range of experimental tasks. The natural question to ask now is whether there are any psychological processes corresponding to the linguist's transformational rules. If there are, they will provide the psychological mapping between the two levels of structure we have discussed.

9.5 Psychological reality of transformational rules

Some early studies of memory suggested that transformational rules might correspond to psychologically real operations. In one Ss were simply asked to remember sentences of a number of distinct syntactic forms, including active declaratives, passive declaratives, active interrogatives and passive interrogatives. Two results emerged which are of interest here: active declaratives were more accurately remembered than other categories of sentence and there was a tendency for subjects' errors to consist of simplifications towards the active declarative, i.e. there were more instances of passives being recalled as actives and of interrogatives being recalled as declaratives than vice versa. On the assumption that passives and interrogatives are derived from structures resembling active declaratives by means of transformational rules, it was natural to suggest that, when asked to remember a sentence, an S broke it down into its corresponding active declarative and stored *this* along with a set of tags to indicate what transformations had applied to it. Thus, (18) would be stored in something like the form suggested by (19).

(18) The rabbit was chased by the cat
(19) The cat chased the rabbit + PASSIVE

This suggestion, known as the *Coding Hypothesis*, can predict the superiority of recall for active declaratives, as their memory representation does not include any transformational tags and hence places a lighter load on the subject's memory capacities. If we make the additional assumption that transformational tags can be lost independently from memory, we can also predict the phenomenon of simplification towards the active declarative. If (18) is stored as (19) and if PASSIVE is lost from this representation, (18) will be recalled as (20).

(20) The cat chased the rabbit

Similarly, if (21) is stored as (22), assuming a rule QUESTION involved in the analysis of interrogatives, we shall be able to explain the tendency for (21) to be recalled as (23) or (24) (or even 20).

(21) Was the rabbit chased by the cat?
(22) The cat chased the rabbit + PASSIVE + QUESTION
(23) Did the cat chase the rabbit?
(24) The rabbit was chased by the cat

Transformations, in the form of tags in memory representations, appear to have an explanatory role to play.

The conclusion of the preceding paragraph was reinforced by an experiment which attempted to *measure* the amount of space transformational tags occupied in short-term memory. That short-term memory has a limited capacity is demonstrated by an attempt to learn a series of digits. For most of us, a string of seven or eight is the longest we can memorise on the basis of one presentation, and this limitation was exploited in the study in the following way.

Ss are presented with sentences of a specified syntactic structure immediately followed by a random string of words. They are instructed to remember the sentence perfectly plus as many of the string of words as they can – there are enough words in the string to ensure that Ss will not get them all right. The Coding Hypothesis has it that (18) is stored as (19) and (21) as (22), and it immediately follows from this that the difference in the number of words from the list recalled along with (18) and the number recalled with (21) provides a measure (in words) of the space used up by the QUESTION tag – this is the only thing which distinguishes the hypothesised memory representations for (18) and (21). Now, rather than using passive declaratives and passive interrogatives to compute this figure, we could use active sentences; any difference between the number of words recalled with an active affirmative sentence and those recalled with a corresponding interrogative will give an *independent* measure of the space used up by QUESTION. In the experiment which was performed along these lines it was possible to compute a number of independent measures for several transformational rules and the major finding of the study was that these measures were reasonably close to each other for each of these rules, i.e. it seemed to make sense to talk about QUESTION occupying X words in short-term memory, of PASSIVE occupying Y words, and so on.

Perception studies, again, provided evidence which could be seen as complementing that arising in the context of work on memory. One very popular paradigm which developed in this connection used a sentence-picture matching task. Very simply, an S is presented with a sentence on a screen; he reads it and immediately presses a button which replaces the sentence with a picture. As quickly as possible S presses one of two buttons to indicate whether or not the sentence is true or false of the picture and the variable we are interested in is reaction-time.

Using this technique, evidence accumulated to suggest that the more complex a sentence was in its linguistic description, the longer it took to process under these circumstances. In particular, it seemed that a small number of transformational rules contributed to perceptual complexity and this gave rise to the *Derivational Theory of Complexity*. According to this theory, given two sentences S_1 and S_2 such that, in a transformational grammar, the generation of S_2 involves all the processes involved in the generation of S_1 plus some additional ones, S_2 will be perceptually more complex than S_1. So, for example, if a passive sentence is assumed to differ from its active counterpart only by the application of PASSIVE, this theory predicts that the passive sentence will be more difficult to perceive. This was exactly what the first experiments in sentence-picture matching revealed and so PASSIVE, along with a number of other transformational rules, was assumed to correspond to some perceptual operation.

Up to now we have adduced evidence for the psychological reality of the two important levels of syntactic structure recognised in transformational grammar and also for the grammatical operations which relate these two levels. With respect to the latter it is now time to introduce some negative evidence and consider its consequences.

9.6 Against the psychological reality of transformational rules

Evidence against the Coding Hypothesis came from a number of studies. In one, Ss are asked to remember a set of active and passive sentences, their recall being prompted by a picture. The picture might be of the total event depicted by the original sentence, of the actor in that event (i.e. of the subject of the sentence if the sentence is active and of the object of *by* if the sentence is passive), or of the acted-upon in the event (i.e. of the direct object of an active sentence and the surface subject of a passive). The Coding Hypothesis is a hypothesis about storage and does not deal with the problem of the interaction between what is stored and contextual factors operating at the time of recall. Accordingly, in the circumstances just described, it can only predict the 'usual' pattern of responses: actives more accurately recalled than passives and a tendency to recall passives as corresponding actives. What emerges, however, is that this pattern is only obtained when the picture shown at recall is of the total event or the actor. If the picture is of the acted-upon, we get the exact opposite of what the Coding Hypothesis predicts: passives are more accurately recalled than actives and there is a tendency for an active to be recalled as its corresponding passive. This is difficult to reconcile with the Coding Hypothesis and seems to point in the direction of active and passive sentences being stored in an identical fashion with the form of the recalled sentence being determined by factors affecting the subject's attention at the time of recall.

The suggestion that transformational tags occupy measurable space in memory also comes under attack with the finding that if the order of recall between sentence and words from the string is reversed on some trials in the study described in the previous section and, furthermore, the S does not know *at the time of the presentation of the stimuli* what order of recall is going to be called for, then the effects of transformational complexity disappear when words from the string are recalled first. The Coding Hypothesis is a hypothesis about *storage*, and there is no reason to believe that Ss are storing the sentences in different ways depending on the recall conditions, as they are ignorant of the recall conditions at the time of storage. The alternative appears to be that transformationally more complex sentences are more difficult to retrieve from memory and that this retrieval process interferes with the subsequent recall of the list of words. Of course, if the list of words is recalled first, there will be no interference from the prior recall of the sentence and the effects of transformational complexity will disappear. Note that this study does provide a niche for transformational complexity in the psychological process of recall, but our point in describing it here is to argue against the reality of transformations in *representations* in memory.

Finally, if we compare the recall of full passives with passives lacking a *by*-phrase, when such sentences are presented in text, we discover embarrassment for the Coding Hypothesis. Briefly, two short stories are constructed, one containing four full passive sentences such as (25), and the other, four agentless passives like (26).

(25) John was shown to his new desk by the teacher
(26) John was shown to his new desk

The two stories are equated for length by using more modifiers (adjectives, etc.) in the one using agentless passives and are presented to Ss to memorise. Recall that in our discussion of (13) above we mentioned a rule deleting unspecified agents in short passives; this is going to apply to (26) along with PASSIVE. It follows that the Coding Hypothesis will predict that short passives will be less accurately recalled than full passives – they involve one additional transformational operation – and that there should be a tendency for short passives to be recalled as full passives (with, say, *someone* as object of *by*) or as corresponding actives (with *someone* in subject position). Neither of these predictions is supported: there are more errors in the recall of full passives than in the recall of short passives and, while there was a strong tendency for full passives to be recalled as corresponding actives, there was little indication of short passives becoming transformationally less complex on recall. The results were more consistent with short passives being stored in a form approximating to their surface structure.

In the light of evidence such as this, attempts to establish connections between *syntactic* operations and the representations of sentences in memory have become rather unfashionable. The very powerful intuition that when we remember a sentence what we remember is the content of the sentence, what the sentence says, and not its syntactic details, dictates the direction of most current research. We shall return to this in Section 8, but first we must pay more attention to the Derivational Theory of Complexity.

In the standard sentence-picture matching experiment described above, Ss are presented with the picture as soon as they have read the sentence. Differences in reaction-time are put down to differences in the time it takes to perceive the sentences, but a moment's reflection will reveal that there is more than sentence perception involved in this task. As well as perceiving the sentence, the S must perceive the picture and compare the results of his perceptions to see whether they match or not. The possibility arises, therefore, that differences in reaction-time are located in one of these processes and not in the process of sentence perception.

To test this possibility a five-second gap is introduced between the presentation of the sentence and the picture, the idea being that this period provides the Ss with ample time to read and understand the sentences. If differences in reaction time are due to differences in difficulty of perception, these difficulties should be over by the time the picture is presented. Accordingly, reaction-time differences should disappear. This is not what happens and, while reaction-times overall are slightly faster than in the condition where there is no five-second gap, the difference between responses for, say, actives and passives, is identical to what it is under the earlier condition. Thus, we cannot locate the difference between actives and passives at the perception stage in this task, and the Derivational Theory of Complexity loses some of its strongest support.

Moving beyond PASSIVE, there has been a good deal of work on other transformational rules which casts doubt on the Derivational Theory of Complexity. To mention just one example here, in some versions of transformational grammar (27) would be regarded as more complex than (28), being derived from a structure resembling that of (28) by a transformational rule known as *particle movement*.

(27) John phoned the girl up
(28) John phoned up the girl

What this rule does should be obvious from the examples and its statement will not concern us here. What is important is that several efforts to demonstrate that (27) is perceptually more complex than (28) (as the Derivational Theory of Complexity demands) were unsuccessful.

From a slightly different perspective, there are a number of demonstrations that there is more to sentence perception than is suggested by the Derivational Theory. In our view, these studies do not provide refutations of the theory, although they are often presented as doing just this. We shall consider one example involving sentence-picture matching.

A variable which we have not considered so far is that of *reversibility*. This is a semantic (or perhaps pragmatic) notion and is concerned with the effects of exchanging subject and direct object expressions in simple sentences. If we perform this operation on (29) we get (30) which is a perfectly good English sentence.

(29) The car bumps the train
(30) The train bumps the car

However, if we try the same thing with (31), we get (32) which is odd in some way (for our purpose we do not have to decide in exactly what way) and extremely unlikely to occur in normal circumstances.

(31) The girl waters the flowers
(32) ?The flowers water the girl

Sentence (29) is reversible and (31) is non-reversible. We can now introduce this variable into a sentence-picture matching task, having half of our sentences reversible and half of them non-reversible. The major finding is that for non-reversible sentences the difference in reaction-time to active and passive sentences disappears, i.e. there will be no such difference for (31) and (33).

(33) The flowers are watered by the girl

It is as if, in this case, syntactic processing can be by-passed. Given that we have a reference to flowers, to watering and to the girl, the only way in which these can be sensibly put together will demand that it is the girl who is doing the watering and the flowers which are getting watered. This process can go ahead independently of the details of active/passive syntax and it seems that in this case (and perhaps in the vast majority of instances in everyday life where utterances have a great deal of contextual support) syntactic rules are not involved in sentence perception.

This conclusion leads to a difficult problem. Assume that we have convincing arguments for surface structures and deep structures being involved in sentence perception (see Sections 3 and 4) but that we lack similar demonstrations in the case of transformational rules (this section). We must ask how the mapping from surface structure to deep structure is achieved, if not by psychological processes akin to transformational rules.

9.7 An alternative to the Derivational Theory of Complexity

Most current views on sentence perception refer to the notion of *strategy*. While there is no generally accepted opinion on the form of such strategies, particular cases are relatively straightforward to come to terms with and we shall mention a number of such examples here. The major point to bear in mind is that strategies are not transformational rules and that, in many cases, they can be seen as representing generalisations based on linguistic experience, generalisations which do not always lead to the correct analysis.

In Section 4 we discussed evidence which indicated the importance of clauses in sentence perception. Equally important, if a listener is to understand a complex sentence, is the requirement that he recognise which clauses are main and which subordinate.

We might suggest, on the basis of statistical counts and stylistic preferences, that native speakers of English favour sentence-structures in which the main clause comes first. Accordingly, we could formulate a strategy of sentence perception, as in (34).

(34) *Main clause first strategy*
The first clause is the main clause *unless it is explicitly marked as subordinate*.

There is some fairly compelling evidence that something like (34) is operative in sentence perception. Most native speakers of English, when confronted with (35), judge it to be ill-formed.

(35) The horse raced past the barn fell

Attempts to interpret it usually include suggestions that an *and* is missing after *past* or after *barn*. But now consider (36) and (37).

(36) The horse which was ridden past the barn fell
(37) The horse ridden past the barn fell

Obviously (37) is related to (36) and many linguists would capture this relationship by postulating a rule which deletes the relative pronoun *which* and the following form of the verb *to be* in (36) to yield (37). This rule seems to be perfectly productive and we can note that it should apply to (38).

(38) The horse which was raced past the barn fell

If it does, it will yield (35) and, at this point, the reader should immediately see the sense in which (35) is well formed and modify his earlier judgement. The immediate question to ask is why there should be a marked difference in response to (35) and (37) and it is this question which (34) helps us with. In the case of the verb *race*, its simple past and its past participle forms are identical (*raced*). For *ride*, however, there is the distinction between *rode* and *ridden*. It follows that a native speaker, perceiving (35) and operating with (34), will be under some pressure to treat *raced* as the simple past of *race* as this will enable him to have an initial main clause *The horse raced past the barn*. But for (37) there will be no such pressure as the unambiguous past participle form *ridden* explicitly marks the clause in which it appears as subordinate. Note that the fact that we *can* eventually perceive the appropriate interpretation of (35) indicates the fallibility of (34) – it is simply an inductive generalisation which is going to be correct *most* of the time.

Of course, it is not in general sufficient for understanding to discern inter-clausal structure; we must also perform an analysis *within* each clause and the findings concerning reversibility in the previous section suggest that probabilistic semantic constraints might be important here. To take account of this, we can formulate a second strategy along the lines of (39).

(39) *Semantic probability strategy*
Clausal constituents are related according to probabilistic constraints.

The most direct piece of evidence in favour of this playing a role in sentence perception has already been introduced in the previous section. There we talked about the possibility of by-passing syntax when probabilistic constraints were strong and (39) is now offered as the explanation for why non-reversible passives take no longer to respond to than non-reversible actives in a sentence-picture matching task.

Additional evidence arises in connection with centre-embedded sentences which we have already seen to be extraordinarily difficult to understand, once they go beyond a single level of embedding (see Chapter 2, pp. 35–6). But an inspection of (40) and (41) should convince the reader that this difficulty can be quite dramatically reduced if we build strong semantic constraints into the sentence.

(40) The dog the monkey the cat chased bit died
(41) The question the girl the lion bit answered was complex

In (40) the cat chases the monkey, the monkey bites the dog and the dog dies, but in terms of our general knowledge of the world, monkeys are, perhaps, as likely to chase cats as to be chased by them, as likely to be bitten by dogs as to bite them, and as likely to die as dogs. In general, there are no semantic constraints operative in (40) and it is extremely difficult to understand. In (41), however, the lion bites the girl, the girl answers the question and the question is complex and here, although probabilistic constraints do not *determine* the interpretation of the sentence (girls *can* bite lions), they point us very clearly towards the correct understanding.

The fact remains that we can correctly interpret, say, (42) which violates probabilistic constraints.

(42) The zebra killed the lion.

This illustrates the fallibility of (39) and also the necessity for additional mechanisms which will come into operation when (39) goes wrong. Taking into account that, *in the absence of probabilistic constraints*, passive sentences take longer to process than corresponding actives (recall that the active-passive difference only disappears for non-reversible sentences), we might consider (43) as a third strategy.

(43) *Canonical sentence strategy*
      In any clause the first NP corresponds to the actor, the V to the action and the second NP to the acted-upon.

In addition to reaction-time data from reversible actives and passives, (43) is valuable in explaining the fact that sentences like (44) are responded to faster in sentence-picture matching than those like (45).

(44) They are fixing benches
(45) They are performing monkeys

In (44) *They* refers to an actor and *benches* to an acted-upon; such a semantic characterisation is not appropriate for (45).

Returning now to (34), it is clear that *marking* of subordination becomes an important concept on this account. We might, therefore, predict that if English offers the option of marking a clause as subordinate or not, the version which is explicitly marked will be easier to process. The technique of *phoneme-monitoring* has been used extensively in investigating this question.

In a phoneme-monitoring study Ss are asked to respond as quickly as possible to the occurrence of a particular sound in a sentence. Reaction-time is viewed as a measure of the complexity of sentence-processing at the time at which the target phoneme appears – the longer the reaction-time, the more complex the processing at that point. Consider this, then, in connection with (46) and (47).

(46) John believes the girl is his sister
(47) John believes that the girl is his sister

Assume that the target phoneme is /g/: Ss respond faster to the /g/ in *girl* in (47) than they do to the similar /g/ in (46). Why should that be?

In (47) *that* marks the clause it introduces as subordinate and the listener to (47) knows, by the time he gets to /g/, that he is in a subordinate clause. For (46), though, there is no such marking, and, as *believe* is compatible with simple NP objects (*John believes the girl*) as well as with *that*-complements, the listener to (46) still has two options available when he gets to /g/. It seems reasonable to assume that keeping open options contributes to complexity; hence, (47) is more complex than (46) at the comparable point. Note that this is the first technique we have introduced which attempts to measure complexity *during* sentence perception as opposed to after it.

Finally, in connection with (34), it has been suggested that it can provide an *explanation* for the form of certain grammatical rules. To illustrate, we have already alluded to the rule which deletes a relative pronoun and the following form of the verb *to be* (cf. 36 and 37). There is a restriction on this rule to the effect that it cannot operate on relative pronouns which refer to the *subjects* of embedded clauses (in (36) *which* refers to the direct object of *ridden*). So, we cannot apply the rule to (48) to yield (49).

(48) The boy who slept in the tent got wet
(49) *The boy slept in the tent got wet

Now, it is obvious that if (49) did exist in English, it would provide processing difficulties comparable to those of (35). Sentence (49) offers a main clause *The boy slept in the tent* and, under the pressure of (34), we analyse it in this way and cannot make any sense of *got wet*. This sort of consideration brings psycholinguistics nearer to its less modest goal (see Section 1) of being able to contribute to linguistic analysis.

There is a large number of problems surrounding strategies which have not been resolved, some of which can be raised on the basis of the examples we have considered here (see Exercise 12 to this chapter). It would be misleading to suggest that there is a well-worked-out theory using this notion. Rather, there are many disparate suggestions which share a distaste for transformational rules in sentence perception, each giving rise to interesting experimental studies. We have seen that similar suspicions arose concerning the involvement of syntactic processes in memory representations and we now turn to how psycholinguistics reacted to this development.

9.8 Semantics and sentence memory

One of the clearest demonstrations that memory representations are not syntactic under certain conditions arises when we present Ss with short stories, each of which contains a *key sentence*. At some point after the S hears this sentence, he is presented with a *test sentence* and has to decide whether it is identical in all respects with any sentence he has heard in the story. The test sentence is constructed in such a way as to bear one of a number of relationships to the key sentence and, of course, on any trial S does not know which sentence in the story is the key sentence. To illustrate, one story which has been used in this sort of study described the invention of the telescope and included (50) as its key sentence.

(50) Galileo, the great Italian scientist, sent a letter about it to him.

The test sentence, which could immediately follow the key sentence or follow it after an interval of 60 or 120 syllables, could either be identical with (50), related to (50) via PASSIVE, related to (50) via another syntactic rule not involving any change in meaning, or related to (50) via switching the subject and indirect object NPs – a switch which involves a marked change in meaning. These last three possibilities are illustrated in (51)–(53).

(51) A letter about it was sent to him by Galileo, the great Italian scientist.
(52) Galileo, the great Italian scientist, sent him a letter about it.
(53) He sent a letter about it to Galileo, the great Italian scientist.

The results of the study were that if the test sentence was presented immediately after the key sentence, Ss would recognise any change, syntactic or semantic. After as little as 60 syllables, however, Ss were almost as likely to respond that they had heard (51) or (52) in the story as they were to respond positively to (50) itself, i.e. after this short period they were not capable of recognising syntactic changes which did not also involve a change of meaning. For (53) subjects' performance was much more accurate and, even after 120 syllables, they were detecting semantic changes with almost 100 per cent accuracy. This seems to indicate that the syntactic details of linguistic material are not usually stored for very long and that it is a representation of a sentence's meaning which a subject has available in his memory under normal circumstances. Note that this does not demand that syntactic details have *no* role in memory. In fact, the results of this study are consistent with such details being available to memory for a short time and it may be that under certain conditions the experimentalist can gain access to this level of representation. It is, perhaps, not insignificant that the present study uses materials in structured story form, whereas most of the earlier memory studies we have mentioned use sentences in isolation as stimuli.

Whether there is anything to this last remark or not, there is also an accumulation of evidence pointing towards semantic levels of representation, even when sentences are presented out of context. So, for example, there is a tendency for sentences using the perfect form of the verb, as in (54), to be recalled using the simple past form, as in (55).

(54) The child has seen the rabbit
(55) The child saw the rabbit

Syntactically this is difficult to explain, as (54) is marked for present tense (*has*) and (55) for past tense (*saw*). Semantically, however, both involve reference to the past – we might say that their semantic representations would include [+Past] – and, from this perspective, their confusion is more readily intelligible.

Again, there is an asymmetry in recall errors for comparative sentences such that (56) is more likely to be recalled incorrectly as (57) than vice versa.

(56) The stream is narrower than the river
(57) The stream is wider than the river

This is put down to the fact that *narrow* is more complex semantically than *wide*, being the *marked* member of the antonym pair, *wide* and *narrow* (see Chapter 7, p. 195). According to this interpretation, *wide* has a more general meaning than *narrow*, being used, for example, to name the dimension of width when it co-occurs with measure phrases (*6 feet wide* v. *?6 feet narrow*), and this has been spoken about in terms of *narrow* possessing one additional feature, when compared with *wide*. Without going into details, it should be clear that this sort of suggestion is attractive from the point of view of explaining the asymmetry in errors for (56) and (57).

Rather more interesting work than the above has taken place within the framework of *Assimilation Theory*. This is a rather difficult position to define but it differs from approaches using semantic features in its emphasis on the importance of background knowledge in 'normal' situations where we might memorise linguistic material. There is evidence to indicate that, for some levels of memory representation, this background knowledge constitutes a necessary condition, i.e. without the knowledge the appropriate representation cannot be set up. This evidence arises when Ss are presented with structured texts and are instructed to comprehend them and remember as much of their content as possible. The texts are chosen to describe unlikely states of affairs but the lexical items and syntactic structures they use are familiar enough. One group of Ss simply hears the text, a second hears the text and is then shown a picture providing an appropriate context for the text and a third group is shown the picture before it hears the text. The results are quite spectacular, with the third group remembering the content of the text much more fully than either of the other two, and this would seem to require that Ss in this group managed to build up a level of representation which they could use in this task. This level of representation was denied the first two groups, despite the familiarity with the lexical items and syntax of the text.

From a slightly different perspective, Assimilation Theory has emphasised the role of *inferences* in memory. In Chapter 7 (see p. 197) we discussed the semantic relation of entailment between sentences and a number of studies have reported a tendency for Ss to recall a sentence which is entailed by a sentence they are asked to remember rather than the sentence itself. Thus, it is quite likely that a S will recall (58) when presented with (59) and vice versa.

(58) The door is not open
(59) The door is closed

One systematic study used sentences like (60)–(63).

(60) Three turtles rested on a floating log and a fish swam beneath it
(61) Three turtles rested on a floating log and a fish swam beneath them
(62) Three turtles rested beside a floating log and a fish swam beneath it
(63) Three turtles rested beside a floating log and a fish swam beneath them

A moment's reflection will show that (60) and (61) are mutually entailing but that this is not so for (62) and (63) – (60) and (61) are referred to as *potential inference* sentences (PIs) and (62) and (63) as *non-inference* sentences (NIs). Ss are presented with a set of sentences including PIs and NIs and are subsequently tested for recognition memory using a carefully constructed set of sentences. This includes PIs which are presented on the first list (OLD PIs), sentences which were entailed by sentences on the first list (NEW PIs), e.g. if (60) were presented in the first list, (61) would be a NEW PI, NIs which were presented on the first list (OLD NIs), and NIs which, while not entailed by sentences on the first list, differed from OLD NIs exactly as NEW PIs differed from OLD PIs (NEW NIs), e.g. if (62) appeared on the first list, (63) would be a NEW NI. The task for Ss was simply to judge whether sentences on the recognition list had appeared on the first list, and the results showed that, while they were perfectly capable of distinguishing OLD NIs from NEW NIs, they were as likely to give positive responses to NEW PIs as they were to OLD PIs, i.e. they could not distinguish between a presented sentence and a legitimate inference from that sentence.

Assimilation Theory has opened up new areas of memory research over the last few years and it seems likely that it will direct investigation for some time in the future. Its major weakness is that it has said little about the details of semantic representations for sentences beyond the fact that such representations must allow the processes briefly described here to take place. In particular, it says nothing about the semantic representation of words and it is self-evident that the understanding process involves 'looking up' the meanings of particular words in some sort of psychological dictionary or lexicon. We now turn to an examination of this idea.

9.9 The psychological lexicon

There are many traditional methods for investigating how words are stored in the psychological lexicon. Common responses in word association tests, where an S is asked to supply the first word he thinks of when the experimenter gives him a stimulus word, reveal the psychological salience of such semantic relations as antonymy, complementarity and hyponymy. *Tall* as a stimulus is likely to lead to the response *short*, *furniture* to *chair*, etc. Of course, such tests also lead to apparently inexplicable responses and this is one of the reasons for their being a favoured psychiatric tool, with the psychiatrist attempting to divine underlying reasons for bizarre associations.

If Ss are presented with a longish list of words and asked to recall them in any order, over a number of trials significant clusterings appear in recall orders. These can often be seen as corresponding to the semanticist's semantic fields, and thus this free recall paradigm gives psychological support to this linguistic construct.

In free sorting tasks Ss are simply presented with a number of words typed on cards and asked to sort them into piles. Typically, sortings will indicate semantic groupings and it is often possible to see Ss' responses as being determined by different levels in semantic taxonomies, e.g. one S may sort into two large piles, representing a [±animate] distinction, where another may choose to recognise further divisions within these two superordinate categories.

A less well known experimental technique has been developed in connection with a particular model of the psychological lexicon – a model which explicitly reflects hyponymic relations – and employs a reaction-time paradigm. The model, developed in the context of an attempt to build a computerised dictionary, assumes that words are stored at nodes in networks. Additionally, each node has associated with it a set of properties which are characteristic of the objects referred to by the word stored at that node (these can, perhaps, be thought of as semantic features). Finally, this property storage is

economical in the sense that a property characteristic of all members of
a class will be stored with the class name and not with the individual
members of the class. A hypothetical portion of such a network
appears in Figure 9.2. Note first that this network mirrors the

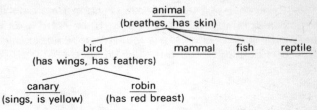

Figure 9.2 *A partial semantic network.*

hyponymic structure of the three-level taxonomy illustrated on p. 196;
evidence for this network will be evidence for the psychological validity of hyponymy. Secondly, in connection with the above remarks,
properties which are characteristic of all animals (breathing and having
skin) are not stored with particular instances of animals (*bird*, etc.).

How can one test the appropriateness of this sort of network as a
representation of the psychological lexicon? Consider (64)–(69).

(64) A canary is yellow
(65) A canary has wings
(66) A canary has skin
(67) A canary is a canary
(68) A canary is a bird
(69) A canary is an animal

Assume that an S is presented with these sentences and asked to judge
whether they are true or false. In terms of Figure 9.2 we might offer the
following impressionistic description of what goes on. For (64), S
enters the network at *canary*, searches the property set stored there
and finds *is yellow*. For (65), he again enters at *canary*, searches and
fails to find so moves up one level to *bird*, searches there and finds *has
wings*. Similarly, for (66), S will have to move up the network, but this
time two levels will be involved. Sentences (67)–(69) differ in parallel
ways, except that no property searches are involved. If something like
this is correct, moving up a level and searching property sets ought to
take time and this is the sort of time which might be measurable using a
reaction-time task. Accordingly, Ss are presented with a large number
of sentences (true and false) constructed along the lines of (64)–(69)
and their task is to respond as quickly as possible, by pressing a button,
with a truth-value judgement. The results are strikingly consistent with
the predictions of Figure 9.2, with the difference in reaction-time to

sentences like (64) and (65) being the same as the difference between (65) and (66) – a measure of the time it takes to move up a level. Similarly, a consistent figure emerges for the time to search a property set, revealed by the differences in reaction-time to (64) and (67), (65) and (68), and (66) and (69).

There is, however, one aspect of such reaction-time data that this theory cannot accommodate: there appear to be regular differences depending on the actual items used in the sentences. For example, (70) will consistently be judged to be true faster than (71).

(70) A robin is a bird
(71) A chicken is a bird

There is nothing in the network model we are considering to tell us why this should be so. According to this model, a robin is a bird and a chicken is a bird and that is the end of the story.

To approach this problem, the suggestion has been offered that semantic categories cluster around stereotypes (see Chapter 7, p. 207) with, for example, some birds being better birds than other birds! A simple experiment to test the feasibility of this suggestion offers Ss a number of category members, as in (72), and asks them to rank them according to degree of birdiness.

(72) *chicken, robin, eagle, ostrich, duck, hawk, sparrow*

The remarkable thing is that Ss *can* do this (they might have regarded the task as meaningless) and that they produce consistent rankings.

Armed with this finding, we can now return to the reaction-time paradigm and examine the effects of degree of category membership (collected in the sort of study just described) on reaction-times. Not surprisingly, it turns out that the more prototypical of the category a member of a category is judged to be, the faster it is judged to be a member of that category.

Another demonstration of the importance of degree of category membership is provided by a novel study in which Ss are introduced to an isolated island and are told that it is populated by several species of birds (say, the set in (72)). They are then told that all members of one of the species contract a highly infectious disease and are asked to judge what proportion of the other species get the disease. A number of interesting findings emerged from this study but, for our purposes, we may merely note two of these:

1 the more prototypical of birds the species that contracted the disease, the higher the incidence of the disease was judged to be in other species, i.e. a bird is more likely to catch a birdy disease from a prototypical bird than from a non-prototypical bird;

2 the effects of the disease were not symmetrical in the sense that more members of species X would be judged to catch the disease if it originated in a prototypical species, than would members of the prototypical species if the disease originated in species X (e.g. Ss are told that all robins – prototypical – get the disease and judge that 30 per cent of eagles get it but, when told that all eagles have the disease, they judge that only 20 per cent of robins get it).

The idea of prototypes in the psychological lexicon is currently a very fashionable one and appears likely to lead to a good deal of exciting work during the next few years. Having introduced it, we shall now bring it to bear on two very important theses which linguists and psycholinguists have discussed during the last forty years or so.

9.10 Universal categories of thought

The two theses alluded to at the end of the previous section are the *Thesis of Linguistic Relativity* and the *Thesis of Linguistic Determinism*. The first of these says, quite simply, that languages can differ without limit and we have already seen that this is opposed by many of the developments in modern linguistics (Chapters 4 and 8; see also Chapter 11). The second, more interesting from the point of view of psycholinguistics, says that the linguistic categories of our native language affect the way in which we think. This position is traditionally associated with the American linguist and anthropologist Benjamin Lee Whorf, and is often referred to as the *Whorfian Hypothesis*. In its strongest form, it claims that our linguistic categories actually *determine* our cognitive categories and that, consequently, our language traps us in a fixed mode of thought. However, the mere fact of translatability of languages argues against this strong form of the hypothesis, and nowadays it is more usual to find a weaker form of it being adopted whereby our linguistic categories *predispose* us to think in certain ways; such predispositions can, though, be overcome.

Strong support for the Thesis of Linguistic Relativity has often been derived from the study of colour lexicons, it being pointed out that there is no straightforward correspondence between the colour terms of the world's languages. This domain has also been explored in connection with Linguistic Determinism, and so it will form the basis of our discussion in this section.

The traditional view that colour lexicons can vary indefinitely was attacked some ten years ago by a study which emphasised the importance of distinguishing between the boundaries of colour terms and the best examples (or prototypes) of such terms. This study confirmed that attention to boundaries yielded no coherent pattern across a number of languages. If, however, native speakers were asked to indicate best examples of colour terms in their language, there were significant clusterings around a small number of points in the colour space. That is to say that, while it is quite likely that there will be no colour term in a language the boundaries of which correspond to English *red*, it is also likely that such a language will have a colour term of which the best example (as judged by native speakers of the language) will correspond to the best example of English *red* (as judged by native speakers of English). This work revealed eleven focal colours which seemed to have some sort of cross-linguistic validity, with languages having basic colour terms focused on a subset of these. Thus, English was claimed to have a full set of eleven terms (*black*, *white*, *red*, *green*, *yellow*, *blue*, *brown*, *pink*, *orange*, *purple* and *grey*). Most European languages shared this pattern (although not, of course, exact correspondences of boundaries) but many languages outside Europe appeared to have less than eleven. In particular, Dani, a language spoken by a people possessing a Stone Age culture in the highlands of New Guinea, appeared to have only two, *mili* and *mola*. In their applicability, these two terms covered most of the visible spectrum and in no sense did their boundaries coincide with those of any English colour terms. Nevertheless, their best examples were judged to coincide with the best example of English *black* and the best example of English *white*. From this it is clear that Dani is consistent with the universalist claims we are considering. Several other possibilities for colour lexicons were also discovered, but it suits our purposes here to emphasise the contrast between English and Dani, as this is going to be vital in our discussion of Linguistic Determinism.

Turning to this, then, the first thing to note is that, as introduced here, it is extremely vague in formulation. If we are going to investigate it experimentally, we shall have to tighten it up considerably. This will involve us in specifying a linguistic variable and explaining what we mean by the claim that this variable affects thinking.

To this end, we can introduce the linguistic variable of *codability* defined over the colours of the colour space. Codability is a number which we associate with each colour in an array and which we compute using three sorts of information:

1 the length of the name a native speaker gives the colour;
2 the time it takes a native speaker to provide a name for a colour;
3 the amount of agreement between native speakers as to what a colour should be called.

The details of the computation need not concern us and we should simply note that the shorter the name a colour is given, the faster the name is supplied and the more agreement there is between native speakers on its name, then the more codable the colour. We now use the colours associated with codability scores in a short-term memory experiment – performance on this task represents what we are going to understand by 'thinking'. The experiment is very simple: Ss are presented with a coloured chip mounted on a card and allowed to look at it for five seconds. It is then removed and ten seconds later the S is shown an array of coloured chips including the one he was previously exposed to. His task is to select this latter from the array.

Using North American Ss, the results of a study of this kind were quite clear-cut: the more codable a colour was (the linguistic property), the more memorable it was (the cognitive performance), and this looks like a straightforward effect of language on thinking. But what if the most codable colours, for North American Ss, were also the focal colours, as defined by the research we have summarised above? The way would be open for the suggestion that, rather than codability causing memorability, focalness causes codability and, indirectly, memorability, i.e. the variables of codability (defined with respect to a particular language) and focalness (assumed to have some universal status, independently of particular languages) would be confounded.

The relevant research has been done and it turns out that, over a range of languages, the most codable colours just are the focal colours. How can we pull these two variables apart? The answer to this question brings us back to the Dani with their relatively impoverished colour lexicon. Precisely because of this impoverishment, codability differences do not exist for the native speaker of Dani where they do for the native speaker of English. Where we might call two distinct colours *green* and *greenish-blue* (thus indicating the higher codability of the first), the Dani will call them both *mili* (or, if they fall on opposite sides of the *mili/mola* boundary, *mili* and *mola*). If, however, focal colours have some privileged psychological position which is independent of language-structure, we would expect to be able to find some reflex of this if we ask Dani Ss to perform cognitive tasks involving colours.

Accordingly, the short-term memory experiment described above has been repeated using Dani Ss and also systematically studying the variable of focalness in the stimuli. Stimuli which an S had to remember could be focal or non-focal and, keeping in mind that the focal colours are not given any special status within the Dani lexicon, Linguistic Determinism would predict no significant differences in Dani performance on these two categories. This is not what was found. Although, overall, Dani Ss were much worse at the task than their North American counterparts (a fact which can, perhaps, be put down to their not using their memories in a way demanded by this sort of task in their everyday lives), they were considerably better at remembering focal colours than they were at remembering non-focal colours, and this finding cannot be explained in terms of Dani language-structure, as the relevant structure is missing.

All of this is consistent, then, with the view that, in the colour space, there are a small number of psychologically salient points. Furthermore, these points possess their salience not because of language-structure, but for some more basic reason – attempts to explain these findings usually refer to universal properties of the human perceptual apparatus and its colour-coding mechanisms. If a language is in the process of becoming more complex in this particular domain, then it will have to recognise the existence of these salient points; it is not free to lexicalise in a completely unconstrained fashion.

Of course, the immediate question to ask concerns whether similar results can be obtained in other parts of the lexicon and there has been some suggestive work in this direction. Whatever the outcome of this work, we think that Linguistic Determinism, while almost certainly having some truth attached to it, must learn to live with the view that there is a universal set of cognitive categories which cannot be limitlessly deformed by individual language-structures. In the next chapter one of the issues to which we shall turn will be that of how such categories might manifest themselves in the developing cognitive and linguistic systems of the small child.

Exercises: Chapter 9

1 Collect a sample of tongue-slips and, for each item in your sample, describe what has gone wrong in the speaker's production.

2 Perform a word association test on a group of subjects. Produce a set of words from a number of distinct syntactic categories having a range of semantic characteristics. Offer them one by one to your subjects with the instruction to write down the first word that comes into their heads. Analyse your results in terms of whether the subjects produce paradigmatic responses (words from the same syntactic class as the stimulus word) or syntagmatic responses (words which can appear in syntactic constructions with the stimulus word) and in terms of the type of semantic relation obtaining between stimulus and response. Attempt to make sense of idiosyncratic responses by consulting your subjects.

3 Perform a sorting experiment by writing a fairly large number of words on cards (say, fifty to a hundred) and giving them to subjects to sort into piles on the basis of similarity of meaning. Select some of your words so that they define what *you* regard as coherent semantic categories and see whether your subjects' behaviour confirms your intuitions. Look for evidence of subjects sorting on the basis of categories which are superordinate to those you have intended them to recognise (e.g. putting all plant names and animal names together on the basis of their all referring to living things). What can you say about sorted piles which do not correspond to your intuitions?

4   Investigate the 'psychological coherence' of constituents by presenting subjects with sentences and pairs of words from the sentences. The subjects' task is to *rate* the relatedness of the pair of words in that sentence along a 5-point scale. If they consider a pair of words closely related they should give the pair 5, if very weakly related, 1, and so on. Test the prediction that pairs of words from the same constituent will be judged more closely related than pairs of words from different constituents. Depending on the amount of time available you might use *all* pairs of words in a sentence or prefer to consider a range of sentences.

5   Select a short passage (100–200 words) which comprises a 'story' (e.g. a short feature in a newspaper). Choose a sentence occurring fairly early in the story that can be passivised. Read the story to subjects and, when you have finished, present them with a test sentence which may be the sentence you have chosen, the passive version of that sentence, or a version of that sentence in which the subject and direct object have been switched. For example, if your story contained *The police chased the thief across the street*, your test sentence might be this or *The thief was chased across the street by the police* or *The thief chased the police across the street*. The subjects' task is to decide whether the test sentence appeared in the story or not. Discuss your results in connection with theories of sentence memory.

6   Repeat Exercise 5 but choose (or construct) a story which contains a passive sentence in the relevant position. Test with that sentence, the corresponding active sentence and the passive sentence with subject and object of *by* switched.

7   Select a small number of semantic categories (e.g. fish, fruits, diseases, occupations, sciences, vehicles) and a number of exemplars of each. Present these exemplars to subjects along with the instruction to rate them with regard to their degree of belonging to the category in question (e.g. degree of fishiness, degree of fruitiness) along a 7-point scale. See whether there is any consistency between your subjects in their ratings and, if there is, attempt to explain it.

8   Repeat Exercise 7 but use pictures as exemplars of subordinate categories. If, for example, you decide to study the category *cow* (subordinate to *mammal*), you should collect (or draw) several pictures of cows taken from different angles, etc., and present these for rating with regard to degree of 'cowness'.

9   Quasi-English is a language exactly like English except that it describes a circle with a gap in it as a *glumph* and a circle as a *glumph without a gap*. Do you think that there are any languages like Quasi-English in this respect? Give reasons.

10   Informally test the suggestion that semantic constraints facilitate the perception of sentences involving more than one degree of embedding. Construct your own materials (using 40 and 41 from the text as models) consisting of a set of semantically constrained sentences and a set of semantically uncon-

strained sentences. Present them to subjects (in written form) and underneath the sentences write a set of questions along the lines of (re. 40 and 41) *Who or what died?*, *Who or what was complex?* See whether subjects take longer and are less accurate in answering the questions for the semantically unconstrained sentences.

11   The following is a North American Indian folk-tale. Allow subjects to read it through twice and test their retention of it after differing amounts of time (e.g. immediately afterwards, after fifteen minutes, after one day, after one week). Look at what aspects of the story are consistently remembered correctly or omitted and try to formulate a generalisation which will explain any pattern you find. Examine the ways in which parts of the story are distorted in recall. Can you offer any explanation for these phenomena?

> One night two young men from Egulac went down to the river to hunt seals, and while they were there it became foggy and calm. Then they heard war-cries, and they thought: 'Maybe this is a war-party.' They escaped to the shore, and hid behind a log. Now canoes came up, and they heard the noise of paddles, and saw one canoe coming up to them. There were five men in the canoe, and they said:
> 'What do you think? We wish to take you along. We are going up the river to make war on the people.'
> One of the young men said: 'I have no arrows.'
> 'Arrows are in the canoe', they said.
> 'I will not go along. I might be killed. My relatives do not know where I have gone. But you', he said, turning to the other, 'may go with them.'
> So one of the young men went, but the other returned home.
> And the warriors went on up the river to a town on the other side of Kalama. The people came down to the water, and they began to fight, and many were killed. But presently the young man heard one of the warriors say: 'Quick, let us go home: that Indian has been hit.' Now he thought: 'Oh, they are ghosts.' He did not feel sick, but they said he had been shot.
> So the canoes went back to Egulac and the young man went ashore to his house, and made a fire. And he told everybody and said: 'Behold I accompanied the ghosts, and we went to fight. Many of our fellows were killed, and many of those who attacked us were killed. They said I was hit, and I did not feel sick.'
> He told it all, and then he became quiet. When the sun rose he fell down. Something black came out of his mouth. His face became contorted. The people jumped up and cried.
> He was dead.

12   Imagine a perceptual device equipped with the strategies (39) and (43) from the text. What will be the result of this device being presented with *The mouse chased the cat*? How will it fare if presented with *The cat was chased by the mouse*? What inadequacies become apparent in the theory of strategies from consideration of examples such as these?

Bibliography: Chapter 9

Aitchison, J., *The Articulate Mammal* (London: Hutchinson, 1976). A very clearly written introduction to experimental work within the transformational paradigm. Does not go into great detail but accurate and stimulating within its self-imposed limitations. Also relevant for Chapter 10.

Clark, H., and Clark, E. V., *Psychology and Language* (New York: Harcourt Brace Jovanovich, 1977). The most comprehensive introduction available including an enormous bibliography up to 1977. Discussion of all the issues raised in this chapter plus many others. To some extent suffers from the authors' desire to develop their own position rather than simply survey the field. Also relevant for Chapter 10.

Fodor, J. A., Bever, T. G., and Garrett, M., *The Psychology of Language* (New York: McGraw-Hill, 1974). A scholarly discussion of the field up to 1974. More difficult than the above books but contains much more theoretical discussion. Necessary reading for anyone wishing to go into psycholinguistics seriously.

Miller, G., and Johnson-Laird, P. J., *Language and Perception* (Cambridge: Cambridge University Press, 1976). The best available survey of work on the psychological representation of words. The authors attempt to develop a theory of their own and, therefore, the text is not introductory. Nevertheless, it contains a wealth of experimental investigations from the history of psychology.

Slobin, D. I., *Psycholinguistics* (Glenview, Ill.: Scott, Foresman, 1978, 2nd edn). A comprehensive introduction by one of the leading workers in the field. This edition contains discussion of some of the recent work on the psychological lexicon. Also relevant for Chapter 10.

There follows a list of papers which are the sources of the findings referred to in the text of this chapter. They are presented in the order in which they are mentioned in the chapter.

Wickelgren, W., 'Distinctive features and errors in short-term memory for English consonants', *Journal of the Acoustical Society of America*, 39 (1966), pp. 388–98.

Coltheart, M., and Geffen, G., 'Grammar and memory: phonological similarity and proactive interference', *Cognitive Psychology*, 1 (1970), pp. 215–24.

Miller, G. A., and Nicely, P. E., 'An analysis of perceptual confusion among some English consonants', *Journal of the Acoustical Society of America*, 27 (1955), pp. 338–52.

Pisoni, D., and Tash, J., 'Auditory property detectors and processing place features in stop consonants', *Perception and Psychophysics*, 18 (1975), pp. 401–8.

Epstein, W., 'The influence of grammatical structure on learning', *American Journal of Psychology*, 74 (1961), pp. 80–5.

Miller, G. A., and Isard, S., 'Some perceptual consequences of linguistic rules', *Journal of Verbal Learning and Verbal Behavior*, 2 (1963), pp. 217–28.

Johnson, N. F., 'The psychological reality of phrase-structure rules', *Journal of Verbal Learning and Verbal Behavior*, 4 (1965), pp. 469–75.

Mehler, J., and Carey, P., 'Role of surface and base structure in the perception of sentences', *Journal of Verbal Learning and Verbal Behavior*, 6 (1967), pp. 335–8.

Fodor, J. A., and Bever, T. G., 'The psychological reality of linguistic segments', *Journal of Verbal Learning and Verbal Behavior*, 4 (1965), pp. 414–20.

Garrett, M., Bever, T. G., and Fodor, J. A., 'The active use of grammar in speech perception', *Perception and Psychophysics*, 1 (1966), pp. 30–2.

Blumenthal, A. L., 'Prompted recall of sentences', *Journal of Verbal Learning and Verbal Behavior*, 6, (1967), pp. 203–6.

Bever, T. G., Lackner, J. R., and Kirk, R., 'The underlying structures of sentences are the primary units of immediate speech processing', *Perception and Psychophysics*, 5 (1969), pp. 225–31.

Forster, K. I., 'Visual perception of rapidly presented word sequences of varying complexity', *Perception and Psychophysics*, 8 (1970), pp. 215–21.

Mehler, J., 'Some effects of grammatical transformations on the recall of English sentences', *Journal of Verbal Learning and Verbal Behavior*, 2 (1963), pp. 346–51.

Savin, H. B., and Perchonock, E., 'Grammatical structure and immediate recall of English sentences', *Journal of Verbal Learning and Verbal Behavior*, 4 (1965), pp. 348–53.

Turner, E. A., and Rommetveit, R., 'Focus of attention in recall of active and passive sentences', *Journal of Verbal Learning and Verbal Behavior*, 7 (1968), pp. 543–8.

Epstein, W., 'Recall of word lists following learning of sentences and of anomalous and random strings', *Journal of Verbal Learning and Verbal Behavior*, 8, (1969), pp. 20–5.

Slobin, D. I., 'Recall of full and truncated passive sentences in connected discourse', *Journal of Verbal Learning and Verbal Behavior*, 7 (1968), pp. 876–81.

Gough, P. B., 'The verification of sentences: the effects of delay of evidence and sentence length', *Journal of Verbal Learning and Verbal Behavior*, 5 (1966), pp. 492–6.

Fodor, J. A., and Garrett, M., 'Some reflections on competence and performance', in J. Lyons and R. J. Wales (eds), *Psycholinguistics Papers* (Edinburgh: University of Edinburgh Press, 1966), pp. 135–79.

Slobin, D. I., 'Grammatical transformations and sentence comprehension in childhood and adulthood', *Journal of Verbal Learning and Verbal Behavior*, 5 (1966), pp. 219–27.

Bever, T. G., 'The cognitive basis for linguistic structures', in J. R. Hayes (ed.), *Cognition and the Development of Language* (New York: Wiley, 1970), pp. 279–355.

Hakes, D. T., 'Effects of reducing complement constructions on sentence comprehension', *Journal of Verbal Learning and Verbal Behavior*, 11 (1972), pp. 278–86.

Sachs, J., 'Recognition memory for syntactic and semantic aspects of connected discourse', *Perception and Psychophysics*, 2 (1967), pp. 439–42.

Clark, H., and Stafford, R. A., 'Memory for semantic features in the verb', *Journal of Experimental Psychology*, 80 (1969), pp. 326–34.

Clark, H., and Card, S. K., 'The role of semantics in remembering comparative sentences', *Quarterly Journal of Experimental Psychology*, 82 (1969), pp. 545–53.

Bransford, J. D., and Johnson, M. K., 'Contextual prerequisites for understanding: some investigations of comprehension and recall', *Journal of Verbal Learning and Verbal Behavior*, 11 (1972), pp. 717–26.

Fillenbaum, S., 'Memory for gist: some relevant variables', *Language and Speech*, 9 (1966), pp. 217–27.

Bransford, J. D., Barclay, J. R., and Franks, J. J., 'Sentence memory: a constructive versus interpretive approach', *Cognitive Psychology*, 3 (1972), pp. 193–209.

Collins, A. M., and Quillian, M. R., 'Retrieval time from semantic memory', *Journal of Verbal Learning and Verbal Behavior*, 8 (1969), pp. 240–7.

Rosch, E. H., 'On the internal structure of perceptual and semantic categories', in T. Moore (ed.), *Cognitive Development and the Acquisition of Language* (New York: Academic Press, 1973), pp. 111–44.

Rips, L. J., Shoben, E. J., and Smith, E., 'Semantic distance and the verification of semantic relations', *Journal of Verbal Learning and Verbal Behavior*, 12 (1973), pp. 1–20.

Rips, L. J., 'Inductive judgements about natural categories', *Journal of Verbal Learning and Verbal Behavior*, 14 (1975), pp. 665–78.

Berlin, B., and Kay, P., *Basic Color Terms: Their Universality and Evolution* (Berkeley, Calif.: University of California Press, 1969).

Brown, R., and Lenneberg, E., 'A study in language and cognition', *Journal of Abnormal and Social Psychology*, 49 (1954), pp. 454–62.

Heider, E. R., 'Universals in color naming and memory', *Journal of Experimental Psychology*, 93 (1972), pp. 10–21.

Chapter 10
Language Development in Children

10.1 Description and explanation in language acquisition research

There are at least three major tasks facing the student of the acquisition of their native language by small children. One of these has already been introduced in Chapter 2 and concerns explanations of the *fact* of language development, the second seeks explanations for the *course* of development and the third involves *descriptions* of different aspects of the child's linguistic system.

The reader will recall that in Chapter 2 we raised the first of these problems in connection with a discussion of innateness, arguing that if it were possible to demonstrate that a particular sort of psychological structure could not be learned solely on the basis of exposure to data of the appropriate kind, then we might be justified in concluding that the outline of the structure is innately supplied. However, this move towards innateness is not the only possible response to the problem created by such a demonstration.

The argument of Chapter 2 depended on accepting a number of assumptions and it is possible to question any of these. Thus, some have argued that it is only *if* we assume that the child acquires a system with the problematic characteristics that the learnability difficulty arises – a response as legitimate as that which postulates innateness simply denies that a system of this sort is acquired. To take a particular example which has given rise to some debate, most of the arguments for innateness have arisen in connection with the assumption that the child acquires a transformational grammar. This approach to syntactic description involves such complexity and such abstractness that, it is claimed, it could not be learned solely on the basis of exposure to data. But perhaps it is not learned at all, and the very fact that it could not be acquired using standard learning mechanisms can be used as an argument for its incorrectness as a theory of adult linguistic competence. Whether one adopts this sort of position or not depends, to a large extent, on one's intellectual background. Of course, the transformational linguist is loath to give up his elaborate formalisms in the light of criticisms from traditional learning theory (for a discussion of learning theory, see Chapter 2, p. 45 ff.); he would rather take the line that learning theory must change. Equally, the learning theorist, brought up in a tradition of over fifty years of experimental investigation, will not happily relinquish his relatively simple ideas on what is involved in learning; he will say that if a system cannot be learned using his well-known principles, then it is not learned.

There is one important point that can be brought to bear on this dispute at this stage: if one group of theorists is to say that the theory postulated by another group is wrong, then it is obliged to offer some alternative. Notoriously, learning theorists who have urged that linguistic theory be modified have failed to deliver any coherent theory of linguistic structure and many would see this as a strong argument against their policy.

A second assumption of the original argument concerned the learning procedures with which the organism (in this case, the child) is equipped. So, the suggestion has been made that we can make richer assumptions about these procedures than those which are typically made in the literature on learning – these latter would normally only involve basic principles of generalisation and discrimination – and that, using these richer procedures, the child will be able to induce the full complexity of linguistic structure. This strategy is often talked about in terms of a *process* approach to the development of language and is contrasted with the alternative *content* approach, whereby the child is actually equipped with innate information about the structure he is to acquire. There are at least two problems with this view.

The first is that, despite the fact that it was originally aired some fifteen years ago, remarkably little progress has been made in being more specific about the nature of the enriched learning mechanisms; it remains a promissory note rather than a useful theory. The second, related to the first, is that it is not clear that if the promise were realised, the position would be distinct, except in emphasis, from the content approach. If the approach is eventually driven to postulate abstract and highly specific learning procedures for the acquisition of language, it is unclear that we have anything which is other than terminologically distinct from the content view.

More substantial, at least in terms of empirical research, than either of the two responses to the problem of learnability discussed so far is the claim that the assumptions about data on which the original argument is based are incorrect. Chomsky himself has repeatedly emphasised the degenerate nature of the input to the child but, in the last ten years, it has become clear that mothers (and other 'caretakers'), when speaking to their children, use language which has special characteristics. On the basis of this, this sort of language is now viewed as an identifiable 'register' (i.e. roughly style, see Chapter 12 for a more detailed discussion) and is referred to as *Motherese*. More will be said in Section 8 below about the characteristics of Motherese but for now we merely wish to contemplate its significance for our general argument. It would be easy to say that Motherese is an ideal *teaching* language given the fact that it is special and that, in particular, it contains hardly any disfluencies or ungrammatical utterances. Subsequently, it might be possible to demonstrate that the problematic properties of the acquired system can be induced from a corpus of data so long as that corpus is Motherese. But this argument prejudges a number of issues which are far from clear. To take just one example, it may be the case that Motherese, rather than being the result of some (unconscious) effort on the part of the mother to teach language, is just a response by the mother to the child's linguistic system; that is, the change in the mother's speech is caused by the child rather than the mother actively affecting the child's development. To some extent the dust has begun to settle on this sort of issue but, for now, we merely wish to make it clear that the *existence* of a special register of Motherese does not guarantee that it has the *teaching function* we are interested in here.

A response of a rather different sort to the learnability problem has come from cognitive and social psychologists. They have claimed that there is nothing specifically linguistic about the systems which the child has to learn and the alternative they offer is to attempt to identify sources for such systems in the child's non-linguistic cognitive development and in his social development. Of course, even if such sources are identified, this does not exclude the possibility that innate knowledge will have to be postulated to account for them. This brief introduction of the role of cognitive and social development in explaining the *fact* of language development leads quite naturally into the second task for the language acquisition theorist.

Typically, organisms that learn to operate with complex structures do not acquire their skills instantaneously; rather, learning is a protracted process with the organism going through a series of *stages*. Certainly this is true of language acquisition in the child and, if we examine this sort of process, one thing that we shall find interesting is a generalisation that one aspect of structure is learned *before* another. Such generalisations point in the direction of there being a *course* of development and workers in child language are concerned not merely to explain the fact of development but also to be in a position to understand this course. Thus, in general, we shall not be content to observe that X precedes Y in language development; we shall also require an explanation for *why* things appear in this order.

Again, when we consider this question, there is a number of alternative types of answer. One, most closely tied to the innateness position, minimises the importance of environmental influences on this process and emphasises the role of biological and maturational factors. Just as in the case of the innatist explanation of the fact of acquisition, this answer arises from an inability to produce an alternative rather than from any direct knowledge of the biological and maturational factors involved. And, again, there are alternatives.

A theorist who wishes to investigate the role of the child's linguistic environment will examine changes in Motherese as the child develops. Ideally, he will be able to argue that earlier appearing aspects of structure can be induced from earlier samples of Motherese and that those aspects of a child's linguistic abilities which only appear late require a more sophisticated input in order to be learned by the child.

Alternatively, it may be possible to discern properties in the child's developing cognitive, social, or perceptual development which can be seen as prerequisites for the child acquiring a particular linguistic structure or procedure. If this is so, we may be in a position to say that the reason for X being acquired before Y is that the child's development in some other domain makes the appearance of X possible before the appearance of Y.

Of course, if we are to seek the sort of explanation alluded to in this section, it is imperative that we have adequate descriptions of different aspects of language development from which we can deduce the generalisations which need to be explained. Description, then, constitutes the third of the major tasks which we referred to at the start of this section. We shall now turn to such descriptions and their associated explanations in different areas of language development. On the whole, the fact of language acquisition has not occupied a central role outside the sort of abstract argument we have presented here. Accordingly, it will not be afforded much discussion until we return to the study of Motherese in Section 8.

10.2 Phonological development

One of the best-known discussions of phonological development is offered by Roman Jakobson in his book *Child Language, Aphasia and Phonological Universals*. Much of what he says there is now regarded as inaccurate and certainly the data on which he based his generalisations are often anecdotal. Against this, however, his work shows remarkable sophistication in its attempt to explain phonological development and is usually taken as a reference point for any discussion of this topic.

Jakobson begins his monograph by noting the existence of the *babbling period*, a period which typically extends from about 6 months of age to 1 year and during which the child produces a very wide range of sounds. These sounds, however, do not appear to have any systematic value for the child in terms of a structured communication system. Often the babbling period is followed by a silent period before the child embarks on phonological development proper, commencing at about 1 year or 15 months. Now, the slightly paradoxical aspect of all this is that when the child begins to acquire his native phonology, he must, apparently, relearn the sounds that he has previously used in the babbling period; that is, to babble a sound is not a sufficient condition for controlling this sound in a structured linguistic system. The way in which the paradox is resolved by Jakobson is for him to suggest that, in phonological development proper, the child is not acquiring sounds as such but *distinctive oppositions* (see Chapter 4), which have a role to play in distinguishing words within his developing system. For these oppositions, Jakobson claims, there is a fixed, universal order of acquisition.

Supposedly, everywhere, whatever language they are learning, children first acquire an opposition between consonants and vowels. As the important idea here is the opposition, any consonant and any vowel will serve to carry it, but often the first consonant is /p/ and the first vowel /a/. With this first opposition the child can construct syllables which offer a syntagmatic combination on which paradigmatic contrasts can be introduced. The first paradigmatic opposition is within the consonant class and is a contrast between oral and nasal Cs. At this point we can imagine a child with a two-word vocabulary, using these basic contrasts. Such a child is likely to have the forms *papa* and *mama* (reduplicated syllables are common in early child speech). The next contrast is also a consonantal contrast and consists of the opposition between bilabial and dental/alveolar, thus giving the child a likely four-item vocabulary, say, *papa*, *mama*, *tata* and *nana*. Up to this point, the consonantal development of all children is claimed to be exactly the same.

According to the theory, the first vocalic opposition follows now with a split between high and low vowels. This would mean that, alongside the four items listed above, the child might control *pipi*, *mimi*, *titi* and *nini*, all eight of these now having distinctive functions for him. Most commonly, there then follows a distinction between high front and high back vowels, yielding the triangular vowel system, /i/, /u/, /a/ (see Chapter 4, p. 108). However, in some cases, the child makes a second height distinction, contrasting a mid vowel with his already functioning high and low vowels; this gives the linear vowel system, /i/, /e/, /a/. Just as for consonants, up to this stage vocalic development is universal.

Later development, while not universal in the above sense, is not devoid of regularity, and Jakobson claims that there is a number of statements which hold true of it. A sample of these appear as (1)–(4).

(1) Children only acquire back consonants after they acquire front consonants.

(2) Children only acquire fricatives after they acquire homorganic stops.

(3) Children only acquire affricates after they acquire homorganic stops and fricatives.

(4) Children only acquire nasal vowels after they acquire corresponding oral vowels.

Note that these statements do not necessarily apply to all children and this is why they do not represent universals of the same type as those which are claimed to characterise the earliest stages of development. A child may *never* acquire (phonological) nasal vowels, e.g. a child learning English, but of course this does not constitute an exception to (4).

Let us for now assume that Jakobson's generalisations are correct and briefly consider the explanation he offers for them. First, he argues that the exceptionless course of early development and the later stages, characterised by (1)–(4) and similar statements, should not be viewed in isolation from other domains of linguistic inquiry. Examination of other areas might reveal interesting correspondences, persuading us that we are on the right track with our generalisations. Jakobson examines two other areas: the distribution of phonological oppositions in the world's languages and the disintegration of language in aphasic patients.

For the former, he suggests that the consonantal system characterised by the oppositions oral v. nasal and bilabial v. dental/alveolar is *minimal* in the sense that no language of the world fails to utilise these oppositions. Similarly for vocalic development, the triangular and linear systems mentioned above represent the minimal vocalic systems in the world's languages. Taken together, these two claims indicate that the child learns first exactly what is universal in the phonological structure of the world's languages. What of later development?

Parallel to (1)–(4) Jakobson formulates what he calls *Laws of Irreversible Solidarity* which are intended to hold true of the distribution of oppositions in the world's languages. Statements (5)–(8) correspond to (1)–(4) in this respect.

(5) If a language has back consonants then it has front consonants.

(6) If a language has fricatives then it has homorganic stops.

(7) If a language has affricates then it has homorganic stops and fricatives.

(8) If a language has nasal vowels then it has corresponding oral vowels.

Thus, very simply, it appears that if Jakobson is correct, having learned the universal core of phonological structure, the child continues by learning the next most frequent sounds (in terms of distribution throughout the languages of the world, not in terms of frequency of occurrence within a language), moving gradually to the sounds which are relatively infrequent.

From aphasia comes an entirely consistent picture, although nowadays virtually no one takes Jakobson's speculations in this area seriously. Nevertheless, his vision is illustrated by his suggestion that the sounds which are most likely to be lost by a patient suffering some language disturbance are exactly those which he will have acquired last as a child (they are also, of course, those which are least common in the languages of the world). Those that will persist, even when a patient suffers massive brain damage, will belong to the universal core, utilising those oppositions which the patient learned first.

The existence of these correspondences from such diverse areas of language requires explanation and, to Jakobson's credit, he has attempted to provide one. Unfortunately, it is involved and not always convincing and we shall not offer a detailed treatment here. We can, however, transmit the flavour of it by considering the first acquired opposition between consonant and vowel. Why should this be the first opposition? Recall that this opposition is typically carried by /p/ v. /a/ and note that these two sounds differ maximally in two ways: (i) acoustically /p/ contains minimal energy and /a/ maximal energy; (ii) articulatorily /p/ involves a total shutting-off of the vocal cavities from the atmosphere, whereas /a/ is a maximally wide vowel. Therefore, if we assume that the child's learning takes account of a 'Principle of Maximal Contrast', we can see that these two sounds contrast optimally on two dimensions, one perceptual and the other articulatory. Suffice it to say here that there is a good deal of evidence for such a principle being useful in learning for both humans and sub-human species and that Jakobson goes on to attempt to apply it consistently to later stages of development. This can be seen, then, as an attempt to explain the order of the acquisition of distinctive oppositions in terms of basic principles of perception and motor behaviour.

We have hinted above that Jakobson's generalisations are far from satisfactory and we now wish to introduce some data which raise problems for his position. The way to appreciate the significance of these data is to ask what a child will do, on Jakobson's account, if he attempts to produce a form employing a phonological opposition which he has not yet mastered. The obvious answer to this is that he will *substitute* some segment from his repertoire for the problematic segment. Thus, on the basis of (1), we might anticipate children going through a stage where they substitute back consonants with front consonants; the pronunciation of *duck* as [dʌt] or of *cut* as [tʌt] is the sort of phenomenon we would expect. Similarly, on the basis of (2), we might expect fricatives to be substituted by homorganic stops, leading to, for example, pronunciation of *that* as [dæt] or *van* as [bæn]. Now, this sort of substitution is, indeed, very common, but unfortunately any suggestion that the child can be seen as using substitution rules along the lines of (9) and (10) rapidly comes to grief.

(9)   /k/ → [t]
(10) fricative → homorganic stop

This can be readily seen by considering the data in (11) where a particular child's pronunciation of various forms is given alongside the forms themselves.

(11) *a light* – [daɪt]   *d daddy* – [dɛdi:]   *g rain* – [de:n]
     b like – [gaɪk]   *e duck* – [gʌk]   *h other* – [ʌdə]
     c lorry – [lɔli:]   *f driving* – [waɪbɪn]   *i chair* – [dɛ:]

In (11)*a–c* we are interested in how the child produces words including /l/ and we can see that it is not the case that /l/ is consistently substituted by some segment in the child's repertoire. In (11)*c* /l/ is produced appropriately, but in (11)*a* and (11)*b* it is produced as [d] and [g]. Similarly, in (11)*d–f*, /d/ is variantly realised as [d] (correctly), [g], or [w], and the first and second columns in (11) illustrate a situation where one sound in the adult system appears to correspond to more than one sound in the child's system. The converse of this appears in (11)*g–i*, where the adult phonemes /r/, /ð/ and /ʧ/ are all produced by the child as [d], i.e. several sounds in the adult system correspond to one sound in the child's productions.

An examination of some of the data in (11) points the way towards a more adequate characterisation of what is going on than that offered by such rules as (9) and (10). If we consider (11)*e*, we can see that the segment which the child substitutes for /d/ is, in fact, matched for place of articulation with the *following* consonant. This is also true of (11)*b*, (11)*c*, (11)*f* and (11)*g* and it appears that assimilatory processes, whereby a segment takes on characteristics of neighbouring segments, may be important in understanding early phonological development (there are, of course, other things going on in 11 with which we are not concerned here). The important thing to be clear about is that processes of this sort are, by definition, *context-sensitive* (see the discussion of coarticulation in Chapter 4). The rules in (9) and (10), however, are *context-free*, simply saying that one segment is substituted by another everywhere. Clearly, such context-free rules are not adequate for representing the sort of variation we find.

There is another phenomenon which suggests that Jakobson's views are, at best, an oversimplification. At first sight it is extremely perplexing. The child from whom the data in (11) come also produced, at the same stage of development, [pʌgəl] when attempting to say *puddle*.

From this we would be likely to conclude that this child simply could not produce the sequence [pʌdəl], but then we discover that the same child, attempting to say *puzzle*, says [pʌdəl]! The child *can* produce the sequence [pʌdəl] but only when he is trying to say something else. Another child illustrates the same phenomenon with his attempts to pronounce *thick* and *sick*. The first of these emerges as [fɪk] and the second as [θɪk]; again, the child *can* say [θɪk] but only when he is trying to say *sick*.

This indicates, at least, that an approach which merely emphasises the acquisition of oppositions is going to be inadequate. It simply is not clear that children do acquire oppositions in any straightforward way – rather, they seem to control oppositions in some contexts and not in others – and it appears that we are going to have to take account of the whole of the child's developing phonological system, where this will include specifications of context-sensitive processes such as those alluded to above, if we wish to come to terms with this.

One way in which this problem has been tackled has been to suggest that the child comes to language learning equipped with a set of *natural phonological processes*. These natural processes can be seen as codifying innate constraints on the production of speech and the assimilations we have referred to above fall easily under this label. Slightly more subtle is the natural process which leads to many obstruents being unvoiced in early child speech. Voicing is unnatural in obstruents because it requires vocal fold vibration which depends upon differences in supraglottal and subglottal pressure (see Chapter 3), while at the same time closing off the vocal cavities from the atmosphere leading to a rapid equalisation of these two pressures. Accordingly, there will be a tendency for voiced obstruents to be unvoiced in the speech of the child until he learns to suppress this natural process. Such suppression is one important aspect of what goes into learning the phonology of one's native language on this view.

Progress in studying natural processes has not been exciting so far and it is likely that even its staunchest proponents would not claim that it offers particularly revealing explanations for the general course of development. But there is a number of recurrent phenomena in development which appear to be amenable to this sort of analysis and it is likely that it will provide a framework for research in the near future.

Before closing our discussion of phonological development, there is one important assumption in our presentation so far which deserves to be made explicit. If we are going to talk about the child possessing substitution rules (context-free or context-sensitive, encoding natural processes), we are required to credit the child with something approximating to the adult phonological form of a word he is attempting to pronounce. Otherwise, there is nothing for the substitution process to operate on and no way to derive, in a systematic way, the child's own form. But are we justified in crediting the child with this sort of representation at a time when he is phonologically immature?

It is a common observation that children's linguistic comprehension exceeds their production in all aspects of language and the assumption we are concerned with is clearly a species of this view. However, appeal to common observation does not constitute serious justification and, while Jakobson himself does not explicitly discuss the issue, others have been more forthright, and it is interesting to look at the sort of argument that has been advanced. Here we mention just two.

The first is straightforward and depends on informal testing of the child's comprehension. We consider a child who does not distinguish *mouth* and *mouse* in his own production and we test his comprehension of this contrast by asking him to fetch pictures of a mouse or a mouth with which we have acquainted the child in various parts of the house. Consistently correct responding under these circumstances leads to the conclusion that the child does perceptually control a contrast that is not present in his own production. Similarly, children will often protest at an adult's attempt to use their own immature forms, saying such things as *Not a guk*, *it's a guk* in response to an adult's suggestion that a particular duck is a guk! Such protests can only be based on the child perceiving the inappropriateness of the adult rendition of his own form and are consistent with the child having knowledge of the appropriate form.

The second argument is rather more complex and invokes the view that, without our assumption, phonological development is inexplicable. We can illustrate this using a simple example. At at early stage of development one child pronounced both *dog* and *doll* as [dɒ]. Furthermore, at this stage the child did not produce any velar consonants. Somewhat later he began to produce velars but only in initial position and, at this time, the child's pronunciation of dog changed to [gɒ], while that for *doll* remained stable as [dɒ]. What are we to make of this?

If we assume that the child controls the adult form of *dog* (/dɒg/), then given the importance of assimilatory processes already alluded to, we can see the pressure for this to be pronounced as [gɒg] as soon as the child can produce velar consonants. But, of course, this child only produces them in initial position to begin with and so, we would expect [gɒ]. With the assumption, we can make some sense of this development; without it, we are completely in the dark.

Arguments such as these notwithstanding, there has been a good deal of scepticism about the assumption and there are several experimental studies aimed at testing it. In one of these the child is asked to identify pictures on the basis of either his own pronunciation of the name of the depicted object or that of an adult. Children do considerably better with adult versions and this provides support for the assumption. Opposed to this, however, is another technique where children are introduced to two play figures who are given nonsense names (e.g. Mr Fap and Mr Vap). They are allowed to play with the figures as the names are used repeatedly and are then asked to do something with one of the figures when both are present. The appropriate choice of figure by the child is intended to indicate perception of the relevant phonological contrast (in this case, voicing).

Results using this technique have indicated that there *is* an order of acquisition for phonological contrasts in perception which is continuing to unfold after the child has begun to produce language, i.e. not all children in these studies controlled all the tested oppositions, despite the fact that they all had some productive language. This, therefore, is inconsistent with the assumption (in its strongest form, whereby the child is required to perceive *all* phonological oppositions if he is producing language) and also contradicts the results of informal testing which we have discussed briefly above. Additionally, there is some support for the view that the order of acquisition of perceptual oppositions is consistent across languages and that it bears some resemblance to the order postulated by Jakobson with which we began this section. The issue of what the child perceives is currently not resolved and will remain the subject of intensive research over the next few years.

10.3 Early syntactic development

Small children usually begin to combine words when they are about 18 months old and most studies of syntactic development have treated this as a natural starting-point. There has been an enormous amount of work done on these earliest steps in syntax and, at the outset, it is important to distinguish two distinct approaches to the area.

The first, popular in the 1960s, owes most, in its methodology, to the school of American structuralism, attempting to define grammatical classes and produce statements governing the co-occurrences of such classes on the basis of a distributional analysis of a corpus of utterances collected from the child. The child is treated as if he were a speaker of an 'exotic' language and no attempt is made to incorporate features of context or guesses as to what the child might mean into the analysis; the approach is known as the *lean* approach. Opposed to it is the *rich* approach, aligning itself, to some extent, with the transformational school of syntax and taking seriously the problem of representing what the child knows about the syntactic structure of the language he is learning. This approach *does* take account of context in an effort to get at what the child is meaning, the belief being that, without this sort of information, it will be difficult to avoid seriously underestimating his structural knowledge.

The lean approach led to the formulation of a number of distributional regularities based on early two-word speech. Thus, it appeared that there was, for each child, a small number of words which occurred particularly frequently in two-word utterances. Furthermore, such words appeared to have strong positional preferences. To take a typical example, the following utterances might well crop up in a corpus collected from a child at this stage.

(12) a *more milk*, *more shoe*, *more baby*, *more outside*, *more train*
    b *mummy gone*, *mummy chair*, *mummy coat*, *mummy up*, *mummy house*
    c *shoe off*, *coat off*, *socks off*, *this off*, *fall off*

In (12)*a* and (12)*b* we find *more* and *mummy* appearing in first position, in (12)*c*, *off* in second position. The terminology that was introduced to describe these regularities involved referring to the fixed-position words as *pivots*, with remaining positionally mobile words belonging to an *open* class. Additional suggestions which had some initial support were that pivots did not appear as one-word utterances, whereas open-class words did, and that pivots did not combine with each other to form two-word utterances, whereas open-class words did. This added up to a sound distributional basis for the distinction and some workers went so far as to suggest that the child's first grammar should be constructed so as to represent these regularities and nothing more. Such a grammar would have the phrase-structure rule of (13), where P_1 refers to the class of first-position pivots, P_2 to the class of second-position pivots and O to the open class.

$$(13) \quad S \quad \rightarrow \quad \left\{ \begin{array}{ccc} P_1 & + & O \\ O & + & P_2 \\ (O) & + & O \end{array} \right\}$$

There are some difficult problems arising from this suggestion, not least of which concerns how the child moves from a grammar employing the grammatical categories P_1, P_2 and O to one using a more standard set (N, V, Adj, etc.). This was tackled in an ingenious way by the suggestion that, although the child's primitive categories do not correspond to any adult category (note, for example, that in (12) both *more* and *mummy* would be assigned to P_1), nevertheless, they honour the adult categories *generically*. That is to say that the child initially puts together a number of adult grammatical categories as one of his primitive categories, not making distinctions which are necessary in the adult language. However, the fact that he does this indicates that he is not innocent of the adult categories – if he were we would anticipate a situation in which different members of the same adult category were assigned to different child categories – and the development of grammatical categories can then be seen as a gradual unfolding of this set of implicit distinctions. Of course, the problem of where the implicit knowledge of the grammatical categories comes from is a real one and the answer that it is innate was the obvious one for proponents of this view to adopt.

Unfortunately, it was not long before the evidence necessary to refute this speculation appeared. In the speech of some children it was necessary to assign some adjectives to a pivot class and others to the open class. This should not happen if the pivot and open classes were honouring adult categories generically.

From a different perspective, work was starting using the rich approach and supporters of this technique were eager to point to phenomena which they believed could not be adequately analysed distributionally. The classic example was put forward at the end of the 1960s by Lois Bloom who, having classified *mummy* as a first-position pivot on distributional grounds, drew attention to the two utterances of (14) produced by one child.

(14) mummy sock

In itself (14) tells us little, but attention to context of utterance revealed that the two tokens of (14) required quite different interpretations. On one occasion it was uttered as the child was picking up her mother's sock; on the other, as the mother was putting the sock on the child. The moral is clear: the first situation reveals that the child is attempting to encode a genitive relation (*mummy's sock*) but is not inflecting *mummy*, and the second suggests that she is concerned with mummy being the instigator of some action on the sock (*mummy is doing something to the sock*) but there is no explicit marking of the action. But this argues that, at some level, the child knows about genitives, about subjects of sentences and about objects of sentences, and representing both tokens of (14) as instances of the grammatical structure $P_1 + O$ fails totally to represent this knowledge.

If this sort of data analysis is permitted, the way is open to postulate other grammatical relations at the two-word stage, and this is exactly what Bloom and many other workers did. The results of these activities were taxonomies of two-word utterances and, while correspondences between different studies were rarely exact, the list in (15) is a fairly representative sample.

(15) *a* subject-verb (*mummy go*)
    b verb-object (*wash baby*)
    c subject-object (*mummy sock* (second interpretation))
    d possessor-possessed or genitive (*mummy sock* (first interpretation))

 e   adjective-noun (*big dolly*)
 f   subject-locative (*sweater chair*)
 g   verb-locative (*jump chair*)

Focusing briefly, now, on (15)*a–c*, we can raise one of the problems that the rich approach faced. These three syntactic relations suggest that the child has all the syntactic machinery to produce subject-verb-object strings. In a standard transformational grammar this sort of competence would be captured by crediting the child with phrase-structure rules along the lines of (16).

(16)   S $\rightarrow$ NP $+$ VP
    VP $\rightarrow$ V $+$ NP

However, this set of rules would enable the child to deal with three-term strings and this he does not do. The solution proposed for this was to postulate a 'transformation' which, given a three-term string, deletes one of the components. But this is uncomfortable for at least two reasons: (i) it is *ad hoc*, i.e. has no application outside the immediate problem context (it is also formally incorrect in that transformational rules are not permitted to delete arbitrary material); (ii) it has all the appearances of a constraint on the child's linguistic productions (i.e. one aspect of his performance) being represented in a theory of his syntactic knowledge (his competence).

 This second problem raises a more general and fundamental one for the investigator intent on producing a grammar to represent the child's linguistic knowledge. It is generally accepted that a speaker's utterances only provide one sort of evidence in this enterprise, and the methodology of grammar-writing for adult languages relies crucially on the availability of native speaker intuitions. For small children, however, we do not have access to such intuitions and, correspondingly, our grammar construction is less constrained. This sort of consideration eventually led to a reduction in interest in grammar-writing for early child speech, the focus of interest switching to semantics. Before we pursue this shift, however, we would like to briefly mention some evidence which suggests that the small child is struggling with something like transformational rules in his acquisition of syntax.

10.4   Transformational rules in language development

One type of evidence which is consistent with children acquiring transformational rules comes from an attempt to interpret the Derivational Theory of Complexity (see Chapter 9, p. 302) in a developmental context. Very simply, this interpretation says that the more complex a sentence-type is in the grammatical description, the *later* it will be acquired by the child. This was discovered to be the case for a number of simple sentence-types including affirmative declaratives, negative declaratives, affirmative interrogatives, negative interrogatives and truncated versions of each of these. These sentence-types are illustrated in (17) and the ordering predictions of (18) were made on the basis of a transformational analysis of the sentences.

(17) *John hit the ball* (affirmative declarative – AD)
    John didn't hit the ball (negative declarative – ND)
    Did John hit the ball? (affirmative interrogative – AI)
    Didn't John hit the ball? (negative interrogative – NI)
    John did (truncated affirmative declarative – TrAD)
    John didn't (truncated negative declarative – TrND)
    Did John? (truncated affirmative interrogative – TrAI)
    Didn't John? (truncated negative interrogative – TrNI)

(18) AD before each of the others
    ND before NI, TrND, TrNI
    AI before NI, TrAI, TrNI
    NI before TrNI
    TrAD before TrND, TrAI, TrNI
    TrND before TrNI
    TrAI before TrNI

In a study of three children and their acquisition of these sentence-types, as revealed by their spontaneous speech, a high proportion of these predictions were confirmed. Against this, however, it is necessary to point out that a number of predictions that would be made for other sentence-types, using a standard transformational analysis, have been shown to be incorrect. To mention just one example, small children begin to use short passives before they use full passives; in the grammar a short passive will be derivationally more complex than a full passive.

Evidence of a different sort comes from the child's acquisition of *Wh*-questions, in which the identity of a particular constituent is queried. A number of *Wh*-questions appear in (19).

(19) *a* What did John hit?
    b Who hit John?
    c Where did John find the ball?
    d How did John hit the ball?

Standardly, these have been derived in transformational grammars by generating the *Wh*-word in the position which makes its relationship with the verb clear. For example, (19)*a* will be derived from a source along the lines of (20).

(20) John did hit what?

In (20) *what* is positioned immediately after the verb indicating its direct object function. Two rules operate on (20) to give (19)*a*: the first of these, *Wh*-movement, takes the *Wh*-word and moves it to the front of the sentence, yielding (21).

(21) What John did hit?

The second inverts the subject of the sentence (*John*) and the auxiliary verb (*did*), giving us (19)*a*. Now, the interesting thing is that some children produce intermediate forms like (21) as they develop *Wh*-questions, i.e. they get the *Wh*-word in the right position, but fail to invert. Such evidence points strongly towards the fact that inversion is something that children have to learn and obviously argues against *Wh*-questions being learned by imitation.

Finally, there is some evidence that children go wrong in interesting ways with some rules that are traditionally analysed as involving movement and deletion. *Wh*-movement is such a rule but, interestingly, the sort of error we are concerned with does not appear in connection with this rule. Consider the simple rule of particle movement. This is usually introduced as deriving sentences like (22) from structures of sentences like (23).

(22) The barber cut my hair off
(23) The barber cut off my hair

What the rule does is copy the particle (*off*) immediately behind the following NP and delete the original occurrence of *off*. Some children appear to get the copying part of a rule like this right without deleting, thus producing utterances like (24).

(24) The barber cut off my hair off

There is currently a good deal of controversy as to why this phenomenon appears to occur with some movement rules and not others, but, again, it indicates that children do not passively imitate the structures they learn and suggest that they entertain structural hypotheses of an abstract kind.

10.5 Semantic development: relational meanings

There are two aspects of semantic development that have been extensively studied. One of these concerns the range of application of single words and will concern us in the next section; the other examines the relational meanings which are encoded in children's early utterances and, since this is not an immediately obvious distinction, we can begin by considering a particular example.

Suppose that a small child says *chair* as he places an object in a chair. We might be interested in the fact that here he uses *chair* to refer to a certain chair and we might inquire as to whether he will refer to other chairs in the same way or whether he will refer to some things we would not regard as chairs using this same word. Such queries are the concern of the next section. Alternatively, we might note that *chair* appears to be playing the role of a location for an object which is not itself represented linguistically in the utterance. Contrast this with a situation in which the child requests that an adult move a chair towards him, again using *chair*. Once more we can wonder about the range of objects to which *chair* might be applied but here, in contrast to our earlier situation, it seems more appropriate to regard the word as representing an object of an action or desire ('You move chair' or 'I want chair'). When we focus our attention on such notions as 'location of an object' or 'object of an action' in such examples, we are paying attention to relational meanings – they are 'relational' because there is some additional entity implicit in the interpretation, an object in the first case and an action in the second.

This way of talking proved attractive to workers in child language for a number of reasons. First, it seemed reasonable to suggest that there might be a relatively small number of such relational meanings in early child speech and it would be interesting to study their development. Secondly, it could be extended naturally to one-word utterances as the above examples demonstrate, thereby establishing some sort of continuity between one-word utterances and later stages of development (recall that studies of syntactic development usually begin with two-word utterances and ignore earlier stages). Finally, in not committing us to grammatical notions like subject and direct object, it avoided the question of where these notions came from – the standard answer to this had been, not surprisingly, that they are innately supplied. Of course, this leaves open two questions. (i) If we provide a semantic characterisation of early child speech in these terms, at the expense of the sort of syntactic approach briefly discussed in Section 3 above, where are we to locate the beginnings of syntax? (ii) Where do the relational meanings themselves come from? The first of these questions has not received any cogent discussion but there has been speculation regarding the second (see below).

Initially, when these ideas were first put forward, their application was restricted to an analysis of two-word utterances. In his monumental work *A First Language*, Roger Brown, one of the foremost scholars of child language, having painstakingly surveyed the difficulties confronting a syntactic approach to two-word utterances, provides a taxonomy of what he calls 'basic semantic relationships'. These 'relationships', listed in (25), account for over 70 per cent of the utterances in which he was interested.

(25) *a* Agent and action (*Daddy throw*)
  b Action and object (*throw ball*)
  c Agent and object (*Daddy ball*, as Daddy throws a ball)
  d Action and locative (*sit chair*)
  e Entity and locative (*teddy chair*)
  f Possessor and possession (*my shoe*)
  g Entity and attributive (*big teddy*)
  h Demonstrative and entity (*that teddy*)

First, note the almost total overlap between (15) and (25), making it clear that they are applicable to the same sets of data. The important difference, however, is that (25) is a *semantic* taxonomy. Accordingly, it is not necessary to postulate abstract unrealised grammatical elements for the relations in (25); as they are not syntactic they do not take on their significance from syntactic relations. Thus, in the case of (25)*c*, we are not forced into recognising the existence of an underlying *verb* as we were in the case of (15)*c*. The (25)*c* schema requires that, at some level, the child has a representation of an action which is not linguistically encoded, but this does not demand crediting him with an abstract and elaborate syntactic system – we merely have to assume that he is capable of representing events and their components.

Secondly, (25) answers an objection to (15) which points out that the subjects recognised as occurring in syntactically oriented studies are, at the two-word stage, almost without exception animate instigators of action, i.e. agents. English subjects fulfil a variety of semantic roles, including agent (26)*a*, experiencer (26)*b* and instrument (26)*c*, but only agents appear at this early stage of child speech.

(26) *a* John opened the door
  b John heard the sound
  c The key opened the door

Therefore, the argument goes, the syntactic notion of *subject* is too abstract for characterising what children of this age know about the language and what is required to represent this knowledge is a more concrete semantic notion. Similar arguments have been put forward for other grammatical relations deemed necessary by (15).

Thirdly, since (25) is a semantic taxonomy, we can investigate its cross-linguistic validity without being concerned about how particular relations are expressed in different languages. There are difficulties in identifying grammatical relations across languages and this will make the generality of (15) dubious. However, there is no reason to believe that the notional categories of (25) cannot be found in all languages, and such cross-linguistic comparisons as have been carried out tend to converge on such a notional set. Languages investigated in this connection include German, Finnish, Turkish, Samoan, and Luo (a tribal language of Kenya) in addition to English, and this has prompted some investigators to suggest that the relations in (25) constitute a developmental universal; all children, no matter what language they are learning, express just these relations first in their two-word utterances.

At this point it makes sense to ask about the source of these relations. Brown resists the inference from universality to innateness by citing some of Piaget's views on early cognitive development, arguing that if Piaget is correct, then the child is equipped with the relevant cognitive categories before he begins language development. Therefore, Brown is attempting to explain the *fact* of these early relations by discovering their source in cognitive development and also their *early appearance* by locating this source in *early* cognitive development.

Piaget's views on cognitive development are, of course, extremely complex and we cannot attempt to summarise them here. However, one of the achievements of the *sensori-motor period* (which, in Piaget's framework, extends from birth to about 18 months – approximately the onset of two-word speech) is what Piaget calls a 'mature object concept'. Before the end of the sensori-motor period, the child is claimed not to distinguish clearly between objects and actions which are performed on them or locations in which they appear. This is illustrated, for example, by occasions when the child, having successfully located an object hidden at a particular location, fails to find it when it is taken to that location again and then, in full view of the child, moved from that location and hidden at a second one; the child, at a certain stage of cognitive development, will search unsuccessfully at the first location. On the basis of this, we might conclude that such a child does not clearly distinguish object from location.

Now, one could argue, clearly if the child is to express an entity-locative relation, he must distinguish the two elements being related. Accordingly, the mature object concept is seen as a prerequisite for the expression of this relation. Although no author has gone into great detail on this issue, there is a general feeling among people working in the field that this sort of argument could be constructed for each of the relations in (25).

Similar arguments have recently been offered for one-word speech, where again a taxonomy of semantic relations has been suggested and attempts have been made to relate these to the child's non-linguistic cognitive development. We shall not pursue this analysis here (see bibliography to this chapter), and we wish to close this section by considering a different, though equally important, question.

If Brown's analysis of the relationship between cognitive development and basic semantic relations is correct, it demonstrates that cognitive development of a certain sort is a *necessary* condition for a certain aspect of linguistic development. However, it does not demonstrate that such cognitive development is a *sufficient* condition for the appropriate expression of the basic semantic relations according to the rules of the language the child is acquiring. This is straightforwardly illustrated by the fact that initially entity-locative utterances lack a preposition where the adult language requires one (i.e. the child says *dolly chair* and not *dolly in chair*). The possibility is therefore raised that there is something specifically linguistic about the *expression* of the basic semantic relations, although the relations themselves are characteristic of general cognition. This has been pursued, in a most interesting argument, by Dan Slobin.

Slobin cites data from the development of children being brought up bilingually in Hungarian and Serbo-Croat, paying particular attention to their expression of the entity-locative relation. What he discovered was that the *same* children were expressing this relation appropriately in Hungarian at a time when they were not doing so in Serbo-Croat (i.e. they said the equivalent of *dolly in chair* when speaking Hungarian but only *dolly chair* when speaking Serbo-Croat). Why should this be?

An examination of the ways in which each language expresses locative notions reveals that they differ in a number of important ways.

(*a*) Hungarian expresses its locative notions only with suffixes whereas Serbo-Croat uses both suffixes and prepositions.

(*b*) All Hungarian suffixes are unambiguous whereas some Serbo-Croat prepositions have the same ambiguity as, for example, *in* in English (*He jumped in the water* can mean either that he jumped when he was in the water or that he jumped into the water).

(*c*) Some Serbo-Croat prepositions 'take' particular suffixes thus rendering the suffix semantically redundant; others allow a choice of suffix.

(*d*) Serbo-Croat suffixes are phonologically conditioned by the stem to which they are attached; Hungarian suffixes are invariable.

It should be clear from this that there is an obvious intuitive sense in which the expression of locative notions in Serbo-Croat is *more complex* than it is in Hungarian. This is independent of the notions which are being expressed and, Slobin suggests, represents a contribution of purely linguistic complexity to the developmental process.

10.6 Semantic development: referential meanings

It is a common observation that, when small children begin to use language, they often use words in a way which is inappropriate from the adult perspective. Thus, stories of children referring to all four-legged animals as *dog* or to all men as *daddy* are well known and the source of much amusement. They do, however, lead to a serious and important question concerning the nature of the child's semantic representation of words.

Concerning the child's first attempts to label aspects of his world, there have been three distinct attempts to approach this question.

The first, put forward by Eve Clark, emphasises the importance of *perceptual* information in the semantic representation of a word. The view assumes that a word's meaning consists of a set of semantic features (see Chapter 7, pp. 203–6) and that, initially, these features encode perceptual information about referents of the word. So, the child perceives a ball and hears the word *ball*, notes that the ball has certain perceptual characteristics (e.g. roundness, redness, squashiness) and establishes a meaning for *ball* on this basis. Now, Clark's claim is that the child might only attend to a subset of the total set of perceptual parameters associated with the ball and, subsequently, establish a meaning for the word which is too general (in the case in question we can imagine that the child only attends to roundness and is thus in a position where he will refer to all round things as *ball*). She predicts, on this basis, that instances of *overextension*, examples of which opened this section, will be explicable in perceptual terms and she herself has cited data indicating the importance of a number of perceptual dimensions in this regard. A small sample of these appears in Table 10.1.

Clark has not been content to cite data which support her position but has also attempted to give that position some explanatory status. On the one hand, it is possible to refer to studies of perceptual development which suggest that the relevant abilities to analyse objects perceptually are present before the child begins to use language – this can be seen as an attempt to explain part of the fact of lexical development by identifying perceptual prerequisites – and, on the other, it has been claimed that the course of lexical development can be predicted if we assume that the child learns the most general features first. Unfortunately, this latter suggestion suffers from a lack of explicitness in the notion 'general feature', although it does display a healthy awareness of the problem of explanation.

In contrast to Clark's emphasis on perceptual features, Katherine Nelson has suggested that it is *functional* criteria which determine initial word use. These functional criteria are seen as emerging from the child's interaction with objects and people and it is indeed the case

Table 10.1 *Some Examples of Overextension*

Perceptual Dimension	Language Being Learned	Child's Form	First Referent	Overextensions
shape	English	bird	sparrows	cows, dogs, cats, any animal moving
shape	English	kotibaiz	bars of cot	large toy abacus, toast-rack with parallel bars, picture of building with columns
sound	Russian	dany	sound of bell	clock, telephone, door-bells
taste	French	cola	chocolate	sugar, tarts, grapes, figs, peaches
touch	Russian	va	white plush dog	muffler, cat, father's fur coat

Source: Adapted from Eve V. Clark, 'What's in a word? On the child's acquisition of semantics in his first language', in T. E. Moore (ed.), *Cognitive Development and the Acquisition of Language* (New York: Academic Press, 1973), pp. 65–111.

that the child's first words tend to refer to aspects of his environment with which he actively interacts rather than to objects which are constantly and invariably present. Two sorts of evidence might be cited in support of this position. First, there are instances of overextension which readily admit a functional explanation but which are difficult to accommodate on a perceptual hypothesis; one of the best examples with which we are familiar is offered by the child who refers to a clothes-brush as *brush* and to a comb and a hair-brush as *comb*. Secondly, in an experimental study, Nelson herself showed that, when confronted with a set of more or less ball-like objects and asked to identify the ball, children of 9 months would initially base their choice on either shape (a ball fixed to a stand) or function (a rubber cylinder free to move). After having been allowed to play with the objects, however, a large number of children changed their choice in the direction of function.

It now seems clear that both perceptual and functional criteria are going to be important in understanding early lexical reference, but in a recent study Melissa Bowerman has questioned one of the basic assumptions of both Clark's and Nelson's positions. Both of these theories hold that a set of criteria (perceptual or functional) constitute necessary and sufficient conditions for the applicability of a word to a referent (in this sense, they are standard semantic feature theories, as discussed in Chapter 7). But now consider the following data cited by Bowerman.

A child initially uses *kick* in circumstances where she is kicking a ball with her foot so that it moves forwards. Subsequently, she uses *kick* when she kicks a floor fan which does not move, when she sees a moth fluttering over a table, when she makes a ball roll by bumping it with the wheel of a car and when she pushes her stomach against a mirror. The suggestion is that these events do not share a criterial set of features determining the applicability of *kick*. Rather, the initial usage determines a *stereotype* (see Chapter 7, p. 207) and subsequent uses are determined on the basis of resemblance to the prototype. Thus, we could regard the initial usage of *kick* as involving three 'features': waving limb, sudden sharp contact and object propelled, with subsequent uses being determined by the presence of *any one* (or more) of these; no single feature or set of features is criterial.

Bowerman provides additional data which point to the same conclusion but it is more interesting at this point to speculate on the source or sources of such prototypes. One obvious source could be the child's linguistic environment, with the child's mother (unconsciously) directing the child's attention to prototypical instances of categories and attaching linguistic labels to them. To our knowledge no research has been undertaken to investigate this possibility. As an alternative, however, we could investigate the child's non-linguistic cognitive development in an attempt to establish that certain prototypes are cognitively salient for the child before he learns the associated linguistic labels. Research in this area is still in a poorly developed state but some initial steps have been taken which relate to our discussion of prototypes in Chapter 9, Sections 9 and 10.

First, there is evidence to suggest that some colour categories exist in very young infants. This is relatively easy to show by adapting infants' attention to light of a particular wavelength. This technique involves projecting the light on to a screen above the horizontal infant and recording eye-movements; after a certain amount of time the infant will cease to be interested in the light and this will be reflected in a sharp drop in the amount of time he spends looking at it. At this point we can either increase or decrease the wavelength of projected light by a fixed amount and, if we have chosen our initial stimulus carefully, one of these transformations will leave us within the same colour category (from the perspective of adult colour categories) and the other will take us across a boundary into a distinct colour category. Of course, from the point of view of the infant we cannot assume that these categories have any reality but it transpires that his attention is immediately recaptured by the wavelength change which involves crossing a boundary whereas this is not so for the change which leaves him within the same category. Recall that this happens despite the fact that the *physical* changes are of the same extent in each case. This, then, would seem to establish the psychological reality of some colour categories long before the onset of speech.

Secondly, using children who have begun to develop language but who do not yet control full colour lexicons, it has been possible to demonstrate that the focal colours of Berlin and Kay (see Chapter 9, Section 10, pp. 317–18) control such children's attention more readily than non-focal colours. This would be consistent with the colour categories being structured around focal colours for children who have not yet mastered the relevant vocabulary. Whether similar sorts of demonstration will appear for other areas of vocabulary must await the outcome of ongoing research but it seems likely to be a dominant question during the next few years.

10.7 The development of speech-acts

One aspect of language development which has been completely ignored so far in this chapter is that which pays attention to the *functions* which the small child's language serves (NB it is important to distinguish this sense of 'function' from that used in the previous section where we were briefly concerned with the functions that various *objects* served. Here we discuss the communicative functions of *language*). In Chapter 7 (pp. 215–16) we introduced some of the basic terminology of speech-act theory and, indeed, this has been applied by some authors to the child's developing system. Probably the most influential approach to functional development, however, is that of Michael Halliday, and it is this approach that we shall pay particular attention to here. Halliday does not present his ideas in terms of speech-act theory but in terms of his own functional framework. Nevertheless, most of his terminology can easily be translated into that used by more standard approaches and, although we shall not indulge in a detailed comparison of this sort here, the reader is referred to the bibliography to this chapter for alternative approaches to functional development.

Halliday suggests that it is possible to identify communicative function in the child's utterances before the child has any recognisable conventional language – he refers to this period of the child's development as that in which the child has a *proto-language* and, in the case of his own son on whom his ideas are based, this extended from about 9 months to 18 months of age. What communicative functions can be identified in this period?

Six functions are postulated by Halliday, with a seventh being added later after the child has made some progress in learning the conventional language system around him. These six functions are:

1 *Instrumental* – involved in the child obtaining objects and satisfying his material needs (e.g. between 9 and 10½ months the child says [nã] when requesting an object). This is the 'I want' function of language.
2 *Regulatory* – involved with controlling the behaviour of others (e.g. between 9 and 10½ months the child says [ɔ̃] with the 'meaning' of 'do that again'). This is the 'do as I tell you' function of language.
3 *Interactional* – involved with using language to interact with others (e.g. between 9 and 10½ months the child says [ø], or several variants of this, to initiate an interaction). This is the 'me and you' function of language.
4 *Personal* – involved in expressing the child's own identity (e.g. expressions of pleasure and interest such as [a] with the 'meaning' of 'that's nice' between 9 and 10½ months). This is the 'here I come' function of language.
5 *Heuristic* – involved in the child using language to explore his environment (e.g. various forms produced by the child between 15 and 16½ months which are interpreted as requesting the name of an object). This is the 'tell me why' function of language.
6 *Imaginative* – involved in using language to create an environment (e.g. various sounds used by the child between 12 and 13½ months to accompany his pretending to go to sleep). This is the 'let's pretend' function of language.

The seventh function, which only appears later, is the *Informative* function, whereby the child seeks to inform an addressee of some fact of which he is previously ignorant. We must now inquire into the strengths and weaknesses of this sort of approach.

Halliday sees one major virtue in his work in establishing continuity between a primitive system of communication – the proto-language – and later conventional linguistic development; both systems can be characterised using the same functional framework. Furthermore, he sees a source for the functions he wishes to identify in his treatment of the adult language (see Chapter 1, p. 23) in his six primitive functions. Thus, he can be seen as attempting to establish a significant developmental continuity from the child's earliest attempts at communication to the fully fledged grammatical system of the adult.

From a different perspective, some of his functions have a good deal of intuitive content and, as already remarked, can be readily identified with functions postulated by other authors working within more standard frameworks. Thus, to mention just two examples, it seems reasonable to identify Halliday's Instrumental and Regulatory functions with the categories of Request Object and Request Action in a taxonomy of communicative functions worked out by the American psychologist Ann Carter. Additionally, Halliday offers an explanation for why the Informative function is late to appear.

His claim is that the six functions listed above are all defined in the social system in which the child is immersed quite independently of language (see Chapter 12, pp. 388–9, for further discussion in a different context). However, in the case of the Informative function, this can only be understood in the context of language. It will, therefore, follow that the Informative function cannot appear until language exists in some form, whereas the other six functions can all be seen as grounded in the child's social milieu and available to him independently of language.

Our view on this argument is that, while it may be correct, it is extremely difficult to evaluate because of a good deal of vagueness in the crucial theoretical concepts. It is fairly easy to accept that, say, the Regulatory function is implicit in the child's social situation; after all it is well known that there are clearly defined power hierarchies in various non-human species which are sustained without the intervention of language. In contrast to this, however, we find it more difficult to see the Heuristic function as originating in some non-linguistic social reality. If we are to take seriously its informal characterisation as the 'tell me why' function, it would seem, no less than the Informative function, to presuppose language. There is another source of worry concerning this argument: if we accept Halliday's claim that the Informative function appears late because it requires language we might be concerned about *how much* language it requires, i.e. all six primitive functions or only some of them. Note that this is not to say that Halliday is incorrect in claiming that the Informative function does appear late; it is his explanation of this fact which is at issue.

One notable omission from Halliday's set of functions, recognised by several other writers on the topic, is the function of directing an addressee's attention to some aspect of the environment in which the child is interested. Many children have, among their earliest words, *see* or *look* or some variant of *that*, *this*, *here*, or *there*. These words are often accompanied by a pointing gesture and appear to have the function in question. A moment's reflection will indicate that it is an extremely important function as, in a sense, to be in a position to say anything about anything a speaker must have routines available for making sure that his addressee can identify what he is talking about. Routines involving the manipulation of attention are exactly what is called for here, and so it should come as no surprise that such routines are relatively easy to identify in the early communicative behaviour of the child.

Overall, theorising within functional frameworks is not highly developed and what we have in the literature·is a set of taxonomies with isolated attempts to establish developmental relations between members of the taxonomies of the sort we have just mentioned.

A claim which is often made is that it is only by paying attention to the child's functional development that we shall be in a position to understand and explain his syntactic development. However, there is little convincing argument to this point and to close this chapter we shall return to syntactic development and examine some recent ideas on the role played by the child's linguistic environment in this process.

10.8 Linguistic environment and language learning

In Section 1 above we pointed out that Motherese, the language which mothers and other caretakers use when talking to small children, has a number of distinctive characteristics. We must now say something about these characteristics.

A number of *prosodic* variables have been studied in this connection. For example, Motherese is slower than talk between adults and word-boundaries are more clearly marked. Regarding pitch, Motherese is pitched higher than adult–adult talk, with a mean pitch approximating to those frequencies to which the infant ear is maximally sensitive. Additionally, it uses a wider pitch-range, allowing for more obvious marking of discourse features such as emphasis.

Turning to *syntactic* variables, Motherese utterances are shorter on average than those adults use to each other, there are fewer instances of complex sentences involving embedding one sentence inside another and there is less use of modifiers and conjunctions. Most important, there are fewer disfluencies including false starts and hesitations in a corpus of Motherese than in a comparable corpus of talk directed to another adult.

This list could be extended considerably but will serve our purposes here in demonstrating the sort of properties which have led to the claim, mentioned earlier, that Motherese is a special register. The important thing to realise at this stage is that the existence of this special register does not guarantee it any status as a teaching language for the reasons already briefly mentioned in Section 1. However, the question of whether the special features of Motherese have any causal role to play in explaining the development of language has recently been the subject of intensive and sophisticated investigation. The results of this work are most interesting and appear to have wideranging implications.

The most revealing study of this type involved collecting spontaneous speech from a group of mothers and their children at two points separated by a six-month interval. A number of measures are defined on the corpus of the mothers' speech at the first point including the percentage of their utterances which are syntactically well formed, the average length of their utterances, the structural complexity of their utterances, the frequency of particular sentence types and several others. At the same time a number of similar measures are defined for each corpus of child speech (at each of the two sampling-points) such as mean length of utterance (in morphemes), number of noun phrases per utterance, average length of noun phrases (in morphemes), number of verb phrases per utterance, average length of verb phrases (in morphemes), extent of inflection of noun phrases and auxiliary structure.

The investigators then compiled correlations between the various measures in the mothers' speech at the time of the first sample and the changes in the various measures between the two samples for the children's speech. Thus, the sort of question they were interested in was whether there was any significant correlation between, say, the length of the mothers' utterances and the children's subsequent development with respect to noun phrase inflections. This sort of correlation would be indicated by those children whose mothers used the longest utterances in the first sample making the most progress in marking noun phrase inflections between the two samples.

In order to rule out the possible effects of the ages of the children and their level of linguistic sophistication on Motherese (recall that it is the effect in the opposite direction in which we are interested), the investigators indulged in some fairly elaborate statistical procedures which had the effect of treating the children as if they were all the same age and at the same level of linguistic sophistication at the time of the first sample. By following these procedures one can be sure that the linguistic variation in the mothers' speech at the time of the first interview is not a response either to the age of the child or to his linguistic sophistication. The question we then ask is whether this maternal variation has any effect on development in the subsequent six-month period.

The results of this study were in many ways surprising. Several variables which had been generally believed to be important in the teaching function of Motherese were shown to have no discernible effects. Thus, the mothers' mean length of utterance had no effect on any of the variables defined on the samples of child utterances. What this means is that it did not make any difference to the child's development with respect to the measures used here whether the mother addressed longer or shorter utterances towards him. A similar conclusion was reached for the number of sentences contained in a single utterance; apparently it made no difference to the child's development in the six-month period whether the mother directed sentences involving embeddings and conjunctions towards him or not. Again, it seemed to make no difference whether the mother used a high proportion of declarative sentences in addressing her child. In general, it transpired that such measures as number of noun phrases per utterance and number of verbs per utterance – measures which relate to the basic content of what the child is trying to say – were completely insensitive to maternal variation.

Nevertheless, there were some effects but, and this is the interesting claim, they were concerned exclusively with details of language learning which are language-specific. For example, it transpired that the child's development of the auxiliary system correlated positively with the mother's tendency to ask yes/no questions. This becomes particularly significant when we note that in English what a yes/no question involves is putting the auxiliary at the front of the sentence, a position we might intuitively regard as psychologically salient. Similarly, the development of the auxiliary system is negatively correlated with the tendency of mothers to use imperatives and this becomes readily explicable when we realise that in English imperatives do not include any auxiliary.

There were additional findings of this nature but in summary it appeared that those aspects of language development which were universal – all children, no matter what language they are learning, have to learn to combine noun phrases and verbs into simple propositions – are insensitive to variations in parental input, whereas those aspects which were language-specific (such as the auxiliary system and inflectional system of English) were affected by one or more of the variables under study.

At this point it becomes possible to ask an important and far-reaching question: if there are aspects of language development which are insensitive to variations in maternal speech, might not these aspects proceed *without* maternal speech?

We have already seen in Chapter 1 (pp. 12 ff.) the results of a number of deprivation studies. Unfortunately, these, as well as suffering from lack of reliable documentation for the most part, are also contaminated by the fact that so many other variables were not 'normal' for the unfortunate children in question, e.g. they did not, typically, receive the usual love and affection or general social contacts that infants being reared in a standard environment have access to. What we are interested in, then, is the possibility of children who are linguistically deprived but who receive all other social stimulation in as near a normal fashion as is possible.

It is felt by one team of investigators that this situation is approximated in the case of deaf children who are being brought up in environments in which the acquisition of sign language is actively discouraged. A group of such children have been studied in Pennsylvania and the remarkable results of this study are that deaf children in these circumstances appear to create *de novo* a system of communication relying on signs which manifests just those properties which we have seen above to be insensitive to variations in maternal input. That is, they develop signs corresponding to noun phrases (these are, typically, *points*, with the child pointing to the object he wants to talk about in the simplest case) and signs corresponding to verbal concepts (these are typically *mimes*). In addition, they begin actively to combine these signs into proposition-like structures in a way which bears certain similarities to those characteristic of the hearing-speaking child. What they do not create is a set of signs enabling them to express notions akin to those expressed by the English auxiliaries or to those expressed by nominal inflections. It would appear, then, on the basis of these two studies that there is a universal core to the world's languages which children will learn independently of variation in input and which, lacking input, they will create from their own resources.

We can note finally that many pidgins (see Chapter 12, pp. 410–11) are characterised by the lack of elaborate inflectional systems and tend only to make available devices for the expression of basic propositional structure. One of the things that happens when a pidgin becomes a creole is that it begins to develop these language-specific facilities, so it would seem that from a quite different direction we have an independent characterisation of what constitutes a basic linguistic system. The emphasis on different varieties of language and on function and interaction that we have met in the last two sections of this chapter leads quite naturally into consideration of language in its geographical and social context; it is to these areas of study that we turn in the last two chapters of the book.

Exercises: Chapter 10

1   Collect a small sample of utterances from a child between 1 and 2 years of age. Devise a descriptive set of categories for the *functions* of the utterances (you might like to start with the functions Halliday has offered, p. 350) and see how confidently you can assign utterances to functions.

2   Up to the age of about 4½ years English-speaking children rarely produce utterances from the following categories: those in which there is a reference to two 'events' and the temporal order of events is not preserved in the linear order of the utterance (e.g. *Daddy's playing (present) with me 'cos he came (past) home*); those which use perfect aspect (e.g. *Daddy has gone to work*); those which express habituality (e.g. *This belongs here*). Before this age, however, children appear to control the necessary syntactic devices to produce such utterances. Why do you think they fail to produce them?

3   The following represent a sample of *negative* utterances from three stages in the development of the expression of negation in small children:

I
no a bad boy
no sing song
no the sun shining
no money
no sit there
wear mitten no
not a teddy bear

II
no pinch me
touch the snow no
this a radiator no
don't bite me yet
don't leave me
he not little he big
that no fish school
I no want envelope
I no taste them

III
Paul can't have one
I didn't did it
Paul didn't laugh
Donna won't let go
that was not me
this not ice cream
Paul not tired
Don't kick my box

Briefly describe the characteristics of these classes of data and comment on how the child's expression of negation differs from the adult's for each stage.

4 Collect or construct a set of exemplars of a particular semantic category (see Exercise 8, Chapter 9). Display them on a page and present them to mothers of small children with the instruction that they should describe the contents of the page to their child. See if there is any consistency in the order in which the mothers choose to describe the exemplars. Does this bear any resemblance to your own rating of the exemplars? Are there any other possible factors you should control for (e.g. position of pictures on page)?

5 The following is a set of word forms produced by a child with the adult form he was attempting in parentheses. For each example describe the differences between adult and child forms and attempt to relate them to some general principles.

[gʌk]	(*dark*)	[gɪk]	(*kiss*)	[mɛn]	(*smell*)
[gɒk]	(*cloth*)	[maɪp]	(*knife*)	[kim]	(*queen*)
[nɔni]	(*noisy*)	[dɒp]	(*stop*)	[gɛgi]	(*taxi*)

6 The following forms have all been attested from children.

What's that is?
What did you bought?
Whose is that is?
I did broke it

Did you came home?
The barber cut off his hair off
I picked up the ball up
Could you get me a banana for me?

Describe how these examples differ from the corresponding adult utterances and, on the basis of your description, try to formulate what they have in common.

7 Instances of inappropriate usage of words which have been cited in the literature include the following.

moon to refer to cakes, round marks on window, writing on windows and in books, round shapes in books, the letter 'O'
tick-tock to refer to gas-meter, fire-hose wound on a spool, bath-scale with round dial

fly to refer to specks of dirt, dust, all small insects, child's toes, crumbs of bread, a toad
chocolate to refer to sugar, tarts, grapes, figs, peaches
dog to refer to muffler, cat, father's fur coat
door to refer to opening box, opening tin, taking limbs off doll

For each of these cases, formulate a hypothesis as to what the meaning of the child's word might be.

8 Children have often been observed to go through three stages in their acquisition of morphological endings (e.g. past tense markers):

(*a*) initially they get irregular endings correct, e.g. *came*, *went*;
(*b*) they over-regularise the regular ending, e.g. *comed*, *camed*, *goed*, *wented*;
(*c*) they get irregular endings correct again.

Discuss why this might be. How would your hypothesis fare if confronted with a child who did not go through the first stage?

9 Children use and understand generalised dimensional adjectives such as *big* and *small* before they master more specialised terms such as *tall* and *short*, *wide* and *narrow*, *deep* and *shallow*. Test whether there might be a straightforward explanation for this in terms of the language the mother uses to the child by producing a set of drawings (for example, of people, cows, buildings) which differ from each other along one dimension (for example, your people might all differ in height or fatness). Offer these sets of drawings to mothers on a page and ask them to talk to their children about them. Note the dimensional adjectives they use. Is there any evidence for such adjectives becoming more specialised for mothers with older children?

10 The following is a set of observations based on children acquiring a variety of languages.

(*a*) Children acquiring Serbo-Croat learn to use locative suffixes before they use locative prepositions.
(*b*) Children acquiring English learn to use *on* and *off* as particles (e.g. *shoes off/on*) before they use them as prepositions (e.g. *on table*).
(*c*) Children acquiring Polish do *not* learn to use *on* and *off* as particles before they use them as prepositions. In Polish the particle is prefixed to the verb.
(*d*) Accusative and dative inflections are early acquisitions for children learning Russian, Polish, Latvian, Finnish and Turkish. They are relatively late acquisitions for children learning German. In German the inflections appear on articles which precede the noun.
(*e*) English articles are late to appear when compared with Bulgarian articles. In Bulgarian the article is suffixed to the noun.

What generalisations can you draw up on the basis of (*a*)–(*e*)? How would you go about explaining such generalisations?

Bibliography: Chapter 10

Bates, E., Benigni, L., Bretherton, I., Camaioni, L., and Volterra, V., 'From gesture to the first word: on cognitive and social prerequisites', in M. Lewis and L. Rosenblum (eds), *Origins of Behavior: Communication and Language* (New York: Wiley, 1977). By far the clearest statement in the literature on the wide range of positions it is possible to adopt on the question of the relationship between linguistic and cognitive development. Not easy reading but repays careful study.

Brown, R., *A First Language* (Harmondsworth: Penguin, 1973). The first report of the results of Brown's massive Harvard project. An original contribution to the field but, in expounding his ideas, Brown reviews an enormous amount of literature in a clear and honest fashion. The presentation of the results of the project is often heavy going.

Dale, P., *Language Development: Structure and Function* (New York: Holt, Rinehart & Winston, 1976). An excellent introduction providing a very competent survey of a number of areas in considerable depth. Does not attempt to be comprehensive.

De Villiers, P. A., and De Villiers, J. G., *Early Language* (London: Fontana/Open Books, 1979). A small book written for readers with no background. A good place to start if you do not feel confident enough to tackle anything more ambitious.

Ferguson, C., and Slobin, D. E. (eds), *Studies of Child Language Development* (New York: Holt, Rinehart & Winston, 1973). A valuable collection of papers including many of the classic studies of syntactic development performed in the 1960s. Also contains an important paper by Slobin on cognition and language, a small part of which is discussed in our text.

Greenfield, P. M., and Smith, J. H., *The Structure of Communication in Early Language Development* (New York: Academic Press, 1976). The most important work on one-word utterances and their semantic properties. Clearly written and well argued.

Halliday, M., *Learning How to Mean* (London: Edward Arnold, 1975). Halliday's major work on language acquisition reporting the development of his own son in great detail. Also relevant to Chapter 12.

Jakobson, R. O., *Child Language, Aphasia and Phonological Universals* (The Hague: Mouton, 1968). Essential for anyone wishing to pursue phonological development. Difficult and obscure in places. See also Chapter 11.

Lock, A. (ed.), *Action, Gesture and Symbol* (New York: Academic Press, 1978). A collection of papers tracing the development of linguistic behaviour back through gesture and non-communicative action. Important papers include those by A. Carter on the functions of early utterances, and by H. Feldman, S. Goldin-Meadow and L. Gleitman on the creation of language by deaf children.

Moore, T. E. (ed.), *Cognitive Development and the Acquisition of Language* (New York: Wiley, 1973). An important collection of papers, most notable for its inclusion of E. Clark's original work formulating her views on lexical development.

Ochs, E., and Schieffelin, B. (eds), *Developmental Pragmatics* (New York: Academic Press, 1979). This collection looks at the development of speech-acts and conversational skills, a fast-growing area of research in language development.

Smith, N., *The Acquisition of Phonology* (Cambridge: Cambridge University Press, 1973). The most systematic attempt to study phonological development from the perspective of generative phonology. Difficult in places.

Snow, C., and Ferguson, C. (eds), *Talking to Children* (Cambridge: Cambridge University Press, 1977). A collection of articles devoted to studying the possible effects of mothers' speech on language development. By far the most sophisticated is by E. L. Newport, G. Gleitman and L. R. Gleitman.

Waterson, N., and Snow, C. (eds), *The Development of Communication* (Chichester: Wiley, 1978). A fairly recent collection of papers of variable quality. Contains one particularly important contribution by M. Bowerman on prototypes in lexical development.

Chapter 11

Comparative Linguistics

11.1 The problem of 'language'

So far in this book we have been content to discuss the structure of language without reference to any problems that might arise in pinning down precisely what are the boundaries of a particular language, such as English. As we shall see in this chapter and Chapter 12, it is far from simple to specify any particular communication system as a language in such a way as to emerge with a relatively homogeneous object of study. The problem is essentially this: if we wish to specify which set of utterances we shall accept as 'English', we have to reckon with the fact that 'English' is spoken in many different ways in different parts of the world – even to the point where mutual intelligibility is doubtful. The temporal limits of a language are no easier to define. While there are clear differences between modern English and the English of Shakespeare's time, most people will be inclined to recognise that both forms of language constitute the same language, namely, English. The English of Chaucer, by contrast, is hardly more recognisable to a speaker of modern English than is modern German. So while there is no historical period to which we can point, claiming that there was a sudden discontinuity of language at that time, nevertheless, normal processes of historical change are capable of effecting quite radical changes in a language over a period of several hundred years. From the point of view of linguistic structure, there is therefore a considerable degree of arbitrariness in what comes to be recognised as a single language and what does not. The unity of 'English' owes as much to political and social circumstances as it does to the purely linguistic properties of the various forms of a language included under that name. Equally striking, however, are the limits to such arbitrariness. In global terms it is probably the rule rather than the exception for people to be bilingual (or multilingual), and their everyday communication may often resemble a random mixture of elements of several languages. In spite of this, different languages remain different in such communities, rather than ending up as an undifferentiated mass of properties chosen at random from the different languages.

This problem – of what linguistic prerequisites exist for the recognition of two forms of language as the same language – is not one which has received a definitive answer as yet. Presumably the phonology, morphology, syntax and vocabulary of the two forms of language will have to be largely similar for such identity to be recognised. *Phonetic* properties appear to be much more variable: English vowel-systems are notoriously variable in dialects, for instance, where a word such as *now* may be pronounced [naɒ] in RP, but [nɛy] in Somerset. But the phonological contrasts are usually retained, so that *now* and other words like it are distinguished from *new*, *no*, *nigh*, etc., in all but a few dialects. There is something of a paradox in the fact that the feature of a language which contributes most to identifying it as a specific language, i.e. its vocabulary, is virtually ignored in most structural linguistic work. The reason for this is that the vocabulary is the easiest part of the linguistic system to manipulate without changing the nature of the language completely – witness the great influx of technical vocabulary into English over the last hundred years or so. Furthermore, whereas languages do not in general differ in the complexity of their grammatical system as a whole (morphological simplicity often being made up for by syntactic complexity), some languages do have greater numbers of words than others, e.g. Modern English has many more words than, say, Modern Eskimo. Note that this does not necessarily mean that individual speakers of English have a greater vocabulary than individual speakers of Eskimo. Given the greater specialisation of functions characteristic of 'advanced' technological societies, a steelworker will use and understand many words unknown to a baker, and vice versa, even though they may both speak English. Many languages of the developing world are facing precisely the problem of assimilating vocabulary at an unusually fast rate, and it is not surprising that English, French, Spanish, Russian, etc., are often used by speakers of other languages in specialised contexts. The problems posed by vocabulary tend to be practical rather than theoretical.

11.2 Types of similarity and their significance

Languages differ or manifest similarities along many different dimensions. English and French, for instance, contrast at various levels: French has front rounded vowels (e.g. [y]), while English does not; English has interdental fricatives ([θ] and [ð]), while French does not; adjectives in English noun phrases precede the noun they modify, whereas those in French more often than not follow the noun. In spite of such differences, French and English are quite similar to each other when they are contrasted with some other languages: they share many phonological contrasts, their sentence-structures are such that a word-for-word translation is often possible, and they share a considerable amount of vocabulary.

In principle we may think of linguists collecting details of such similarities and differences for any two or more languages in the world. By itself, however, this would be a fairly pointless exercise; such contrasts are only important when we can interpret them as showing something about language in general, or about the historical relationship between two languages. Such interpretations fall into four categories, either providing an account of universal features of languages, or providing a classification based on typological, genetic, or areal factors. Before we go into the results and methods of these approaches, it is worthwhile considering the general implications of these different approaches to language comparison.

According to one set of positions, of which Chomsky's (as sketched in Chapter 2) is merely the latest, the purpose of linguistic theory is to relate general properties of language to those aspects of individual speakers or the language-community which may be taken as determining the nature of language, whether these are cognitive, perceptual, or social in nature. For those who follow this line of thought, universal properties of language, and those properties which form one of a small range of alternatives, are the major focus of interest, as they give us clues as to the organisational principles on which language is based. If all languages contain a phoneme which has an alveolar or dental stop as its most frequent allophone, then this must indicate that alveolar or dental stops are particularly favoured in some way, either in terms of the organisation of the vocal tract, or in terms of ease of perception or some other general principle. A linguistic theoretician will be concerned to find an account of language which deals satisfactorily with a large number of such facts. From this point of view, historical relationships of languages will be of use mainly as a check against assuming a property to be universal merely because it is shared by a number of genetically or areally related languages. (In fact, there are more subtle ways in which the study of historical relationships can contribute to theoretical linguistics, but we shall not be concerned with them here.)

Another position, which is complementary to, rather than inconsistent with, the first, seeks to discover historical relationships between languages; ideally, it should relate to historical and archaeological findings about movements of peoples, conquest, assimilation, etc. All these factors, even simply contact between peoples at some period, leave their mark on the language of the linguistic communities affected by them, and it is often possible to reconstruct such events through traces in the language of modern descendants of such peoples. On the whole, as we shall see, the structural properties of a language will not be a reliable guide to its historical relationship with other languages; rather, we have to turn to the form of specific morphemes and words, which will correspond regularly to those of another language if there is a historical relationship to establish. From this perspective, universal properties of languages, and typological classifications, are relevant mainly as a supplementary tool, since a feature of a language which is either universal, or one of a small number of possibilities which all languages must choose from, is manifestly unsuited to the demonstration of relationship with some other specific language. For example, if two languages have a five-member vowel-system (i, e, a, o, u), this can be no indication of historical relationship, as such vowel-systems are extremely common in the languages of the world. If, however, two languages have the same word for 'man', this may well be evidence of a historical relationship.

During the nineteenth century, linguistics (or 'the science of language') was concerned almost exclusively with the study of languages in their historical relationships. However, each of the areas we have mentioned is currently under active investigation, and all have led to interesting results. Below, we shall consider them in turn, although inevitably most attention will be devoted to historical linguistics, which of these fields has the longest history of serious study, and the most impressive results.

11.3 Universals and typology of language

If 'linguistic universal' is to be understood as a specific property possessed by all languages, then there are relatively few known cases of genuine linguistic universals, and those that exist are, in appearance at least, fairly banal. The universal occurrence of a *t*-phoneme may well follow from general principles of articulatory or auditory salience. All languages are said to possess pronoun-systems which distinguish three persons and two numbers, i.e. there are forms for 'I', 'you' and 'he/she/it', with plurals such as 'we' and 'they'. It is indeed difficult to conceive of a language in which such distinctions were inexpressible. While it is likely that we shall discover more such principles as our knowledge of languages increases, there is sufficient variety in the languages of the world to cast doubt on the possibility of gaining a satisfactory general picture of the structure of all languages if we limit ourselves to statements of this type.

A more interesting type of universal statement is one which predicts that if any language has a certain property, it will also have some other property. For instance, there are languages which have nasal vowels (e.g. French, Polish), and there are languages which do not have (phonemic) nasal vowels (e.g. English, Russian), but in languages which do have such vowels, there always exist corresponding non-nasal vowels. In other words, the occurrence of a nasal vowel phoneme in a language implies the occurrence in that language of a non-nasal vowel phoneme with otherwise identical articulatory properties, but not vice versa. Such principles are known as *implicational universals*;

they are of interest because they often suggest connections between linguistic phenomena which are not apparent from a superficial consideration of those phenomena. Of course, implicational universals are in no sense explanatory, but they suggest many more phenomena for which an explanation must be found than would emerge from descriptions limited to a single language. In this example involving nasal and oral vowels, we would expect a distinctive feature theory to account for the fact that there is a special relationship between nasal and oral vowels. Both of the systems of distinctive features that we considered in Chapter 4 deal with this aspect satisfactorily: nasal vowels are specified in the same way as corresponding oral vowels, but for an extra feature of nasality. Many other implicational universals (or claimed universals, as no individual linguist can obtain a fully reliable impression of all languages) pose greater difficulties. But there is another aspect to the explanation of the relationship of nasal and oral vowels: why are nasal vowels not the universally occurring set, with oral vowels depending on them for their occurrence? One approach to this problem has been to claim that certain linguistic features are more *marked* than others – in the case of phonology, markedness usually involves some extra articulation, some deviation from the position of rest of articulators, as well as a more restricted distribution across languages, and within individual languages which make use of such phonological material.

Implicational universals are not restricted to phonology. In syntax, one well-known set of implicational universals relates to possible sequences of constituents within the sentence. In a number of languages (e.g. Welsh, Samoan, Hebrew, Tagalog) sentences typically begin with a verb; such languages always have prepositions as markers of the relationship between noun phrases and other elements within the sentence. The converse does not follow, as can be seen from English or French, which have prepositions but which do not typically begin sentences with a verb. With a very small number of exceptions (e.g. Amharic), those languages which typically end sentences with a verb (e.g. Japanese, Turkish, Quechua, Yidiny) have postpositions – relational words like prepositions except that they follow the noun phrase. Similarly, verb-initial languages always have auxiliary verbs preceding the main verb (as in English *was smoking*), while verb-final languages have auxiliary verbs following the main verb. When a whole range of unrelated languages is compared in this way, it is fairly typical for trends to emerge which fall down only in a few instances. The position of genitive (possessive) modifiers, for instance, typically correlates with the occurrence of postpositions or prepositions. Where genitive modifiers follow the head noun, a language is likely to have prepositions (e.g. French *la plume de ma tante* 'the pen of my aunt', where *de* is a preposition, and the genitive modifier *de ma tante* follows the head noun *plume*). Conversely, genitive modifiers generally precede the head in languages which have postpositions (e.g. Japanese *Taro no hon* 'Taro's book', where *no* is the postposition, and the modifier *Taro no* precedes the head noun *hon*). English, however, is largely a prepositional language, but it frequently has genitive modifiers preceding the head noun (*John's book*). This is complicated by the fact that the *'s* genitive marker can plausibly be considered a postposition in English, while genitive modifiers of a different sort follow the head (*the property of the school*). Amharic, on the other hand, is a clear example of a language with prepositions but genitive modifiers preceding the head noun (e.g. *ya-šum baqlo* 'the chief's mule', where *ya* is the genitive preposition, and *ya-šum* is the modifier of the head noun *baqlo* 'mule'). Such languages are rare, however. It is difficult to evaluate the status of such trends: it may be that there is a genuine implicational universal available to us but the existing formulation is too imprecise to capture it. Alternatively, it has been suggested, some languages might genuinely be unstable in some sense – in the course of change from one set of orders to another, or artificially influenced by some other language; if such a position could be supported, the fault would lie not with the formulation of universals, but in the expectation that all languages should be stable enough to conform with them. However, such a position is fraught with conceptual difficulties; it is perhaps safer to recognise that there is a lot that we do not know about languages.

A set of implicational universals is likely to define a typology of languages, in so far as they tend to relate linguistic features in a small number of groupings. To pursue the word-order example, we can define a typology in terms of whether the verb typically occurs at the beginning of a sentence, at the end of a sentence, or in the middle of a sentence. (Of course, it is also possible that some languages have no one order which can be called 'typical'; most linguists would, however, claim that such languages do not exist.) Verb-initial languages, as we have seen, will also have prepositions and postponed genitive modifiers; verb-final languages will have postpositions and preposed genitive modifiers. Verb-medial languages may be of either sort. In terms of frequency of occurrence, a whole range of other features may be added to this typology: although there are many languages which behave rather differently, there is an intensive clustering of verb-initial languages which have the properties enumerated in Table 11.1, and there are rather more verb-final languages which have the properties enumerated in Table 11.2. Other typical verb-initial languages include Arabic, Berber, Gaelic, Jacaltec, Malagasy and Zapotec. Typical verb-final languages include Avar, Bengali, Dargva, Gilyak, Mongolian, Nama, Tamil and Turkish. There appears to be some **geographical basis for these groupings: the languages of the Indian**

Table 11.1   *Characteristic Properties of a Verb-Initial Language*

Properties	*Example: Welsh*
The verb is typically the first word in the sentence	Gwelodd y dyn y ci saw the man the dog 'The man saw the dog'
There are prepositions	am y ci 'about the dog'
Modifiers (adjectives, genitives, relative clauses, etc.) follow the head noun	ci plentyn dog child 'the child's dog'
Auxiliary verbs precede the main verb	bydd y dyn yn gweld y ci will the man in see the dog 'the man will see the dog'
Question words (like *who*, *what*, etc., in English) occur at the front of the sentence	beth yr hoffet ti ei weld? what that would-like you its see 'what would you like to see?'

Table 11.2   *Characteristic Properties of a Verb-Final Language*

Properties	*Example: Japanese*
The verb is typically the last word in the sentence	Biru wa momo o tabeta Bill subj. peach obj. ate marker marker 'Bill ate the peach'
There are postpositions	gakkoo ni 'at school' school at
Modifiers precede the head noun	Biru no momo 'Bill's peach' Bill 's peach
Auxiliaries follow the main verb	Biru wa momo o tabenakatta Bill subj. peach obj. eat neg. 'Bill didn't eat the peach'
There is no characteristic position for question words	Biru wa nani o tabeta? Bill subj. what obj. ate 'What did Bill eat?'

subcontinent, and the languages of North-East Asia, are all fairly consistently verb-final. However, as can be seen from the lists of languages, these word-order features are not distributed on a purely geographical basis, and no explanation for their distribution is likely to be forthcoming from that source.

It is conventionally estimated that there exist somewhere between three and six thousand distinct languages still spoken today. No definitive answer exists, of course, because of the difficulties noted above of giving a precise definition to the notion 'a language'. Only a relatively small number of these languages have been investigated in sufficient detail to allow us to place them with reference to the sorts of research into language universals described above. Both in practical and in theoretical terms the detailed study of little-known languages is an urgent task: in practical terms, the survival of small communities is to a large extent dependent on the maintenance of their language; from a purely theoretical point of view, no proposal relating to the characteristic properties of human language (see the programme sketched in Chapter 2) can be considered established unless it has been shown to account satisfactorily for the full range of variation to be observed in the languages of the world. Even in terms of relatively superficial properties of grammar, the last two decades have seen the description of linguistic phenomena quite unlike anything we might have been led to expect from a study of the more easily accessible languages of the world. It is highly unlikely that the next two decades will fail to bring up more data to force us to revise our grammatical preconceptions.

11.4 The nature of language change

Languages change with time. Across all the linguistic levels that we have examined in this book, Modern English differs to some extent from the English of previous centuries, as even a superficial reading of the literature of these periods will show. The same would be true of any language at any time, although we often lack the historical records which would show this directly. More important, language change does not proceed along predetermined paths; two communities speaking the same language originally will find their languages gradually diverging, unless the need for intercomprehensibility is maintained by continuous contact. Linguists are fortunate in having certain very well-documented instances of such divergences – notably, the breakdown of Latin into the Modern Romance languages (French, Italian, Romanian, Spanish, etc.). These various Modern Romance languages are clear cases of distinct languages – in their standard varieties they are usually not mutually comprehensible to their speakers, and the many differences between them are strikingly obvious. At the same time, the historical records show that they did not spring up as distinct languages all of a sudden, but rather that they have been diverging in gradual steps for many hundreds of years. Essentially the same processes of change can be observed in all the other European languages, where written records have been kept for hundreds of years. We have already seen that the drawing of language-boundaries at some point in historical processes of this sort is a fruitless exercise; the illusion of discreteness of change is perhaps reinforced by the standardised nature of most 'literary' languages – notions of 'good English' and 'bad English', for instance, are largely a consequence of such attempts at standardisation (see Chapter 12, p. 391, for discussion).

Change in vocabulary is probably the most readily apparent form of language change. At the same time, the determinants of changes in vocabulary are so manifold, and so intertwined with the circumstances of life at the time of change, that it is all but impossible to formulate general principles relating to these changes. The fact that the concept represented by *phlogiston* was shown to be untenable around the end of the eighteenth century, and that a novel word, *oxygen*, gradually became accepted as the name of the gas which formed the basis of a revised set of concepts, owes little to the nature of linguistic organisation, except in so far as all scientific activity is dependent on language-like representations. The specific morphemic make-up of a word such as *conurbation* is a familiar one in English, but the word itself is a novel one, and it refers to a specifically modern phenomenon. The history of vocabulary mirrors the history of society: words are created as new objects arise to be referred to; words are lost as objects fall into disuse. Nevertheless, the history of vocabulary can provide us with examples of the types of change which occur at other linguistic levels as well. Different words may be used at different periods for much the same meaning; a *footpad* is little different from a *mugger*, but the former is clearly obsolete, while the latter is a fairly recent term. Words may be borrowed from one language to another; English is packed with borrowed words, mainly from Romance, but with a fair number of individual words from the most varied languages – e.g. *bungalow* from Hindi, and used to indicate a specifically Indian type of one-storey dwelling, with a thatched roof. This word also illustrates another type of change – generalisation of meaning; it is now commonly used to refer to any type of single-storey house. Words may also become more specific in meaning; *meat*, which once meant 'food' in general, is now restricted to the meaning of food consisting of the flesh of animals. A word may be lost for no obvious reason; *betimes* is a perfectly good word meaning 'early', but it is no longer in current use. Such changes fall into a fairly restricted set of categories – loss and acquisition (via borrowing, or by conscious invention), and change of meaning, either by a change in the generality of its reference, or by extension to some concept felt to be related.

Grammatical (morphological and syntactic) change is also clearly apparent from an inspection of earlier and later forms of the same language, but in this case it is hardly plausible to invoke the 'outside world' as a cause of these changes. The use of a second person singular pronoun in English, and associated forms of verb agreement (*thou hast*), has been lost in most dialects of Modern English; 'reasons' adduced for such changes are likely to be unconvincing, especially given the fact that many languages which are rather similar to Modern English in grammatical structure (French, German, etc.) retain this feature. Nor do changes universally apply in the same direction; both the Modern Germanic languages (German, Dutch, Scandinavian, English, etc.) and the Modern Romance languages are characterised by a relative poverty of inflectional morphology, and a corresponding rigidity of the word-order of their sentences, when they are compared with earlier forms. Thus, (1) and (2) are corresponding sentences in Latin and French.

(1) Puer amat puellam
(2) Le garçon aime la fillette } 'The boy loves the girl'

In (1), each word is marked for the function it fulfils in the sentence: *puellam*, for instance, indicates by its final *-m* that it is a direct object, and that it is singular. In (2), by contrast, the syntactic role of the noun phrases is completely unmarked morphologically. So it is natural that (1) may be reordered as (3) in Latin without any oddness, while (4) is unacceptable in French.

(3) Puer puellam amat
(4) *Le garçon la fillette aime

Such changes are not, however, a necessary fact of the development of languages. The modern Slavonic languages have lost little of the morphology, and none of the freedom of word-order, characteristic of the older forms of Slavonic; Finnish and Hungarian (in no way related to the other European languages we have been discussing) have actually added to the complexity of their nominal morphology, and now possess fourteen and twenty-two cases respectively, as opposed to the five or six that scholars generally recognise as having occurred in their parent language.

The extent to which borrowing affects grammatical structure is rather less clear, but borrowing of derivational morphology is rather common. English provides multiple examples of this, as it has borrowed so much vocabulary from French that many of the derivational processes that are implicit in the borrowed words may be regarded as a semi-productive part of English derivational morphology; abstract nominal suffixes, such as *-ation* or *-ment*, prefixes such as *sub-* or *re-*, etc., – all these are of Romance origin.

As with vocabulary, so with syntax and morphology; we can classify types of changes which have occurred, but it is far from clear that there are principled constraints on the types of grammatical change that are possible. Admittedly, certain types of change are observed relatively frequently, but the range of languages over which syntactic variation has been systematically observed is so restricted that we cannot be sure that factors of genetic relationship or geographical proximity do not determine the narrow range of observed changes. However, the case of phonology seems rather more promising; historical phonology was intensively developed during the nineteenth century, and many of the most impressive results of linguistics were in this field. Simply by virtue of the size of their basic units, phonological data occur with greater abundance in texts than grammatical data. However, there are problems here as well. The occurrence of a particular syntactic construction in a text is directly observable, as long as we understand the text; but the phonological and phonetic properties of the text can only be deduced, if at all, by indirect means. Orthography is by its very nature conservative, and the various factors such as style of text, accuracy of scribes and readability of text all affect the reliability of the impressions that we gain regarding the phonological properties of those texts. None the less, a variety of techniques – whether relating to phonological constraints on poetry, loan words, or the interpretation of occasional errors – or (where they exist) attempts at grammatical description by contemporaries, have been developed over a long period, which enables us, within limits, to gain a fairly accurate impression of these phonological properties.

Phonological changes (usually referred to, in line with tradition, as *sound changes*) are of many and varied types, as are other types of language change. But what is significant about sound change is that, no doubt partly because a vastly greater number of such changes have been studied, there appears to be a significant degree of directionality in the changes which are possible. In other words, there are certain general types of sound change which are relatively frequent, while the reverse order of change is unknown or infrequent. This fact holds out the possibility of formulating principles of sound change – a possibility which will be central to any attempt to reconstruct earlier forms of language, as we shall see in the next section.

At this point we shall simply point to two types of change which are relatively common: assimilations and palatalisations. Assimilations (see Chapters 4 and 8) are changes which apply usually to consonant clusters, making one of the consonants closer to an adjacent consonant in some respect. We find in Latin, for instance, a rather common suffix -*tus*, which forms passive participles from verbs. When this suffix is attached to a verb stem ending in a voiced consonant, e.g. *ag*- 'act', this stem-final consonant is devoiced, assimilating to the initial consonant of the suffix – *actus*. In the development from Latin to Italian, such consonant clusters further assimilate in terms of place of articulation: Latin *exactus* 'exact' corresponds to Italian *esatto*, Latin *noct*- 'night' becomes Italian *notte*, Latin *septem* 'seven' results in Italian *sette*, and so on. Similarly, the history of Russian provides an example of assimilation: as a consequence of the loss of certain short vowels, consonant clusters are formed, and these undergo assimilation in voicing; Old Russian *kŭde* 'where', on losing the short vowel, has come through to Modern Russian as *gde*, just as Old Russian *bŭčela* 'bee' is now *pčela*. Such examples could be multiplied endlessly: assimilation is a very common type of change, while the reverse order of change is exceedingly scarce, at least in the sort of consonant clusters we have been looking at.

Palatalisation involves a change of specific types of consonants to (alveo-)palatal affricates or fricatives (see the discussion in Chapter 4, Section 9; this use of the term is, of course, to be kept sharply distinct from 'palatalisation' as the name of a secondary articulation). Again, the development of Latin into Italian provides a convenient example: the Latin and Italian words for 'food' are respectively *cibus* and *cibo* in the conventional orthographies. In Latin the initial consonant is a [k] (or [c]), while in Italian it is a [ʝ]. The same point holds for pairs like *cingulum* and *cingolo* 'belt', or *celare* (in both languages) 'hide'. The same is true of the voiced equivalents, e.g. Latin *gemellus* 'twin' (with a [g] (or [ɟ])), Italian *gemello* with a [dʒ]). All these changes take place before a front vowel. In a different phonetic context, the same process can be seen at work in the development of French, where it applies before the vowel /a/ (in Latin). Thus, Latin *cantare* 'sing' corresponds to Modern French *chanter* (beginning with [ʃ]), but in Old French it was the affricate [ʝ] which occurred in that position. Similarly for a mass of other words, such as *campus–champ* 'field', *carus–cher* 'dear', etc. Again, palatalisations of this sort are very common among sound changes which are reliably attested. The reverse process is apparently unknown. The fact that sound changes fall into classes which are in some way limited is one of the factors which enable us to go beyond the study of change in attested language states, and attempt to reconstruct language states which must have existed, but of which we have no direct historical record.

These are but two of the many types of sound change which emerge from a study of languages in change. There is virtually no class of phonological phenomena which has not undergone change in some language within recorded history. There is, however, a further type of change which has to be dealt with separately. Sound changes, by altering segments in specific contexts, may result in morphological irregularity: under conditions which remain problematic, the morphological system may reform itself in such a way as to maintain regularity. This is one aspect of a process known as *analogy*. For instance, in the early history of Russian, short vowels were lost, being either omitted altogether or made into long vowels. This rule operated in the following steps.

(*a*) A short vowel is lengthened when the next vowel is also short (e.g. /ĭ/ becomes /e/). This can be seen as applying from right to left, so that it has the effect of converting a sequence of short vowels into alternating long and short vowels.

(*b*) Remaining short vowels are deleted.

A Russian town was called *Smolĭniskŭ*, in its citation form, the nominative case. The first rule applies to change it to *Smolĭneskŭ*, and cannot apply again, as there are no other short vowels where the next vowel is itself a short vowel. Deletion of the remaining short vowels yields *Smolnesk*. However, oblique case forms of nouns ended in full vowels rather than the short vowel /ŭ/, e.g. the genitive form was originally *Smolĭniska*. This time rule (*a*) applies to yield *Smolenĭska*, and rule (*b*) gives *Smolenska*. The nominative and genitive case forms therefore have different stem forms, and the situation was subsequently simplified by analogy in favour of the oblique case forms, i.e. the nominative form became *Smolensk*. The peculiar thing about analogy is that it does not apply equally to all forms: Russian contains many nouns in which, because of the loss of short vowels, nominative and oblique forms are different, e.g. *rot* 'mouth' (nom.), *rta* 'mouth' (gen.). Analogy often has the effect of making sound change more difficult to observe, although it is seldom applied on such a scale as to render such observation impossible.

11.5 Change and reconstruction

To discover genetic relationships between languages, and establish some details of the 'ancestor language' common to two attested languages, we need to have recourse to techniques of reconstruction. We may do this for purely linguistic reasons to discover more about processes of language change and the interrelationships of languages – or as an auxiliary to other historical disciplines. All such techniques, however, rest on an assumption, without which rational consideration of the historical relationships of languages would be impossible – usually known as *uniformitarianism*. This is the assumption that those features of languages (or any other phenomenon) which are directly observable today, and which we wish to claim are general features of language, will also be true of languages of which we have no direct experience. If the next language we come across could in principle be entirely different from those we have met previously (if, for instance, duality of structure were not characteristic of some language), then we would have no basis for deciding anything about the structure of ancestor languages. The same principle applies also to the types of language change that we can observe: if we were to admit, for instance, that before historical records started the reverse of palatalisation was quite common, but only ceased to be so at some time before records started, then we would also be violating the principle of uniformitarianism, and reconstruction techniques would be impossible. It is important to realise that this assumption is a metaphysical one; there is nothing in the facts of language which forces us to adopt it. If we fail to adopt it, however, the whole enterprise of historical reconstruction of languages becomes impossible.

Establishing a genetic relationship between languages is done by showing that they correspond systematically in some ways; to take up a familiar example, it is possible to show that words of similar meaning in French and Italian are systematically related, in the sense that a particular sound of French may correspond to some other particular sound in Italian. Thus, where French has *chanter* 'sing', *cher* 'dear' and *chef* 'head' (in the sense 'head of an organisation'), which all begin with [ʃ], Italian has *cantare*, *caro* and *capo*, with the same meaning as the cognate words in French, but with initial [k]. Of course, given our discussion in the previous section, we know that this reflects a sound change which has taken place in French in its development from Latin, but it should be clear that, were we not in possession of extensive documentation on Latin, we might still be able to reconstruct the ancestor form from a comparison of French and Italian. Such comparisons allow us to establish genetic relationships: why should we then wish to go further in reconstructing the form of the ancestor language? There are several reasons for this. Our reconstructions will have to make up a plausible language, and therefore constitute a check on the validity of the comparative method; similarly, the correspondences established can be checked for plausibility in terms of the sound changes (or other changes) which they involve as a prerequisite. Historical linguists will also be interested in relationships of considerable remoteness: it is well established that modern languages such as English, German, Dutch, etc., are genetically related in the Germanic language family. Germanic itself is an Indo-European language, on a par with Romance, Celtic, Greek, Slavonic, Indo-Iranian, etc. There are various hypotheses about the relationships which Indo-European might have with a number of other reasonably well-established language families – Uralic, Altaic, Afro-Asiatic, etc. While the relationship between the individual Germanic languages is evident from the modern forms of these languages, it is doubtful if Indo-European could so readily be imagined if only the modern forms of the languages were available for comparison; it would be more difficult still to establish historically more remote relationships. Reconstructed forms of language, on the other hand, may themselves be compared with each other, and therefore put us in a position to probe much more deeply into language relationships than we would be able to otherwise.

At the same time, it must be said that reconstruction has its limits: the outstanding nineteenth-century Indo-Europeanist August Schleicher felt himself in a position to write a fable in his reconstructed Indo-European language. For more than a century now, however, historical linguists have been much more circumspect about the status of their reconstructions. As will be seen in Chapter 12, language use is much too complex for us to be able to assume that we could have any direct insight into how language was used many millennia ago.

Having sketched out the general motivation for reconstruction, we can now turn to some specific techniques; we shall base the initial discussion on sound change. Three possible effects of sound changes – morphological irregularity, many-to-one relationships between two languages, and specific unidirectional correspondences between two languages – lie at the basis of our ability to reconstruct phonological systems. It is obviously possible, given that sound changes apply in specific contexts to specific segments, that such changes may lead to morphological irregularity. The case of the Latin suffix – *tus*, considered in the previous section, provides an example of this; the assimilation of the stem-final consonant to the initial consonant of the suffix results in the existence of two allomorphs of the verb stem (i.e. in this case *ag-* and *ac-*). Such allomorphy is usually a reliable indication of an earlier sound change. Such a situation is found in Russian, for instance, where many verbs show alternations between a stop and a palatal affricate; e.g. *tek-ut* 'they flow', but *teč-ot* 'it flows', *xoč-u* 'I want', but *xot-it* 'he wants', and so on. This alternation reflects changes which occurred across the whole Slavonic linguistic area. It is not difficult to see that, in view of our earlier discussion about palatalisation as a historical process, the palatal affricates in such alternations are the later development. A similar alternation which reflects sound change can be observed in the English vowel-system, with such forms as *profane*, *profanity*, *sincere*, *sincerity*, *derive*, *derivation*, and so on. This reflects the historical change which took place in English known as the Great Vowel Shift, whereby the whole system of English tense vowels was reorganised, while the system of lax vowels remained as before. It is of some interest that this sort of alternation is normally derived in a generative phonology from a single underlying base form (see Chapter 8, p. 248), which suggests strongly that Modern English contains sufficient information for us to be able to reconstruct the change. The reconstruction of change in this way, usually through morphological alternations, is known as *internal reconstruction*.

If we compare two languages and find that a pair of phonemes in the one language shows a regular correspondence with a single phoneme in the other, and furthermore that there are no obvious conditioning factors for the division of the one phoneme into two, then we shall generally choose the more differentiated language as representing the ancestor language in this respect. For instance, in the two Tungusic languages Ewenki and Manchu, an initial /l/ in Ewenki can correspond to either /l/ or /n/ in Manchu.

Ewenki	Manchu	
loko	lakja	'hang'
largi:	largin	'mess'
lo:gdi	loqdi	'thick'
lamu	namu	'sea'
laŋ	naŋgu	'trap'
lombocon	njomoʃon	'a type of fish'

If we assume that the change from some ancestor language took place in the direction of Ewenki, then we are able to postulate two entirely determinate changes: putative initial /l/ remains unchanged, while initial /n/ is changed to /l/ in Ewenki. If we were to assume the reverse order, i.e. the one in which Ewenki represented the ancestor language in this respect, we would be forced to postulate a change of initial /l/ to /n/ which occurs only in some subset of words. There is little doubt which is the preferable solution.

We have pointed out in the previous section that certain changes are apparently unlikely to occur in the reverse order; this fact can be made use of in comparative reconstruction where two languages differ from each other in terms of one of these unidirectional correspondences. For instance, the various Inupiaq Eskimo dialects differ from each other in terms of the types of consonant cluster which occur; we find correspondences such as the following.

Eastern Eskimo	Western Eskimo	
qimmiq	qipmiq	'dog'
kimmik	kikmik	'heel'
minŋiq	mitŋiq	'jump'

It should be clear that Eastern Eskimo dialects make use of assimilation to a much greater degree than Western Eskimo dialects. Given the observation that assimilation in consonant clusters is a natural process, while the reverse is not, we are forced to the conclusion that Western Eskimo represents the original situation in this respect.

The same point can be made as regards palatalisation; again, such correspondences are commonplace – we cite another Tungusic example, with the following data from Ewenki and Manchu.

Ewenki	Manchu	
tari	tare	'that'
to:ki:	toxo	'elk'

Ewenki	*Manchu*	
tura:ki:	turaki	'crow'
timi:	ʧimari	'in the morning'
tire	ʧiru	'press'

It is clear from these data that /t/ in Ewenki and Manchu corresponds except before /i/, where Manchu has the affricate /ʧ/. Given what we have said about palatalisation, the Ewenki form here clearly cannot be considered as derived from the Manchu form. An incidental point to note about this example and the previous one from Tungusic is that we have been led to two conclusions about the ancestor language of Ewenki and Manchu, one of which sees it as more directly related to Ewenki and the other to Manchu. This is a fairly typical situation in comparative linguistics: it would be quite unusual to find a language which consistently retained features of the ancestor language, while other languages diverged from this. All languages change.

Using techniques such as these (although naturally of considerably greater complexity), it is possible to reconstruct many features of ancestor languages even when the relationship between two families is quite remote. The outstanding example of this is, of course, Indo-European, although the extent to which reconstruction is possible even where languages have no recorded history is very striking, e.g. in the Americas or Australia. However, the techniques we have described encounter problems of a practical nature with all languages, and perhaps the most serious of these involves borrowing. All languages, as we have seen, go in for borrowing from other languages – especially of vocabulary, but also of grammatical and phonological properties where the relationship of the two language-communities is intimate. If two languages have a series of phonologically related words, how are we to justify the claim that these go back to a period when the two languages had a common ancestor, rather than postulating borrowing at some period? It is clearly no use arguing for the antiquity of the proposed sound changes, as this would also be consistent with borrowing at a still earlier period. It has sometimes been claimed that such problems are entirely insoluble within linguistics, but the consensus has been and is that certain areas of vocabulary and grammar are more central to the functioning of language than others, and therefore less liable to change. For instance, if a language possesses grammatical categories such as tense or agreement on the verb, case or number on the noun, it is not difficult to envisage the loss of these categories (cf. the loss of case endings between Latin and Modern French), but it is most unlikely that a language would borrow the markers of such categories from another language. Similarly, it is not difficult to see why a language might import from another language words denoting, say, a novel substance, such as *tea* or *titanium*, but there is unlikely to be a language in which there is no word for *nose*, and consequently the need for borrowing such a word is not likely to arise very often. The number of established correspondences is also a relevant factor, and might at times override these other factors; but a systematic comparison of groups of languages provides the investigator with a whole range of interrelated correspondences, and ultimately it is the overall picture of the relationship of languages which will enable us to test the validity of individual correspondences.

While the problems involved in phonological reconstruction concern, on the whole, the minutiae of such an enterprise, the problem with syntactic reconstruction relates to whether it is possible at all. This may simply follow from the fact that the accumulated wisdom on syntactic change is so much scantier than what is known about phonological change, or alternatively syntactic change may really be different from phonological change in principle. There are few problems when the languages involved are relatively homogeneous: it would be weird, for instance, to reconstruct the proto-language of the modern Turkic languages as being anything other than a verb-final language, in which modifiers precede the modified word, and there are postpositions. Apart from a few Turkic languages which are known to have been heavily influenced by Indo-European languages (e.g. Gagauz), the modern Turkic languages consistently have these characteristics. But such homogeneity is not characteristic of Indo-European languages, for instance: VSO (Celtic languages such as Welsh, Breton, etc.), SOV (Indo-Iranian languages such as Persian and Hindi) and SVO (English and French, among others) are all attested as basic orders of transitive sentences in Indo-European languages, while other languages of the same family may either allow considerable freedom of word order (Slavonic languages such as Russian and Czech), or have variant orders in different contexts (e.g. German, where SVO is the natural order in main clauses, while SOV is the basic order of subordinate clauses). Furthermore, while it is clear that phonological change often leaves a residue of morphological irregularity which can act as a signal of its occurrence, those aspects of syntax which have been claimed to represent similar residues are by no means clearly so. For instance, English contains nominal compounds such as *animal lover*, or *dog owner*, which have a clear semantic relationship to verb phrases such as *loves animals* and *owns a dog*; one might wish to suggest that this type of compound represents a fossilised form of verb-final syntax in English, as opposed to the verb-object construction in the productive category of verb phrases in Modern English. But then again, perhaps it merely relates to the fact that simple forms of nominal modification in English typically occur before the noun. Arguments of this type are far from being universally accepted in diachronic syntax.

In establishing correspondences between languages and reconstructing ancestor languages, the historical linguist is implicitly subscribing to the *family tree* model of language relationships. According to this conception, the historical relationships of a set of languages are representable in tree form, each node representing a language (attested or reconstructed), and divergent branches representing the process of splitting up of a language into two or more distinct languages. For instance, a partial classification of the Turkic languages yields the family tree in Figure 11.1. As a model of the real relation-

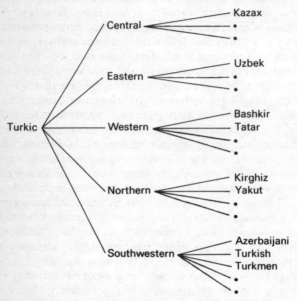

Figure 11.1   *A family tree for the Turkic languages*

ships between languages, such a tree-structure is a considerable oversimplification, as we shall see. However, it is an accurate reflection of the type of language relationship presupposed by the methods of reconstruction which we have been discussing. To arrive at a more realistic model of language change, it is first necessary to appreciate the ways in which dialects interact, and in which linguistic areas are formed.

11.6   Linguistic geography

No language is an entirely homogeneous object. The factors which condition such variation as is found within a language are many and various – ranging from the geographical position of the speech-community to the age, sex and socioeconomic status of individual speakers. We shall consider these latter factors in more detail later (Section 7 below and Chapter 12), but the traditional form of dialectology has concerned the geographical spread of linguistic features. No speaker of English can be unaware of the existence of such variability; even within the British Isles there are large numbers of remarkably distinct forms of English (e.g. compare Belfast with Glasgow, Newcastle, Norwich, Cockney, etc.), while a specialist trained in the variety of British English dialects can distinguish hundreds of distinct accents. The most obvious distinguishing features are phonetic: particularly the vowel-systems of English dialects show massive variation, which to an extent involves phonological variation as well. One well-known case is the distinction made in Norwich English between a [uː] vowel in words such as *road*, *rose*, *moan*, etc., and a [ɒu] diphthong in words such as *know*, *rows*, *mown*, etc. In other words, Norwich speakers control a phonemic distinction which is no longer made in most other dialects of English. Conversely, in many dialects of Northern England, standard /ʌ/ and /ɒ/ are merged, so that *cut* and *put* rhyme. Given this range of variation, the remarkable thing is that English-speakers *can* understand each other; at least passively, speakers of English must have at their disposal a wide range of phonetic realisations of each phonological contrast. There is little doubt that mass communications and greatly increased mobility of population in this century have evened out some of the major dialect differences in English. None the less, it could hardly be claimed that British English was particularly homogeneous.

On the whole, dialect differences in the British Isles relate to accent, and a certain amount of specialised local vocabulary. Compared to these, the grammatical differences which exist among these dialects are relatively insignificant. There is a great deal of variation among forms of the verb *be*, which is always among the most irregular forms in Indo-European languages. Some dialects use *be* as the finite form of the present tense of this verb, while others use a variant, such as *bin*. It is not clear that any genuine syntactic differences between these dialects can be found. However, there are certain forms of British English, e.g. some Irish dialects, which appear particularly grammatically deviant when viewed from the perspective of standard British English. Studies of such dialects cite sentence forms such as *I saw him, goin' to Mass o' me* (i.e. when I was going to Mass) or *'Twas a loss to the country Michael to die* as fairly typical of the deviations of these dialects from standard British English syntax. It is no coincidence that the use of such constructions is found in areas of bilingualism with a language (Irish Gaelic) of genuinely different structure from English. Differences of a similar order can be found in the English spoken in

Africa or India, although in these cases the speakers of English may not in fact be native speakers.

Dialects, by their very nature, differ from each other; on the whole, dialects in close geographical proximity to each other differ less than widely separated dialects. And yet nothing that we have so far looked at relating to language change could lead us to expect this to be the case. If we imagine that three dialects developed from a single 'super-dialect' at some early stage in the differentiation of separate languages, we would be entitled to expect that they would develop quite separately from each other. However, this does not happen. Furthermore, dialects do not differ from each other in a 'hierarchical' manner; two adjacent dialects are likely to share a number of linguistic features, but other neighbouring dialects may share further linguistic features with only one of them. A 'family tree' model of dialect relationships is quite unable to cope with situations such as these – quite normal situations at that. A more adequate approach to such differentiation is known as the *wave* model, viewing changes as radiating out from a centre. This approach is not intended to account for the fact that changes begin at a certain centre, nor to explain why they are accepted in adjacent dialects or why they stop before they engulf all dialects; it is simply a way of envisaging the distribution of changes which more or less adequately reflects the observed results.

A well-known case of dialect differentiation adds a further refinement to this view. Northern German dialects as a whole differ from the Southern German dialects in that a Northern voiceless stop will often correspond to a Southern fricative or affricate. For example, the Northern dialects have *ik*, *maken* and *dat* (respectively 'I', 'make' and 'that'), while the Southern dialects have *ix*, *maxen* and *das* corresponding to them. The Southern forms represent the innovation, as other Germanic languages are closer to the Northern forms in this respect. However, the situation is complicated by the fact that in Western Germany, while the northernmost and southernmost dialects are as described, there are some intermediate dialects. Some speakers would say *ix*, but *maken* and *dat*; rather farther to the south, there are speakers who say *ix* and *maxen*, but still *dat*. Looked at from the point of view of diffusion of language change, the fricativisation of *k* progressed farther north than the fricativisation of *t*, and farther in *ix* than in *maxen*. It is obviously possible to view this phenomenon as involving diffusion in wave-like fashion northwards from the centre of the change in Southern Germany. More important, it illustrates the over-simple nature of a notion of sound change which is couched entirely in terms of one sound developing into another, as if such a change took place other than relative to specific words.

This is by no means an isolated example. With a little study of dialect atlases, it is simple to extract similar cases. It is known that, corresponding to voiceless initial fricatives in standard British English, some parts of the south-west of England use a voiced fricative. In fact, the spread of this feature, at least in rural dialects is highly uneven; *furrow* is pronounced with initial [v] in Devon, Cornwall, Somerset, Dorset, Wiltshire, Hampshire and parts of Monmouthshire, Herefordshire, Gloucestershire, Berkshire, Surrey and Sussex. Pronunciation of *finger* with a [v] is more restricted – not being found, for instance, in Surrey, Sussex, Berkshire, or parts of Hampshire. Much of Somerset and Cornwall retains a voiceless fricative in *saddle*, although in *seven*, voicing is more common. In *swearing*, initial [z] is widespread only in Devon and parts of Hampshire. The overall picture is that only Devon and the south-western parts of Hampshire are consistently marked by initial voicing of fricatives: the spread of this feature to other areas is patchy.

We have emphasised at the beginning of this chapter the arbitrary nature of the division between languages and dialects; it is natural, then, to ask whether there is a point at which forms of language can become so different that changes may not spread across the boundary between them. Can a feature of one language be transmitted to an adjacent but totally different language? We have already seen that it can; in its simplest form it is called borrowing. But essentially such transference of features across languages must be responsible for the existence of *linguistic areas*. Possibly the best-documented of these is the Indian subcontinent, the north of which is populated on the whole by speakers of Indic languages, related to other Indo-European languages, while the south contains predominantly speakers of Dravidian languages, which are genetically quite distinct. What makes this a linguistic area is that these languages share a range of features which cannot be explained by common ancestry: in phonology, they all have a series of retroflex stops, while syntactically they are all verb-final languages, have case-marking systems in which the subject of a transitive verb is set apart from subjects of intransitive verbs and objects of transitive verbs (a phenomenon known as *ergativity*) and do not co-ordinate finite verb phrases, but instead use non-finite forms (gerunds) for all but the final conjunct. These and many other features are common between Indic and Dravidian (and the Munda languages, such as Santali and Sora), and can only be understood as having involved some kind of transference of features from one language to another, although the precise mechanism of such transference is a matter for speculation. India is by no means exceptional in constituting a linguistic area: the small number of reliably documented cases owes more to the reluctance of linguists to devote time to this problem than it does to the scarcity of plausible candidates.

11.7 Mechanisms of linguistic change

Up to this point, where we have been discussing linguistic change, we have used a mode of expression which implicitly attributes independent existence to forms of language: languages 'change', one form is 'replaced by another', and so on. Behind this mode of speech, however, we have to be in a position to understand how 'language change' relates to the speech of individual speakers. If we look at any specific postulated sound change (e.g. the change of [k] to [ʧ] in the development of French), it is utterly implausible to suggest that a whole language-community suddenly changed its mode of speech, or that a new generation of speakers suddenly began to speak in a different manner from the preceding generation. And yet, such a change manifestly took place.

This problem has led to a whole range of unconvincing attempts to explain how languages change, one of the most popular being that changes take place in imperceptible stages. At the same time, a phonemic description of a language can be seen as one way of putting continuous parameters of phonetic variation in some sort of discrete framework; if such a position is valid, then linguists would be forced to accept that phonological change was sudden – a form either does or does not constitute one realisation of a phoneme.

Dialects, on the other hand, may be regarded as living embodiments of different linguistic changes; whatever changes have occurred within the history of a single language will generally be reflected in the diversity of dialects within that language – the case of the stop-fricative alternation in German dialects illustrates this nicely. But as long as dialects are regarded as being quite separate from each other in terms of the speakers that constitute them, there can be little progress in determining how such dialect variation actually relates to the changes which occur within a language. This *impasse* has been at least partially resolved in recent years by work on urban dialect surveys initiated by the American sociolinguist William Labov. We leave a detailed description of this work until Chapter 12; what concerns us here is the way in which sound change can be observed in progress, and its major features specified.

The first point which Labov and others have noted is that there is consistent variation across age-groups within a single speech-community. In New York English, for instance, the pronunciation of postvocalic /r/ (in words such as *car* or *port*) in the upper socioeconomic groups correlates inversely with age, i.e. younger speakers use it a lot, while older speakers hardly ever use it. This sort of observation can be compared with older descriptions of the speech of a particular group, and such checks confirm that such an age-related distribution does indeed reveal a linguistic change in progress. In the light of this type of evidence, it becomes clear why previous scholars considered language change to be unobservable; without large-scale surveys which control for such variables as socioeconomic class and age, any variation will indeed appear random. Some indication of what further progress such a change is likely to make can be gained from a number of different factors relating to the use and evaluation of such forms. Tests eliciting different styles of speech (the most formal being used for the isolated pronunciation of words from a list) show that the use of postvocalic /r/ in New York increases with formality of style – when it might be expected that people will be trying to be 'correct'. This tendency is especially marked among the 'lower-middle class', a group whose use of this feature in spontaneous speech is minimal. Further, evaluation tests, carried out by testing people's assessment of a recorded voice, with the same speaker alternately using and not using the feature being evaluated in the recording, show that a speaker using postvocalic /r/ is consistently rated by younger New Yorkers as belonging to a higher prestige group than the same person without this feature. This is yet another illustration of the passive 'multidialectalism' of speakers: New Yorkers are well aware of both the linguistic and the social status of many features of speech which they nowhere make use of in their own spontaneous speech. There is no reason to believe that New Yorkers are exceptional in this respect.

The general picture of language change that emerges from studies of this sort is one of speech characteristics of a minority of speakers gradually asserting themselves as prestige features. Their prestige with other groups of speakers then leads these groups to mark them as 'desirable' forms, even though the effect on their everyday linguistic behaviour may be minimal. It is at the point where the values of one social group are adopted by those of another group that changes of this sort move out of the narrow group in which they have developed. In a socially static community, such changes would not take place; it is doubtful if such a community could exist.

Such an approach to language change is far from constituting an explanatory theory of the nature of language change in general. Questions of the interaction of different languages in multilingual societies, or of the interaction of geographical dialects, are not integrated into such an account. The question of whether there are purely linguistic constraints on changes in language-systems remains unanswered. Many other problems remain to be cleared up, even within the framework as it is set up. There is little doubt, however, that work in this tradition represents a significant conceptual advance, in allowing us for the first time to see possible connections between macroscopic questions of language change, and detailed facts about the use of language by individual speakers, to which we now turn.

Exercises: Chapter 11

1   The table on p. 385 presents the distribution of morphological properties of certain types in a range of languages. Assuming that this sample is representative, establish a set of implicational universals on the basis of these data.

2   Any analysis such as that of Exercise 1 involves assumptions; identify the assumptions in Exercise 1 which involve a genuine (i.e. non-implicational) universal.

3   Are any of the implicational universals that you formulated in Exercise 1 more 'natural' than the rest? Do any follow from the nature of the phenomena they involve?

4   Examine the following passage, and describe those syntactic and lexical features which differ from those of Modern English.

In the year 1666 (at which time I applied myself to the grinding of optick glasses of other figures than spherical) I procured me a triangular glass prism, to try therewith the celebrated phaenomena of colours. And in order thereto, having darkened my chamber, and made a small hole in my window-shuts, to let in a convenient quantity of the sun's light, I placed my prism at its entrance, that it might be thereby refracted to the opposite wall. It was at first a very pleasing divertisement, to view the vivid and intense colours produced thereby; but after a while applying myself to consider them more circumspectly, I became surprised, to see them in an oblong form; which, according to the received laws of refraction, I expected should have been circular. They were terminated at the sides with straight lines, but at the ends, the decay of light was so gradual that it was difficult to determine justly, what was their figure; yet they seemed semicircular. (Isaac Newton, in *The Philosophical Transactions of the Royal Society*, 1672.)

5   Of the following English words, some are of modern origin, while others have been used for centuries. Try to guess which is which, then check in a reliable historical dictionary (e.g. the *Oxford English Dictionary*). Have any of these words changed in meaning? How do they relate to the different types of vocabulary change?

abscond	*anthropologist*	*arthropod*	*boggle*
bulldozer	*inmate*	*know-how*	*knuckleduster*
morphology	*occipital*	*perspex*	*sandpaper*
sociologist	*structural*	*submarine*	*supersonic*
syndicate	*titter*	*transplantation*	
urban	*xylophone*		

6   The borrowing of vocabulary may take place when two speech-communities are in contact, but other factors also contribute to the borrowing of words into a language. Using an etymological dictionary, collect some samples of Latin-derived words in English (and other words formed on the same pattern), and draw out a rough typology of the different ways in which these words have come into the English language.

	Russian	English	Eskimo	Dyirbal	Jacaltec	Akan	Mandarin Chinese	Quechua	Hindi	Maori
Nouns marked for case	yes	no	yes	yes	no	no	no	yes	yes	no
Nouns marked for number (sing./pl.)	yes	yes	yes	no	no	yes	no	yes	yes	yes
Nouns marked for dual number (i.e. if there are two)	no	no	yes	no	no	no	no	no	no	no
Nouns categorised for gender or class	yes	no	no	yes	yes	no	no	no	yes	no
Verbs marked for tense	yes	yes	yes	yes	no	yes	no	yes	yes	yes
Verbs agree with subject in person	yes	yes	yes	no	yes	no	no	yes	yes	no
Verbs agree with subject in number	yes	yes	yes	no	yes	no	no	yes	yes	no
Verbs agree with object	no	no	yes	no	yes	no	no	yes	no	no
Adjectives agree in gender with nouns	yes	no	no	no	no	no	no	no	yes	no

7 The following words occur in the related Tungusic languages Ewenki and Nanaj. What correspondences can be derived from them?

Ewenki	Nanaj	English gloss
huleptēn	pun'ektē	ashes
hukite	puxi	belly
hegdi	egdʒi	big
huw	pū	(to) blow
ukun	kū	breast
ulē	xule	(to) dig
ejēn	xejē	(to) float
dil	dʒili	head
edī	edʒi	husband
hennen	pejnē	knee
sā	sā	know
bū	bū	give
halgan	palgā	leg
kumke	kunke	louse
beje	beje	man
hokto	poqto	road
urumkūn	xurumi	short
sann'an	sann ā	smoke
kulin	qolā	snake
koto	qoto	knife
koro	qoro	anger
hīwē	pīwē	sharpen
hog	xoj	(to) chop
han'an	pan'ā	shadow
dilgan	dʒilgā	voice

8 Do any of the correspondences in Exercise 7 give any grounds for suggesting what the ancestor form common to these two languages might have looked like?

Bibliography: Chapter 11

Bloomfield, L., *Language* (London: Allen & Unwin, 1933). An introduction to linguistics by one of the greatest American linguists: chs 18–27 are still a standard discussion of historical linguistics and dialectology.

Emeneau, M. B., 'India as a linguistic area', *Language*, 32 (1956), pp. 3–13. A comparison of the linguistic features of Indic, Dravidian and Munda language groups.

Greenberg, J. H., 'Some universals of grammar with particular reference to the order of meaningful elements', in J. H. Greenberg (ed.), *Universals of Language* (Cambridge, Mass.: MIT Press, 1963), pp. 73–113. The statement and justification of forty-five universals of morphology and syntax.

Jakobson, R. O., *Child Language Aphasia and Phonological Universals* (The Hague: Mouton, 1968). Contains important material on implicational universals in phonology. See also Chapter 10.

Lehmann, W. P. (ed.), *A Reader in Nineteenth Century Historical Indo-European Linguistics* (Bloomington, Ind.: Indiana University Press, 1967). Contains many of the seminal articles which contributed to the nineteenth-century reconstruction of Indo-European, most of them still more readable than similar modern works.

Lehmann, W. P., *Historical Linguistics: An Introduction* (New York: Holt, Rinehart & Winston, 1973). Goes in much greater detail into the material of Sections 4–7 of this chapter.

Ullman, S., *Semantics: An Introduction to the Science of Meaning* (Oxford: Blackwell, 1962). A solid account of traditional semantics, including extensive discussion of change in vocabulary.

Weinreich, U., Labov, W., and Herzog, M. I., 'Empirical foundations for a theory of language change', in W. Lehmann and Y. Malkiel (eds), *Directions for Historical Linguistics* (Austin, Texas: University of Texas Press, 1968), pp. 99–188. A programmatic statement of the importance of detailed study of synchronic linguistic variability for our understanding of language change.

Chapter 12

Sociolinguistics

12.1 Language and socialisation

Chomsky's approach to language has permeated the main body of this book, and it is important to remind ourselves here of the emphasis he lays on the psychological aspects of language, going as far as regarding linguistics as a branch of psychology whose ultimate object would be the discovery and formal description of the mental structures which make possible the acquisition and subsequent use of language. Approaching language in this way, namely, from within the organism itself, the core structural properties of language at the levels of syntax, phonology, etc., are supposedly accounted for by the genetically programmed properties of the language faculty in the mind, ultimately by the anatomical structure of the brain areas concerned with language. From such a standpoint, it is more apposite to talk of language *developing in* the child than of the child learning language, in a way similar to the growth of arms and legs in the human organism, or of wings in birds.

It is also in principle possible to look at language from outside the organism, i.e. abstracting from the mental states that may be thought to underlie linguistic performance and concentrating instead on its interpersonal, or social, aspects. This is the stand taken by Halliday, among others. We have already referred to Halliday's emphasis on function and communication in Chapter 1 (pp. 23–5) and to his functional approach to child language in Chapter 10 (p. 349 ff.), so only a brief word will be in order here concerning his attitude on the putative polarity between language as a mental phenomenon and language as a social phenomenon which can be seen as underlying much of the debate within linguistics.

At the basis of Halliday's model of language is the act of interaction between the subject (child or adult) and his environment. The environment is seen as the social fabric where the individual is placed as a social being. Meaning emanates, or is constructed, from the situation in which this 'primary act' finds its realisation, and from the total culture which envelops the situation, language being a system for encoding the meaning potential of the environment – Halliday talks of language as a way of constructing a 'social semiotic'. Various aspects of the 'primary act' are manifested in functions of language and these are claimed to be at the origin of language, both ontogenetically and, more speculatively, phylogenetically. Note the complete reversal of Chomsky's worldview here – while for Chomsky man is genetically equipped with certain mechanisms (including a language mechanism) which define the scope of, and put limits to, object formation by humans (including the formation of mental objects and, presumably, of social constructs as well), Halliday shifts the focus on to the social fabric, from which the developing child would supposedly construct his own reality and, ultimately, his language. Alongside its role as reality-builder and intimately interacting with it, language is viewed as the most important means for the transmission of social structure from one generation to the next. Figure 12.1 gives a schematic representation of the linking chain between social order and meaning. Implicit in this model is the claim that an analytical understanding of language presupposes an understanding of society, i.e. of the system of social meanings (social semiotic) out of which language grows. One social theory which is particularly relevant in the present connection has been advanced by the British sociologist Basil Bernstein, incorporating language as a central component of social structure: Halliday has more than once expressed his sympathies with Bernstein's views.

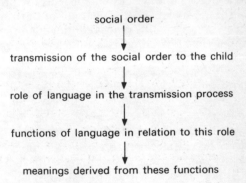

social order

↓

transmission of the social order to the child

↓

role of language in the transmission process

↓

functions of language in relation to this role

↓

meanings derived from these functions

Figure 12.1   *Schematic representation of the relationship between society and language.*

Source: Halliday, 1975, p. 5.

For Bernstein, the mode of social interaction is primarily contingent on social class and the principal socialising agent is the family. For instance, some families (*person-oriented* families) place the emphasis on the individual, and thus the interaction is based on personal appeal and on verbal justifications involving the expression of causal relationships, while in others (*position-oriented* families) the social roles of the members are rigidly delimited, and the interaction typically involves the use of an imperative mode. For example, a child does not want to kiss his grandfather, and the mother can either tell him 'I don't want none of your nonsense' (positional orientation) or, say, 'I know you don't like kissing Grandpa, but he is unwell, and he is very fond of you, and it makes him very happy' (personal orientation) (Bernstein, 1971, p. 158). It is important to realise from the outset that Bernstein's ideas have raised a cloud of criticism, and we shall refer to several of these objections as the exposition proceeds. For example, regarding language socialisation, there is important empirical evidence from the work of the American sociolinguist William Labov that the peer-group rather than the family is mainly responsible for the person's *vernacular* (the style based on automatic patterns of articulation and with no audio-monitoring, that is, more loosely, the style which comes most naturally to the speaker). From a more general and politically oriented standpoint, Harold Rosen assigns a major socialising role to working-class organisations and to the media, which Bernstein entirely glosses over, and he also points at the oversimplistic nature of Bernstein's taxonomy of social class, with only two groups (middle class and (lower) working class) being set up on the basis of only two variables (occupation and education).

As suggested above, Halliday sees language as the primary tool for the perpetuation of the social order. The tenor of Bernstein's theory is that there are overt language differences contingent on social class, but it must be realised that this alone is insufficient to draw inferences about the existence of substantive differences in meaning or in higher cognitive structure. In an early paper (1958, repr. in Bernstein, 1971, pp. 23–41), Bernstein indeed made the suggestion that the middle class may possess a greater power for abstract thinking, possibly causing class differentiation as regards perception of content and structure of objects. In work reported in 1962 (1971, pp. 76–94) he tested the reality of putative class differences in verbal planning, hypothetically correlated with the number and distribution of hesitations during a discussion on the abolition of capital punishment and, although the experiment yielded positive results, it also confirmed the independence of verbal behaviour with respect to non-verbal intelligence scores – in this connection, the often-advanced interpretation of Bernstein's theories as élitist and reactionary is perhaps a little surprising.

12.2 Language varieties

A word about language varieties is necessary at this point in order to understand fully the import of Bernstein's claims. Linguistically, the world is a true mosaic (see Chapter 11), and any attempt to draw boundaries beyond the individual faces ultimately arbitrary decisions. At the lower end of the scale we can place the *idiolect* as defined by Bernard Bloch (1948, p. 7): 'the totality of the possible utterances of one speaker at one time in using a language to interact with one other speaker' (but cf. in this connection the notion of 'linguistic repertoire' on p. 392 below). Theoretically, it would be possible to chart out all the features of geographically adjacent idiolects, the result being a complex network of *isoglosses* (an isogloss is a line defining the geographical distribution of one linguistic feature); a bundle of isoglosses can be said to define a *dialect*. It is difficult to specify criteria for distinguishing between a dialect and a *language*. Probably the two most commonly cited (though misguided) criteria are mutual intelligibility and possession of literature. According to the first, only mutually unintelligible varieties can be accorded the status of independent languages, but there are varieties of English which are not mutually intelligible (intelligibility is, of course, a relative notion, and varieties can be more or less mutually intelligible), and, on the other side of the coin, many 'independent' languages (e.g. Portuguese and Spanish) differ from one another far less than some 'dialects', as in the case of those of Chinese or Arabic. Regarding the requirement that a body of literature be associated with a language, leaving aside the ontogenetic and phylogenetic priority of the spoken language (see Chapter 3, Section 1), literature, whether written or oral, is clearly a sociocultural product not to be confused with language, and no linguist would want to maintain that there are varieties of speech which are *structurally* so primitive that they cannot serve as the instrument for literary creation (but see the discussion on pidgins in Section 8 below).

In general, the opposition between language and dialect bears on *prestige* and is usually associated with political or, at any rate, ethnic affirmation, and newly independent states typically promote their speech variety to the category of language – in Norway, for instance, the official Danish was gradually displaced after independence in 1814 in favour of several local varieties, some of them hardly distinct from the language of Denmark. Often, in the process of elevation to official language, the local dialect must undergo *standardisation*, i.e. it must be made into an instrument functionally apt for utilisation at such levels of community life as law-making, education, the administration of justice, etc. Standardisation typically involves the selection of one dialect or the amalgam of several, and the codification of this variety through regularisation of the orthography, the lexicon, the morphology and even the pronunciation and the syntax, after which *loyalty* to the language as a symbol of national identity is expected (but is not always forthcoming) from the citizens of the state. Standardisation is one of the most important facets of *language planning*, an area which takes us into the domain of what is usually called the *sociology of language*.

The situation of Arabic deserves some discussion in that it exemplifies what Charles Ferguson has labelled *diglossia*. It is typical of the Arab world that the *high* variety of the language (the official language of the state) is not used by the local population, who instead communicate in a *low* variety. In a diglossic situation, the high variety usually represents an older, fossilised state of the language (e.g. Classical Arabic or Katharevusa Greek), or a prestigious variety associated with some neighbouring or formerly colonising nation (e.g. High German in Switzerland and French in Haiti), while the low variety is made up of local dialects (some more prestigious than others) which have undergone centuries of evolution and thus become distinct from the old language. Note that, strictly speaking, in these societies diglossia is accompanied by bilingualism, a term which refers to the possession of more than one language (or dialect) by an individual (either a *compound bilingual*, the two or more languages forming an integrated system in his mind, or a *co-ordinate bilingual*, with separate systems). The presence of diglossia and bilingualism gives rise to the phenomenon of *code switching*, a situation summarised by Joshua Fishman in the phrase 'who speaks what language to whom and when'. The *linguistic repertoire* of any particular individual can (but need not; see the discussion on register on p. 404 ff. below) include more than one language or dialect, Fishman again giving the hypothetical example of a Brussels civil servant, who may speak French at the office, standard Dutch at the social club and a local variety of Flemish at home. Code switching provides an excellent window for observing the interrelationship between *microsociolinguistics* (concerned with individual behaviour) and *macrosociolinguistics* (concerned with the role of language in the society).

Variation between languages or between dialects involves differences at all linguistic levels (phonology, syntax, etc.); yet the speech differences between social classes are hypothesised by Bernstein to be restricted to the semantic level. The term he uses in this connection is *code*, different codes supposedly corresponding to different conceptions of the world as determined by the social semiotic. This distinction is important, and highlights the causal relationship claimed to hold between social organisation and code.

12.3 Class, codes and control

Bernstein's proposal is that two codes, *restricted code* and *elaborated code*, are made use of as part of ordinary social intercourse – for example, restricted code is typical in the opening phases of a cocktail party (cf. e.g. the high level of lexical predictability), while elaborated code is more likely to be used when, for instance, expressing views on politics. Knowledge of appropriate code use is supposedly an integral part of social skill, and the working class is claimed to violate middle-class conventions by extending the use of the restricted code to situations which according to middle-class values would call for the use of the elaborated code.

The main body of Bernstein's empirical research aims at establishing the lexical and syntactic correlates of the putative semantic differences between the codes, a task that can be seen as contradictory from the viewpoint that syntax is, at least to a large extent, independent from semantics. The central theme is the higher lexical and syntactic predictability of the restricted code, but it remains unclear whether 'predictability' is meant to refer to frequency alone, or whether it must be negatively related to Chomsky's notion of creativity discussed in Chapter 1 (p. 5). Other salient features of the restricted code as described by Bernstein are the use of simpler and shorter items, and its less logical and more affective nature, manifested in a lower incidence of connectives, a more frequent use of 'sympathetic' devices, and so on. Table 12.1 summarises a list of such features given in Bernstein (1959, in 1971, pp. 42–60), which still retains much of its original heuristic value in spite of some important subsequent qualifications.

Note that, as suggested earlier, restricted code must not be confused with dialect. In the set of sentences below (adapted from Trudgill, 1975, p. 93), (1) represents standard language (cf., for example, the use of *gentlemen* as against *blokes*) and restricted code (the syntax is particularly simple and does not include any subordination), (2) elaborated code and dialect, (3) standard language and elaborated code and (4) restricted code and dialect.

(1) The gentlemen were crossing the road and a car knocked them down.
(2) The blokes what was crossing the road got knocked down by a car
(3) The gentlemen who were crossing the road were knocked down by a car
(4) The blokes was crossing the road and a car knocked them down

Conflicting results emerge from much of the empirical work testing the hypothesis. In Bernstein's 1962 study (1971, pp. 76–94), the middle-class subjects used a higher proportion of subordinations, complex verbal stems, passives, adjectives (both common and uncommon ones), adverbs, conjunctions and 'egocentric' sequences (e.g. including expressions such as 'I think'), whereas the working-class subjects showed a preference for 'sociocentric' sequences (e.g. with tags such as 'you know') and for using personal pronouns (especially *you* and *they*). While similar results were obtained by Lawton (1968) in an extension of the test to the written language, an additional

Table 12.1   *Summary of Bernstein's Description of Restricted and Elaborated Codes*

	Restricted Code	Elaborated Code
Experience encoding	condensation of meaning in stock words, phrases, or sentence structures	verbal elaboration for the expression of differentiated, individualised experience
Conceptual content	confusion of the reason with the conclusion;	complex conceptual hierarchy
	use of devices of sympathetic circularity (tag questions, 'you know', etc.);	
	frequent use of idiomatic phrases;	
	frequent use of short questions and commands	
Sentence structure	use of simple, short, unfinished sentences;	use of complex sentences
	preferent use of the active voice	
Connectives (i.e. conjunctions and prepositions)	simple and repetitive; preferent use of conjunctions	frequent use of prepositions to indicate logical relationship and temporal and spatial contiguity
Qualifiers (i.e. adjectives and adverbs)	rigid and limited use	discriminative selection
Subject impersonal pronouns (*it, one*)	infrequent	frequent

individual interview showed the working-class boys to be capable of using the elaborated code. Also, in Robinson's (1965) test the two classes exhibited lexical differences in an informal letter written to a sick friend, but not in formal letters addressed to a school governor. These two sets of results indicate that the context of situation is an important variable that can only be neglected at the investigator's risk. Labov (1972c) reports that dramatic changes took place in the previously highly non-verbal behaviour of an 8-year-old when the interviewer returned accompanied by the child's best friend, bringing with him a supply of crisps, and further reducing the asymmetry of the situation by sitting on the floor and using taboo words and topics. Also, he remarks that silence can often be interpreted as an indication of a high level of communicative competence (see Chapter 2, p. 42), since in a situation of asymmetry 'anything [the child says] can literally be held against him. He has learned a number of devices to *avoid* saying anything in this situation, and he works very hard to achieve this end' (p. 185). A parallel interpretation can be given to the results of Hawkins's (1969) experiment, where two groups of children were set the tasks of telling a story based on four picture-cards and of describing three painting reproductions. The working-class children used a higher proportion of pronouns referring to the actual pictures, while the middle-class children used more elaborate noun phrases including qualifiers, intensifiers, etc. From one perspective this dearth of exophoric pronouns (i.e. pronouns referring to the non-linguistic context) in middle-class performance can be viewed as an instance of redundant and clumsy behaviour, since both the investigator and the pictures were there while the task was being carried out. These apparent contradictions have not received proper accommodation within Bernstein's framework.

For Bernstein, as for Halliday, it is the mode of socialisation that mediates the formation of the linguistic code from the social semiotic. Bernstein and Henderson (1969, in Bernstein, 1973, pp. 24–47) tested the hypothesis that the middle class places a greater importance on language in the area of personal relationships than for the transmission of practical skills, by asking mothers a hypothetical question on the difficulties that mute parents would experience in performing with the child activities related to practical skills, cognition, affection and morality. The results led to the association of middle-class families with a personal orientation, with the emphasis on the child's autonomy, and of working-class families with a positional orientation, with the child's autonomy much reduced (see p. 389 above). Cook-Gumperz (1973) administered a questionnaire under various guises to mothers and children with the purpose of collecting evidence on the mothers' speech behaviour and of gathering samples of the children's speech in various contexts. The questions bore on the areas of child preparation for infant school, the orientation of the mother to the language, and the type of language used by the mother in her explanations to the child, including aspects of social control, and the results appeared confirmatory of Bernstein and Henderson's. Both studies, however, are subject to the criticism that the inference of actual behaviour from answers given to hypothetical questions is illegitimate.

The following statement illustrates Bernstein's neutrality regarding the possible aesthetic or intellectual evaluation of the codes (1971, p. 186).

One of the difficulties of this approach is to avoid implicit value judgments about the relative worth of speech systems and the cultures which they symbolize. Let it be said immediately that a restricted code gives access to a vast potential of meanings, of delicacy, subtlety and diversity of cultural forms, to a unique aesthetic the basis of which in condensed symbols may influence the form of the imagining.

Despite these good intentions, however, the theory has often been seen as containing an implicit indictment of the restricted code and its users, and labels such as 'verbal deprivation' and 'deficit hypothesis' are not uncommon. Notoriously in the USA, and to some extent in Britain, the incidence of working-class failure in the school curriculum has been attributed to linguistic handicap, and several programmes of compensatory education have been proposed. In one, devised in America by Bereiter and Engelmann in the mid-1960s, a series of rather crude behaviouristic drills (see Chapter 2, pp. 32–3, for a discussion of behaviourism) are proposed, which treat socially disadvantaged native speakers of English as if they were strangers to the language. The authors show, moreover, a high degree of linguistic naïvety, as when they judge elliptical answers to be deficient in some way – in all likelihood, the answer *No. The pencil is not red. The pencil is blue* to the question *Is the pencil red?* would be considered boringly pedantic in everyday discourse by all social classes. More important, non-standard varieties of English do not inhibit the construction of logical arguments any more than their more prestigious counterparts, as Labov has gone to great pains to show. For instance, the use of double negatives in black English vernacular (BEV) and other substandard varieties has been repeatedly condemned as illogical, and a sentence such as *I don't know nothing* has been claimed to be synonymous with *I know something*, rather than to express the meaning of standard English (SE) *I don't know anything* in those varieties. But Labov has shown that this phenomenon is rule-governed, negative concord being *obligatory* in BEV for all indefinites within a clause. He also attacks the myth that verbal deprivation is the norm in communities outside the official culture, and he comments that in the BEV community 'we see a child bathed in verbal stimulation from morning to night' (1972c, p. 163). He moreover suggests that the supposed 'verbality' of the middle class can be more realistically viewed as mere 'verbosity' (cf. the discussion on Hawkins's experiment above) and he contrasts the interview behaviour of a 15-year-old member of a New York street gang with that of an upper-middle-class, educated black man, the former producing a tight argument in BEV on the subjects of life after death and the colour of God, while the latter conceals a rather mediocre standard of thinking with extra verbiage and the use of a few OK words such as 'science' and 'culture'.

From a different angle, Dittmar, one of Bernstein's critics, regards the issue of codes as one related to the needs of production in post-industrial societies, where the priority given to information-processing requires the handling by the worker of systems with features closer to those of the elaborated code. To conclude this discussion, while admitting to the delicate nature of the issue, we can point at the desirability of maintaining objectivity as much as possible in research. Also, the code theory does not prejudge what action, if any, must ensue from its findings and, were these to be unambiguous, proletarisation of the school would in principle be just as possible a solution as the enforcement of middle-class codes. In our opinion, while the proponents of the hypothesis will do well to pay heed to the criticisms that have been advanced relating to the methodology of their investigations, the choice of sociological and linguistic variables (the latter, for instance, have tended to concentrate on aspects of surface structure to the exclusion of more abstract levels) and the dangers of interpreting language differences as evidence for non-linguistic cognitive differences, there are aspects of the research accumulated by Bernstein and his associates which remain worthy of attention and must be dispassionately evaluated.

12.4   Variable rules

The question of the logicality of non-standard varieties and their rule-governedness is important enough to warrant closer attention here. Omission of the copula *be*, for example, has been adduced as further evidence for the non-logicality of BEV, but it also occurs in some well-established literary languages (e.g. Russian) and, further, Labov's research indicates that there is an underlying copula in BEV, and that its frequent omission in surface structure is the result of the principled operation of a deletion rule which is, moreover, intimately related to the contraction rule of SE. We shall now turn to the analysis of this phenomenon.

Labov points out that the copula is obligatory in BEV in comparative constructions, in tag questions, for emphasis and in various other cases, and he relates these apparent idiosyncrasies to the requirement, shared with *be* contraction in SE, that the form which is a candidate to undergo the reduction operation must not bear a high degree of stress. This explains the ill-formedness of (5)*b* in SE and of (5)*c* in BEV as reductions of (5)*a*.

(5) *a* John is in charge of the house during the day. Tom is at night
    b *John is in charge of the house during the day. Tom's at night
    c *John is in charge of the house during the day. Tom at night

On the other hand (6)*a* can be contracted to (6)*b* in SE and reduced to (6)*c* in BEV, since the degree of stress on *is* is negligible.

(6) *a* Tom is wild
    b Tom's wild
    c Tom wild.

So far, Labov has shown that copula deletion in BEV, like copula contraction in SE, is not erratic. This finding supports Chomsky's claim that human languages and their dialects are rule-governed, and it goes a long way towards vindicating the linguistic respectability of BEV. It has been suggested by generative grammarians, moreover, that many instances of language variation are limited to surface structure. The next step in Labov's description of the present phenomena is more innovatory, and potentially could have far-reaching repercussions for linguistic theory.

Labov observes that neither *be* contraction nor *be* deletion is a *categorical* rule, i.e. that the full form of *be* does in fact alternate with the contracted form or with zero in the relevant environments. To call these rules optional, however, would conceal the fact that they exhibit systematic variation, thus violating his *Principle of Accountability*, which he formulated (1972a, p. 94) as in (7).

(7) *Principle of Accountability*
    any variable form (a member of a set of alternative ways of 'saying the same thing') should be reported with the proportion of cases in which the form did occur in the relevant environment, compared to the total number of cases in which it might have occurred.

The introduction of statistical properties in competence rules represents a major departure from Chomsky's more abstract conception of grammar as critically separate from actual behaviour, and is related to Labov's claim that there is a higher degree of regularity in community grammar than in idiolectal grammar.

In Labov's formulation, each rule is associated with a factor Φ which quantifies its application probability – the value of Φ will be 1 in categorical rules, but in *variable rules* a factor k_o characteristically restricts the application of the rule, as expressed in (8).

(8) $\Phi = 1 - k_o$

The factor k_o is typically a function of the environment of the rule. For example, in the case of copula contraction, the rule applies semicategorically to the form *am*, and is next most likely to contract tensed forms preceded by a pronoun. Lower in the scale of likelihood are cases where none of the above conditions obtains but the tensed form is followed by a verb, and so on.

12.5 Social variables

In addition to these environmental variables, the factor k_n is associated with an *input probability* (p_o) contingent on social variables such as class, age and sex, and on register (see Section 6 below), and a *product model* which assumes mutual independence of constraints, suggests that k_o be computed according to (9).

(9) $\quad k_o = (1 - p_o)(1 - v_i)(1 - v_j) \ldots (1 - v_n)$

where each v_k refers to the probability associated with one environmental feature. This yields (10) as a formula for computing Φ.

(10) $\quad \Phi = 1 - (1 - p_o)(1 - v_i)(1 - v_j) \ldots (1 - v_n)$

A value of 1 for any of the variables in this formula will, of course, make the rule categorical since k_o will be 0 and Φ, 1. A value of 0 for any of the variables will mean that that variable has no effect on the computed value of Φ as $1 - 0 = 1$.

As an illustration of the role of *social class* in the determination of p_o, we shall mention the findings of the British sociolinguist Peter Trudgill in his investigations in the city of Norwich concerning the pronunciation of the vowels of the words *knows* and *nose*, identical in RP ([əʊ]), but not so in Norwich, where there is a tendency to pronounce the former as [ɒu], and the latter as [uː], as has already been mentioned in Chapter 11 (p. 379). Crucially, however, while the two segments showed an almost 100 per cent rate of differentiation in working-class informants, middle-class subjects often approached (though seldom consummated) merger, i.e. in their pronunciation both [ɒu] and [uː] shifted considerably in the direction of [əʊ]. Interestingly, in some stages of approximation the speakers are unable to perceive the differences they are objectively making, a fact that has important consequences for the theory of phonology, and for linguistic theory in general. First, this situation lends credence to the idea that linguistic description must be neutral between speaker and hearer. Secondly, it casts a strong shadow of doubt on the operational viability of the minimal pair test, traditionally of incalculable value for phonology (see Chapter 4, p. 97). Finally, not only the informant, but the linguist as well, may fail to perceive the articulatory differences made by the speaker, and thus it is possible that some historically recorded mergers between sounds are not such in reality, and this would explain the otherwise mysterious subsequent separate evolution of apparently formerly merged sounds.

The social stratification of phonological variables has been a well-established fact since Labov's early work, and we shall refer here to his study of the variable (r) in New York City (it is customary to enclose variable segments in brackets). Labov's subjects were the salespeople of three Manhattan department stores, selected as representatives of three different social groups on the basis of their location, their price and advertising policies, their physical layout, and the wages and working conditions of their employees. In order to overcome the *Observer's Paradox*, i.e. the fact that the investigator has to observe the people whose unobserved speech he wants to investigate, Labov carried out a series of rapid, anonymous interviews in the guise of a customer asking for directions which would require the answer *Fourth floor* – with two occurrences of the variable (r) – repeated once by the informant at the investigator's request (*Excuse me?*). As predicted, the scores for [ɹ] pronunciation were highest for the socially highest store (62 per cent), next highest for the middle store (51 per cent) and lowest for the low-class store (21 per cent).

Before the Second World War, New York City was a non-rhotic (i.e. *r*-less) area under the influence of the prestige pattern of New England, but the military upheaval brought along a shift towards the American *r*-pronouncing norm, and the stratification of (r) as a social variable. This dating is hypothesised on the basis of behavioural differences correlated with *age* – there is a sharp increase in positive attitude to the use of [ɹ] for all classes and in actual use for the upper middle class with informants under the age of 40 (see Chapter 11, p. 382), i.e. with those subjects who had not gone past the adolescent period at the time of the conflict.

The data from the New York (r) survey also showed a higher sensitivity of the lower-middle class to the variable, and this sensitivity is central to Labov's theory of language change (see Chapter 11, p. 383). For instance, while the highest status group shows a negative correlation between incidence of the prestige variant and age, as would be expected from what was said in the previous paragraph, this pattern is reversed for the second-highest status group. Also, all subjects tended to correct their output in the direction of the prestige norm as speech became more formal, but the change was substantially more marked with lower-middle-class informants. This *hypercorrection*, Labov suggests, is indicative of the greatest *linguistic insecurity* of this social group, and creates a contrast with the uppermost class, safely anchored in its superior socioeconomic status, and with the lower class, who do not regard change in linguistic behaviour as a means of social promotion. A recent study on code switching in a Northern Irish village also shows a positive correlation between linguistic behaviour, as related to variable rules, and social ambition, measured in terms of the informant's keenness to 'get on in the world'.

Further, the study of sociolinguistic variables has given quantitative empirical confirmation to the common impressionistic observation that the speech of women is more 'refined' than that of men, as manifested by their lower usage of taboo words and of other *stigmatised* forms. Thus in Trudgill's Norwich study women used higher percentages of the prestige variant [ŋ] for the variable (ng) (as in *going*), and lower-middle-class females also showed the greatest shift away from the local pronunciation [n], thereby confirming Labov's findings regarding the highest index of linguistic insecurity for the second-highest status group. Interestingly, however, in the case of men it was the third-ranked status group (the upper-working class) who showed greatest hypercorrection.

Confirmation of the importance of *sex* as a sociolinguistic variable comes from the results of *subjective reaction tests*, which also add further evidence for the existence of important differences between the systems of social stratification in the USA and in Britain. In his survey of New York's Lower East Side, Labov asked the subjects to rate several speakers recorded on tape along a scale of occupational suitability, and he then asked them to indicate which of four alternative pronunciations of the given variables was closest to their own usage. His findings can perhaps be related to Sapir's experiences with native Amerindians (see Chapter 4, p. 100), in that the subject's perception appears closer to his intention than to the actual physical sound he produces, with informants from the lower-middle class showing greatest sensitivity to the presence of stigmatised variants in the speech of others, while consistently over-reporting their own performance in the direction of the prestige norm. Similar behaviour was exhibited by women when reporting on the variable (ju) (as in *Hugh*) in Trudgill's Norwich study, but the male speakers tended to under-report their use of the standard variant [ju] in the direction of the local pronunciation [ʉ], a fact that suggests that their favoured target is not the standard prestige norm, but rather the pattern of working-class speech, which can therefore be said to possess *covert prestige*. This type of behaviour can speculatively be related to the lack of embourgeoisement of the British working class and its relatively greater maintenance of cultural standards of its own, as well as to the existence of connotations of masculinity in working-class speech, possibly associated with the stereotype of toughness and roughness characterising working-class life. There is, however, some interesting evidence against a greater attribution of masculinity to non-standard speech, from the subjective reactions of a heterogeneous sample to female-spoken RP and Lancashire speech, with RP speakers paradoxically being rated high both for traits associated with femininity *and* for traits that are best related to masculinity, possibly because of an association between RP and social power (a masculine trait), and because of the greater availability of expensive fineries (a feminine trait) which accompanies social power. The use of such attitude tests is an important tool of research, and it forms part of the study of the *social psychology of language*.

Trudgill's findings on the variable (o) (as in *box*) provide an elegant illustration of the interaction between the various factors represented by social class, age, sex, stigma, hypercorrection and covert prestige, and how the systematic study of linguistic variants in *apparent time* (as shown by their social stratification) can shed light on language changes that take place over *real time*. The greater linguistic insecurity of women would lead us to expect that the occurrence of the local variant [ɑ] would be lower among working-class females than among working-class males, but the data indicate just the opposite. Middle-class females, on the other hand, do show a greater incidence of the prestige RP variant [ɒ] than males, probably as a result of conscious imitation of the standard (what Labov calls *change from above*, i.e. from above the level of awareness), to which they have easy access. Moreover, the use of [ɑ] in working-class females decreases with age. All these strange facts can be brought to order when account is taken of the geographical distribution of the variants [ɑ] and [ɒ], the former restricted to the city of Norwich, and the latter being the prevalent form in the surrounding area of Norfolk, from which it is rapidly being unconsciously adopted by working-class men (thus representing *change from below*). The result is that the traditional Norwich form [ɑ] is becoming more and more restricted to older working-class women, for whom the Norfolk forms are relatively inaccessible – the identity between the newly introduced male working-class [ɒ] and the prestigious RP [ɒ] is, of course, purely coincidental.

There is an additional social variable which has recently been receiving some attention, and for which it may be possible to claim a greater objective reality than for social class. A recent study by Lesley Milroy of three working-class communities in Belfast is focused on the construct *social network*, a basic unit of interaction constituted by a 'focus' (the subject being studied) and a number of 'points' (the individuals with whom the focus interacts), and based on the presence of transactions (usually exchanges). Networks have a high or a low 'density', depending on whether there is mutual interaction between the points or not, and network ties are 'uniplex' or 'multiplex', i.e. single-stranded or multi-stranded (e.g. when the relations between the focus and the points are simultaneously based on kinship, work, leisure, etc.).

Milroy's hypothesis is that there exists a significant correlation between scores in language variables and scores in the network strength-scale, which quantifies multiplexity and density, and which in the present study was set up on the basis of membership of a territorially based and high-density cluster (a 'cluster' is a network zone with relatively high density), the possession of substantial kinship ties within the neighbourhood, the sharing of the workplace with at least two others of the same sex from the area, and the spending of leisure-time with workmates. It must be noted here that, although the linguistic importance of the peer-group is well known, at least since Labov's Harlem study, in which members were divided up into core members, secondary members, peripheral members and entirely marginal individuals or 'lames', Milroy's quantitative approach also permits the inclusion of extra-group subjects and the individual analysis of each speaker.

All eight phonological variables supported the hypothesis, thus confirming the importance of social network as a social variable. As an illustration, we shall mention the case of Paula and Hannah, two middle-aged women from the same area with very similar socioeconomic circumstances (they are both unskilled workers and so are their husbands). Paula's network score was 2 out of 5, and Hannah's 0, and this small difference was reflected in their linguistic behaviour, with Paula showing a consistent closer approximation to the norms of the vernacular.

Like Milroy, Jenny Cheshire worked out an index of adherence to the vernacular culture in her study of three peer-groups of largely 11–15-year-old boys and girls in two adventure playgrounds in Reading. The linguistic variable was the non-standard use of the suffix -s in present tense verb forms other than the third person singular, which is disfavoured by the presence of a following complement marked for subject and for tense (e.g. *I reckon they should pull our troops out*), and favoured in verbs with a special vernacular meaning (e.g. *we fucking chins them with bottles*, where 'chin' has the meaning 'hit on the chin'). The index of adherence for boys was worked out on the basis of the boy's status in the group, his degree of 'toughness' and his degree of job ambition. Predictably, there was a positive correlation between higher index scores and higher frequency of non-standard -s forms. Interestingly, in the case of girls it was found that their overall lower degree of integration to the vernacular culture (otherwise quite difficult to quantify) did not necessarily result in a decrease in the rate of non-standard forms, although there was indeed a rather sharp decrease when the recordings were made in the more formal school setting, a fact which takes us back to the earlier general discussion on the influence of the context of situation on language behaviour.

12.6 Register

In Chapter 10 (p. 328) we used the label *register* in connection with Motherese, and in the previous section we mentioned the existence of hypercorrection in the linguistic behaviour of the social group with aspirations of upward mobility (the lower-middle class in the USA and the upper-working class in Britain). When social class variation is plotted on a graph against degree of speech formality, hypercorrection appears as significant increase in the steepness of the line relating the scores in the less formal to those in more formal styles of speech, and on occasions such a line crosses over the one representing the scores of the next-highest statusful social group. Figure 12.2 shows a typical, if

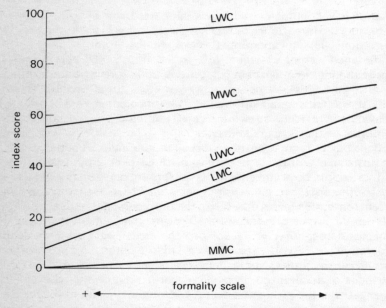

Figure 12.2   *Hypothetical example of the distribution of a linguistic variable by social class (LWC = lower-working class; MWC = middle-working class; UWC = upper-working class; LMC = lower-middle class; MMC = middle-middle class). Note the sharper gradient of the lines corresponding to the UWC and LMC.*

somewhat stylised, pattern of social stratification (NB a higher score corresponds to an overall broader local pronunciation). In the light of this it is little wonder that the isolation of contextual styles has been an important concern for sociolinguists.

   In the semi-formal context of the interview it is, of course, easier to elicit forms of speech closer to the formal than to the casual end of the continuum, but different degrees of formality must be distinguished. First, there is the *careful speech* the respondent will tend to use when answering interview questions (the Norwich questionnaire, for instance, included questions on the local background of the informant, on a few Norwich words, on Norwich itself, and on subjective attitudes to the speech of others). Next comes the *reading style* – the subject is usually requested to read out a passage including the relevant variables, possibly dealing with everyday topics and written in an informal style to induce a greater degree of naturalness in the subject, who can also be advised to read it as if, for instance, spoken by a young man. Still more formal is the style elicited by reading out a *word list* including the variables, or by the recitation of a list of items known by heart by the respondent, such as the days of the week or the list of cardinal numbers. The greatest amount of conscious attention, and thus formality, is expected from the reading of *minimal pairs*, which typically cause the greatest shift towards the standard prestige norm.

The safest way of obtaining informal casual speech is, of course, outside the interview situation, by means of such techniques as rapid and anonymous exchanges with individuals of fixed 'social address' (e.g. salespeople, as in Labov's earlier-mentioned (r) study, policemen, taxi drivers, beggars, etc.), candid observation of speech in open situations (e.g. trials or political debates) or of large numbers of people in public places such as buses, and collection of data from the media, particularly from free conversations or debates. Labov further proposes the use of direct interviews at the scenes of disasters, where the strong emotional loading interferes with the conscious monitoring of speech. Attention shift can also be experimentally induced. One method, for instance, sets the subject the task of filling in (dummy) blanks to distract attention away from the actual variables embedded in the sentences. Another technique consists in questioning the informant about the position of his tongue while he pronounces the word with the relevant variable, since attention is then directed to the tongue rather than the variable. A particularly simple test involves the repetition of a sentence or word by the subject, who has been found to reinterpret the stimulus in agreement with his own vernacular (speakers of BEV, for example, typically applied negative concord). More sophisticated techniques include the removal of auditory feedback by feeding white noise through earphones, or of visual cues from the experimenter by having the subject turn his back to him.

The evidence available from the existing sociolinguistic research indicates that it is possible to obtain approximations to casual speech in an interview, and Labov uses the term *spontaneous speech* to differentiate it from the casual speech which occurs in genuinely informal contexts. Spontaneous speech is likely before the interview begins, with the subject interacting with other household members, and as a result of interruptions by a third person (particularly effective in the case of telephone calls) during the course of the interview itself. But also as a part of the interview the subject may indulge in long, rambling diversions, to be encouraged by the interviewer, who can also use questions leading to the production by the subject of children's rhymes and the like, which usually elicit a markedly casual, pre-adolescent type of speech. Informal speech also emerges with an interview question on a situation where the informant may have found himself in serious danger of being killed, the idea being that, as in the case of the disaster mentioned earlier, emotion will take over and attention will get distracted (in a more optimistic vein, Trudgill substituted a request for a humorous situation, since, as he phlegmatically remarks, the lives of Norwich people appear to be more uneventful than those of New Yorkers). Finally, when the interview is over the experimenter can continue chatting with the subject at an informal level, behaving as if he were a normal employee who has just finished his job and is enjoying a few moments of relaxation. Naturally, an even smaller degree of influence of the Observer's Paradox occurs when the test is carried out in a setting of group interaction (natural or experimental), with the investigator as a participant observer, and in her Belfast study Milroy approached the communities as 'a friend of a friend' (technically, a second-order network contact, i.e. a contact connected to the points immediately linked to the focus), exchanging various services (e.g. car lifts) in return for being allowed access to the group's speech.

It can readily be seen from the foregoing discussion that the one crucial factor determining style is the amount of attention given to his speech by the subject, and Labov has elaborated a list of *channel cues* indicative of attention shift. They relate to modulations of the production mechanism affecting the whole of speech, and include change in tempo, pitch range, volume of breathing, or rate of breathing. Very important is (frequently nervous) laughter, particularly common while recounting the danger-of-death situation, and which relates to rate of breathing, the greater use of air making it necessary for the speaker to take a sudden breath at the next pause, and this can be detected in the recording given the appropriate techniques. In contrast to the social variables mentioned in the previous section, the quantification of register is ostensibly difficult, but Labov suggests that it might ultimately be possible to correlate degree of attention to physical variables such as the noise level in the experimental technique mentioned earlier, or, even more strikingly, to the size of pupil dilation while speaking.

12.7 Community grammars

Speech variations correlated with register or with social factors typically happen along a continuum from the broad vernacular to the prestige norm. In some communities, however, the absence of a monolithic prestige norm allows the speakers a range of choices as they shift away from the vernacular when formality of style increases, and this is indeed the case in the three Belfast communities studied by Milroy, which showed little sign of adherence to a middle-class norm. In all cases, however, both linguistic behaviour and performance in attitude tests reveal the existence of a shared stock of unconscious knowledge concerning the social value of linguistic variables, and on this basis we can define a *speech-community* as the set of speakers who participate in the same set of linguistic norms.

A broader concept of speech-community is advanced by John Gumperz to include knowledge of non-linguistic communicative behaviour, best related to Hymes's idea of communicative competence (see Chapter 2, p. 42), and concerning such things as the role and meaning of silence, the norms governing the physical distance between the interlocutors (possibly related to wider territorial constraints), the interpretation of humour, etc. The basic unit within this approach is what could be called the *speech-event*, which can be regarded as a sociolinguistic version of the speech-act (see Chapter 7, p. 215), and communities have been found to make use of ritualised speech-acts (e.g. insults) incomprehensible to the outsider (for instance, Labov mentions the expression *Your mother is a duck* used as a ritual insult in a Harlem adolescent peer-group). These areas inevitably take us away from language as a subject of study in itself, and into what has been called the *ethnography of speaking*.

In his Norwich study, Trudgill goes further than postulating a shared set of sociolinguistic norms for the speech-community, and claims that a common grammar, or *diasystem*, must be hypothesised as well. On the one hand, he shows that it is possible to derive the phonetic forms subject to sociolinguistic variation from a common set of underlying phonological forms (see Chapter 8, Section 4). There is also some measure of empirical evidence for the diasystem. Not only are the different varieties mutually intelligible, but members of the Norwich speech-community possess the active skill of imitating the whole repertoire of accents (e.g. for humorous effect) in a way not possible for non-local pronunciations. Also, and very importantly, there appears to be such a thing as a 'Norwich voice', described by Trudgill in terms of the construct *articulatory setting*, which refers to a set of particular muscular adjustments in the larynx or in the vocal tract which globally influence phonetic dimensions such as phonation, pitch, loudness, displacement of organs, tenseness and nasalisation. Thus the harsh, metallic impression typical of a Norwich voice can be related to a tendency towards creaky voice (see Chapter 3, p. 70), high pitch-range, loudness, upward displacement of the larynx, fronting and lowering of the tongue's centre of gravity, muscular tension and nasalisation, which can all be viewed as different manifestations of one central controlling factor, namely, a tendency towards high muscular tension. Interestingly, the incorporation of articulatory setting in the formalisation of the diasystem may bring along a substantial simplification in the composition of individual rules, many aspects of which can be interpreted as individualisations of the overall articulatory setting. In the present context, moreover, the capacity shown by Norwich speakers for regulating the articulatory setting in accordance with specifically local norms provides additional empirical evidence for the reality of the speech-community.

Different from Trudgill's diasystem is Charles Bailey's concept of *panlectal grammar*, in that it includes varieties of the language for which there is no direct evidence that they belong in the competence grammar of any one speaker. Bailey's approach differs from Chomsky's in some important ways. First, it involves a refocusing of language theory on the social dimension, i.e. an abandonment of Chomsky's notion of competence and a return to Saussure's idea of *langue*, where the locus of the language is placed in the speech-community (more broadly redefined along the lines just suggested) rather than in the individual speaker. Also, Bailey proposes that Chomsky's programmatic concern with completely homogeneous speech-communities be replaced by the hypothesis that the child is continually revising his internalised grammar, in an effort to come to grips with the wide range of varieties which he inevitably comes across. Note that, as well as extending the speaker's competence into domains unrelated to performance, this proposal entails the integration of synchronic linguistics with historical linguistics and dialectology, thus blurring Saussure's dichotomy synchrony-diachrony within a pan-chronic approach.

The formalisation of panlectal grammars has been carried out in the framework of the implicational model originally proposed by David DeCamp, the basic idea of which is that some code switches take implicational precedence over others. The psychological claims implicit in this model show important differences from those in Labov's, since, rather than involving the speaker in frequency-monitoring, it endows him with a set of discrete choices which control a range of implications. Derek Bickerton, for instance, has questioned the possibility of the human mind being able to process percentage variability, especially in the absence of group members (sociolinguistic variability is still expected in non-social speech), but Cedergren and D. Sankoff have pointed out the existence of a large body of literature documenting probabilistic aspects of mental processes.

The implicational model is particularly well suited to the description of linguistic variation in communities such as those in the Caribbean where an official European language coexists with different degrees of a local variety related to it. The description typically matches actual linguistic behaviour with sets of isolects, where an *isolect* is defined as any set of rules in the panlectal grammar differing from other adjacent sets of rules by only one rule or, possibly, by the alternation of two rules only. The use of implicational scales, moreover, permits the maintenance of Chomsky's discrete approach to rule formalisation, since analysis of the continuum is possible through the postulation of different isolects, each containing discrete rules only (Labov's model, of course, characteristically involves the use of non-discrete rules).

The model has been applied by Bickerton to the analysis of the distribution of the complementisers *tu* and *fu* (both equivalent to SE *to*) in a basilectal area of Guyana (the term *basilect* refers to the broadest type of local speech, while *acrolect* describes the varieties close to the standard language; intermediate areas in the continuum are referred to as *mesolect*). Table 12.2 gives the implicational scale for

Table 12.2 *Matrix containing the Seven Possible Isolects for the Three Environments Specified, as Corresponds to a Wave Model, where the Categorical Spread of a Feature is preceded by a Period of Inherent Variation*

	Inceptive Verbs	Psychological Verbs	Other Verbs
1	F (=*fu*)	F	F
2	T (=*tu*)/F	F	F
3	T	F	F
4	T	T/F	F
5	T	T	F
6	T	T	T/F
7	T	T	T

the isolectal distribution of *tu* and *fu* on the assumption of three different deep structures depending on whether the dominant position is occupied by an inceptive verb (e.g. *begin*), a psychological verb (e.g. *want*), or some other type of verb that can be followed by a *tu*/*fu* complementiser (e.g. *come*). The grid predicts that no T will occur to the right of F, and the prediction is borne out well by the data – only two of the twenty-eight speakers interviewed in the small 'Hindu' village of Bushlot violated the putative constraint. Because the focus of implicational scales is on the individual's rather than the group's behaviour, it is possible to attempt to explain these idiosyncrasies, if admittedly only in a *post hoc* manner. One of the informants was a dynamic well-travelled character, simultaneously an enthusiastic supporter of traditional mores, while the other was an old, poor woman originating from an 'African' village, where mesolectal features are more dominant than among rural 'Hindus', who remain closer to the basilect. Note finally that, as well as allowing for individual variation, the implicational approach permits us to do away with the fixed social variables characteristic of Labov's model, thus allowing for a greater degree of cross-fertilisation between linguistics and sociology.

12.8   Pidgins and creoles

The linguistic situation in Guyana exemplifies well the type of linguistic variation particularly common in the Caribbean and in other areas where there has been intense social intercourse between members of drastically different cultures. The origins of such present-day language continua must be sought in history, usually involving large, and often forcible, movements of population of various racial and linguistic origins. Cases of borrowing such as those mentioned in Chapter 11 (p. 368) can be seen as examples of language hybridisation, typically favoured by contact situations, although it can be prevented by barriers such as a negative attitude to the other language or social group, or the existence of radical structural differences or an excessive semantico-semiotic contrast between the two languages. Language mixtures are abundant throughout history and, in a broad sense, they are part and parcel of all speech-events for, as the creolist Robert Le Page suggests, they stem from the interaction between the individual participants and the context – typically, individuals have a strong tendency to modify their speech to approximate that of the groups with which they wish to identify, in such a way that a speech-act can be regarded as a projection of the individual's identity.

An interesting example of language mixture is provided by the jargon formerly used by Italian immigrants in Argentina ('cocoliche'), characterised in its first stage by the importation of Italianised Spanish lexicon, then by the introduction of phonetic modifications in the direction of the local Spanish, and finally by the occurrence of more important morphosyntactic changes. Although as a system cocoliche was highly predictable (cf. *langue*), the continuous incidence of new arrivals and the progressive integration of the older ones into the local variety of Spanish made it extremely unstable at the individual level (cf. *competence*). Crucially, however, if the circumstances are different, language mixtures may undergo a substantial degree of stabilisation, particularly when the mixture is not based on the language of any of its users and when these belong to more than two language groups.

In such cases, a *pidgin* is likely to arise. Pidgins are drastically simplified systems used for purposes of trade (the word 'pidgin' probably
represents the Chinese pronunciation of 'business') and basic social
exchange in situations of linguistic heterogeneity. Among their features are the total absence of the copula *be*, a dramatic reduction in
morphological forms, an avoidance of redundancy at all levels, the use
of repetitive devices with a grammatical function, the frequent use of
paraphrases to replace single lexical items, the poverty of their vocabulary, etc. As has been pointed out (Chapter 10, Section 8), there
are strong parallels between pidgins, on the one hand, and simplified
registers (such as those used in all languages to talk to babies, foreign-
ers, deaf people, and so on) and the initial stages of child language, on
the other. Two well-known theories of the origins of pidgins derive
from this observation. For Bloomfield, pidgins originate from the
baby-like talk employed by masters with their (ordinarily black) servants, possibly a contemptuous imitation of the speech used by the
servants themselves, while for Robert A. Hall, Jr, they arose by spontaneous generation as a result of the need for communication. Interestingly, Ferguson has remarked that such simplified forms of speech are
universal in their basic shape, although containing some language-
specific characteristics, a situation which might point in the direction of
innateness.

Pidgins are auxiliary linguistic codes connected to a very specific
set of circumstances, and their eventual death is inevitable unless
they become the native language of the young generation through
creolisation. It may be rewarding to look at pidginisation as a case of
second language learning where there is a normal input (the languages
of the various groups involved in the situation) and a restricted output
(the pidgin), while in creolisation the input is restricted (the pidgin)
and the output normal – creoles are in effect considered normal
languages by most scholars, and on the way from pidgin to creole there
is characteristically a large increase in both vocabulary and number of
grammatical devices. Interestingly, this creation has been seen as
evidence for the existence of an innate language faculty (see Chapter 2,
p. 47 ff.), supplementing the deficiencies of the pidgin input, but there
has also been some suggestion that, at least in their initial stages,
creoles may indeed be defective languages which create a handicap
situation for their speakers.

There are at present over 6 million creole speakers in the world, with
the largest concentration in the Caribbean, but with some important
nuclei in West Africa and South-East Asia. As well as the creoles
related to European languages (of which French-based creoles are the
largest numerically, with some 4½ million speakers), there are others
connected to Arabic, Swahili and other African languages. Also worth
mentioning are Police (or Hiri) Motu in Papua-New Guinea, which is a

pidginised form of Hanuabada Motu (one of the 750 languages of the island), and Chinook Jargon, an Amerindian pidgin formerly widespread throughout the Pacific West Coast.

Some remarkable similarities between various creoles contrast with this apparent diversity. On the one hand, French creoles are mutually intelligible from places as far apart as Mauritius (in the Indian Ocean), Haiti, Martinique and other Caribbean islands, and Louisiana in the USA. Also, and maybe even more surprisingly, some remarkable similarities (both lexical and structural) exist across most of the European-based creoles, even though the main body of their lexicons is related to languages as diverse as English, French and Dutch. To answer the challenge posed by this fact, and contrasting with Bloomfield's and Hall's polygenetic theories, Keith Whinnom has advanced a monogenetic hypothesis according to which all such creoles are genetically related, having originated from å Portuguese pidgin spread since the sixteenth century throughout West Africa and the Far East, perhaps itself the descendant of the old medieval Lingua Franca or Sabir associated with Mediterranean trade and the crusades. The key aspect of the evolution process would be *relexification*, whereby the pidgin's lexicon (which, it must be remembered, is particularly restricted) is renovated in the direction of the lexicon of the dominant language, while the basic structure is left unaffected. Attractive as it is, there are some important difficulties with this theory, since, on the one hand, it still fails to account for the similarities which also exist with other pidgins and creoles unrelatable to such a hypothetical Portuguese ancestor and, on the other, it makes nonsense of the attested policy of separating slaves of the same linguistic group to prevent communication. An alternative theory purports to explain the similarities on the basis of the common linguistic background of the slaves, mostly of West African stock, the differences being attributed to the existence of different degrees of acculturation, related to the intensity of the contact with Europeans and to differences in the choice of group for target identification (the metropolis, the original country of the slaves, or the local creole society).

The situation where the official language is the same as the language which constitutes the base vocabulary of the creole and where a formerly rigid social stratification has broken down brings about what DeCamp has termed the *postcreole continuum*, and this is the situation existing in Guyana which has been examined earlier. The usual outcome is the merger of the creole with the standard, leaving behind a trail of dialectal variation indistinguishable from that traditionally studied within the framework of nineteenth-century historical linguistics (see Chapter 11, p. 380), and possibly associated with social variables of the kind described by Labov. When the two aforementioned circumstances are absent, the creole can either be relegated to the lower 'patois' status or be elevated to the category of official language, thus undergoing standardisation and use extension (cf., for example, Bahasa Indonesia and New Guinea Pidgin or Tok Pisin, currently involved in a series of very interesting linguistic and sociopolitical problems).

12.9 Conclusion

Pidgins and creoles occupy a particularly privileged position in linguistic research, because of their relevance to areas as diverse as language planning, social variation, language history, language acquisition, both by adults and by children, and so on. They therefore constitute an appropriate topic to bring this book to a close. Before doing so, however, it will be well to take quick stock of the current state of linguistics.

Arguably, Chomsky's revolution in the 1950s irreversibly changed the tone of linguistic research and a very considerable, at times spectacular, body of work has since been accumulated. One of Chomsky's great insights was, of course, to redirect the object of inquiry of the discipline on to the human mind, and, as pointed out in Chapter 2 (p. 38), he advocated a central role for linguistic intuitions as data. But this introspectionism is not without problems, as the history of psychology bears witness (see Chapter 2, p. 33, and resort to the investigator's dialect has often been the final line of defence, if a rather unproductive one since it offers no solution to the endless disputes that have arisen over the grammatical status of various data. Direct elicitation with other subjects does not circumvent the introspection problem, and it brings in the risk of producing results under the influence of the experimenter's expectations, empirically attested in other areas of behavioural research. Chomsky himself has never suggested that intuitions be given the final word, but his caution has frequently gone unheeded in the course of actual linguistic practice. The problematic nature of such a stand is highlighted by the fact that whatever empirical evidence there is confirms the tendency for the intuitions of linguists to be at variance with those of the bulk of the population. It is the opinion of many that linguistics cannot go on building on such shaky ground.

The answer is not to throw away the baby with the bathwater and revert to pre-Chomskyan linguistics, but rather to take advantage of the wide range of discoveries which have taken place since Chomsky started writing about a quarter of a century ago. For instance, Labov's findings strongly indicate that neglect of the social aspects of language can have unfortunate consequences. Besides the 'experimenter effect' mentioned in the previous paragraph, the subject frequently falls victim to 'linguistic dishonesty' (i.e. attributing to himself a higher rate of use of prestige variants than is objectively the case), itself the result of subtle, but none the less real, social forces, which must therefore be reckoned with by the researcher. All this points in the direction of there being advantages in community as against individual grammars, and to the possibility of systematically exploiting what Labov called the 'Saussurean Paradox' (the individual side of language, *parole*, can only be studied in the context of social speech, while its social aspect, *langue*, is best analysed through the observation of particular individuals). Labov's imaginative contributions in the area of methodology of empirical research are invaluable, and as a final illustration we shall report on an experiment designed to test the possible equivalence of the English *be* and *get* passives.

Sentences like (10) and (11) have sometimes been considered synonymous, although the implication of agency on the part of the subject in (10) has occasionally been noticed.

(10) He got arrested to prove a point
(11) He was arrested to prove a point

There is of course, a clear stylistic differentiation between these two sentences, and the interesting question is whether the more frequent use of (10) in colloquial speech reflects a semantic tendency towards subject-agency in this register.

Labov set up an experiment to test the validity of this hypothesis, by asking members of the public to 'help with a traffic survey', with the interviewer recounting the supposedly real story of a man who came to a pedestrian crossing while the 'no crossing' sign was on and a policeman was standing in the vicinity; no cars were coming, and the man crossed the street, and he got arrested. The underlined phrase was varied for different tests in the experiment into got arrested to test the law, was arrested and was arrested to test the law. The subject was asked the question 'Do you think that was the right thing to do?' and, Labov suggests, one would expect him to interpret 'that' as referring to the arrest in the straight passive, and to crossing the street if the grammatical subject 'he' is taken as the agent. Note that the informant is quite unaware of the real object of the test (in fact he thinks it has to do with the ordering of traffic!), and thus there is no appeal to linguistic introspection and no interference from the experimenter's effect. Interestingly, the prediction was only borne out when the purpose clause 'to test the law' was present; otherwise, the use of *get* and *be* in passives appeared to function exclusively as a social variable. Contributions like this, added to those of psycholinguistics, language acquisition, comparative linguistics, animal communication and other areas of language study, provide us with perspectives which complement the findings of theoretical linguistics. Many linguists are becoming conscious of the need to take account of such perspectives, and this growing awareness cannot but contain the promise of an optimistic and exciting future for linguistics.

Exercises: Chapter 12

1 Make a list of activities involving the use of language in which you ordinarily engage (e.g. conversations with your friends and family, participation in an academic seminar, shopping at the local grocer's, party-going), and try to elucidate which may be said to call for a restricted code and which for an elaborated code. Justify your decisions on the basis of the general conversational structure of each of the situations.

2 In the list below, indicate the sentences that allow for copula contraction, and check whether your choices correlate with a lower degree of stress on the copula when it remains uncontracted in those sentences.

(*a*) he is out shopping; (*b*) you are not seen; (*c*) there she is; (*d*) she is going to try hard next time; (*e*) where is it?; (*f*) you are, I fear; (*g*) she is here, I fear; (*h*) we are in business; (*i*) who is it for?; (*j*) she is there; (*k*) how clever she is!; (*l*) you are clever, though.

3 Conduct two informal tests on attitudes and stereotypes, one related to languages and dialects, and one to their speakers. Ask a small sample of people to give a rating along the corresponding scale A and B respectively. In the sample you may wish to monitor variables such as age, sex, and, say, occupation, and to advance some reasons for any differences you may find in response patterning.

Scale A

	very	fairly	fairly	very	
lazy					precise
unpleasant					pleasant
ugly					pretty
weak					strong
rough					smooth
slow					fast
dull					lively
arrogant					modest
tense					relaxed
uneducated					educated

For languages and dialects (choose languages and/or dialects with which the informants are reasonably familiar, either through direct experience or through, for example, television).

Scale B

	very	fairly	fairly	very	
intelligent					stupid
friendly					unfriendly
honest					dishonest
responsible					irresponsible
determined					timid
interesting					boring
well-bred					uncouth
co-operative					unco-operative
trustworthy					untrustworthy
active					passive

For speakers (ideally, you ought to record a friend on tape saying the same thing in different accents; if you cannot get hold of a reasonable imitator, try at least to find voices which are similar in pitch, loudness, etc.).

4   In informal conversational situations it is possible to omit the deleted parts of the following sentences. Work out the rule(s) which govern such deletions.

(*a*) ~~you are~~ going home, aren't you?; (*b*) ~~are you~~ coming for coffee?; (*c*) ~~you have~~ been out running again, haven't you?; (*d*) ~~you~~ haven't been moaning again, have you?; (*e*) ~~have you~~ been with Mary recently?; (*f*) ~~she~~ wants more coffee, does she?; (*g*) ~~he is~~ knocking on the door, isn't he?; (*h*) ~~did~~ she come yesterday?; (*i*) ~~have you~~ collected your mail already?; (*j*) ~~she has~~ recovered from her illness, hasn't she?

5   Cross-classify each of the transcripts below with regard to code (restricted, elaborated), dialect (standard, non-standard) and style (formal, casual). What additional information on the transcripts would increase confidence in your classifications?

(*a*) He going fishing and he catching a fish and it . . . he got hold of the . . . that and pulled him in the water and then they got in a boat and saving him.
(*b*) Yes well he's not the sort of person who cares but I expect after these people who've murdered somebody they're in a state of madness and they don't know what they're doing you know.
(*c*) Why? I'll tell you why. 'Cause, you see, doesn' nobody really know that it's a God, y'know, 'cause I mean I have seen black gods, pink gods, white gods, all colour gods, and don't nobody know it's really a God. An' when they be sayin' if you good, you goin' to heaven, tha's bullshit, 'cause you ain't goin' to no heaven, 'cause it ain't no heaven for you to go to.

(*d*) Well to teach you things so that when you grow up you you'll be able to have a fairly good job according to your brain and be able to get on in life and if you didn't have schooling then well the world would be a dead loss, people wouldn't know much and it just be an ignorant place.

(*e*) Every hafpenny she had had gone . . . paying for storage of furniture and she had dogs and . . . all er so I just let her live here, like, but she used to have a catering there as well, like Mrs Crighton. When I come home I'd have a three course dinner, and I couldn't leave a handkerchief down it was washed and ironed. I was made up because I didn't have to do nothing to help her.

(*f*) Bit of advantage hanging them, isn't it . . . sort of person who's lost their well say a person's husband what's murdered well he's after about 20 years and he's free again well he'll, might start again. You'd want to see him hanged, wouldn't you and out of the way.

(*g*) I have personally never had a dream come true. I've never dreamt that somebody was dying and they actually died, (mhm) or that I was going to have ten dollars the next day and somehow I got ten dollars in my pocket. (Mhm). I don't particularly believe in that, I don't think it's true. I do feel, though, that there is such thing as – ah – witchcraft.

(*h*) So er the purpose of education is when you grow up suppose you get a better job than you would if you didn't learn. And you get more money and it helps you in more ways than one.

6   Ask a small sample of people differing in age, sex, occupation and/or geographical origin to recount the events taking place in a short cartoon story (e.g. Charlie Brown). Choose some of the parameters put forward by Bernstein as characteristically differentiating speech codes (e.g. use of subordination, frequency of qualification, etc.) and for each of them quantify the results of your survey in terms of the social variables. Construct a graph for each speech parameter by plotting social variables against speech parameter scores. Advance some explanations for any patterns that emerge.

7   Translate the two equivalent creole passages below into standard English. Point out some of the differences between the mesolectal passage (*a*) and the basilectal passage (*b*), and advance possible explanations for them.

(*a*) Wans opan a taim die woz a jengklman huu had wan uondli daata. Har niem woz Pini. Shi woz a gie an dandi gorl. She didn laik tu taak tu eni an eni man. Shi laik a gie fain man to taak tu. Shi staat to taak tu a man. θingkin ðat it woz soch a wandaful man hantil aattaword shi gat kalops bai taakin to di man, and aafta taakin tu di man, di man slipt har. Shi muon an krai aal die antil aaftaword, shi get in toch wit anada man huu shi fiil dat dat woz muor wandaful dan di fors wan. Bot luo, aafta shi gat mari, insted it woz a man, it woz a bul-kou. (NB kalops = 'pregnant'.)

(*b*) Wantaim, wan man en ha wan gyal-pikni nomo. Im en niem Pini. Im ena wan priti gyal fi-truu. Im neba laik fi taak tu eni an eni man. Im laik a nais buosi man fi taak tu. Im taat taak tu wan man, tingk se a soch a wandaful man; Bot im get kalops aafta im taak tu di man. An aafta im taak tu di man, di man slip im. Im muon an krai aal die so tel aaftawod im get iin wid wan neda man we im tingk se im muor wandaful dan di fors wan. Bot luo, afta im marid, steda man, a bulkou im marid.

8   Many of the world's languages possess grammaticalised forms of address along the formal–informal scale similar to Old English *you –thou*, but Modern Standard English has lost all such overt morphological differences. Not surprisingly, however, very subtle distinctions persist through resources such as the use of various vocative forms – professional title followed by surname (*Dr Peachey*), non-professional title followed by surname (*Mrs Senior*), first name (*Thaddeus*), nickname (*Taddy*), surname (*Smith*), family title followed by first name (*Uncle Sam*), *love* or *dear*, *sir* or *madam*, *governor* or *mate* or *squire*, etc. Holding the situation and/or the social status constant, construct hypothetical implicational scales for various sets of forms. Check the resulting 'isolectal' series with 'idiolectal' data for which you have some empirical evidence, and advance some explanations for any distributional gaps that may emerge.

9   It is an open question whether there is significant social variation in the distribution of at least some of the semantic features of English. For instance, in a sentence like *All inhabitants don't know English*, the quantifier *all* may or may not attract the negation *not*, and the sentence can therefore be interpreted as synonymous with *None of the inhabitants know English* or with *Not all the inhabitants know English*. In order to test this issue, choose a small sample of people differing with respect to such variables as age, sex, occupation, or geographical origin, and ask them whether each of the ten sentences below is true or false of (i) France, (ii) a remote village in China.

(*a*) all inhabitants don't know English; (*b*) all people are not black; (*c*) all people don't know Mandarin; (*d*) all people don't own a car; (*e*) all people aren't Socialist; (*f*) all people don't use chopsticks; (*g*) all people don't eat rice; (*h*) all people can't sing the Internationale; (*i*) all people haven't been to Peking; (*j*) all people haven't blond hair.

Comment on your results with the aid of the theoretical constructs introduced in this chapter (e.g. frequency-graphs or implicational scales).

Bibliography: Chapter 12

Bernstein, B., *Class, Codes and Control*. Vols 1 and 2 (London: Routledge & Kegan Paul, 1971 and 1973). Vol. 1 contains the most important of Bernstein's papers laying down the foundations of the code hypothesis, and Vol. 2 has important additions by several of his collaborators, including Hawkins's (1969) study on reference and the nominal group, and Bernstein and Henderson's (1969) experiment on the relevance of language to socialisation; as noted in the text, the reader will no doubt notice some seemingly contradictory results and unclarities, but the body of this work remains essential for those interested in the theory of codes.

Bickerton, D., *Dynamics of a Creole System* (Cambridge: Cambridge University Press, 1975). This is Bickerton's major study, where he presents the results of his survey of the language situation in Guyana and its implications for creole studies and for linguistic theory in general, including a brief discussion on implicational scales.

Bloch, B., 'A set of postulates for phonemic analysis', *Language* 24 (1948), pp. 3–46.

Chambers, J. K., and Trudgill, P., *Dialectology* (Cambridge: Cambridge University Press, 1980). An excellent introduction to this important area of linguistics; it discusses several topics included in this chapter, such as language and dialect, language and social variables, isoglosses, variable rules, implicational scales and others. Also relevant for Chapter 11.

Cook-Gumperz, J., *Social Control and Socialization* (London: Routledge & Kegan Paul, 1973). This is the study referred to in the text of class differences in children's and mothers' responses to a questionnaire, indicating the existence of more than one type of family-structure.

Dittmar, N., *Sociolinguistics* (London: Edward Arnold, 1976). This is a translation of the original German, and almost half of it is devoted to the discussion of the deficit hypothesis; apart from this relative imbalance, it is an erudite presentation of the subject, most useful for consultation.

Giglioli, P. P. (ed.), *Language and Social Context* (Harmondsworth: Penguin, 1972). A useful collection of readings from the angle of the sociology of language and the ethnography of speaking; it includes papers by Hymes on ethnographies of communication, Goffman on situation, Searle on speech-acts, Bernstein on codes, Labov on non-standard English and on language and social context, Gumperz on the speech-community, Ferguson on diglossia, Brown and Gilman on the pronouns of power and solidarity, and others.

Halliday, M. A. K., *Learning How to Mean* (London: Edward Arnold, 1975). See also Chapter 10.

Halliday, M. A. K., *Language as Social Semiotic* (London: Edward Arnold, 1978). A good presentation of the author's ideas on the interrelationship between language-structure, meaning and society, with the emphasis on language function; it contains some useful references to Bernstein's theories and to the way they integrate in Halliday's conception of language.

Hawkins, P. R. (1969), 'Social class, the nominal group and reference', in Bernstein, 1973, pp. 81–92.

Hudson, R. A., *Sociolinguistics* (Cambridge: Cambridge University Press, 1980). A very coherent and stimulating presentation of the subject, which will well repay reading; despite the slight slant towards the ethnography of speaking, most aspects of sociolinguistics receive a fair treatment, and arguably it qualifies as an exemplary general textbook in sociolinguistics.

Hymes, D. (ed.), *Pidginisation and Creolisation of Languages* (Cambridge: Cambridge University Press, 1971). A most useful collection on the subject, including papers by DeCamp on the development of pidgin and creole studies, Whinnom on linguistic hybridisation, Ferguson on pidgins and simplified registers, DeCamp on postcreole continua, Labov on system in creole languages, and many others; recommended.

Labov, W., *The Social Stratification of English in New York City* (Washington, DC: Center for Applied Linguistics, 1966). This is Labov's pioneering study on modern sociolinguistics; it includes a thorough survey of the methodology, and an analysis of the social and linguistic variables in the city, with important references to language change.

Labov, W., *Language in the Inner City* (Philadelphia, Pa: University of Pennsylvania Press, 1972a). A collection of papers on Black English, including one on copula delection, with a presentation of variable rules.

Labov, W., *Sociolinguistic Patterns* (Oxford: Blackwell, 1972b). This excellent volume incorporates many of Labov's previous studies on sociolinguistic methodology and practice, dealing with matters such as the stratification of (r)in New York, the isolation of contextual styles, hypercorrection and language change, the study of language in its social context, etc.; highly recommended.

Labov, W., 'The logic of nonstandard English' in P. P. Giglioli (ed.) (1972), pp. 179–215 (Labov, 1972c, in text).

Labov, W., *What Is a Linguistic Fact?* (Lisse: Peter de Ridder Press, 1975). Labov's criticisms of the traditional practice of transformational linguists, coupled with suggestions for improvement; sharp and to-the-point, it is well worth reading.

Lawton, D., *Social Class, Language and Education* (London: Routledge & Kegan Paul, 1968). This is a good summary and critique of the theories put forward by Bernstein and his collaborators, complemented with the report of the author's own experimental study and with general chapters on education and on language and thought.

Milroy, L., *Language and Social Networks* (Oxford: Blackwell, 1980). This is the original report on Milroy's survey of the linguistic correlates of social networks in three Belfast communities and of the theoretical implications of the findings; clearly written and often insightful, it is recommended.

Pride, J. B., and Holmes, J. (eds), *Sociolinguistics* (Harmondsworth: Penguin, 1972). An anthology dealing with most aspects of broad sociolinguistics with sections on bi- and multilingualism, which includes a paper by Fishman on domains of language behaviour, standard and national language, dialectal and stylistic variation, and speech acquisition and proficiency; useful as an introductory survey.

Robinson, W. P., 'The elaborated code in working class language', *Language and Speech*, 8 (1965), pp. 243–52. Social class differences in the use of code do not show up in an experiment involving the writing of formal letters, thus pointing to the importance of context of situation.

Rosen, H., *Language and Class* (Bristol: Falling Wall Press, 1972). A short leaflet containing a critical look at Bernstein's theories, ostensibly from a politically committed standpoint.

Trudgill, P., *Accent, Dialect and the School* (London: Edward Arnold, 1975). A general discussion on language variation and prescriptivism and their repercussions on educational programmes; it includes a chapter on verbal deprivation.

Trudgill, P. (ed.), *Sociolinguistic Patterns in British English* (London: Edward Arnold, 1978). A very important collection of Labov-type sociolinguistic work done recently in Britain; in addition to an introduction where Trudgill defines the subject-matter of sociolinguistics, it contains, among others, papers by the Milroys on Belfast networks, Douglas-Cowie on language and social ambition in a Northern Irish village, Cheshire on substandard English in Reading, and Elyan and others on the perceived 'androgyny' of RP English.

Trudgill, P., *The Social Differentiation of English in Norwich* (Cambridge: Cambridge University Press, 1974). This is a pioneering application of Labov's methodology to sociolinguistic research in Britain, giving a fascinating picture of the demographic, social and linguistic realities of Norwich, also most useful at the methodological level.

Valdman, A. (ed.), *Pidgin and Creole Linguistics* (Bloomington, Ind.: Indiana University Press, 1977). A recent, up-to-date collection on the subject, including papers by DeCamp summarising the development of pidgin and creole studies, Bickerton on pidginisation and language acquisition, and Le Page on pidginisation and creolisation.

Addenda to Bibliographies

Aitchison, J., *Language Change: Progress or Decay* (London: Fontana, 1981). A remarkably lively introduction to historical linguistics addressing the fundamental questions of how and why languages change, how linguists observe and find out about change, and how and why languages begin and die. In tackling these issues, the author presents and draws from various other linguistic areas, including (classical) historical linguistics, variability theory, developmental psycholinguistics and creole studies, thus successfully providing the beginner with a basic conceptual framework covering a broad spectrum of linguistic theory.

Allwood, J., Andersson, L. G., and Dahl, Ö., *Logic in Linguistics* (Cambridge: Cambridge University Press, 1977). An introduction to logic written with students of linguistics in mind. Useful for the beginner, but sacrifices some explicitness and accuracy when more complex topics are tackled. A good place to continue after Chapter 7.

Anderson, S. R., *Phonology in the Twentieth Century* (Chicago: University of Chicago Press, 1985). A very useful history of twentieth-century linguistics with the focus on phonology. The exposition is more historical than formal, with a generous scattering of biographical notes on all the major figures. The different sections are organised around the theme of the tension between rules and representations, and past theories are integrated into a general view of the subject. Besides its historical contribution, the book provides a very adequate introduction to some of the topics included in this book, such as the linguistic ideas of F. de Saussure, the theory of the phoneme (Trubetzkoy, Jones, Sapir, Bloomfield, Twaddell), Prague structuralism, Jakobsonian distinctive features, the American pregenerative school and the emergence of generative phonology.

Atkinson, P., *Language, Structure and Reproduction* (London: Methuen, 1985). This is a general introduction to the sociology of Basil Bernstein, with a good coverage of his views on language codes and on the interaction between language and social reality. In addition, the author addresses the issue of the many misinterpretations of Bernstein's work and endeavours to redress the balance.

Bauer, L., *English Word Formation* (Cambridge: Cambridge University Press, 1983). A textbook-like presentation of the field of morphology, with the focus on derivation and word formation in general. It provides a good taxonomy of the various procedures available, with a discussion of the parameters which affect their productivity and regularity. There is ample exemplification from English, and references to general linguistic theory are made whenever appropriate.

Chomsky, N., *Rules and Representations* (Oxford: Blackwell, 1980). Chomsky's ideas on the relevance of linguistics for traditional philosophical and psychological questions, along with some fairly technical discussion of particular aspects of syntactic theory. The more general sections have determined the tenor of much debate on the significance of linguistics in this decade.

Chomsky, N., *Knowledge of language* (New York: Praeger, 1986). A recent statement of Chomsky's philosophical and psychological views. Very similar to earlier works on these themes, but changes in terminology and emphasis are important for an understanding of current debate. General discussion in the early pages is followed by fairly technical linguistic exposition which the beginner is likely to find extremely difficult.

Cruse, D. A., *Lexical Semantics* (Cambridge: Cambridge University Press, 1986). A detailed presentation of the topic, referred to in Chapter 7 of this book. Undoubtedly the most accessible, and yet quite thorough, examination of the meaning relations between words, also discussing the methodological problems arising in the field of lexical semantics.

Cruttenden, A., *Intonation* (Cambridge: Cambridge University Press, 1986). A compendium of different approaches, it usefully taxonomises such aspects as the basic parameters of intonation and the inventory of English tones and their meanings. It laudably attempts to repair the confusion likely to arise from the conceptual and terminological inconsistencies of the various authors, but the reader should be warned that a perhaps disproportionate attention is given to some of the areas, e.g. English tonology.

De Luce, J., and Wilder, H. T. (eds), *Language in Primates* (New York: Springer-Verlag, 1983). A most useful collection on the topic. Directly relevant are the introduction by the editors summarising the issues and the history, an informative and critical paper by Terrace on Nim, a presentation of project Chantek by Miles and an evaluation of the overall findings by Fouts. In addition, there are other papers on more general issues concerning apes, language and the apes experiments.

Downes, W., *Language and Society* (London: Fontana, 1984). Contains two main strands that the author brings together at the end in an attempt to unify the various perspectives within a functionalist framework. The first two-thirds usefully develop some of the main issues in variability theory, the social psychology of language and the sociology of language, intelligently intertwined in the presentation. The latter part relates to utterance meaning, i.e. pragmatics (cf. Chapter 7, Section 6, in this book) and discourse analysis.

Dowty, D., Wall, R., and Peters, S., *Introduction to Montague Semantics* (Dordrecht: Reidel, 1981). A clear introduction to the most technically demanding variety of logical semantics. Rather difficult, but very important for anyone who wishes to go further with modern semantics. Goes well beyond the material in Chapter 7.

Elliot, A., *Child Language* (Cambridge: Cambridge University Press, 1981). An attractively written introduction which would be a good way to go further into this area after reading this book. Tends not to engage theoretical issues, which has the advantage of avoiding certain complexities but the disadvantage of leaving some of the arguments rather flabby.

Fasold, R., *The Sociolinguistics of Society* (Oxford: Blackwell, 1984). An excellent introductory but informative survey of what we have called the 'sociology of language' in the main text of this book (Chapter 12, p. 391). The multifarious aspects of the area are reviewed in a clear and stimulating style, including a basic but instructive chapter on statistical techniques.

Particularly welcome is the geographically catholic coverage of data. Very pedagogical; each chapter includes a summary and a list of objectives.

Fletcher, P., and Garman, M. (eds), *Language Acquisition* (Cambridge: Cambridge University Press, 1986, 2nd edn). A large collection of articles covering all the major areas of language acquisition research. Written with the introductory student in mind, but still presupposing rather a lot. Of clear relevance to Chapter 10.

Fodor, J.A., *Modularity of Mind* (Cambridge, Mass.: MIT Press, 1983). A defence of the view that the mind is divided into separate components, each devoted to a specialist task. The argument relies heavily on language, but the whole text is a stimulating, if sometimes difficult, experience. Relevant for Chapter 2.

Fodor, J. D., *Semantics: Theories of Meaning in Generative Grammar* (New York: Crowell, 1977). Surveys attempts to integrate semantic theories with syntactic theories. Contains a useful discussion of philosophical theories. Relevant for Chapter 7.

Hawkins, P., *Introducing Phonology* (London: Hutchinson, 1984). A very clear, graded and thorough presentation of most of the topics included in Chapter 4 of this book, in particular phonemic analysis, phonological systems, phonological processes and distinctive features. It additionally deals with intonation and phonological variation. Despite the explicit disclaimer, it is also relevant for generative phonology.

Jackendoff, R., *Semantics and Cognition* (Cambridge, Mass.: MIT Press, 1983). An attempt to integrate semantic and psychological considerations, and it contains a wealth of descriptive problems and proposed solutions. The somewhat idiosyncratic notation makes it a difficult book to read, but it is likely to be a landmark in the investigation of a new and difficult area.

Jeffers, R. J., and Lehiste, I., *Principles and Methods for Historical Linguistics* (Cambridge, Mass.: MIT Press, 1979). Reviews the main aspects of language change introducing concepts, theories and terminology amidst generous exemplification. A useful bibliography follows each topic. While the main focus is on the facts and theories of sound change, in line with tradition, it also includes syntactic, lexical and sociolinguistic aspects of language history, and there is a short discussion on writing and the philological method.

Katz, J. J., *Language and Other Abstract Objects* (Oxford: Blackwell, 1981). An attack on the view that linguistics should be concerned with human psychology. Katz maintains that the proper subject-matter of linguistics should be a certain class of abstract objects – languages – and this provides a Platonist interpretation of linguistics. Provides a different slant on the discussion in Chapter 2.

Lass, R., *Phonology* (Cambridge: Cambridge University Press, 1984). A major work only to be tackled after some exposure to the subject. Strewn with data, its theoretical eclecticism bordering on scepticism makes it into a synthesis of authors and approaches. It reinterprets much of the traditional literature, clarifies the terminology and makes explicit many unstated assumptions. All analyses are intelligently argued through in the wider context of methodology of science. The book is of special use for phonemic and classical structuralist theory, but it includes important discussions on generative and postgenerative theory and on some less well-known models, as well as on phonological variation and change.

Leahey, T. H., *A History of Psychology* (Englewood Cliffs, NJ: Prentice-Hall, 1980). An excellent summary of the history of psychology, including lengthy discussion of introspectionism, behaviourism and Chomsky's psychology of language. Develops many of the issues of Chapter 2, but also contains much material not discussed in this book.

Levinson, S. C., *Pragmatics* (Cambridge: Cambridge University Press, 1983). A clearly written introductory account of the major areas of pragmatics, including lengthy chapters devoted to presupposition, conversational implicature and speech acts. Amply illustrated and containing detailed criticisms, it is necessary reading for anyone wishing to explore the semantics-pragmatics boundary.

Matthei, E., and Roeper, T., *Understanding and Producing Speech* (London: Fontana, 1983). An accurate and reasonably up-to-date discussion of experimental psycholinguistics, raising issues to do with both the production and perception of speech. Relevant to Chapter 9.

McCawley, J. D., *Everything That Linguists Ever Wanted to Know about Logic* (Oxford: Blackwell, 1981). A comprehensive account of semantic and pragmatic phenomena from a logical perspective. Contains a wealth of examples and problems, but is rather idiosyncratic in its use of notation. Relevant for Chapter 7, but also discusses issues in the area of interaction between syntax and semantics.

Morris-Wilson, I., *English Phonemic Transcription* (Oxford: Blackwell, 1984). A collection of exercises on phonetic transcription – reading from phonetic texts and transcribing from ordinary orthography. A key is provided for the latter at the end of the book. The interesting, often witty, passages succeed in taking the drudgery out of what could otherwise be a forbidding task.

Petyt, K. M., *The Study of Dialect* (London: Deutsch, 1980). A very well-documented and clear introduction to dialectology. Besides dealing with traditional approaches and with the history of the subject, it has chapters on the more modern structuralist, generative, and sociolinguistic versions, presented by means of informative outlines of the essential literature. As follows from its comprehensiveness, this work will also be useful for other related disciplines, such as historical linguistics or sociolinguistics.

Piattelli-Palmarini, M. (ed.), *Language and Learning: The Debate between Noam Chomsky and Jean Piaget* (Cambridge, Mass.: Harvard University Press, 1980). Proceedings of a conference which took place in 1975 where Chomsky and Piaget were invited to present their views on language learning to a distinguished set of commentators. The result is an extremely stimulating collection, with the contributions of Chomsky, Fodor and Putnam being particularly recommended. Useful for Chapter 2 and Chomsky's general philosophy of language.

Pullum, G. K., and Ladusaw, W., *Phonetic Symbol Guide* (Chicago: The University of Chicago Press, 1986). An excellent, very thorough survey of the various systems of phonetic transcription in existence. The clear layout makes cross-comparison an easy task. Useful given the fact that not all writers (e.g. many in the American tradition) adhere to the IPA alphabet.

Roach, P., *English Phonetics and Phonology* (Cambridge: Cambridge University Press, 1983). This book provides a basic but sound grounding in the phonetic system of English, especially in the areas of articulation and intonation. Particularly suitable for the beginner, native and non-native alike, because of its clarity of presentation and pedagogical structure, which includes a generous supply of tables and diagrams.

Terrace, H. S., *Nim* (London: Eyre Methuen, 1980). An excellent presentation of one of the major ape projects, successfully incorporating the human and the anecdotal into a rigorous account of the ape's successes and failures. It includes a pointed summary of prior research and a programmatic statement with suggestions to facilitate the task of future workers. One of the appendices contains a valuable presentation of ASL, generously illustrated, as is also the rest of the book. Highly recommended as a pleasurable but still scholarly introduction to the subject.

Wanner, E., and Gleitman, L. R. (eds), *Language Acquisition: The State of the Art* (Cambridge: Cambridge University Press, 1982). A very important collection of articles covering most of the central empirical and conceptual issues in the field. The articles are contributions to research and often presuppose considerable knowledge. However, the introductory paper, written by the editors, is a valuable overview of many crucial issues.

Wells, J. C., *Accents of English*, 3 vols. (Cambridge: Cambridge University Press, 1982). A survey of the pronunciation of English in all the world regions where it is either a mother tongue or a historical legacy of current sociopolitical significance. All major English accents are carefully dealt with, Received Pronunciation and General American in particular, but some minor ones are also discussed, the necessarily rather broad mesh still allowing for a fair degree of descriptive detail. The second volume is entirely devoted to the British Isles, and the first contains a general survey of the main divergences found in English worldwide, both at the phonetic and at the systemic level, with a historical interpretation of them. The first chapter lays down the general framework, which uses phonetic description, phonological analysis, sociolinguistic stratification and sound change.

Author Index

Subject Index